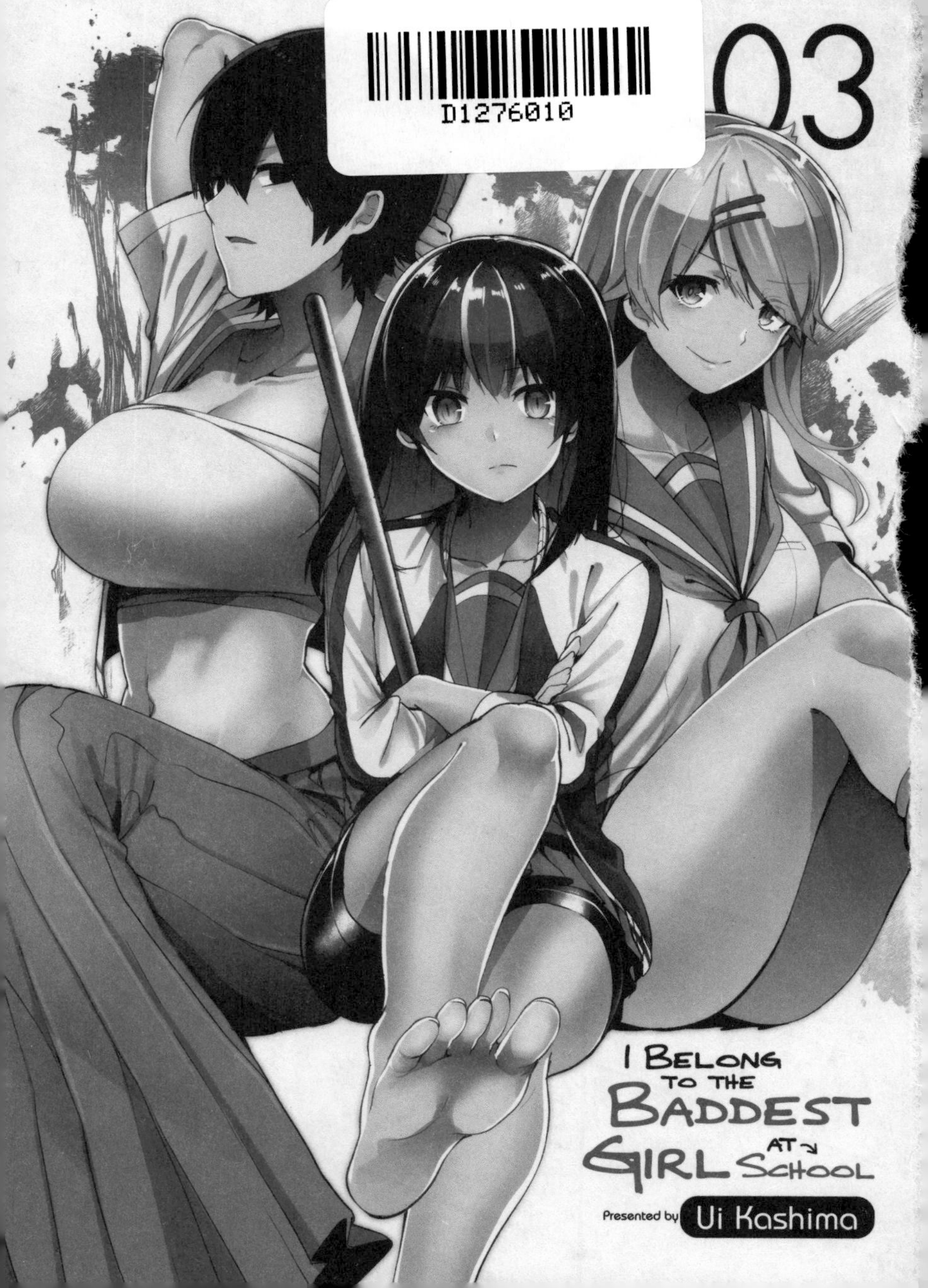
03
I BELONG TO THE BADDEST GIRL AT SCHOOL
Presented by Ui Kashima

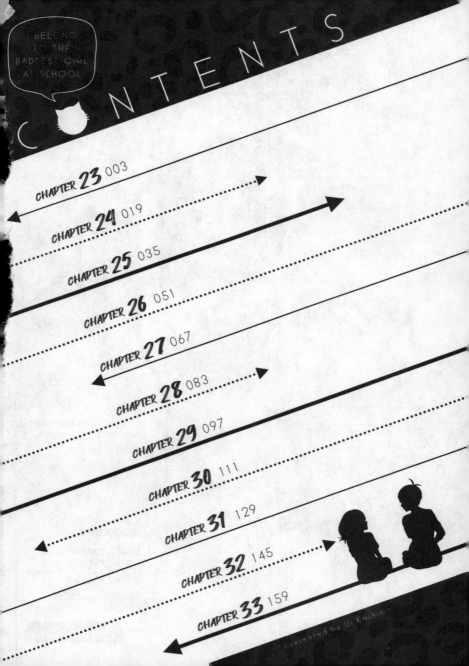

CONTENTS

I BELONG TO THE BADDEST GIRL AT SCHOOL

Presented by Ui Kashima

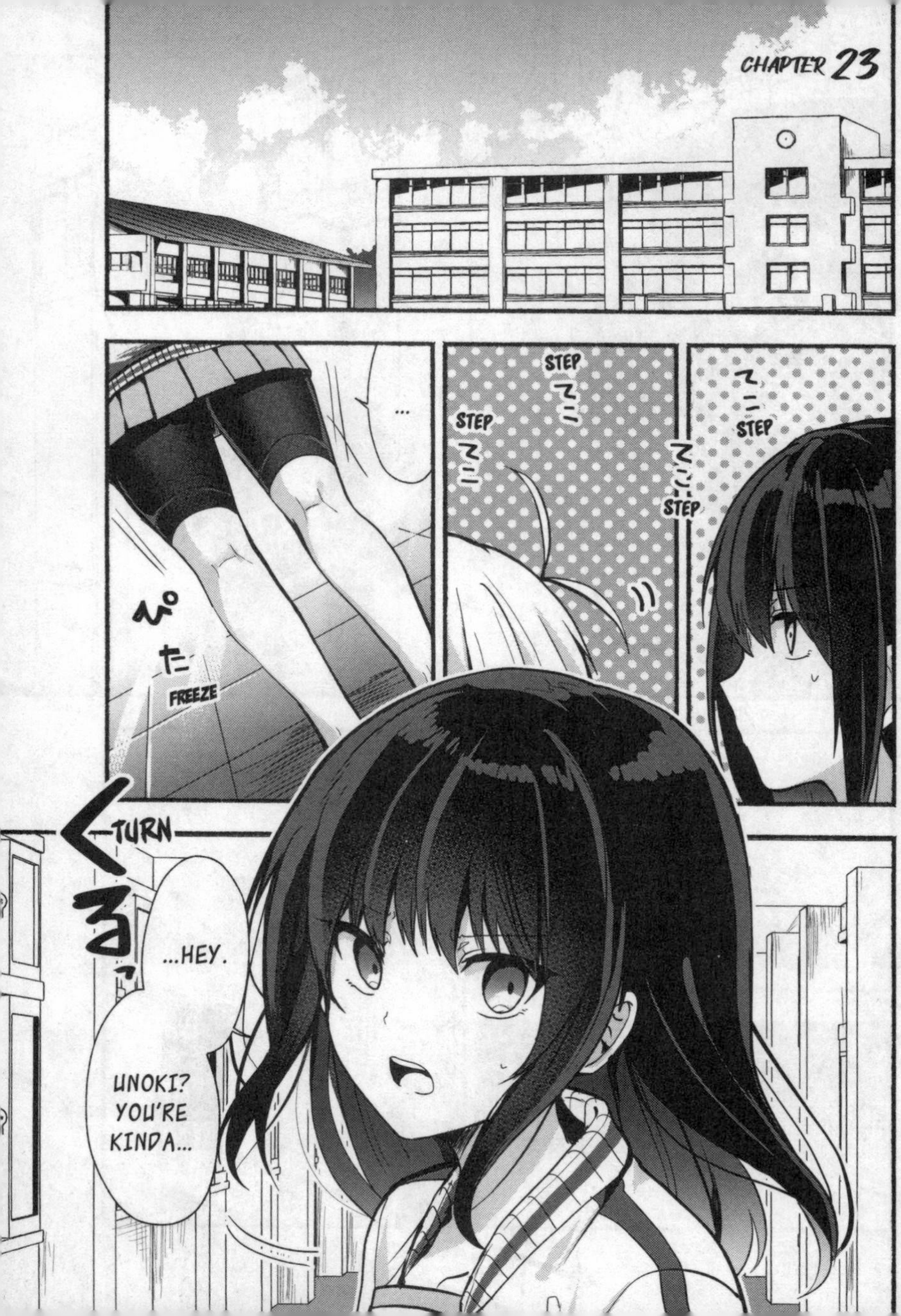
CHAPTER 23
てこ
STEP
てこ
STEP
STEP
てこ
STEP
てこ
...
ぴた
FREEZE
くる
TURN
...HEY.
UNOKI? YOU'RE KINDA...

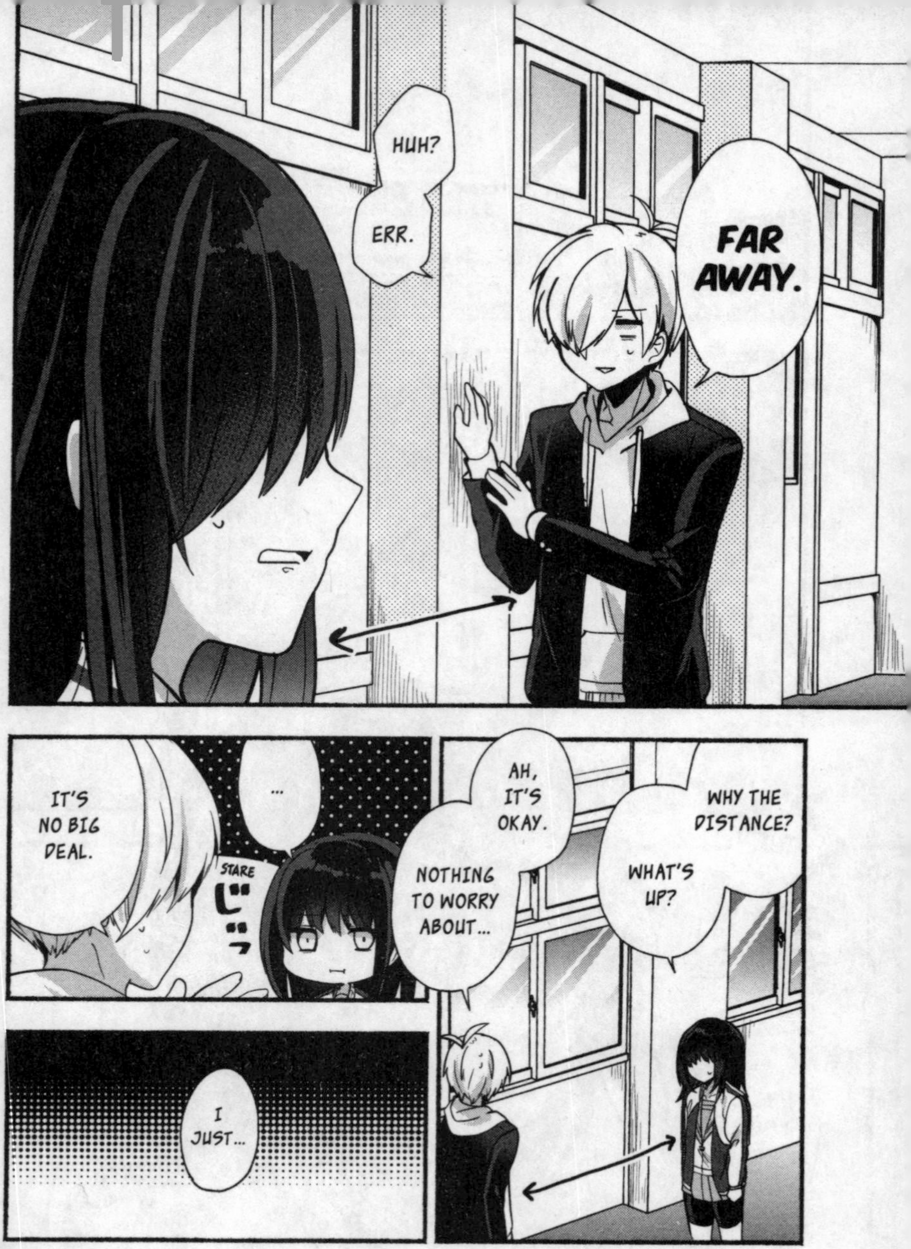
FAR AWAY.
HUH?
ERR.
WHY THE DISTANCE?
WHAT'S UP?
AH, IT'S OKAY.
NOTHING TO WORRY ABOUT...
...
STARE
IT'S NO BIG DEAL.
I JUST...

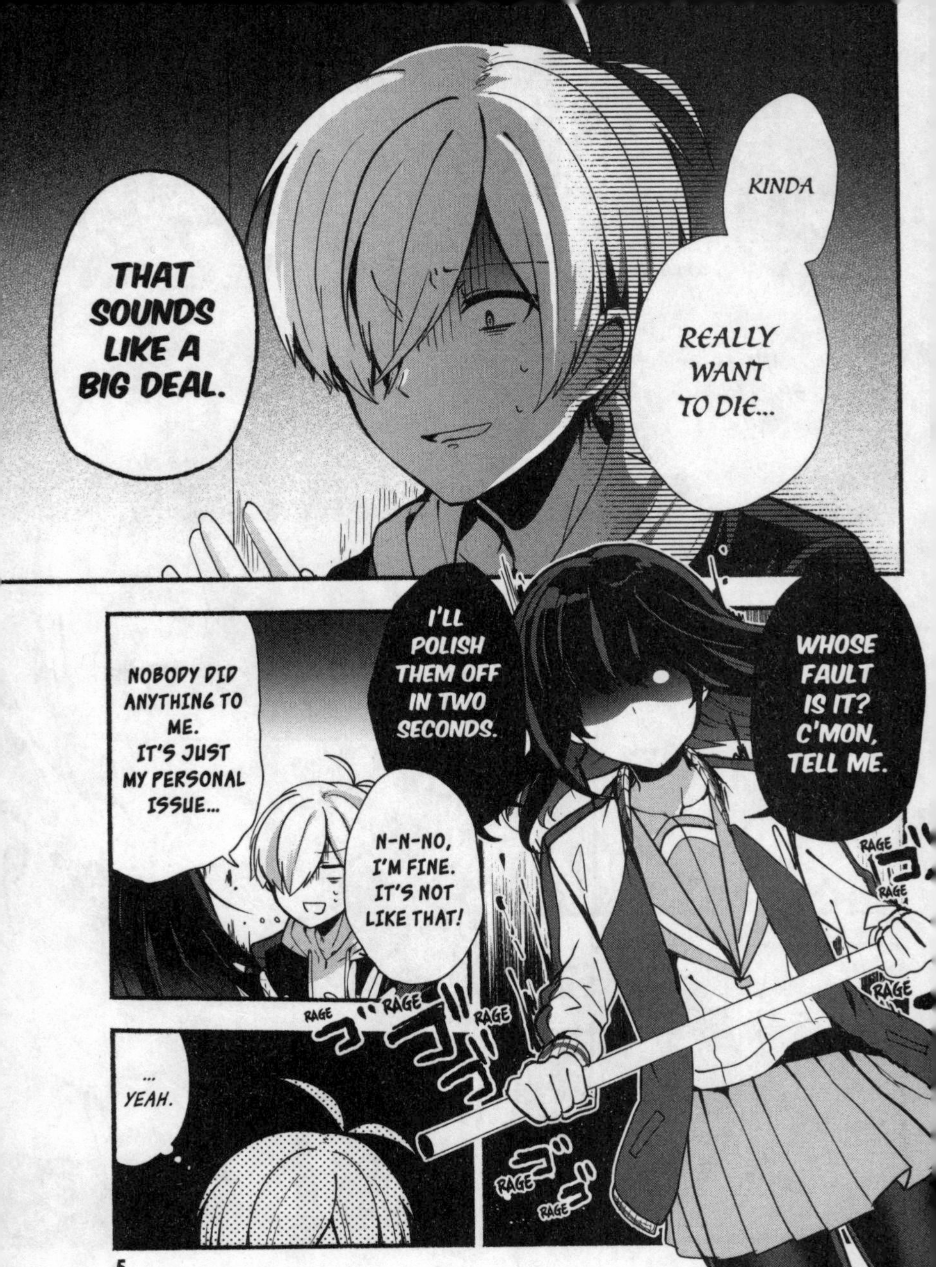
KINDA
REALLY WANT TO DIE...
THAT SOUNDS LIKE A BIG DEAL.
WHOSE FAULT IS IT? C'MON, TELL ME.
I'LL POLISH THEM OFF IN TWO SECONDS.
RAGE
RAGE
RAGE
RAGE
RAGE
RAGE
RAGE
RAGE
N-N-NO, I'M FINE. IT'S NOT LIKE THAT!
NOBODY DID ANYTHING TO ME. IT'S JUST MY PERSONAL ISSUE...
... YEAH.

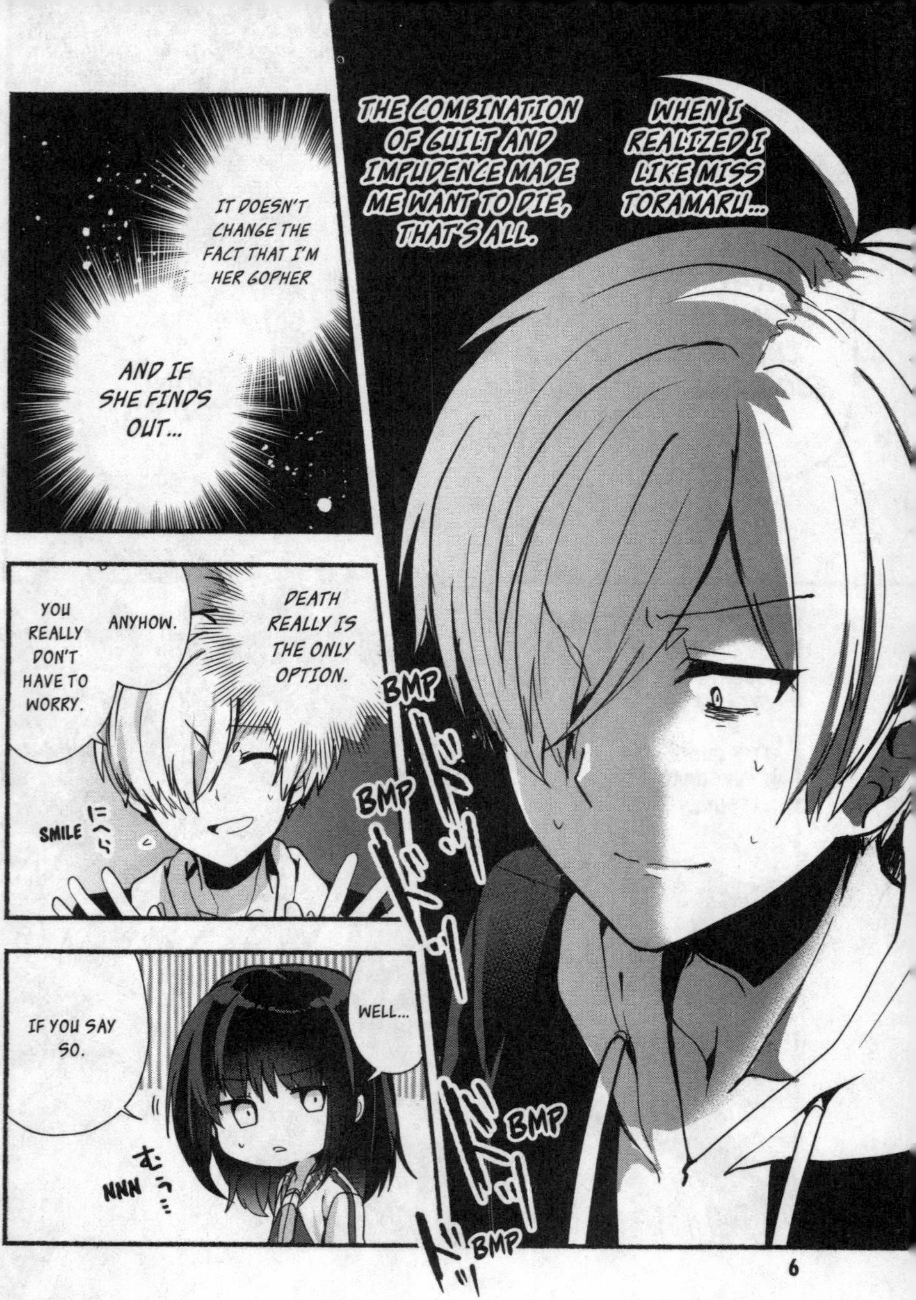
WHEN I REALIZED I LIKE MISS TORAMARU...
THE COMBINATION OF GUILT AND IMPUDENCE MADE ME WANT TO DIE, THAT'S ALL.
BMP
BMP
BMP
BMP
IT DOESN'T CHANGE THE FACT THAT I'M HER GOPHER
AND IF SHE FINDS OUT...
DEATH REALLY IS THE ONLY OPTION.
ANYHOW.
YOU REALLY DON'T HAVE TO WORRY.
SMILE
にへら
WELL...
IF YOU SAY SO.
NNN
むっ...

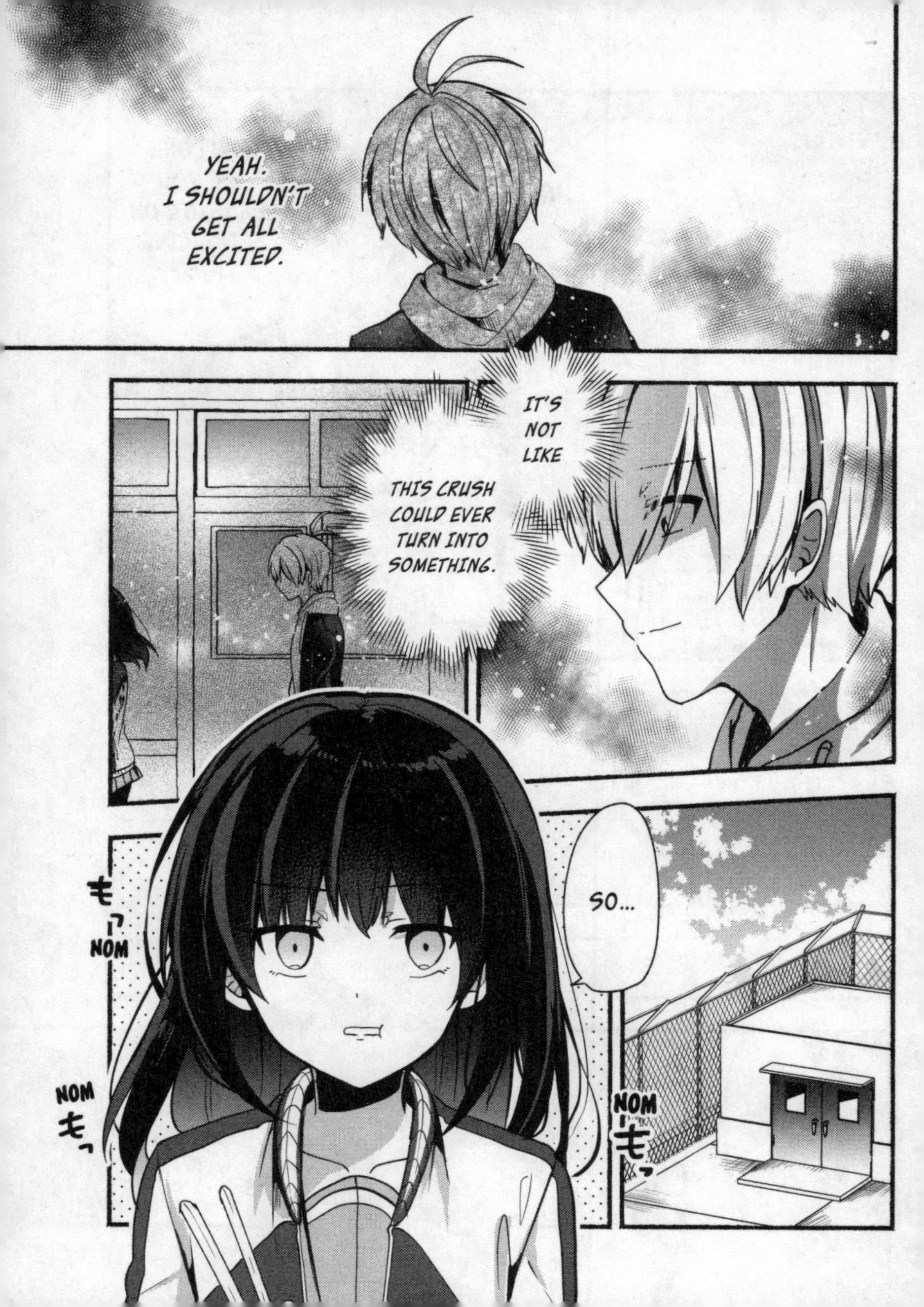
YEAH. I SHOULDN'T GET ALL EXCITED.
IT'S NOT LIKE
THIS CRUSH COULD EVER TURN INTO SOMETHING.
SO...
NOM もっ
もっ NOM
NOM もっ

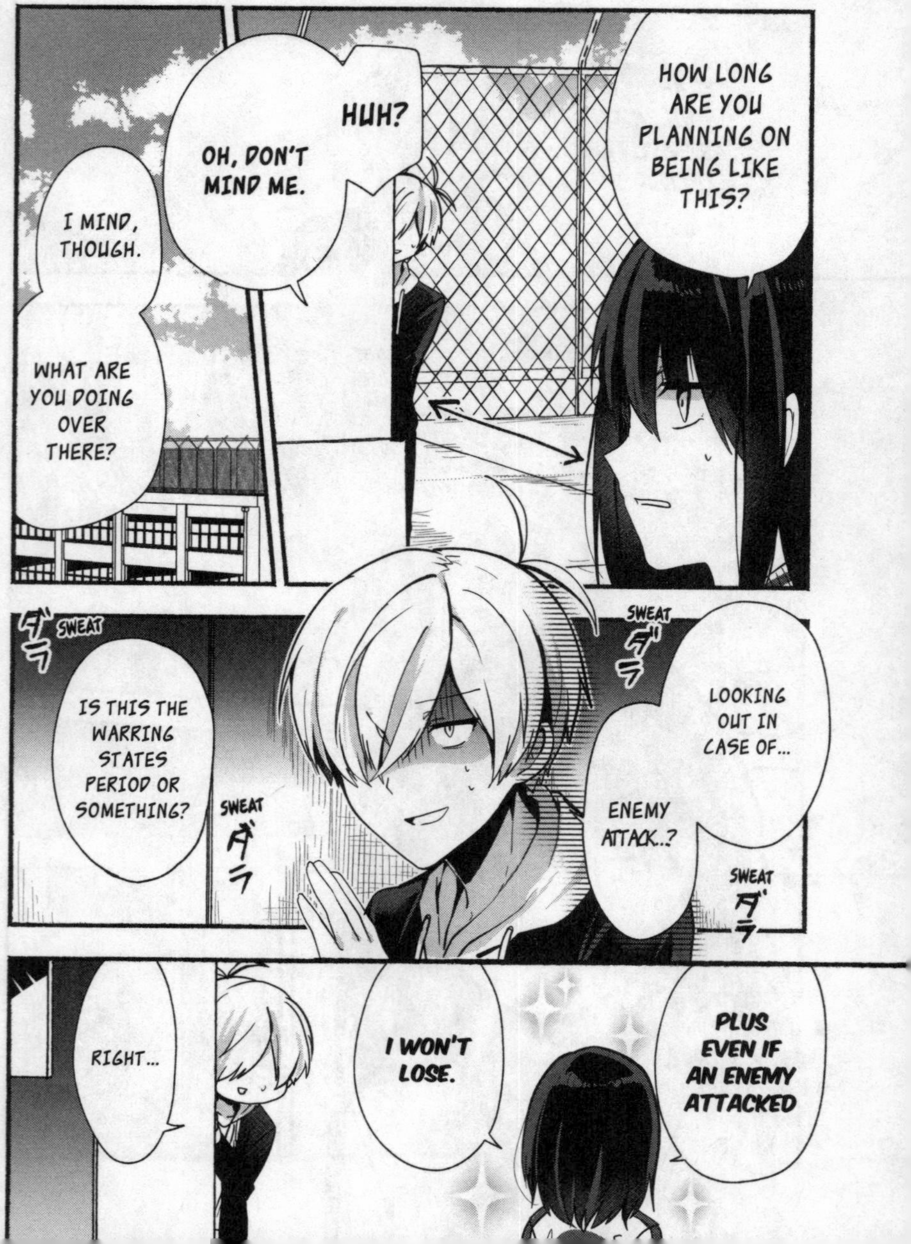
HOW LONG ARE YOU PLANNING ON BEING LIKE THIS?
HUH?
OH, DON'T MIND ME.
I MIND, THOUGH.
WHAT ARE YOU DOING OVER THERE?
SWEAT
LOOKING OUT IN CASE OF...
ENEMY ATTACK..?
SWEAT
SWEAT
IS THIS THE WARRING STATES PERIOD OR SOMETHING?
SWEAT
PLUS EVEN IF AN ENEMY ATTACKED
I WON'T LOSE.
RIGHT...

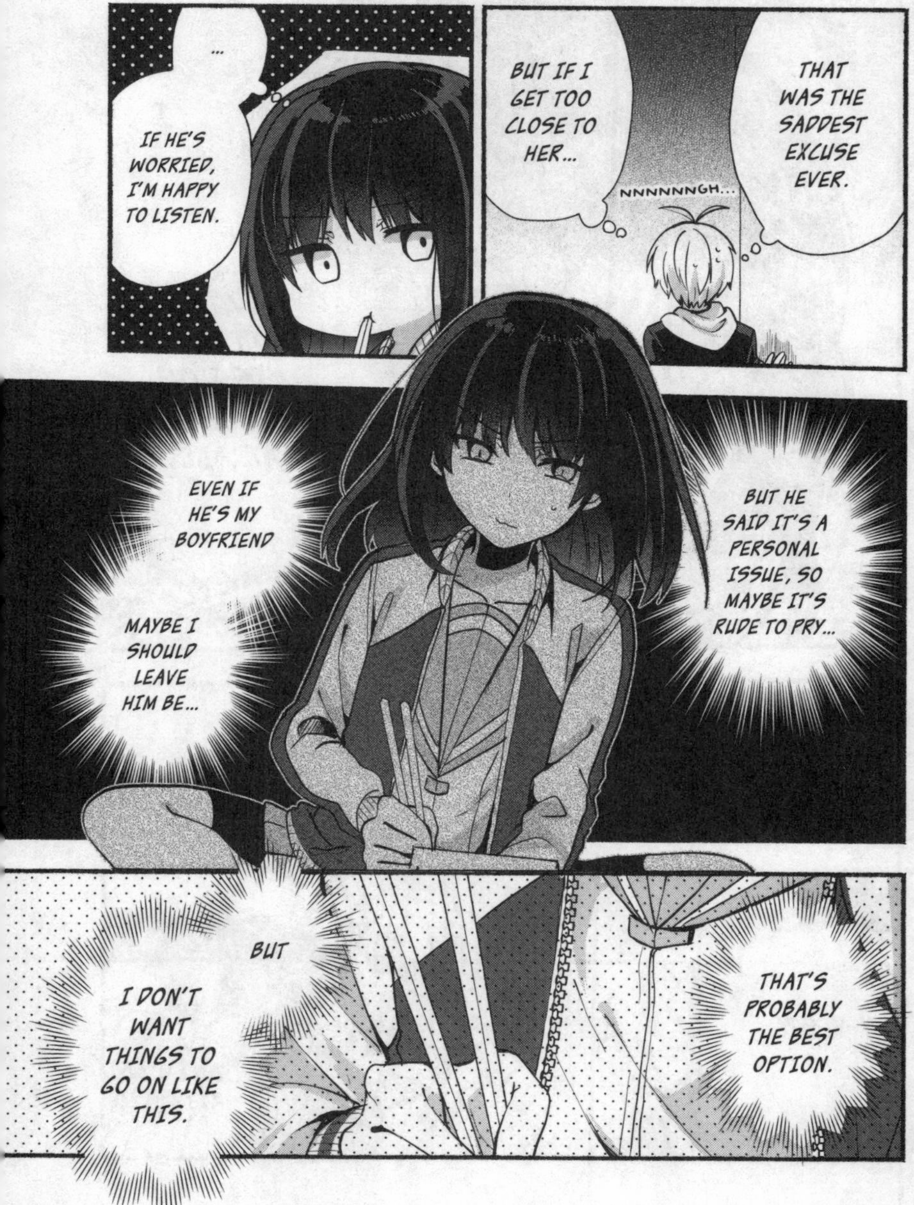
THAT WAS THE SADDEST EXCUSE EVER.
BUT IF I GET TOO CLOSE TO HER...
NNNNNNGH...
...
IF HE'S WORRIED, I'M HAPPY TO LISTEN.
BUT HE SAID IT'S A PERSONAL ISSUE, SO MAYBE IT'S RUDE TO PRY...
EVEN IF HE'S MY BOYFRIEND
MAYBE I SHOULD LEAVE HIM BE...
THAT'S PROBABLY THE BEST OPTION.
BUT
I DON'T WANT THINGS TO GO ON LIKE THIS.

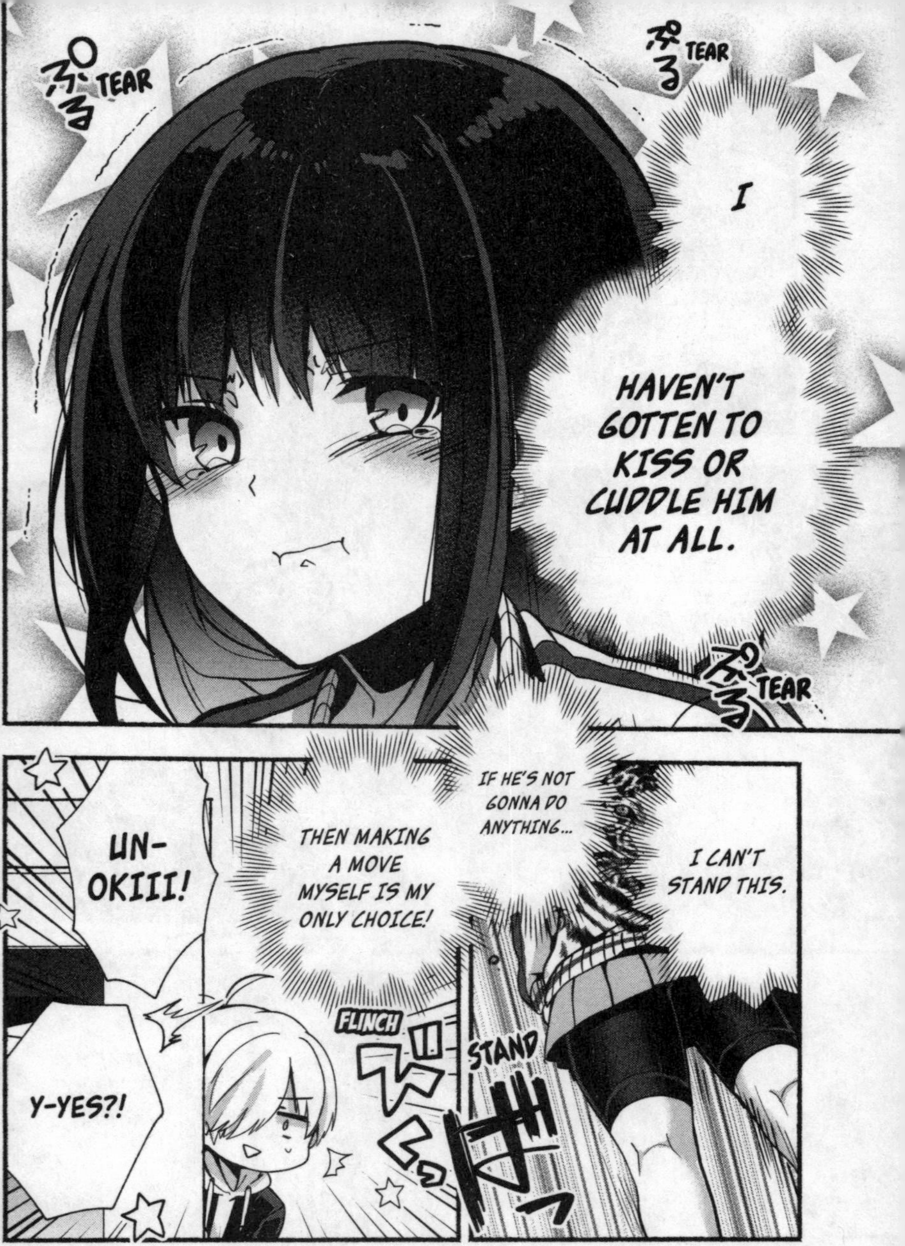

ぷる TEAR
I
HAVEN'T GOTTEN TO KISS OR CUDDLE HIM AT ALL.
ぷる TEAR
ぷる TEAR
I CAN'T STAND THIS.
IF HE'S NOT GONNA DO ANYTHING...
THEN MAKING A MOVE MYSELF IS MY ONLY CHOICE!
STAND
FLINCH
UN-OKIII!
Y-YES?!

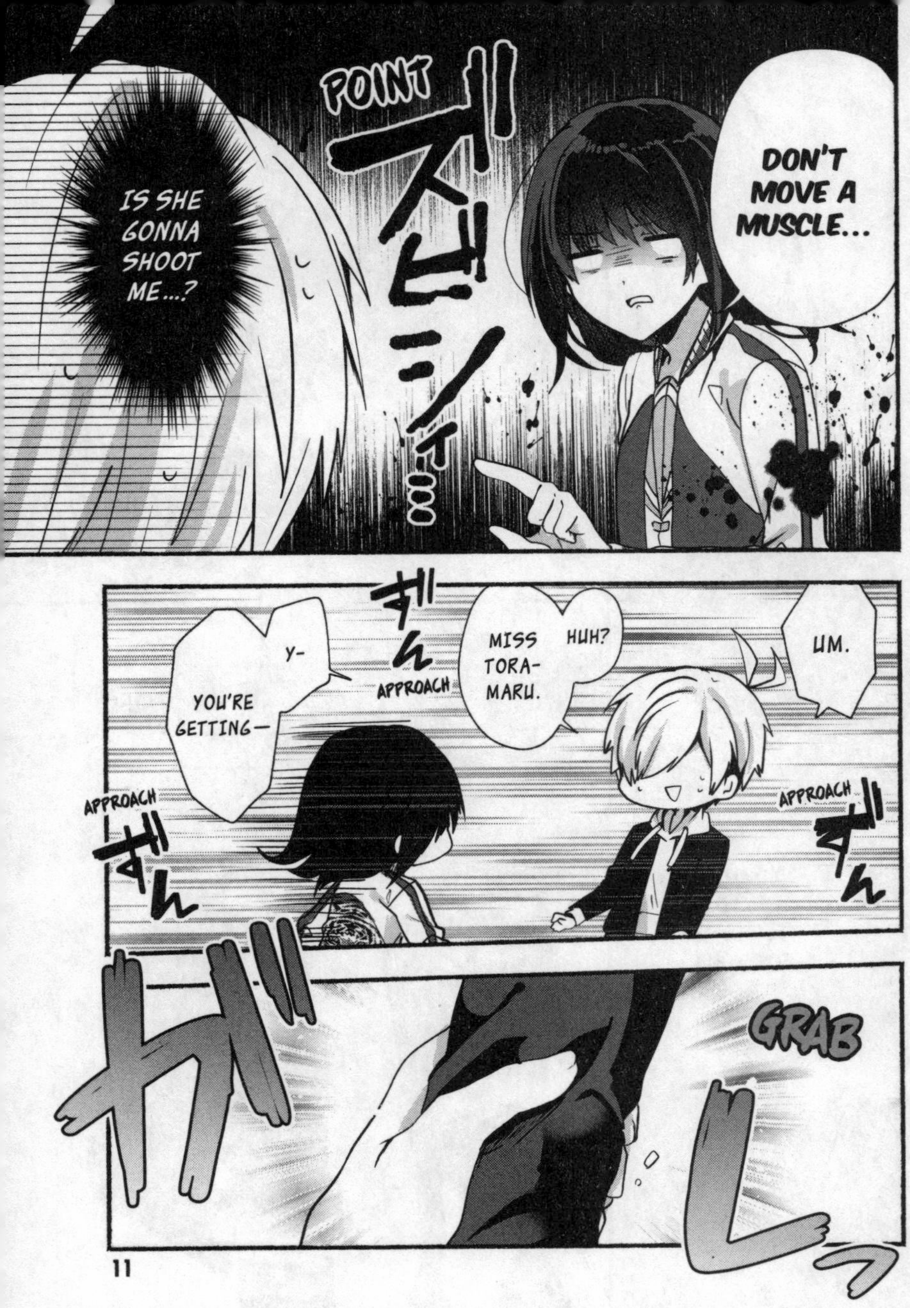
DON'T MOVE A MUSCLE...
POINT
IS SHE GONNA SHOOT ME...?
UM.
APPROACH
HUH?
MISS TORA-MARU.
APPROACH
Y-
YOU'RE GETTING—
APPROACH
GRAB

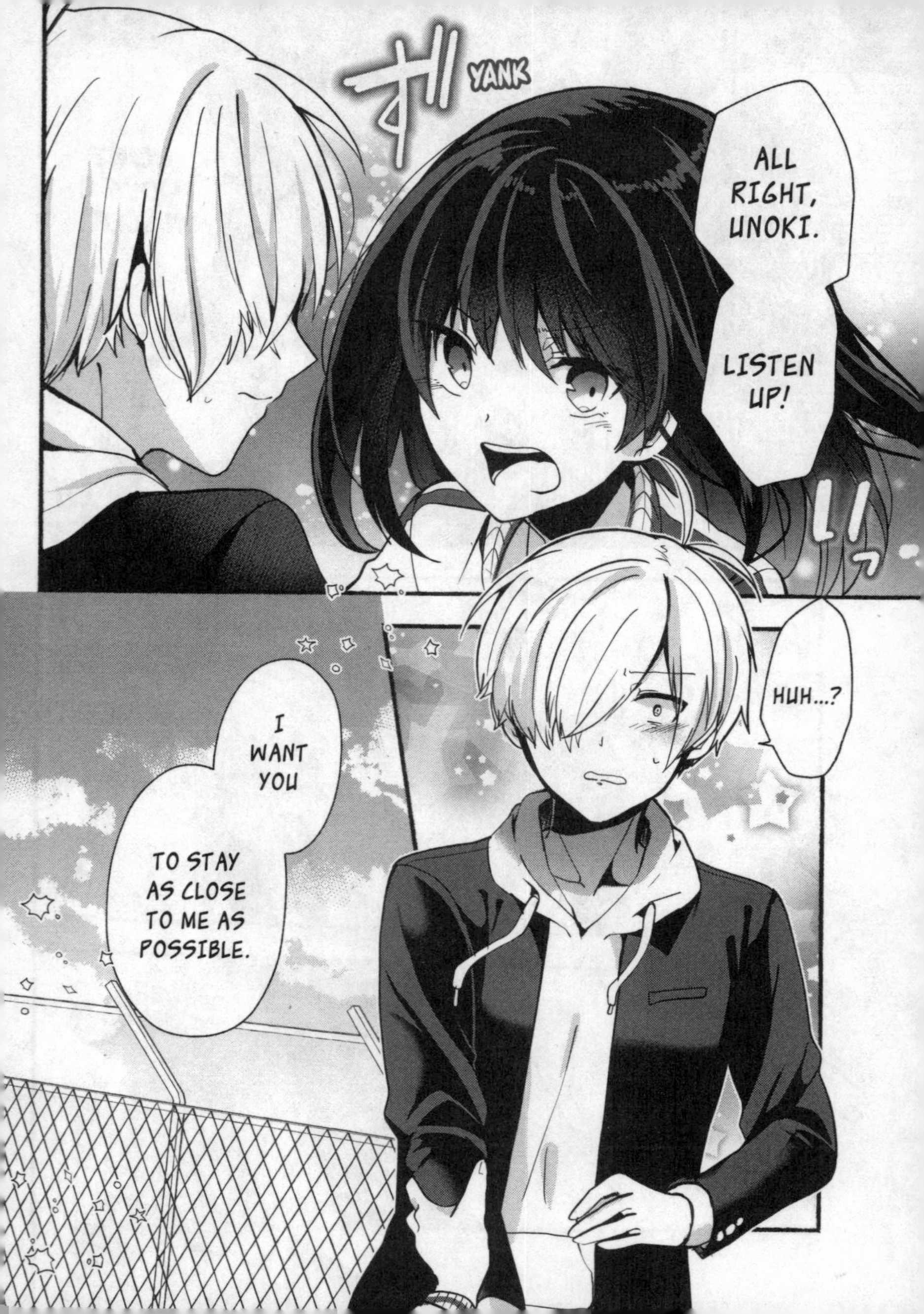
YANK
ALL RIGHT, UNOKI.
LISTEN UP!
HUH...?
I WANT YOU
TO STAY AS CLOSE TO ME AS POSSIBLE.

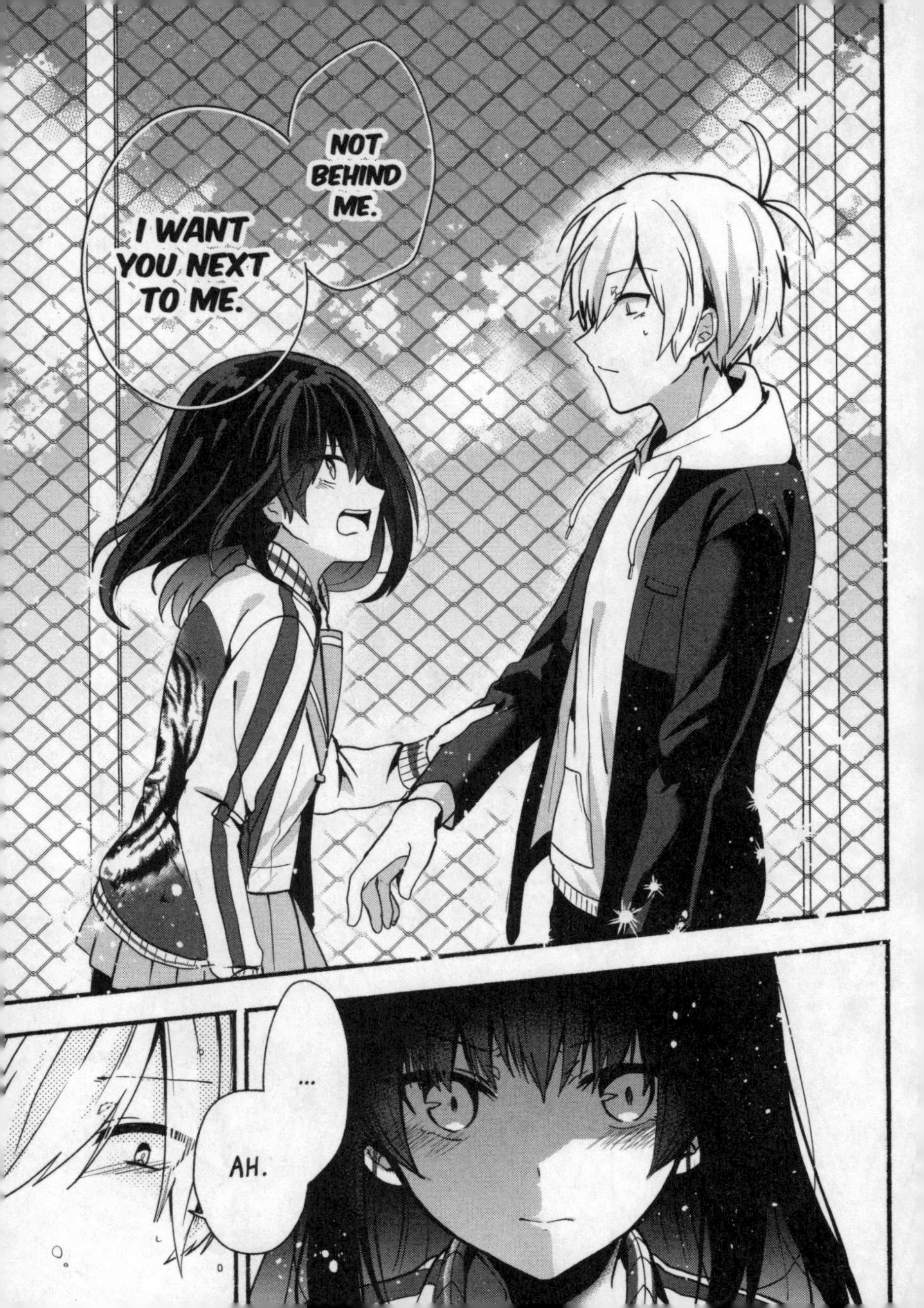
NOT BEHIND ME.
I WANT YOU NEXT TO ME.
...
AH.

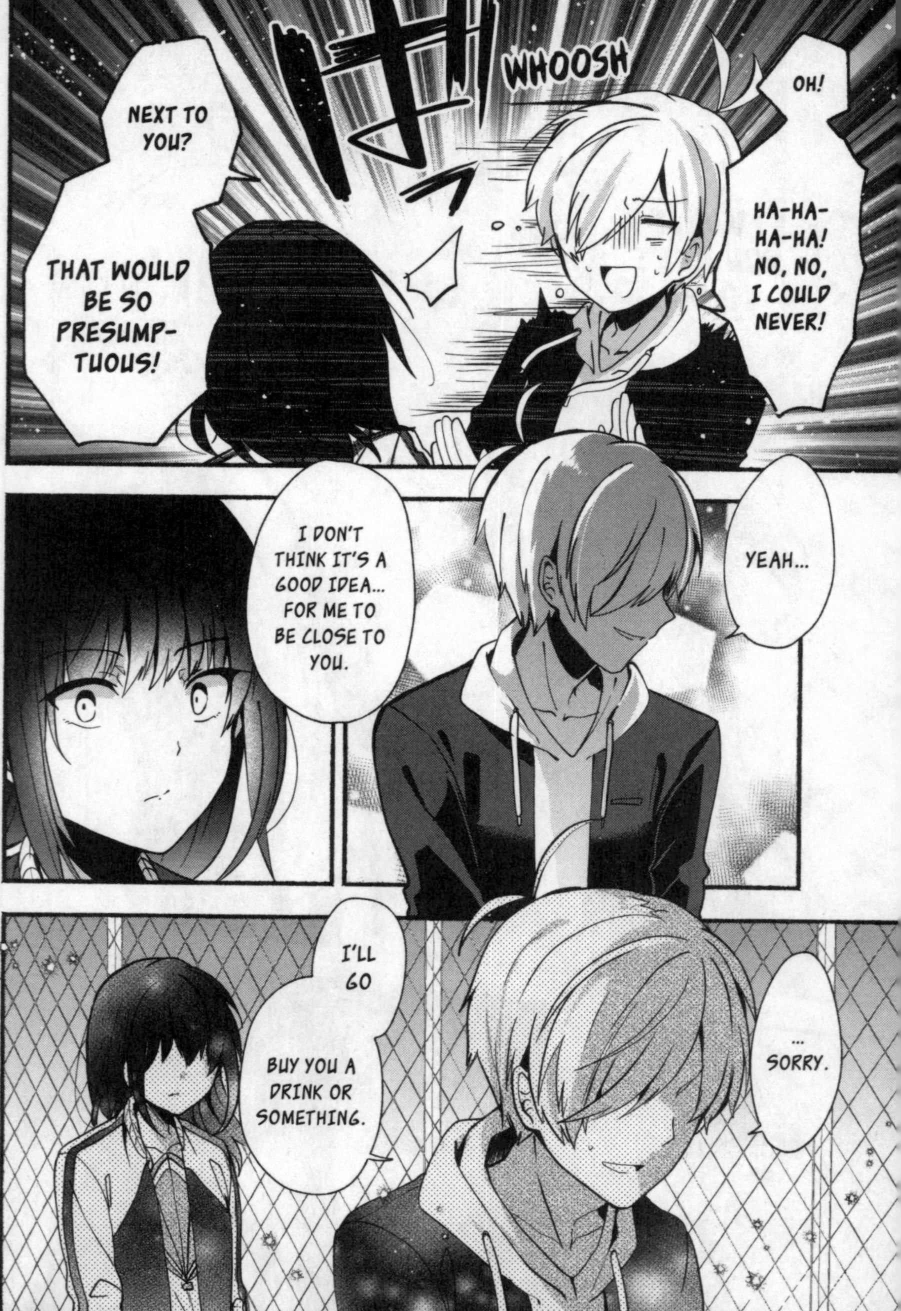
OH!
WHOOSH
HA-HA-HA-HA! NO, NO, I COULD NEVER!
NEXT TO YOU?
THAT WOULD BE SO PRESUMP-TUOUS!
YEAH...
I DON'T THINK IT'S A GOOD IDEA... FOR ME TO BE CLOSE TO YOU.
...SORRY.
I'LL GO
BUY YOU A DRINK OR SOMETHING.

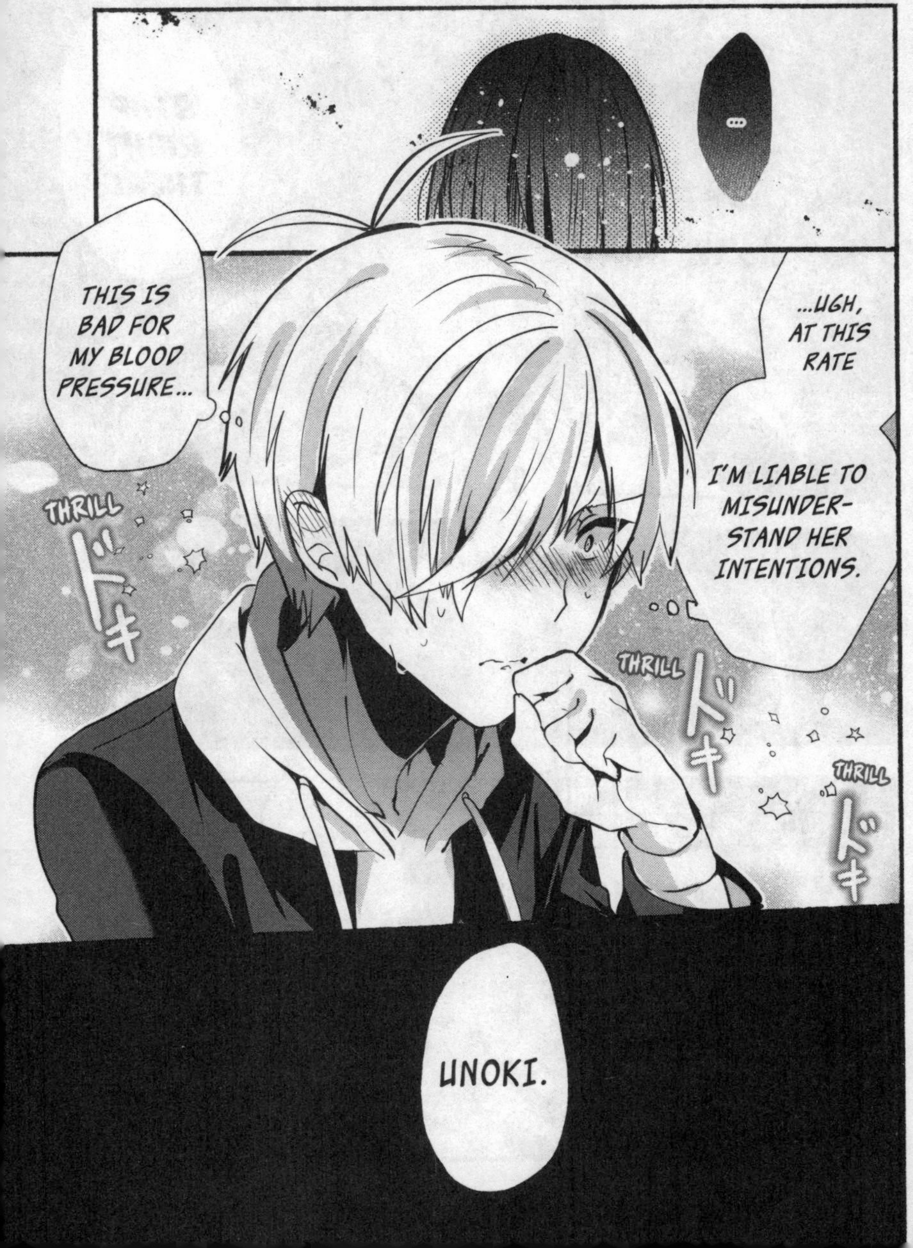
...
...UGH, AT THIS RATE
I'M LIABLE TO MISUNDERSTAND HER INTENTIONS.
THRILL ドキ
THRILL ドキ
THIS IS BAD FOR MY BLOOD PRESSURE...
THRILL ドキ
UNOKI.

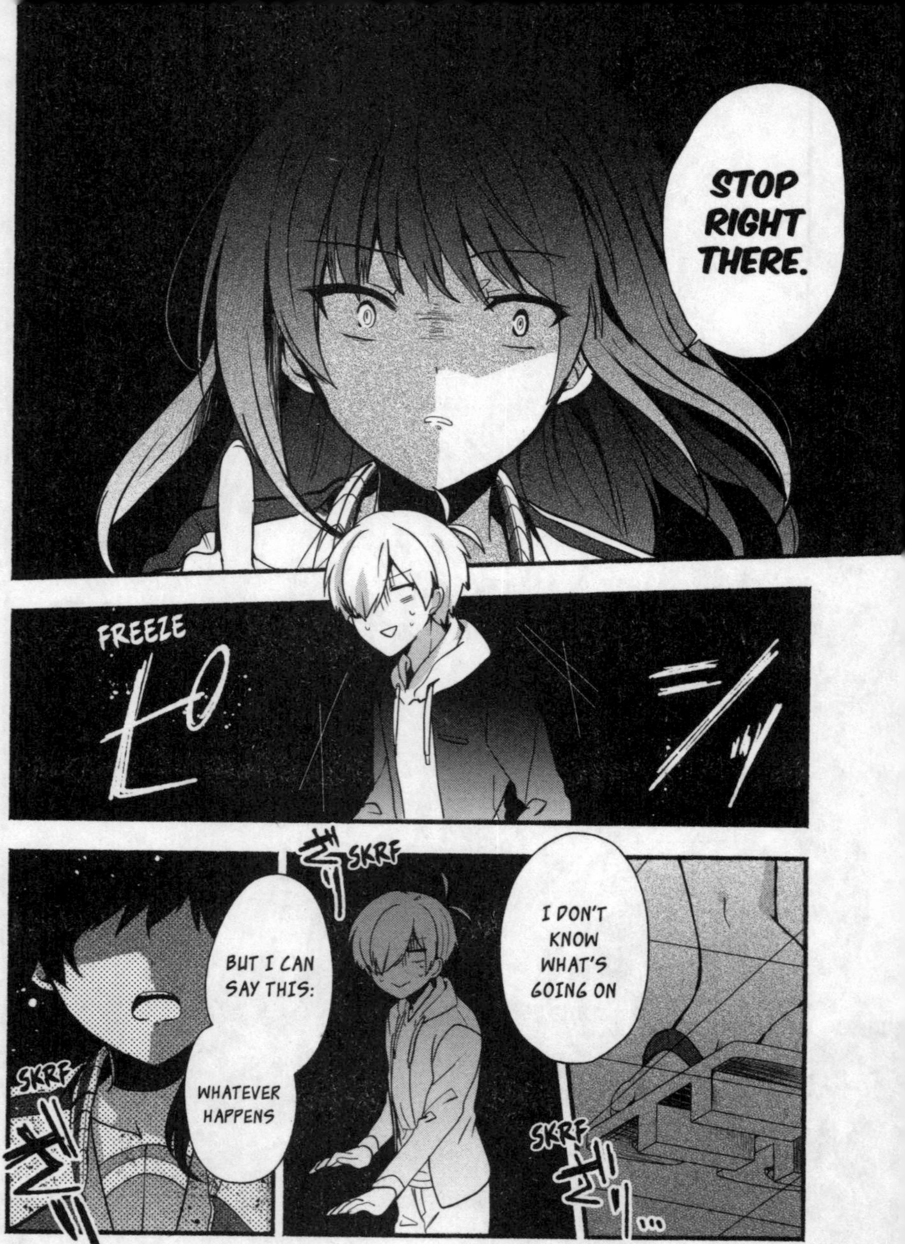
STOP RIGHT THERE.
FREEZE
I DON'T KNOW WHAT'S GOING ON
SKRF
SKRF
BUT I CAN SAY THIS:
WHATEVER HAPPENS
SKRF

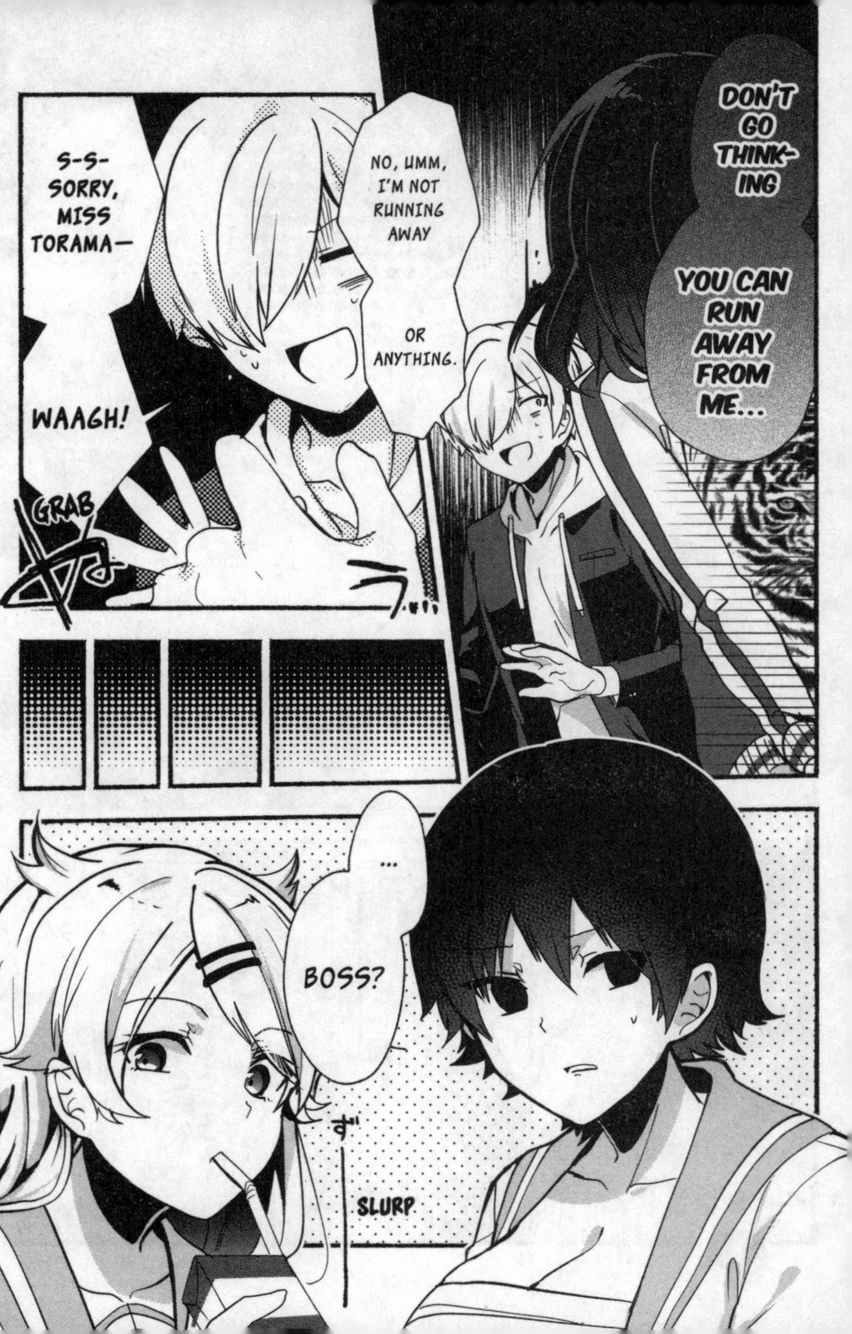
DON'T GO THINKING
YOU CAN RUN AWAY FROM ME...
NO, UMM, I'M NOT RUNNING AWAY
OR ANYTHING.
S-S-SORRY, MISS TORAMA—
WAAGH!
GRAB
...
BOSS?
ず
SLURP

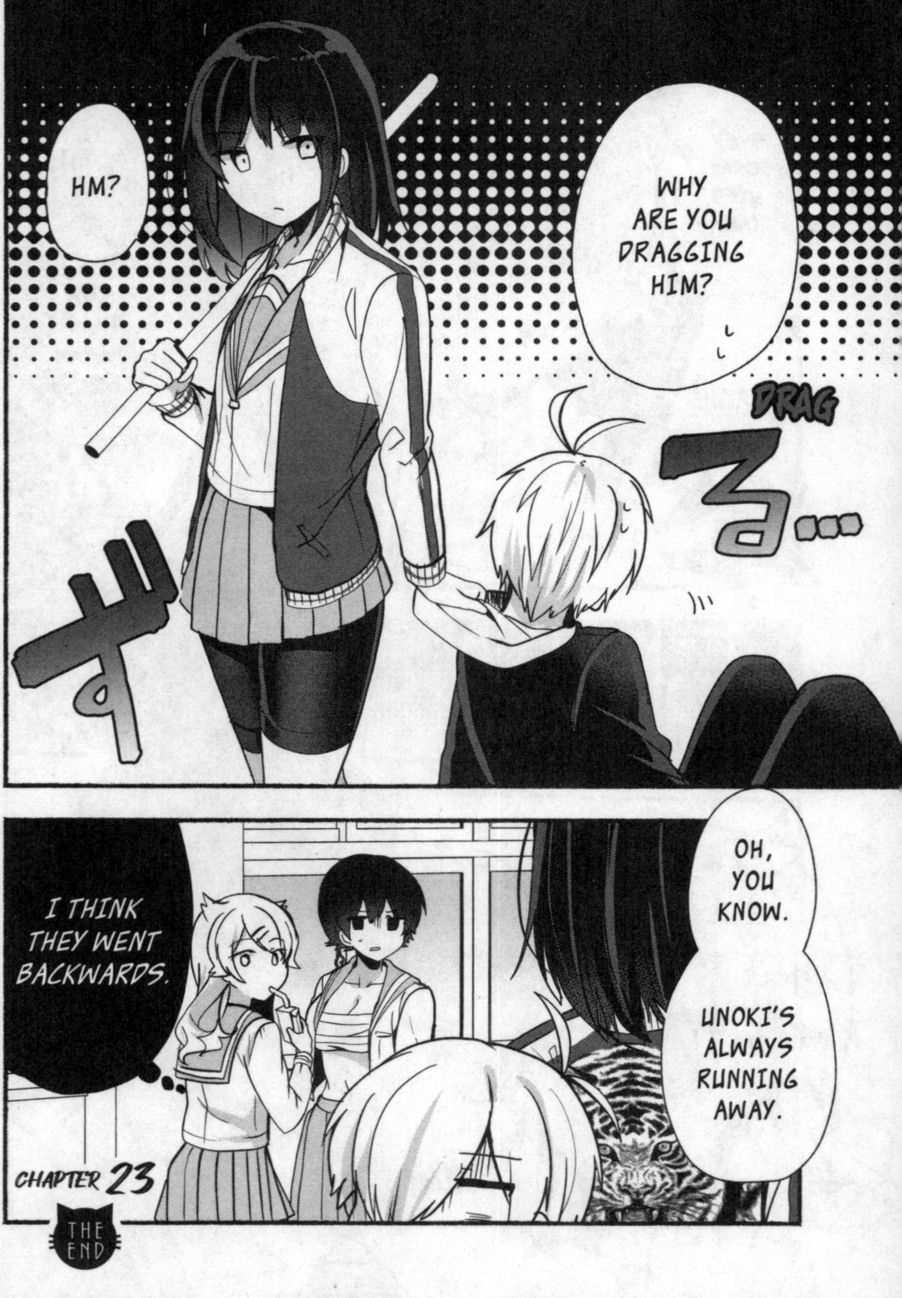
WHY ARE YOU DRAGGING HIM?
DRAG
る...
ず
HM?
OH, YOU KNOW.
UNOKI'S ALWAYS RUNNING AWAY.
I THINK THEY WENT BACKWARDS.
CHAPTER 23
THE END

CHAPTER 24

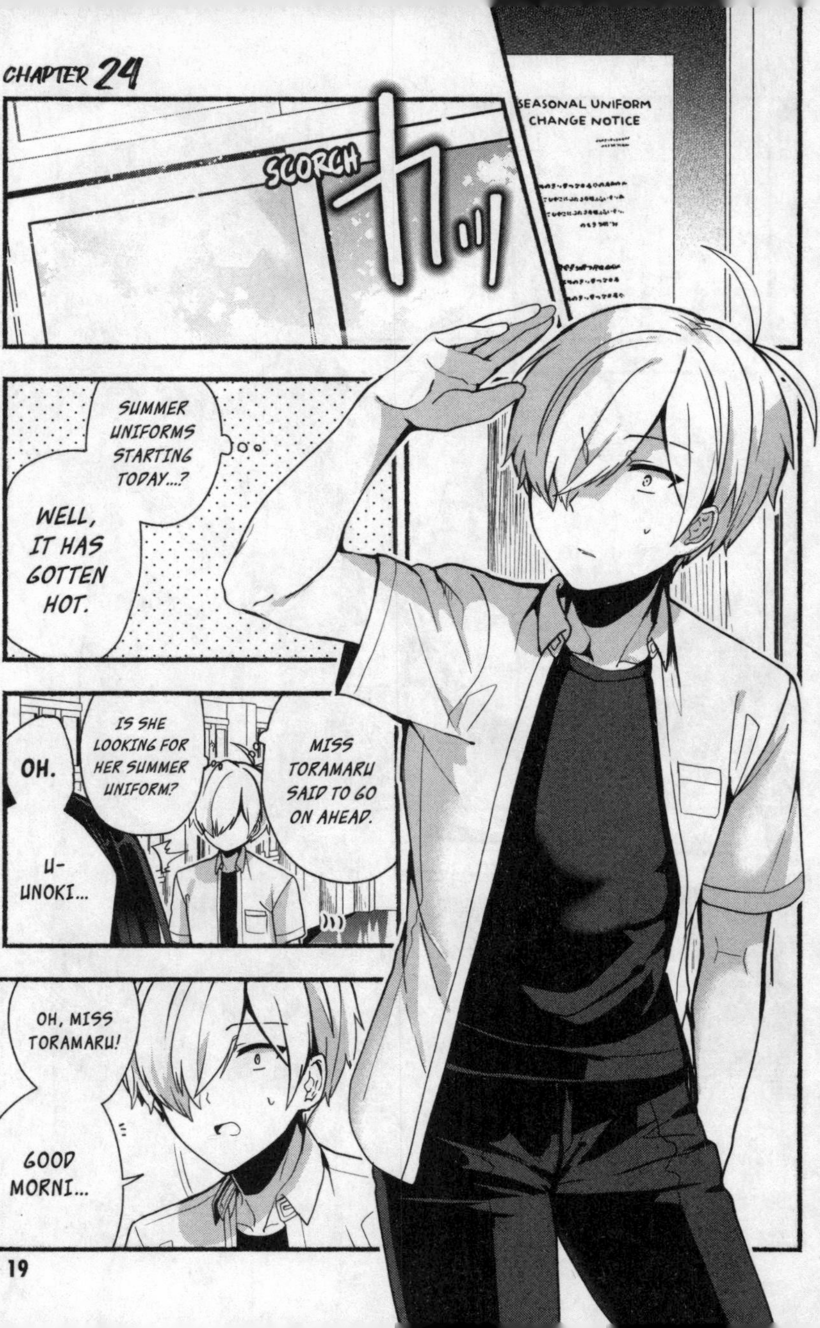

SEASONAL UNIFORM CHANGE NOTICE
SCORCH
SUMMER UNIFORMS STARTING TODAY...?
WELL, IT HAS GOTTEN HOT.
MISS TORAMARU SAID TO GO ON AHEAD.
IS SHE LOOKING FOR HER SUMMER UNIFORM?
OH.
U-UNOKI...
OH, MISS TORAMARU!
GOOD MORNI...

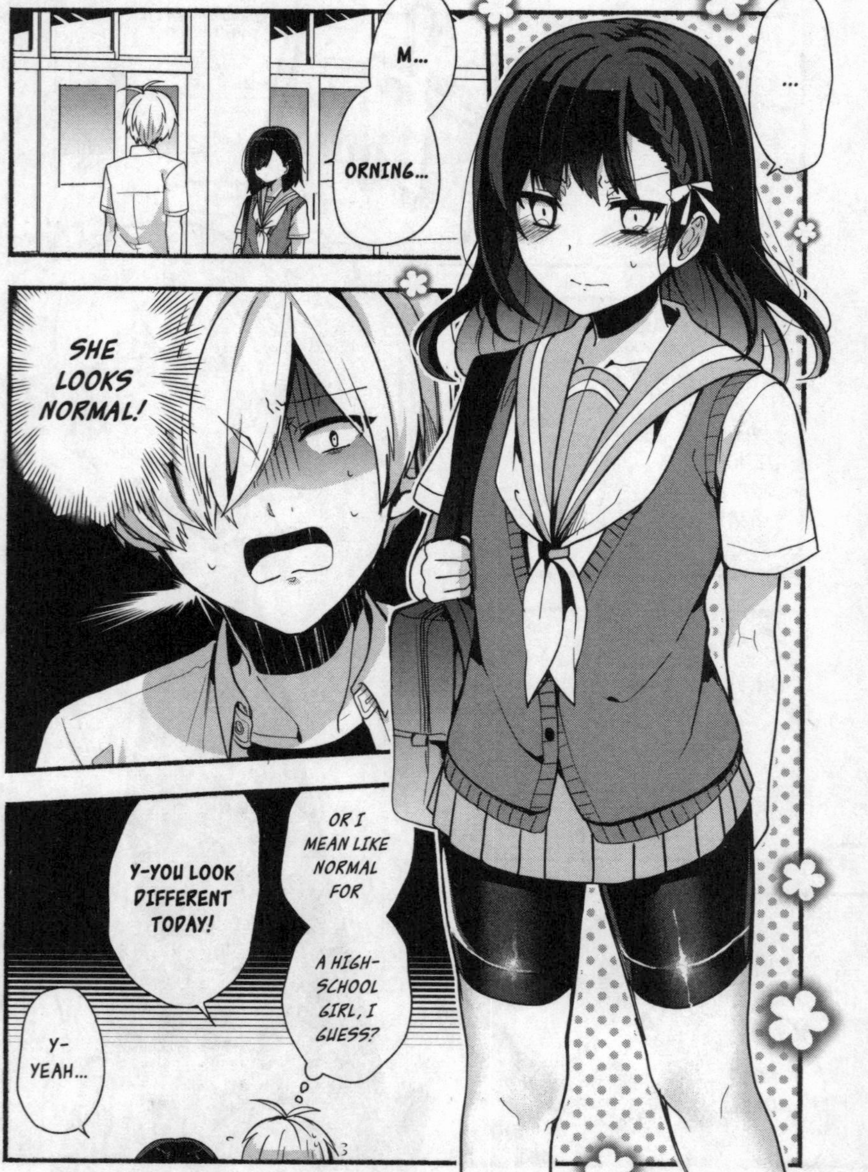
...
M... ORNING...
SHE LOOKS NORMAL!
Y-YOU LOOK DIFFERENT TODAY!
OR I MEAN LIKE NORMAL FOR A HIGH-SCHOOL GIRL, I GUESS?
Y-YEAH...

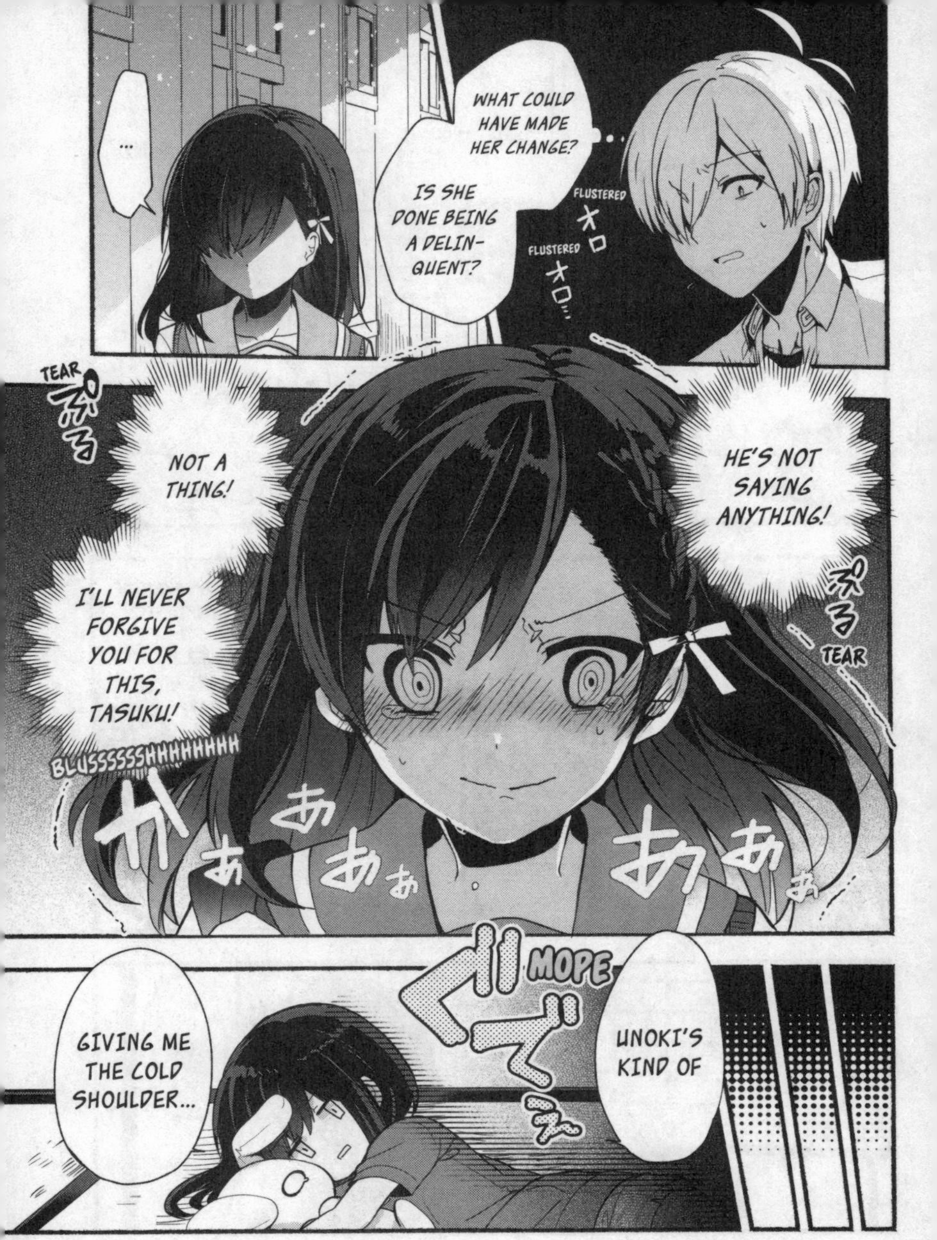
WHAT COULD HAVE MADE HER CHANGE?
IS SHE DONE BEING A DELINQUENT?
FLUSTERED
オロ
FLUSTERED
オロ...
...
HE'S NOT SAYING ANYTHING!
ぷる
TEAR
NOT A THING!
TEAR
ぷる
I'LL NEVER FORGIVE YOU FOR THIS, TASUKU!
BLUSSSSSSHHHHHHHH
かあぁあぁあぁあぁ
MOPE
ぐでん
UNOKI'S KIND OF
GIVING ME THE COLD SHOULDER...

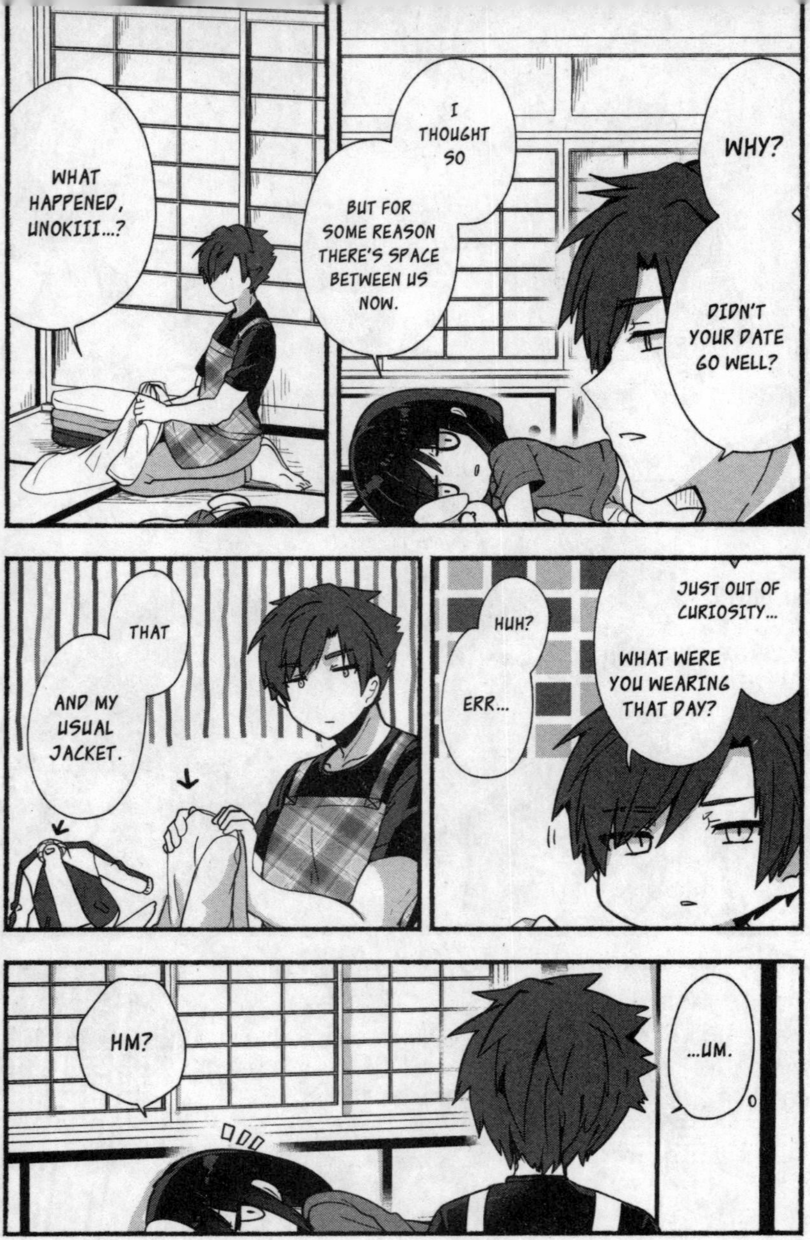
WHY?
DIDN'T YOUR DATE GO WELL?
I THOUGHT SO
BUT FOR SOME REASON THERE'S SPACE BETWEEN US NOW.
WHAT HAPPENED, UNOKIII...?
JUST OUT OF CURIOSITY...
WHAT WERE YOU WEARING THAT DAY?
HUH?
ERR...
THAT
AND MY USUAL JACKET.
...UM.
HM?

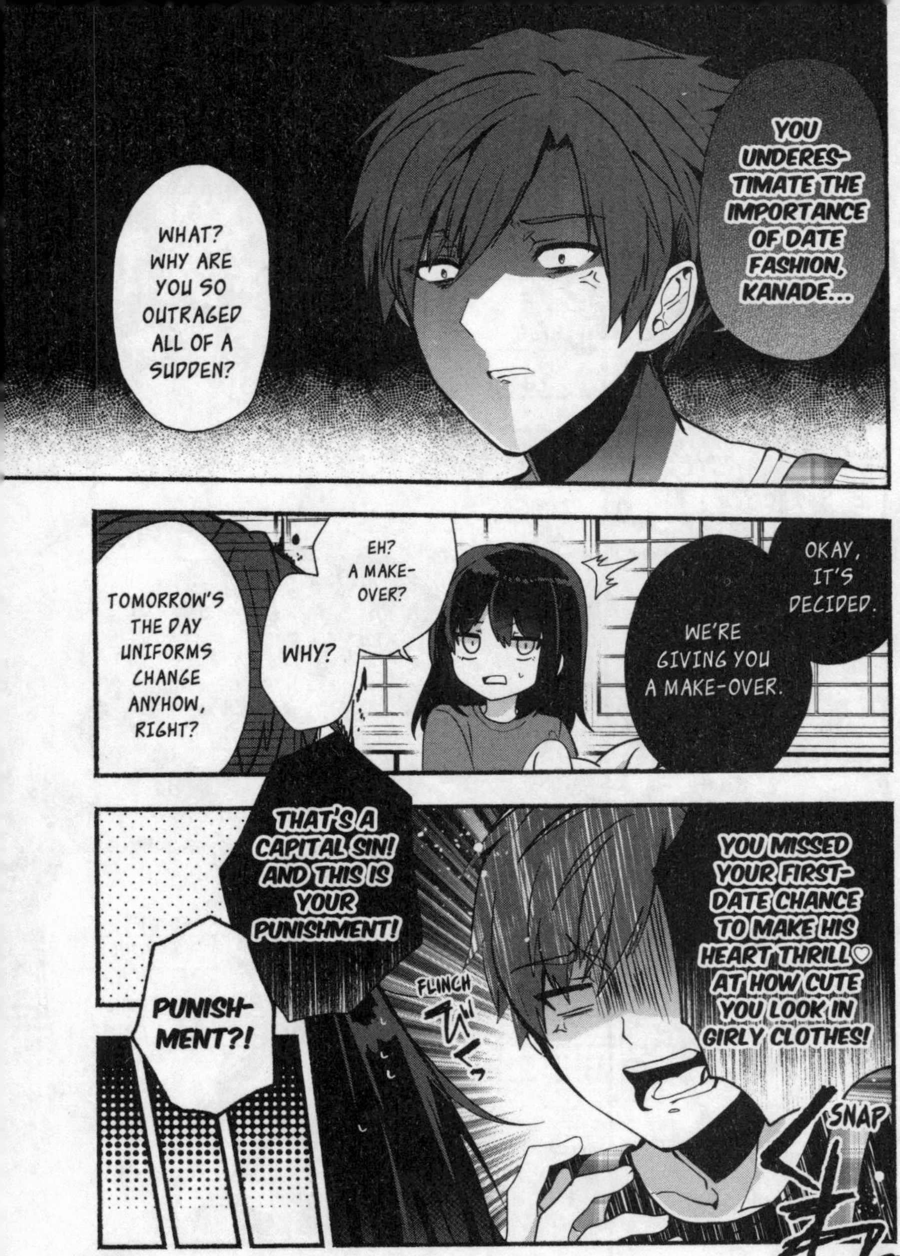
YOU UNDERESTIMATE THE IMPORTANCE OF DATE FASHION, KANADE...
WHAT? WHY ARE YOU SO OUTRAGED ALL OF A SUDDEN?
OKAY, IT'S DECIDED.
WE'RE GIVING YOU A MAKE-OVER.
EH? A MAKE-OVER?
WHY?
TOMORROW'S THE DAY UNIFORMS CHANGE ANYHOW, RIGHT?
YOU MISSED YOUR FIRST-DATE CHANCE TO MAKE HIS HEART THRILL♡ AT HOW CUTE YOU LOOK IN GIRLY CLOTHES!
THAT'S A CAPITAL SIN! AND THIS IS YOUR PUNISHMENT!
FLINCH
PUNISHMENT?!
SNAP

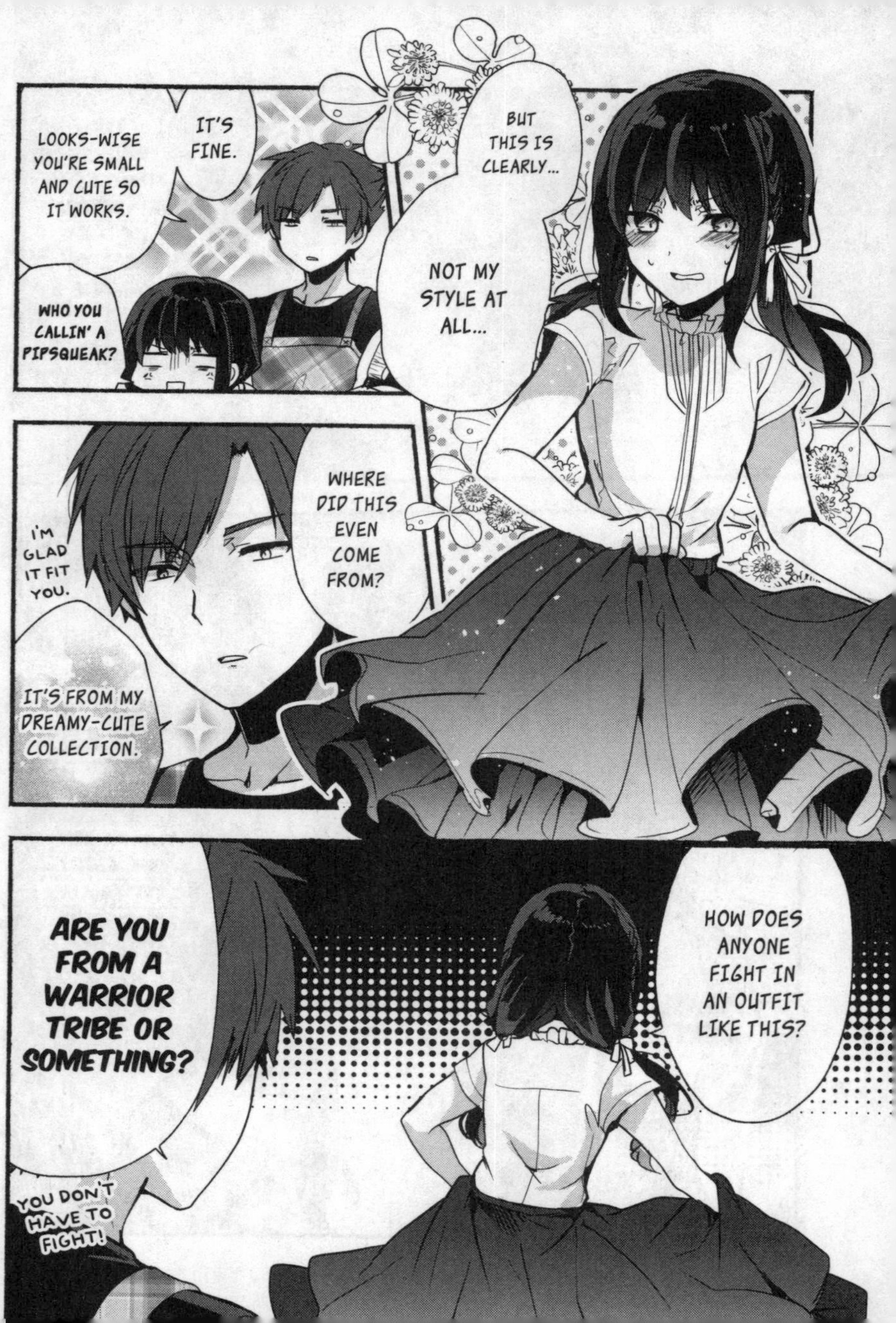
BUT THIS IS CLEARLY...
NOT MY STYLE AT ALL...
IT'S FINE.
LOOKS-WISE YOU'RE SMALL AND CUTE SO IT WORKS.
WHO YOU CALLIN' A PIPSQUEAK?
WHERE DID THIS EVEN COME FROM?
I'M GLAD IT FIT YOU.
IT'S FROM MY DREAMY-CUTE COLLECTION.
HOW DOES ANYONE FIGHT IN AN OUTFIT LIKE THIS?
ARE YOU FROM A WARRIOR TRIBE OR SOMETHING?
YOU DON'T HAVE TO FIGHT!

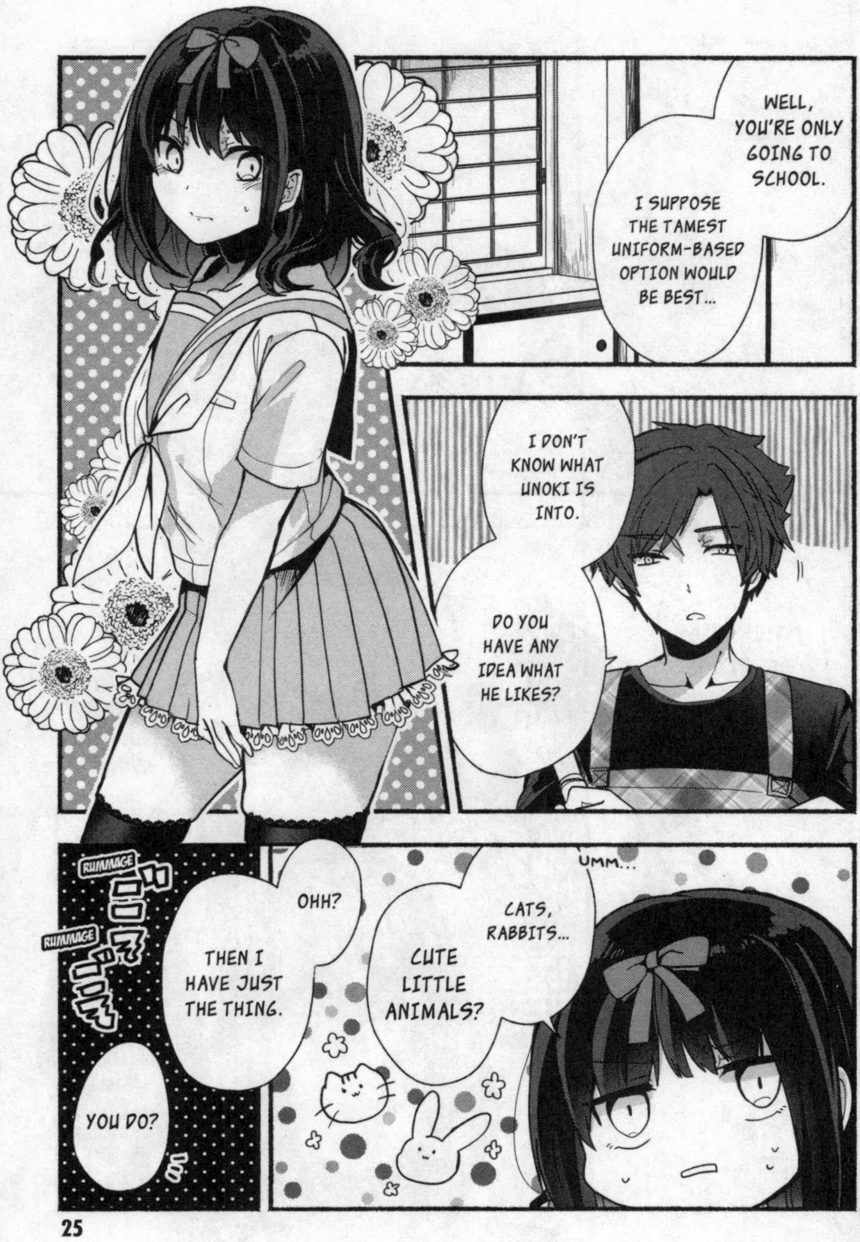
WELL, YOU'RE ONLY GOING TO SCHOOL.
I SUPPOSE THE TAMEST UNIFORM-BASED OPTION WOULD BE BEST...
I DON'T KNOW WHAT UNOKI IS INTO.
DO YOU HAVE ANY IDEA WHAT HE LIKES?
UMM...
CATS, RABBITS...
CUTE LITTLE ANIMALS?
OHH?
THEN I HAVE JUST THE THING.
RUMMAGE
RUMMAGE
YOU DO?

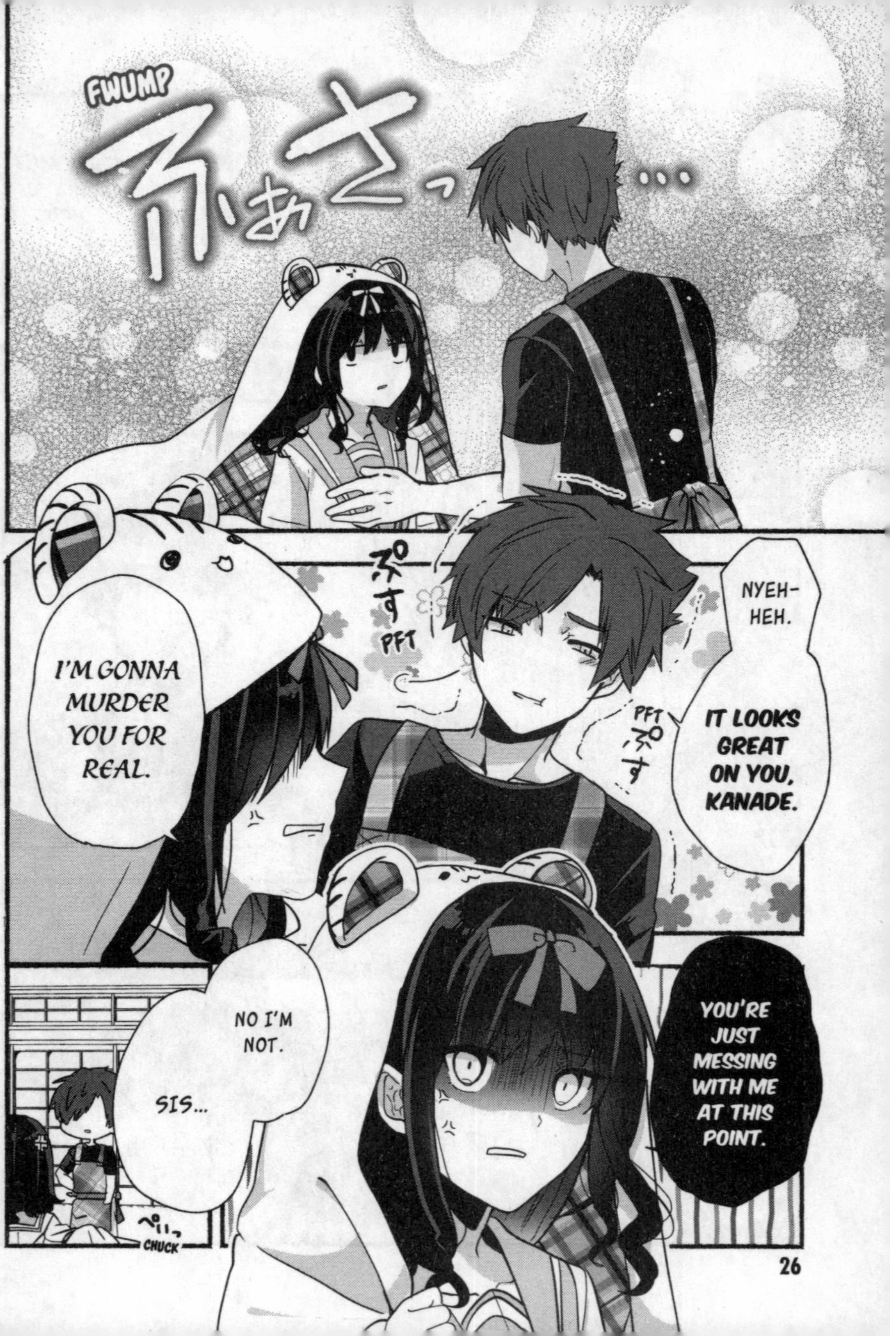
FWUMP
ふあさっ…
ぷす
PFT
NYEH-HEH.
IT LOOKS GREAT ON YOU, KANADE.
PFT
ぷす
I'M GONNA MURDER YOU FOR REAL.
YOU'RE JUST MESSING WITH ME AT THIS POINT.
NO I'M NOT.
SIS...
ぺいっ
CHUCK

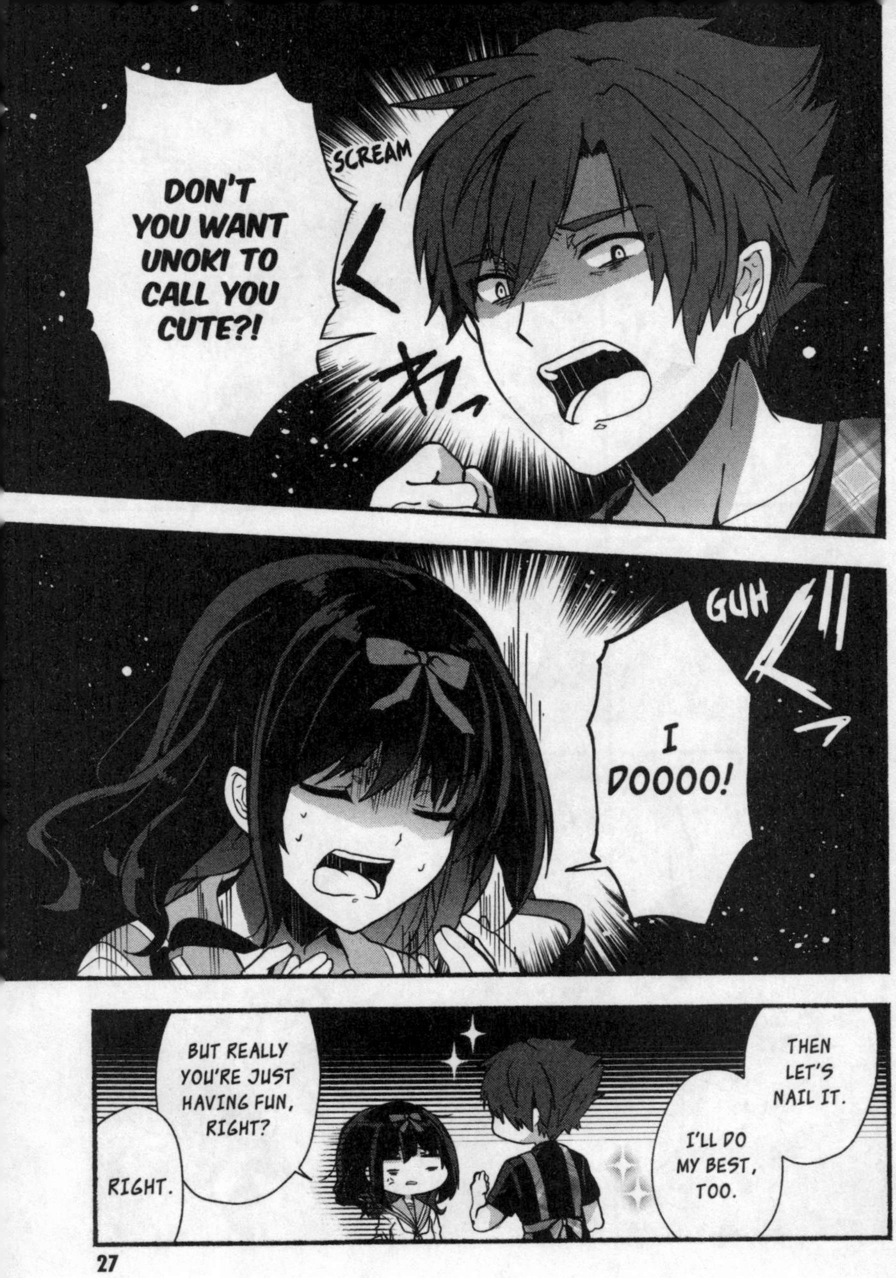
SCREAM
DON'T YOU WANT UNOKI TO CALL YOU CUTE?!
GUH
I DOOOO!
THEN LET'S NAIL IT.
I'LL DO MY BEST, TOO.
BUT REALLY YOU'RE JUST HAVING FUN, RIGHT?
RIGHT.

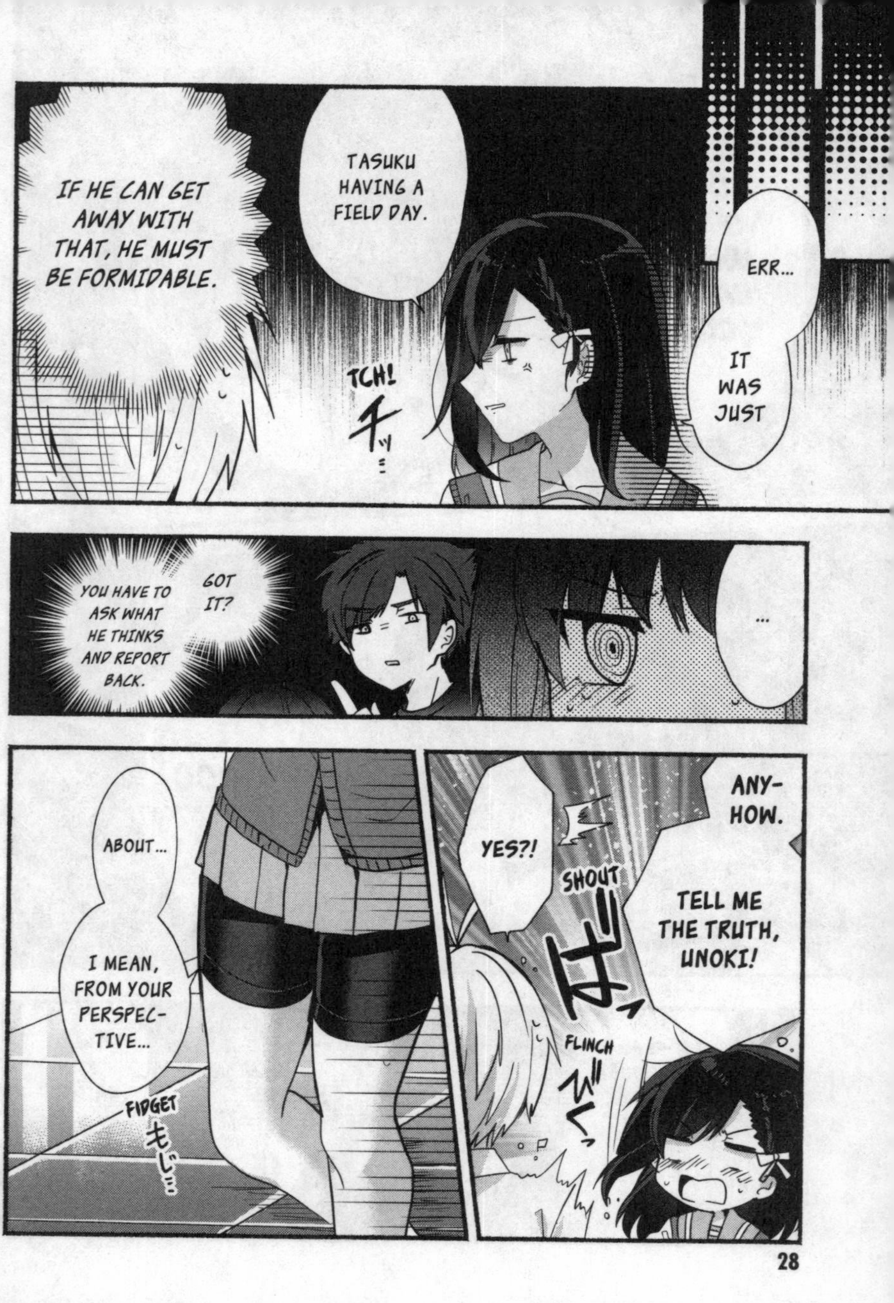
ERR...
IT WAS JUST
TASUKU HAVING A FIELD DAY.
TCH!
チッ
IF HE CAN GET AWAY WITH THAT, HE MUST BE FORMIDABLE.
...
YOU HAVE TO ASK WHAT HE THINKS AND REPORT BACK.
GOT IT?
ANY-HOW.
TELL ME THE TRUTH, UNOKI!
YES?!
SHOUT
ばっ
FLINCH
びくっ
ABOUT...
I MEAN, FROM YOUR PERSPEC-TIVE...
FIDGET
もじ...

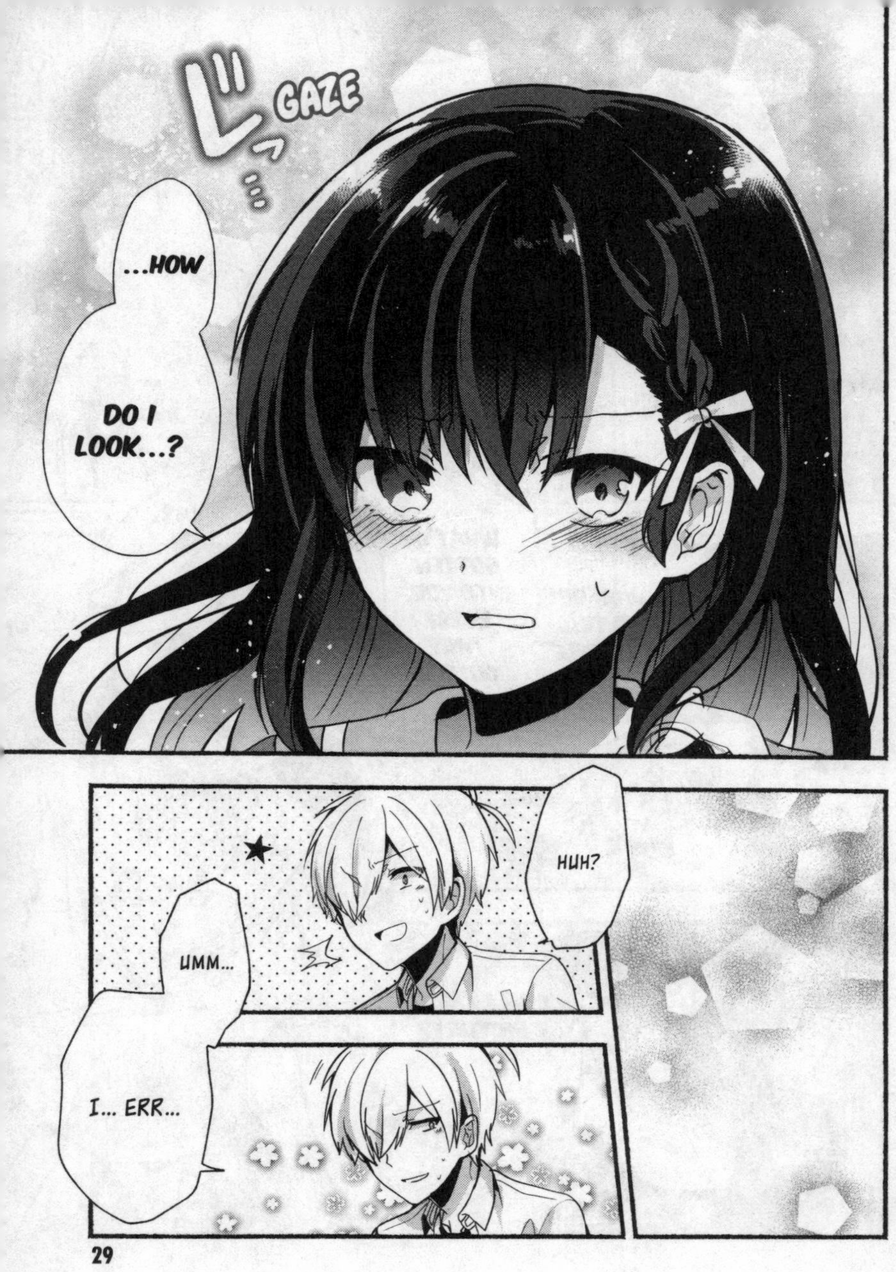
ジ
GAZE
...HOW DO I LOOK...?
HUH?
UMM...
I... ERR...

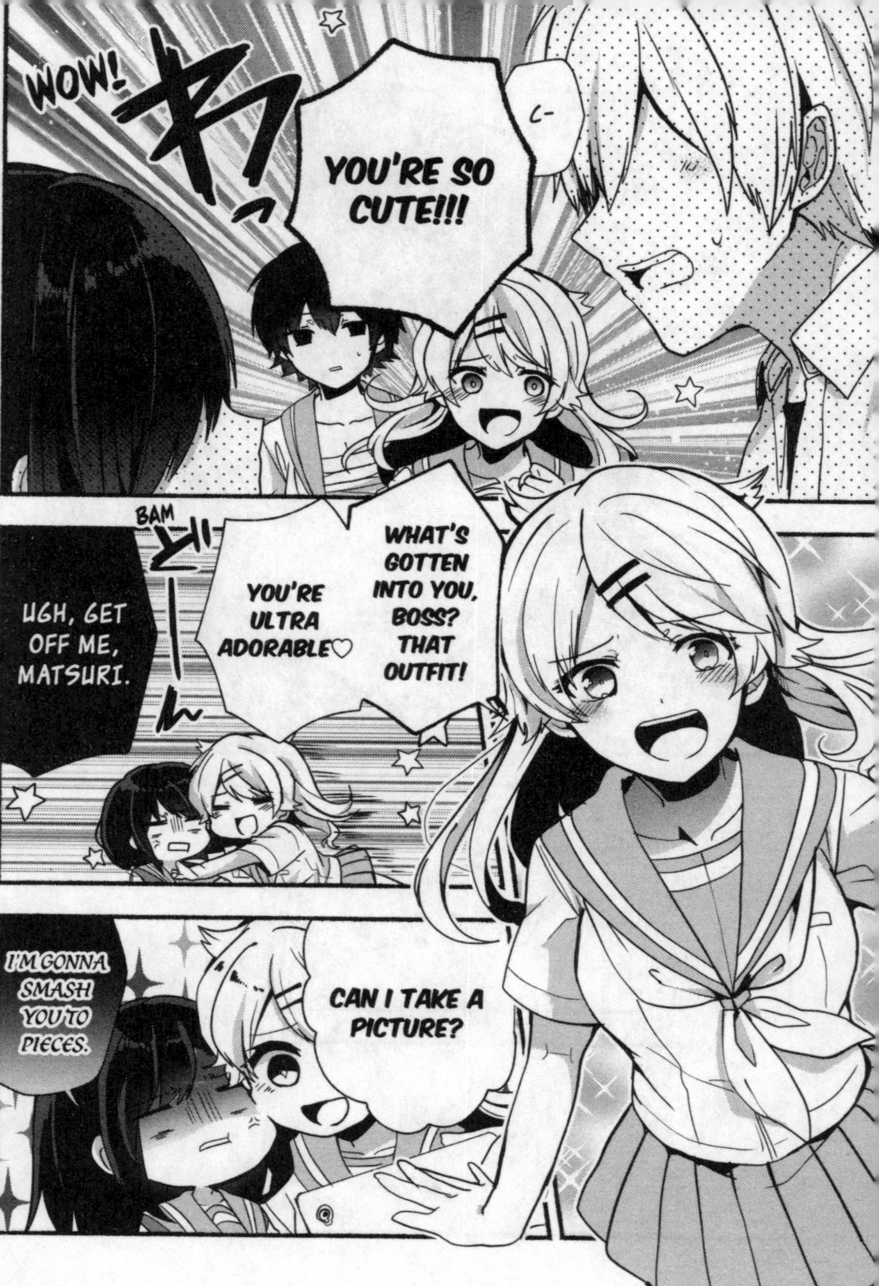

WOW!
YOU'RE SO CUTE!!!
BAM
WHAT'S GOTTEN INTO YOU, BOSS? THAT OUTFIT!
YOU'RE ULTRA ADORABLE♡
UGH, GET OFF ME, MATSURI.
CAN I TAKE A PICTURE?
I'M GONNA SMASH YOU TO PIECES.

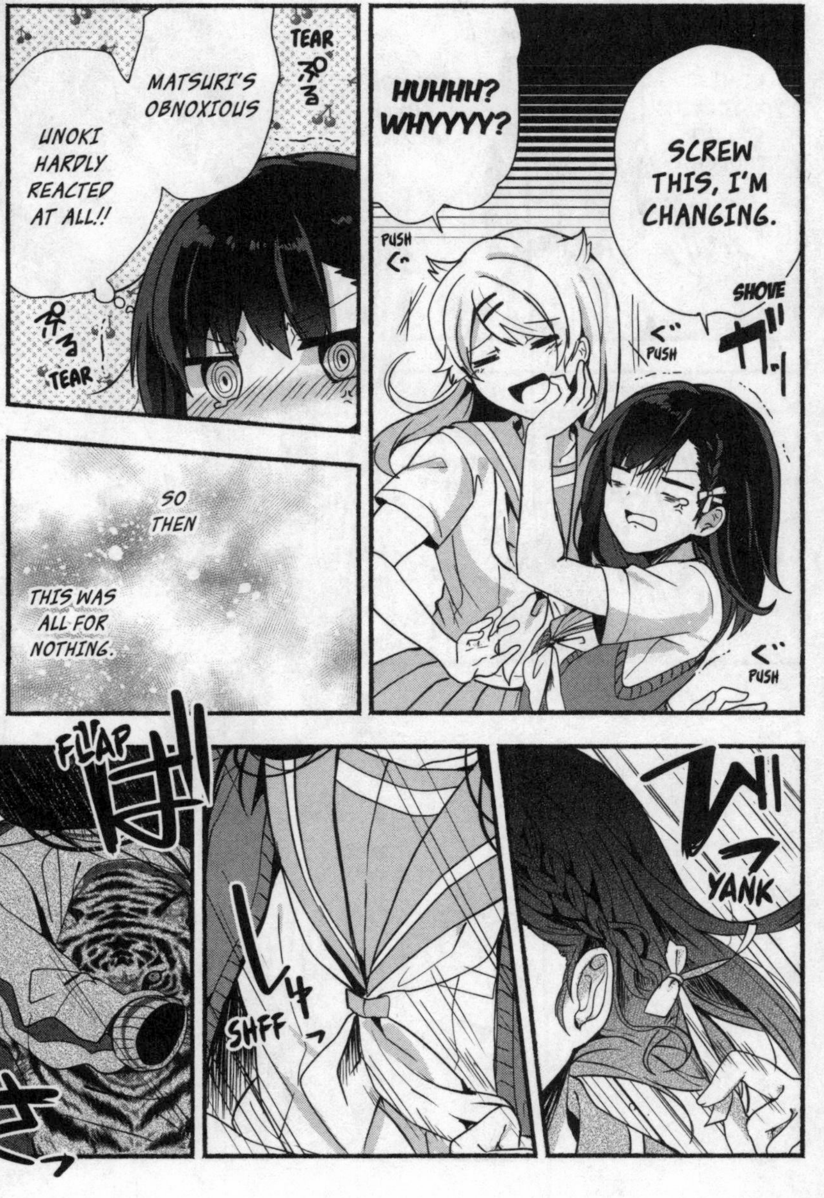
SCREW THIS, I'M CHANGING.
HUHHH? WHYYYY?
SHOVE
PUSH
PUSH
PUSH
TEAR
MATSURI'S OBNOXIOUS
UNOKI HARDLY REACTED AT ALL!!
TEAR
SO THEN
THIS WAS ALL FOR NOTHING.
YANK
SHFF
FLAP

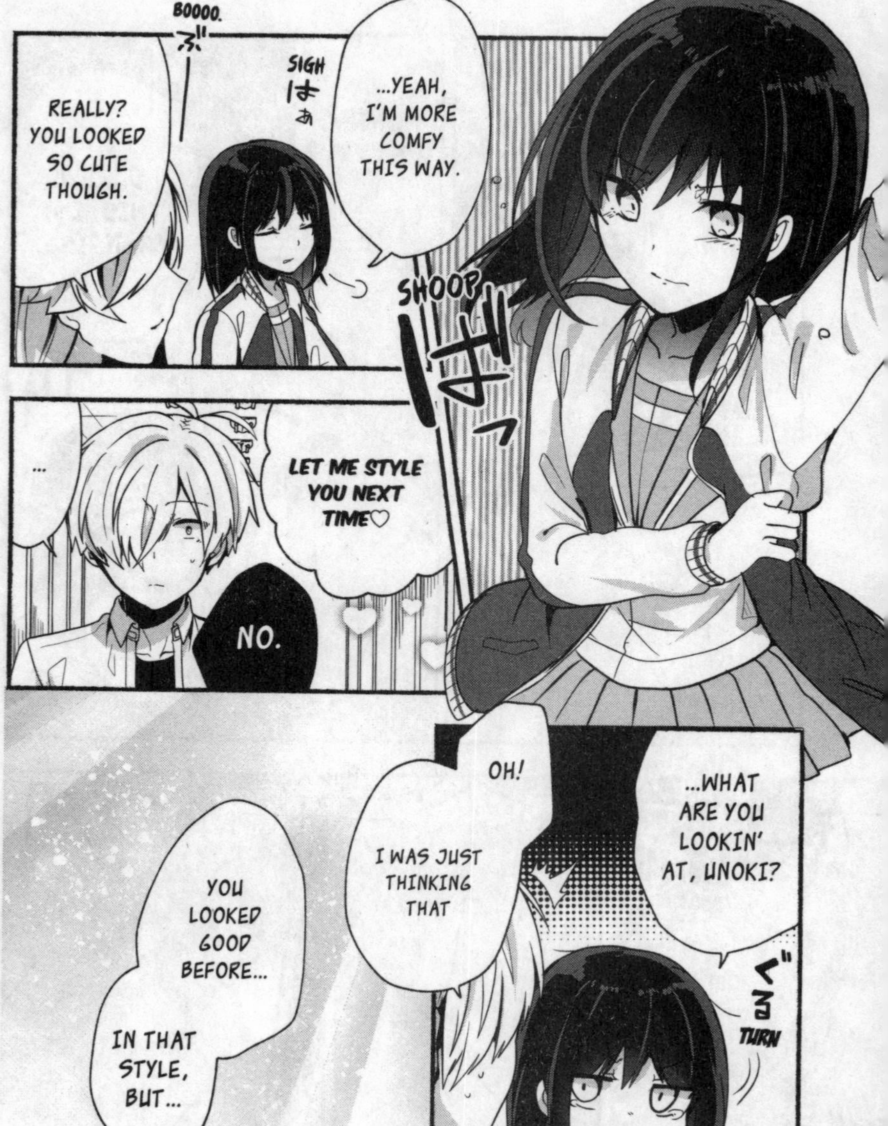
SHOOP
ぱっ
...YEAH, I'M MORE COMFY THIS WAY.
SIGH
はぁ
BOOOO.
ぶー
REALLY? YOU LOOKED SO CUTE THOUGH.
LET ME STYLE YOU NEXT TIME♡
...
NO.
...WHAT ARE YOU LOOKIN' AT, UNOKI?
TURN
OH!
I WAS JUST THINKING THAT
YOU LOOKED GOOD BEFORE...
IN THAT STYLE, BUT...

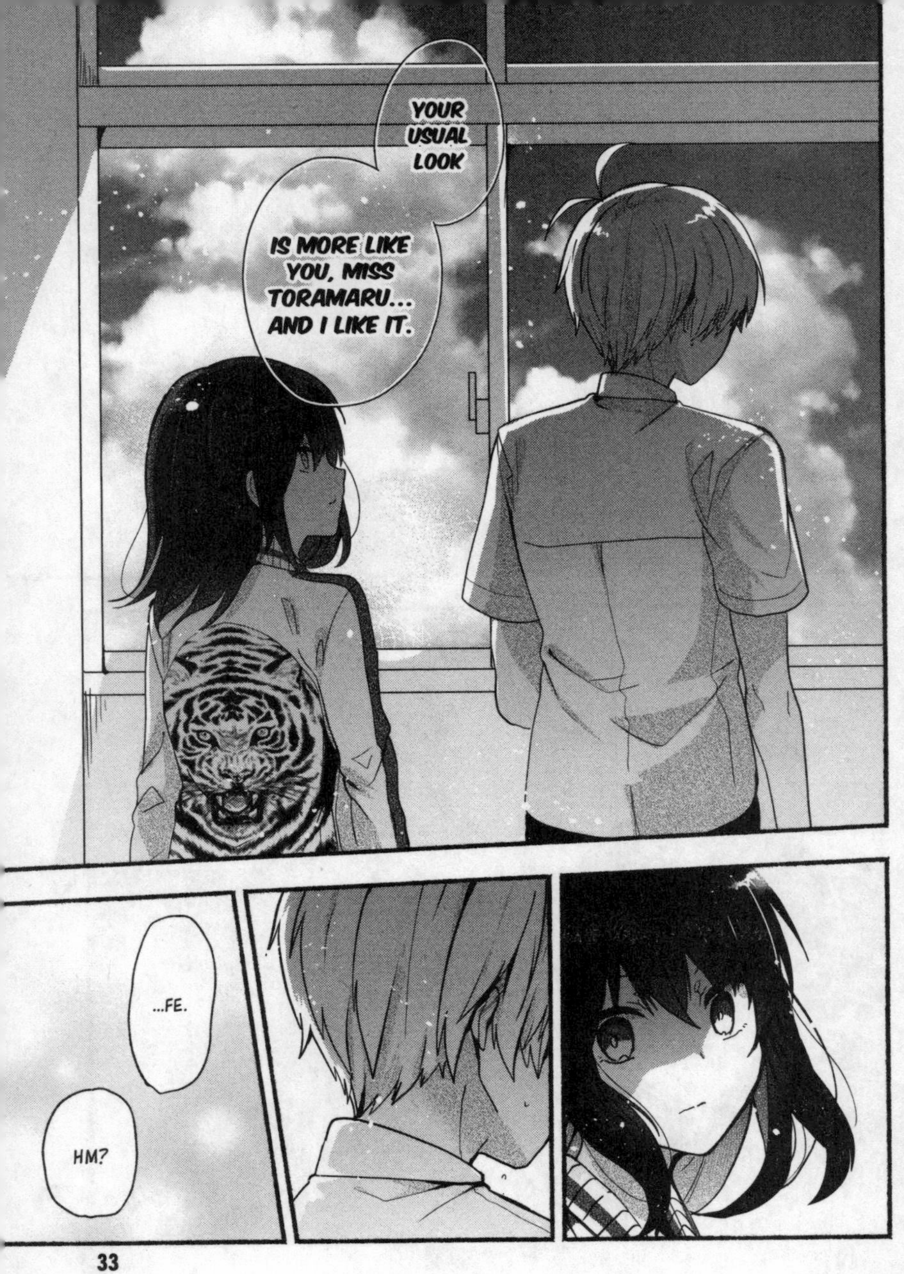
YOUR USUAL LOOK
IS MORE LIKE YOU, MISS TORAMARU... AND I LIKE IT.
...FE.
HM?

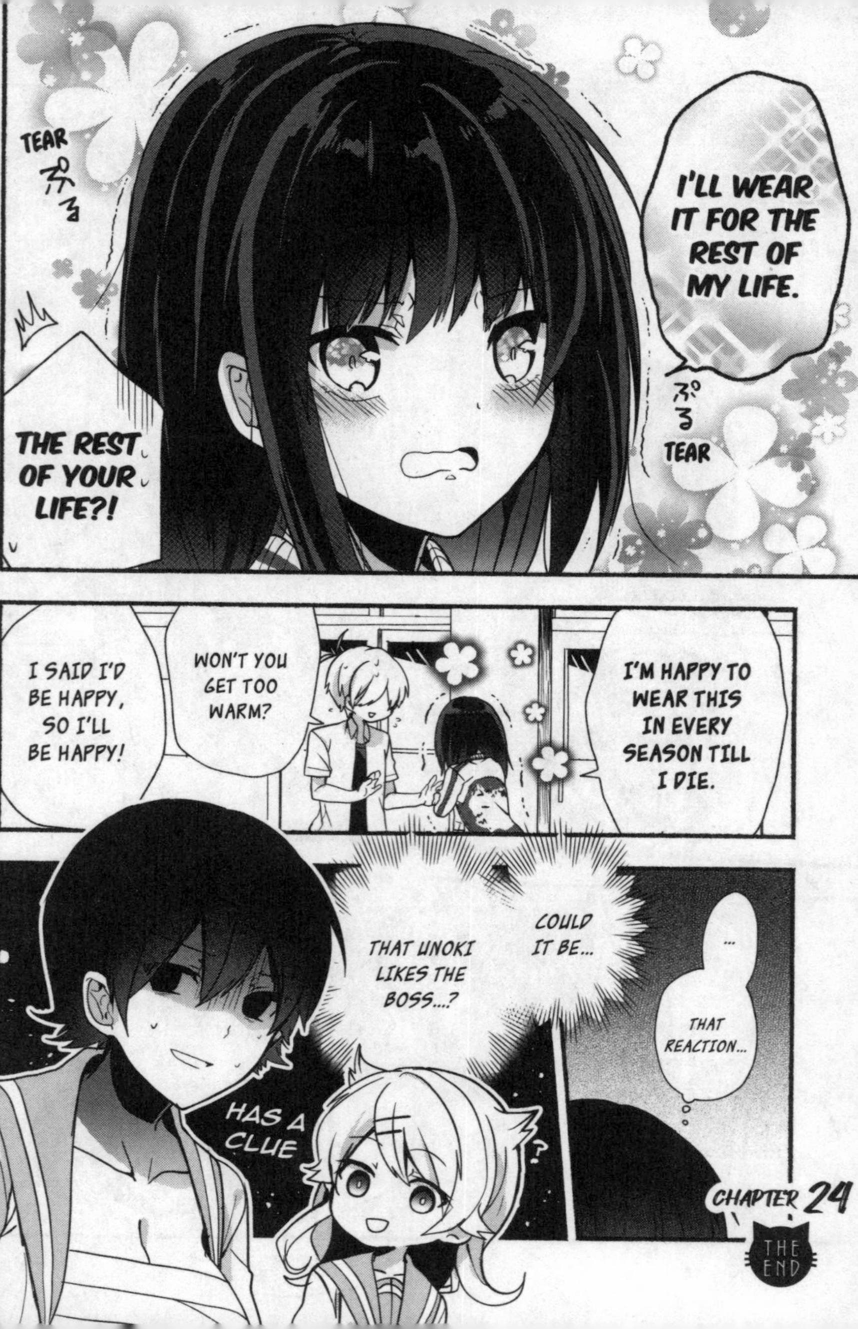
I'LL WEAR IT FOR THE REST OF MY LIFE.
ぷる
TEAR
TEAR
ぷる
THE REST OF YOUR LIFE?!
I'M HAPPY TO WEAR THIS IN EVERY SEASON TILL I DIE.
WON'T YOU GET TOO WARM?
I SAID I'D BE HAPPY, SO I'LL BE HAPPY!
...
THAT REACTION...
COULD IT BE...
THAT UNOKI LIKES THE BOSS...?
HAS A CLUE
CHAPTER 24
THE END

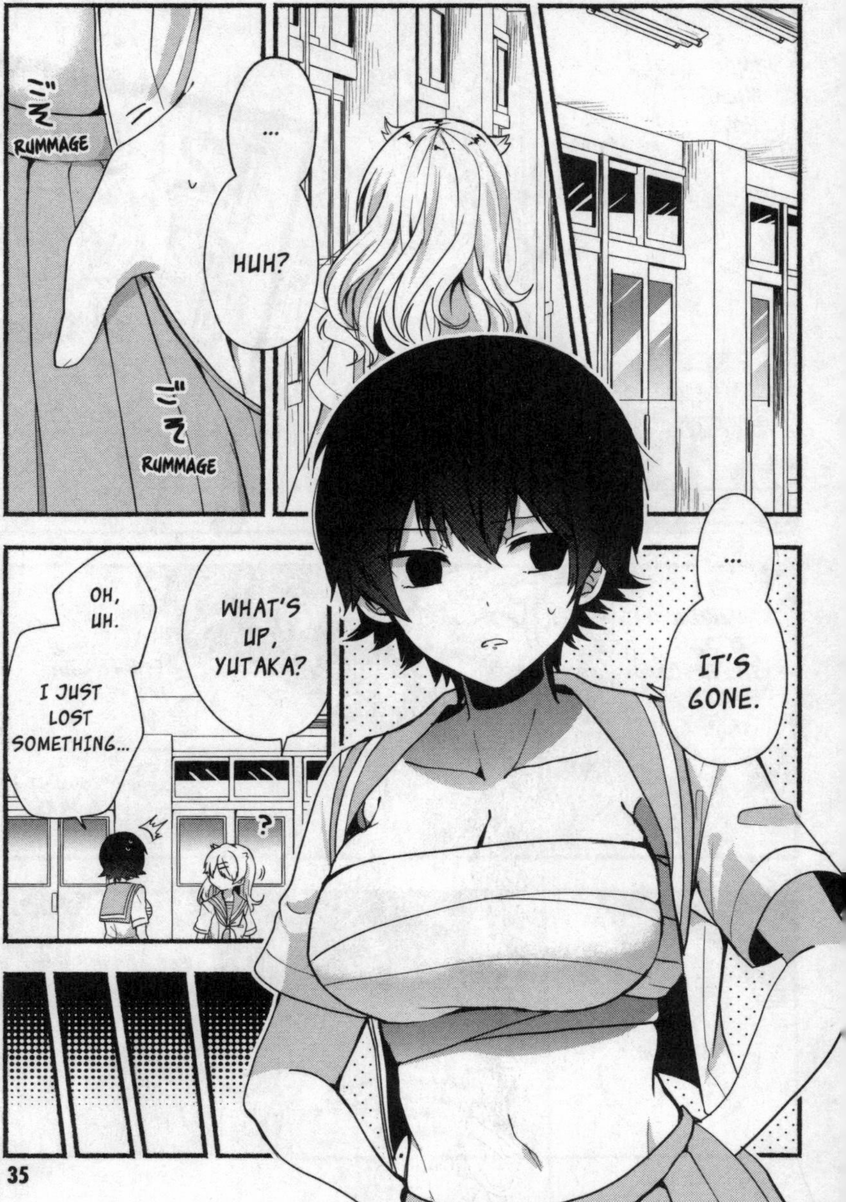
...
HUH?
ごそ
RUMMAGE
ごそ
RUMMAGE
...
IT'S GONE.
WHAT'S UP, YUTAKA?
OH, UH.
I JUST LOST SOMETHING...
?

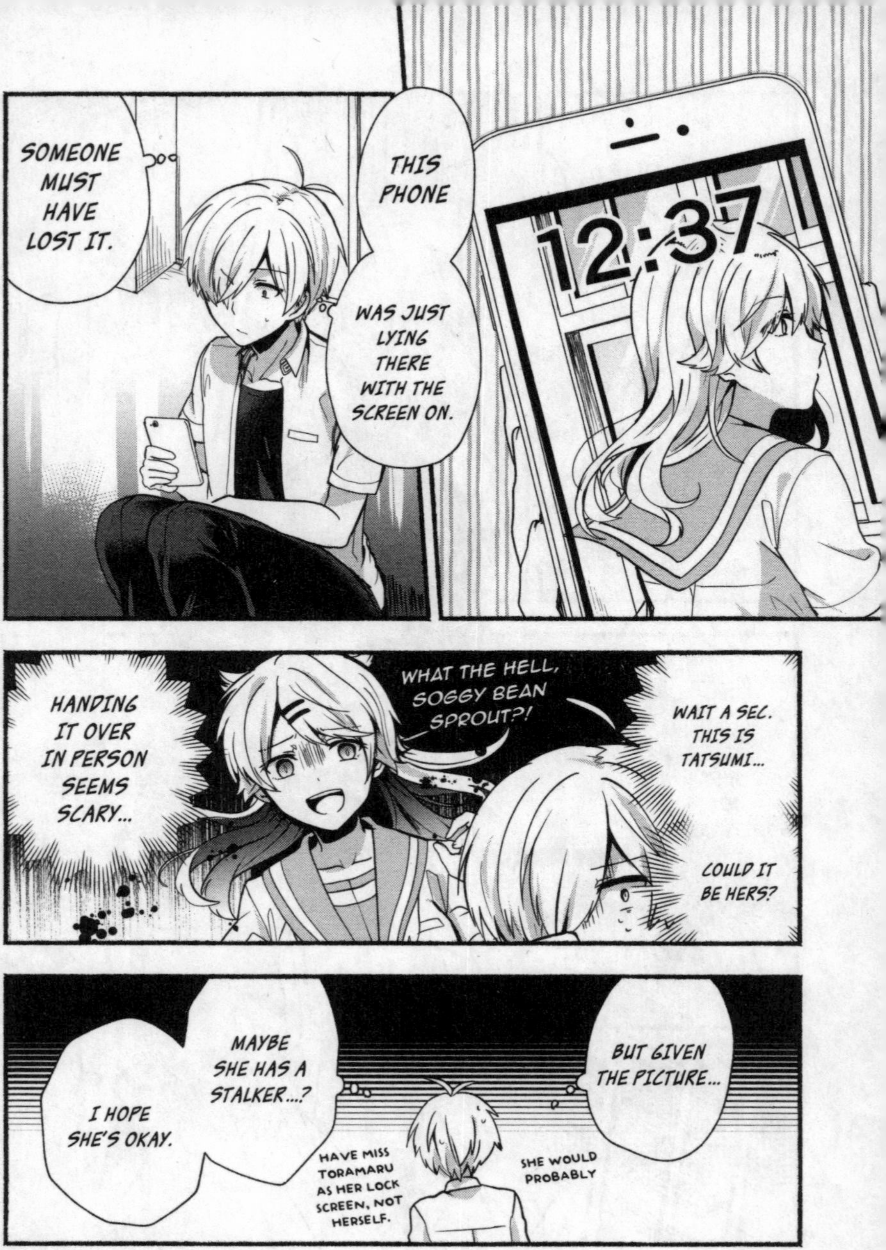
12:37
THIS PHONE
WAS JUST LYING THERE WITH THE SCREEN ON.
SOMEONE MUST HAVE LOST IT.
WAIT A SEC. THIS IS TATSUMI...
COULD IT BE HERS?
WHAT THE HELL, SOGGY BEAN SPROUT?!
HANDING IT OVER IN PERSON SEEMS SCARY...
BUT GIVEN THE PICTURE...
SHE WOULD PROBABLY
HAVE MISS TORAMARU AS HER LOCK SCREEN, NOT HERSELF.
MAYBE SHE HAS A STALKER...?
I HOPE SHE'S OKAY.

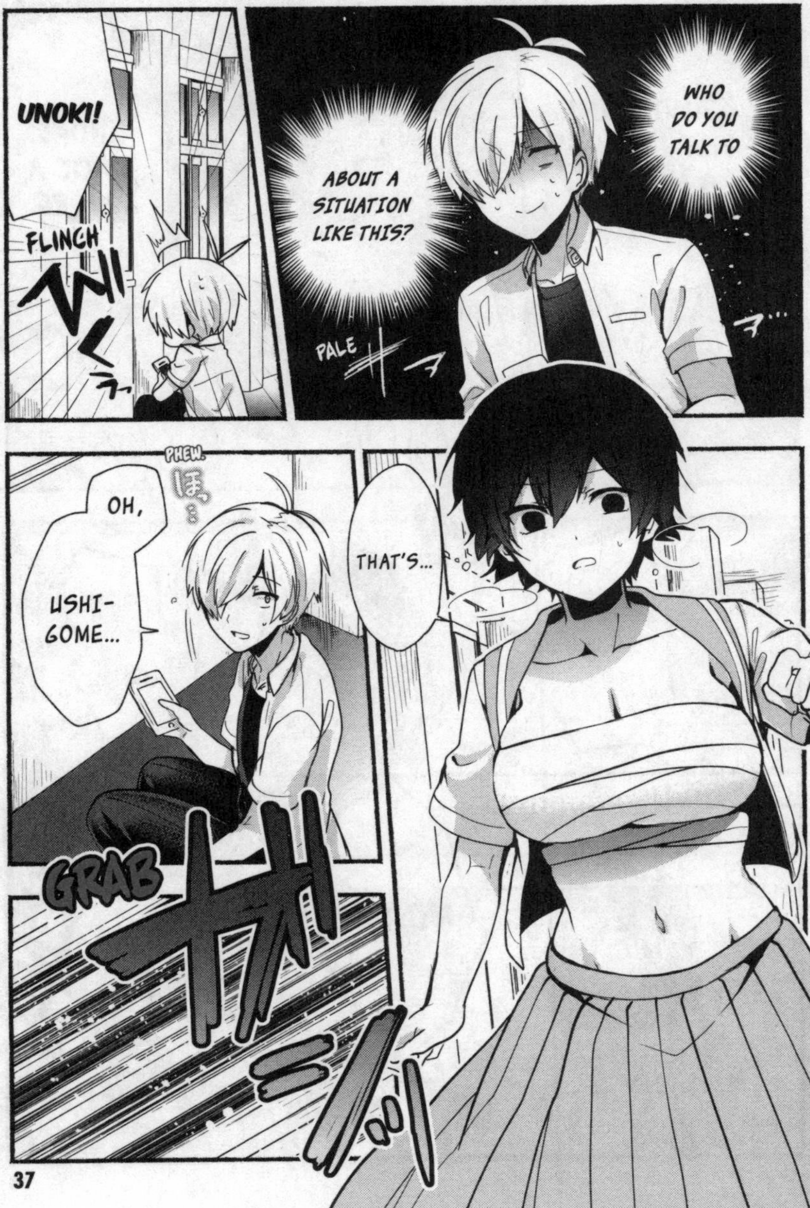

WHO DO YOU TALK TO
ABOUT A SITUATION LIKE THIS?
PALE
UNOKI!
FLINCH
THAT'S...
PHEW.
OH,
USHI-GOME...
GRAB

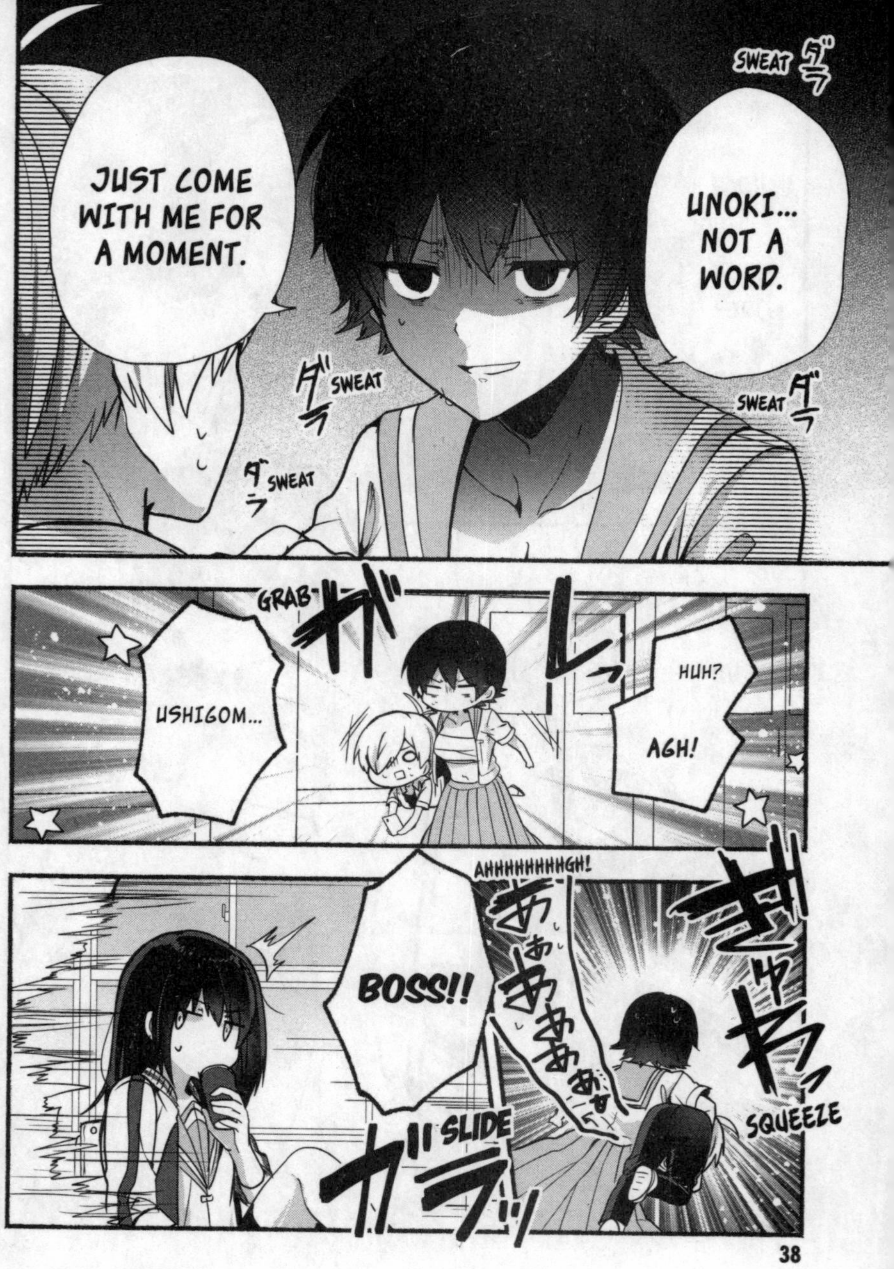
SWEAT
UNOKI... NOT A WORD.
SWEAT
JUST COME WITH ME FOR A MOMENT.
SWEAT
SWEAT
HUH?
AGH!
GRAB
USHIGOM...
SQUEEZE
AHHHHHHHHGH!
BOSS!!
SLIDE

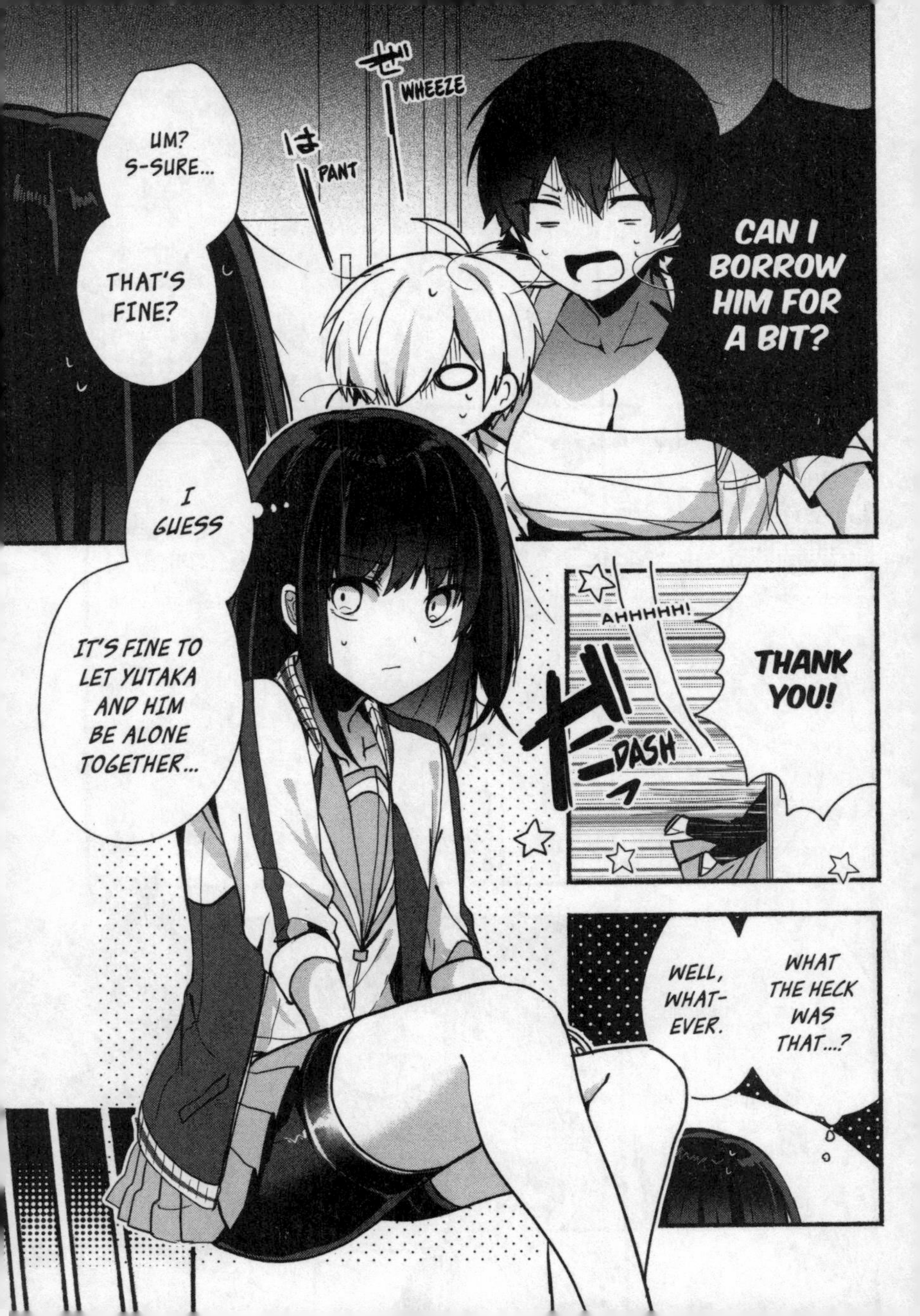
CAN I BORROW HIM FOR A BIT?
ぜ WHEEZE
は PANT
UM? S-SURE...
THAT'S FINE?
I GUESS
AHHHHH!
THANK YOU!
DASH
WHAT THE HECK WAS THAT...?
WELL, WHAT-EVER.
IT'S FINE TO LET YUTAKA AND HIM BE ALONE TOGETHER...

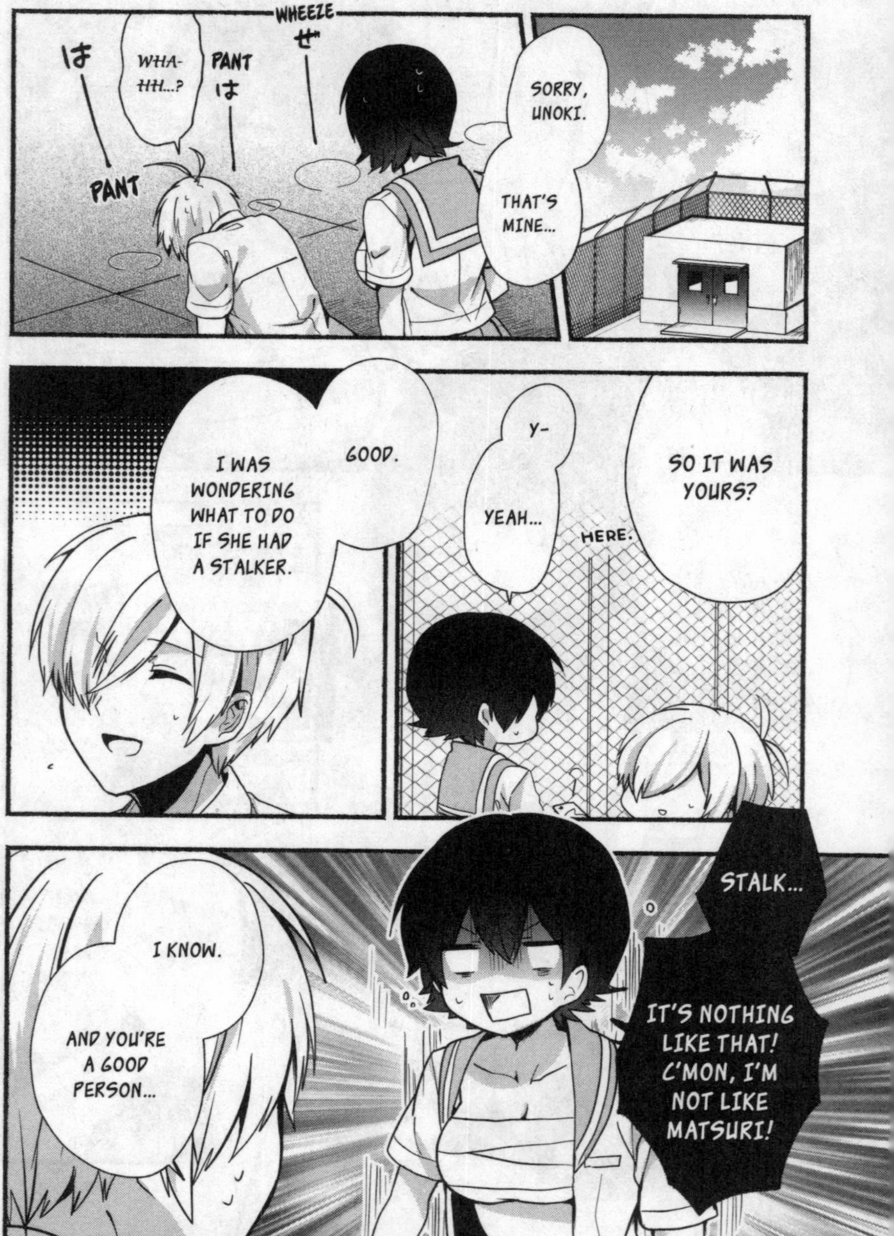
SORRY, UNOKI.
THAT'S MINE...
WHEEZE
ぜ
PANT
は
WHA-HH...?
は
PANT
SO IT WAS YOURS?
HERE.
Y- YEAH...
GOOD.
I WAS WONDERING WHAT TO DO IF SHE HAD A STALKER.
STALK...
IT'S NOTHING LIKE THAT! C'MON, I'M NOT LIKE MATSURI!
I KNOW.
AND YOU'RE A GOOD PERSON...

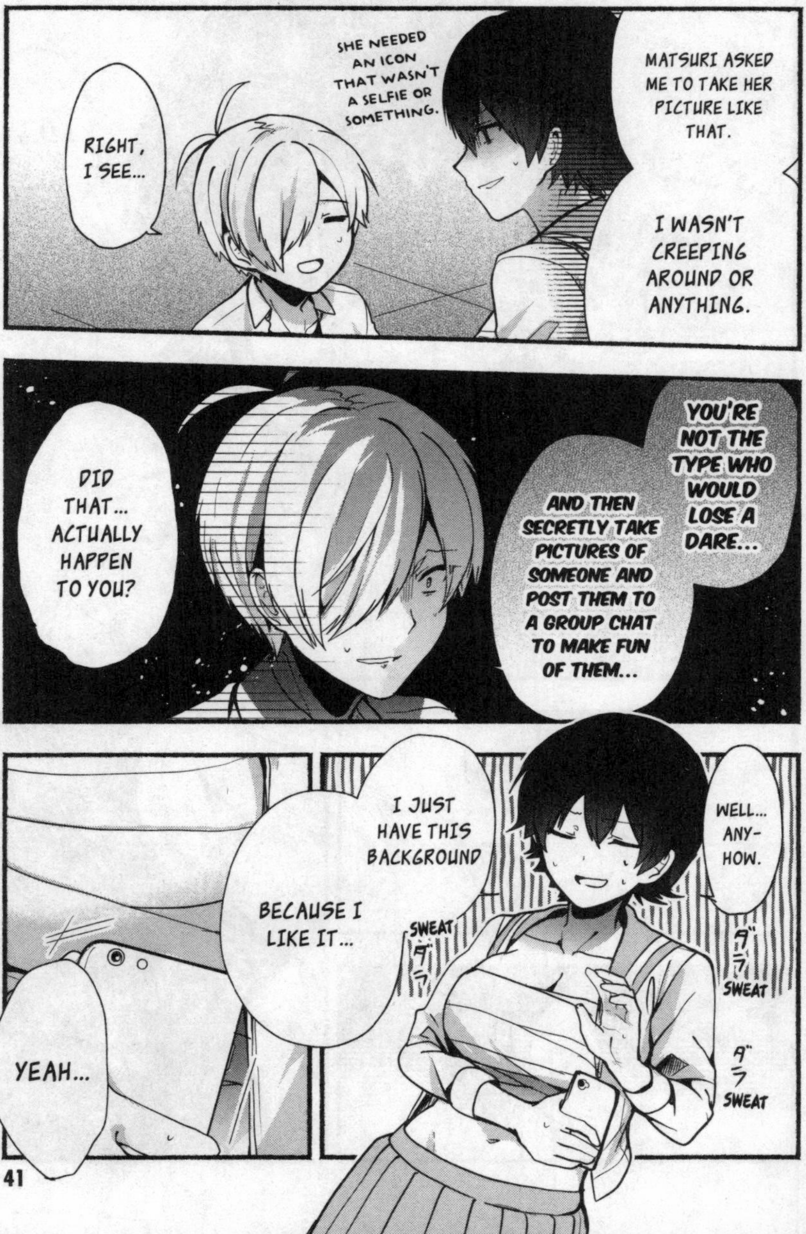
MATSURI ASKED ME TO TAKE HER PICTURE LIKE THAT.
SHE NEEDED AN ICON THAT WASN'T A SELFIE OR SOMETHING.
I WASN'T CREEPING AROUND OR ANYTHING.
RIGHT, I SEE...
YOU'RE NOT THE TYPE WHO WOULD LOSE A DARE...
AND THEN SECRETLY TAKE PICTURES OF SOMEONE AND POST THEM TO A GROUP CHAT TO MAKE FUN OF THEM...
DID THAT... ACTUALLY HAPPEN TO YOU?
WELL... ANY-HOW.
ダラ SWEAT
ダラ SWEAT
I JUST HAVE THIS BACKGROUND
BECAUSE I LIKE IT...
SWEAT ダラ
YEAH...

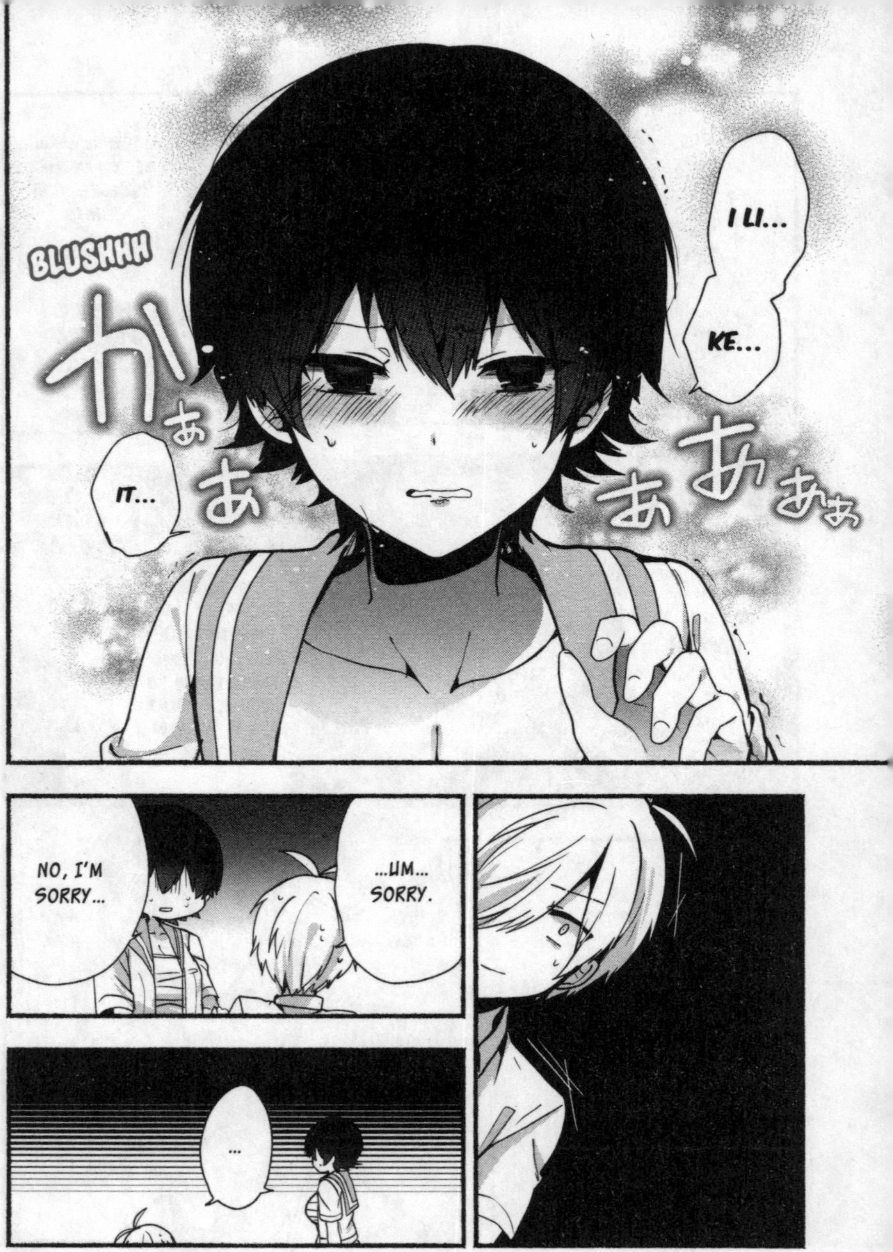
I LI...
KE...
IT...
BLUSHHH
かぁああぁぁ
...UM... SORRY.
NO, I'M SORRY...
...

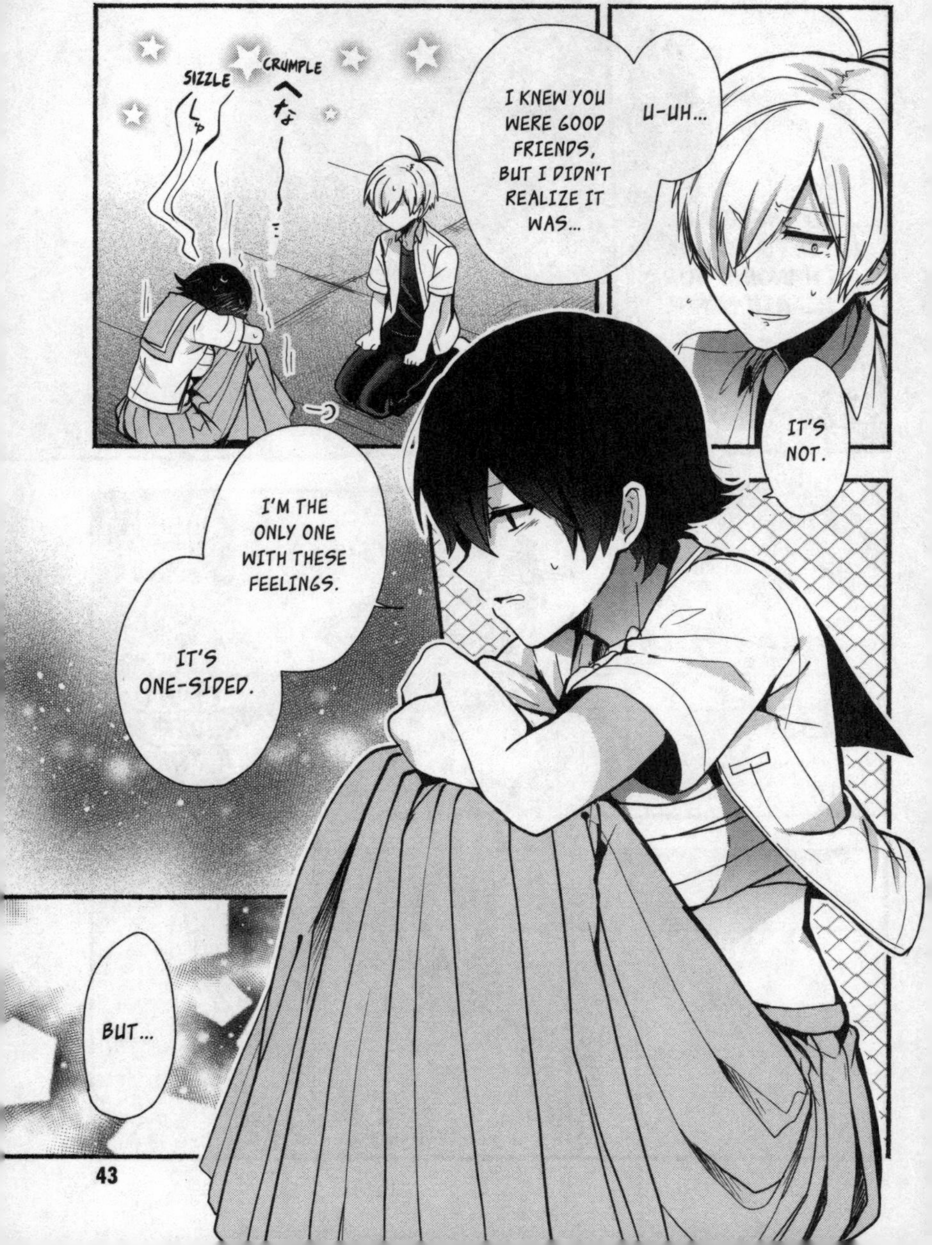
U-UH...
I KNEW YOU WERE GOOD FRIENDS, BUT I DIDN'T REALIZE IT WAS...
CRUMPLE
へな
SIZZLE
しゅ
IT'S NOT.
I'M THE ONLY ONE WITH THESE FEELINGS.
IT'S ONE-SIDED.
BUT...

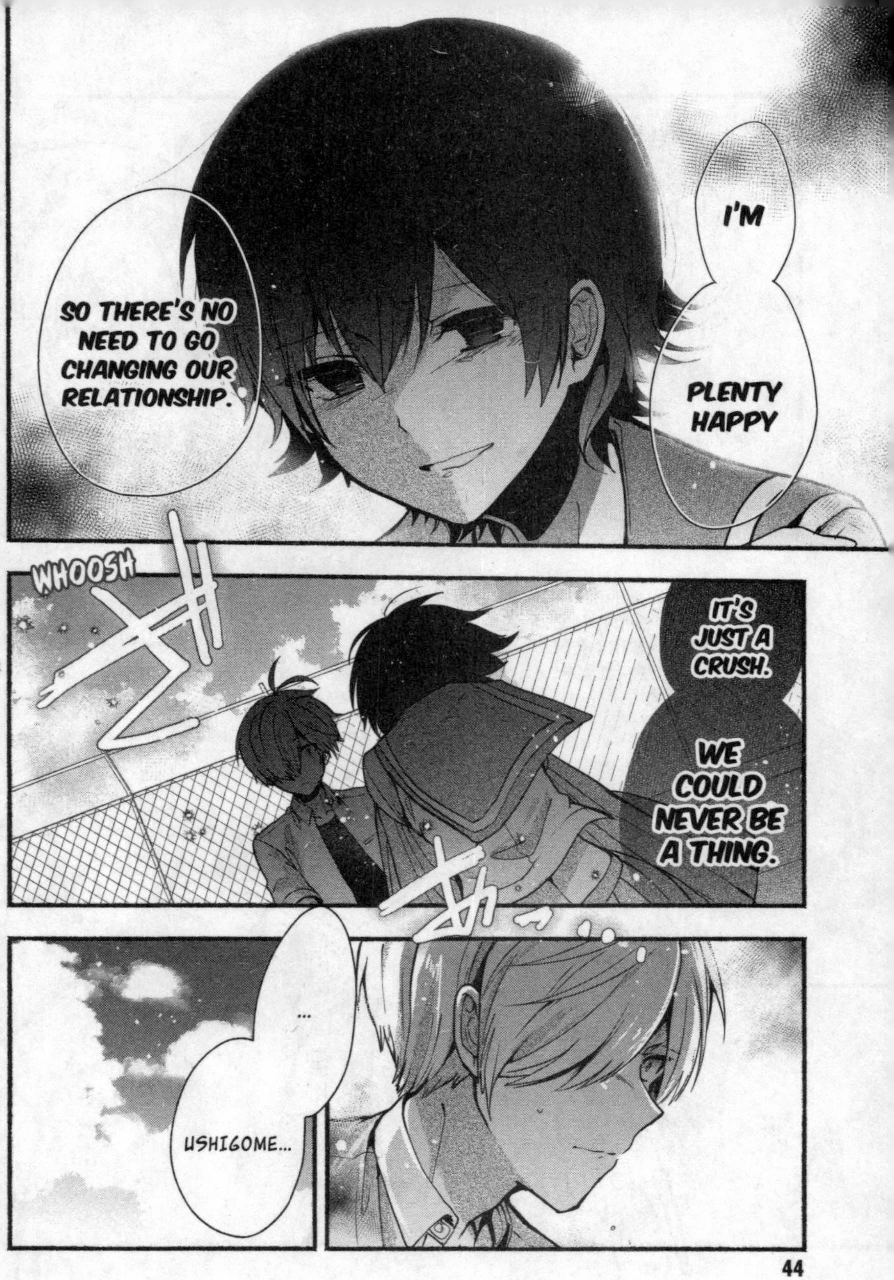
I'M PLENTY HAPPY
SO THERE'S NO NEED TO GO CHANGING OUR RELATIONSHIP.
IT'S JUST A CRUSH.
WE COULD NEVER BE A THING.
WHOOSH
...
USHIGOME...

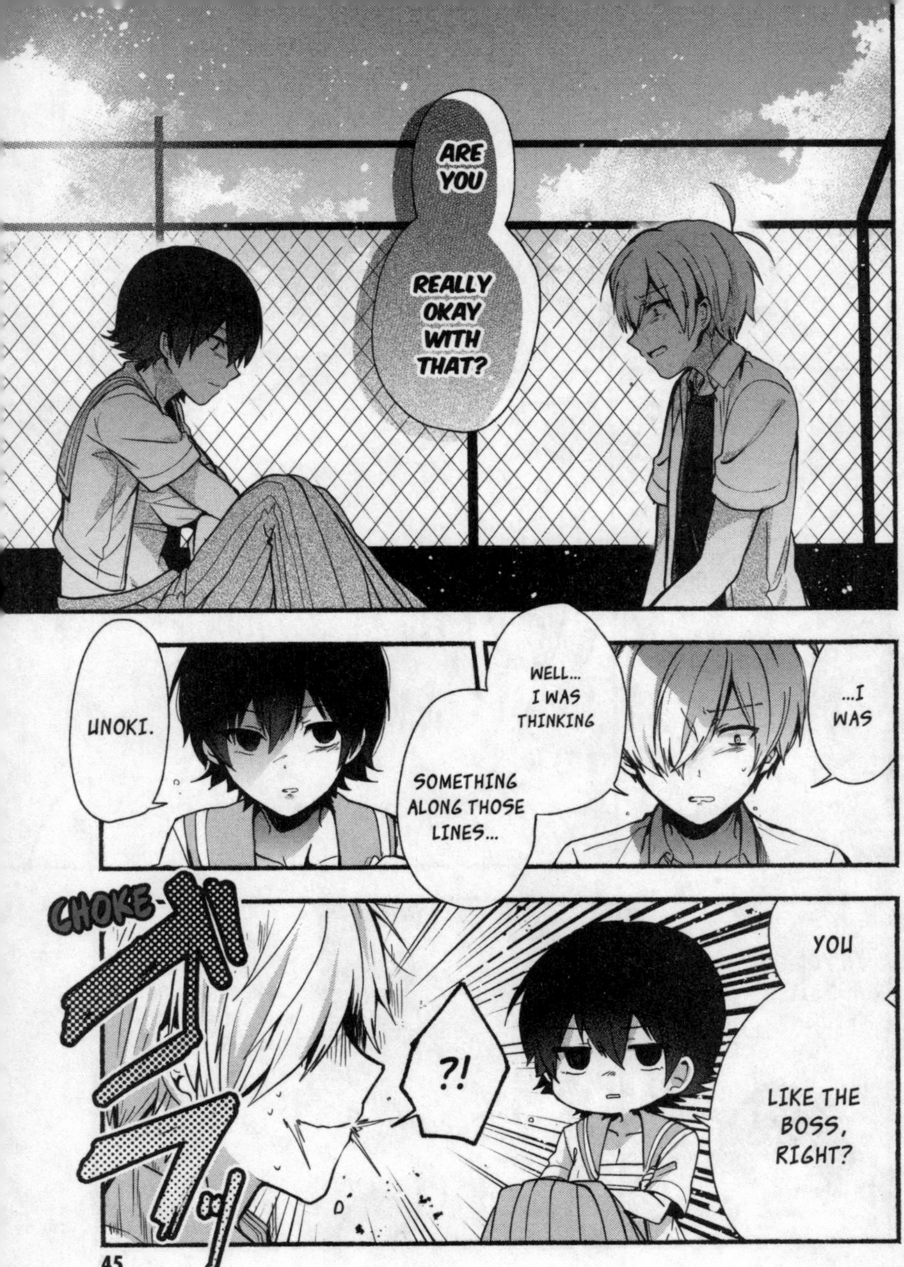
ARE YOU REALLY OKAY WITH THAT?
...I WAS
WELL... I WAS THINKING SOMETHING ALONG THOSE LINES...
UNOKI.
YOU LIKE THE BOSS, RIGHT?
?!
CHOKE-

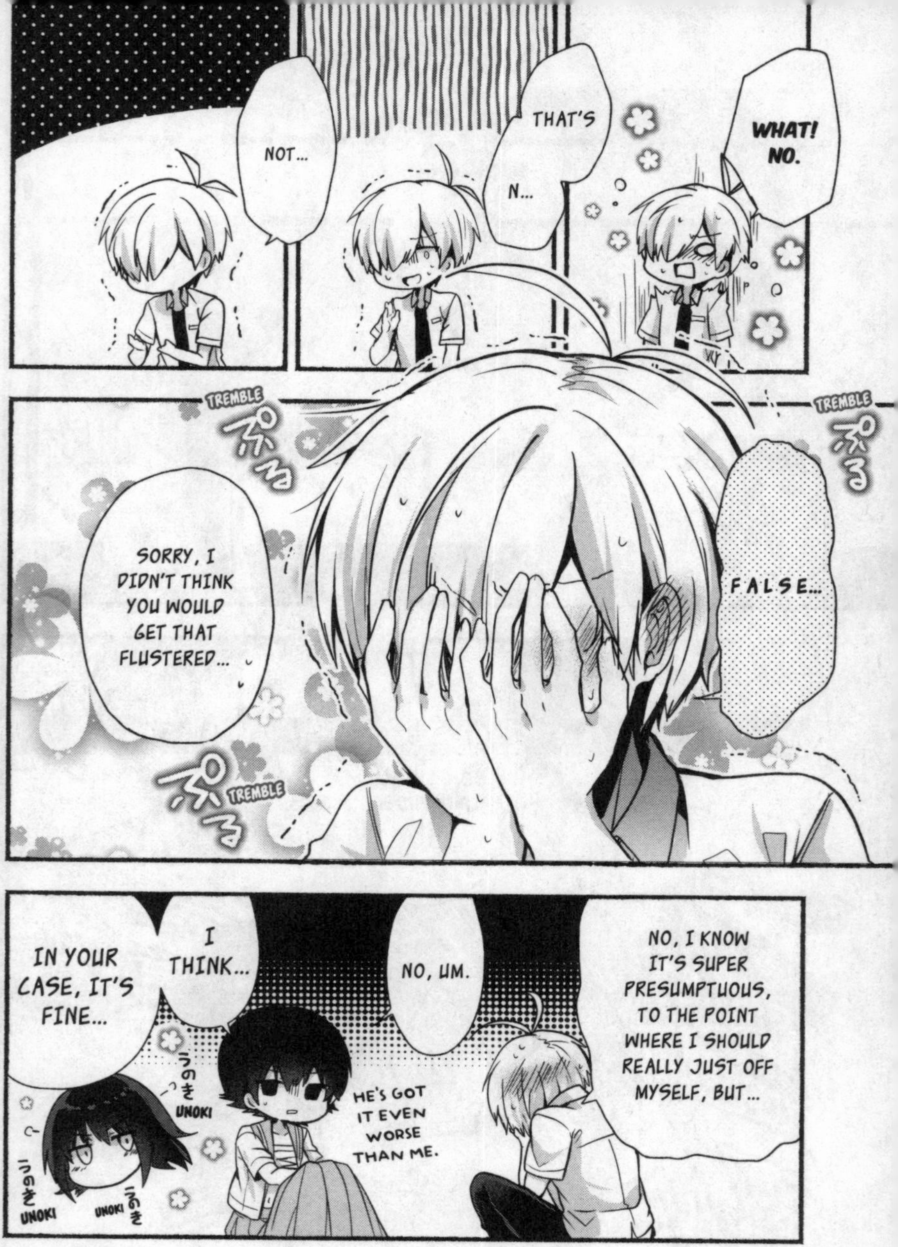
WHAT! NO.
THAT'S
N...
NOT...
TREMBLE
ぷる
FALSE...
TREMBLE
ぷる
SORRY, I DIDN'T THINK YOU WOULD GET THAT FLUSTERED...
TREMBLE
ぷる
NO, I KNOW IT'S SUPER PRESUMPTUOUS, TO THE POINT WHERE I SHOULD REALLY JUST OFF MYSELF, BUT...
NO, UM.
I THINK...
IN YOUR CASE, IT'S FINE...
HE'S GOT IT EVEN WORSE THAN ME.
うのき
UNOKI
うのき
UNOKI
うのき
UNOKI

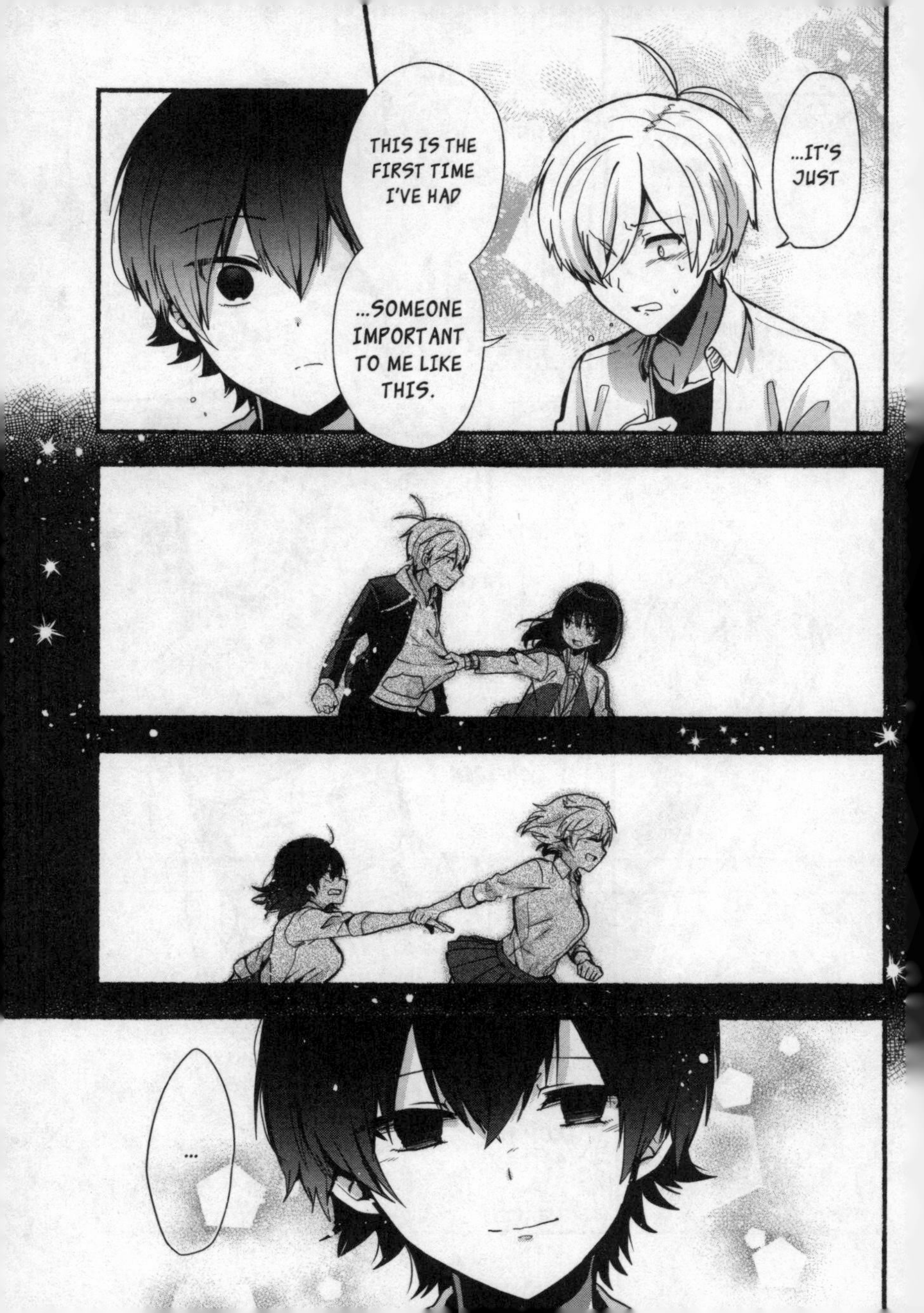
...IT'S JUST
THIS IS THE FIRST TIME I'VE HAD
...SOMEONE IMPORTANT TO ME LIKE THIS.
...

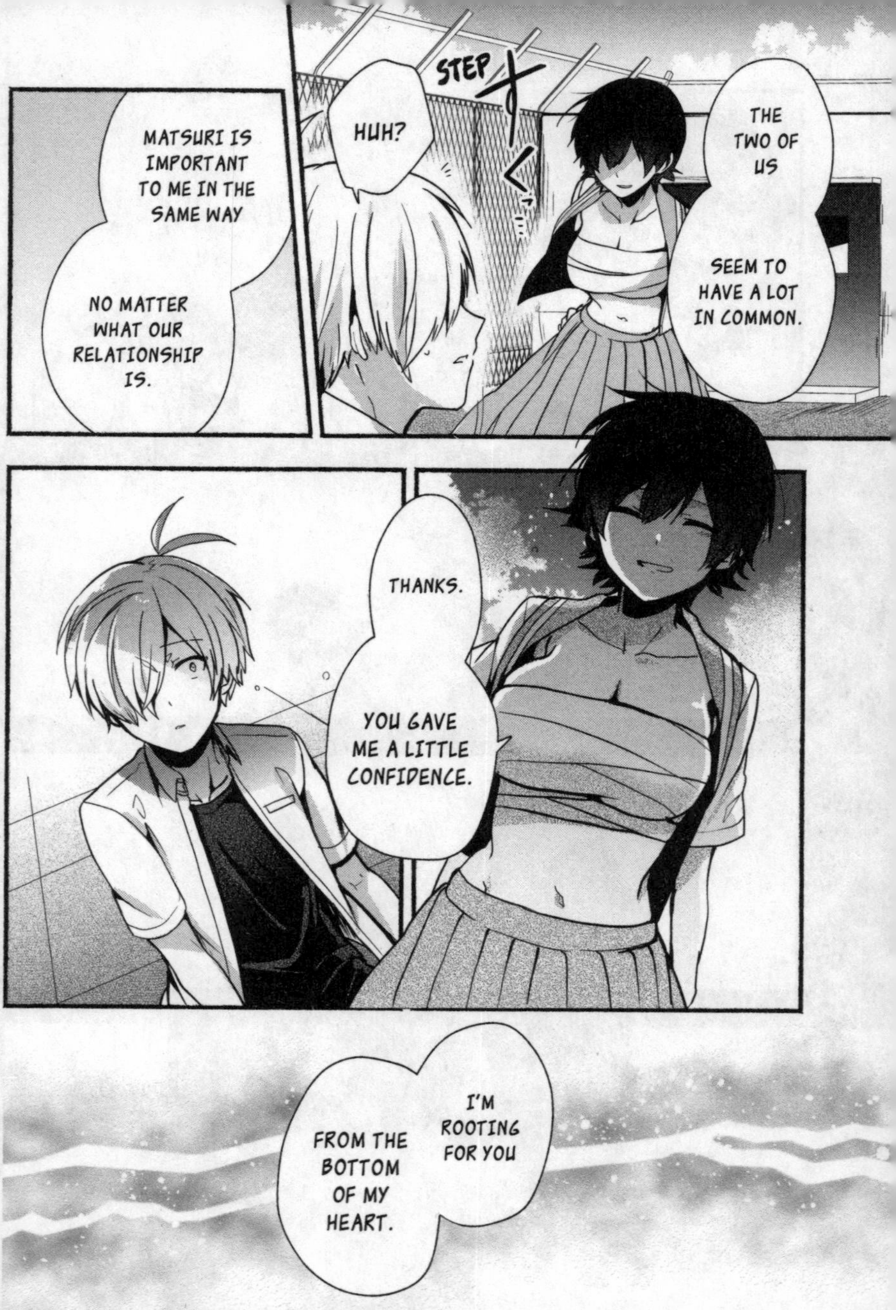
THE TWO OF US
SEEM TO HAVE A LOT IN COMMON.
STEP
HUH?
MATSURI IS IMPORTANT TO ME IN THE SAME WAY
NO MATTER WHAT OUR RELATIONSHIP IS.
THANKS.
YOU GAVE ME A LITTLE CONFIDENCE.
I'M ROOTING FOR YOU
FROM THE BOTTOM OF MY HEART.

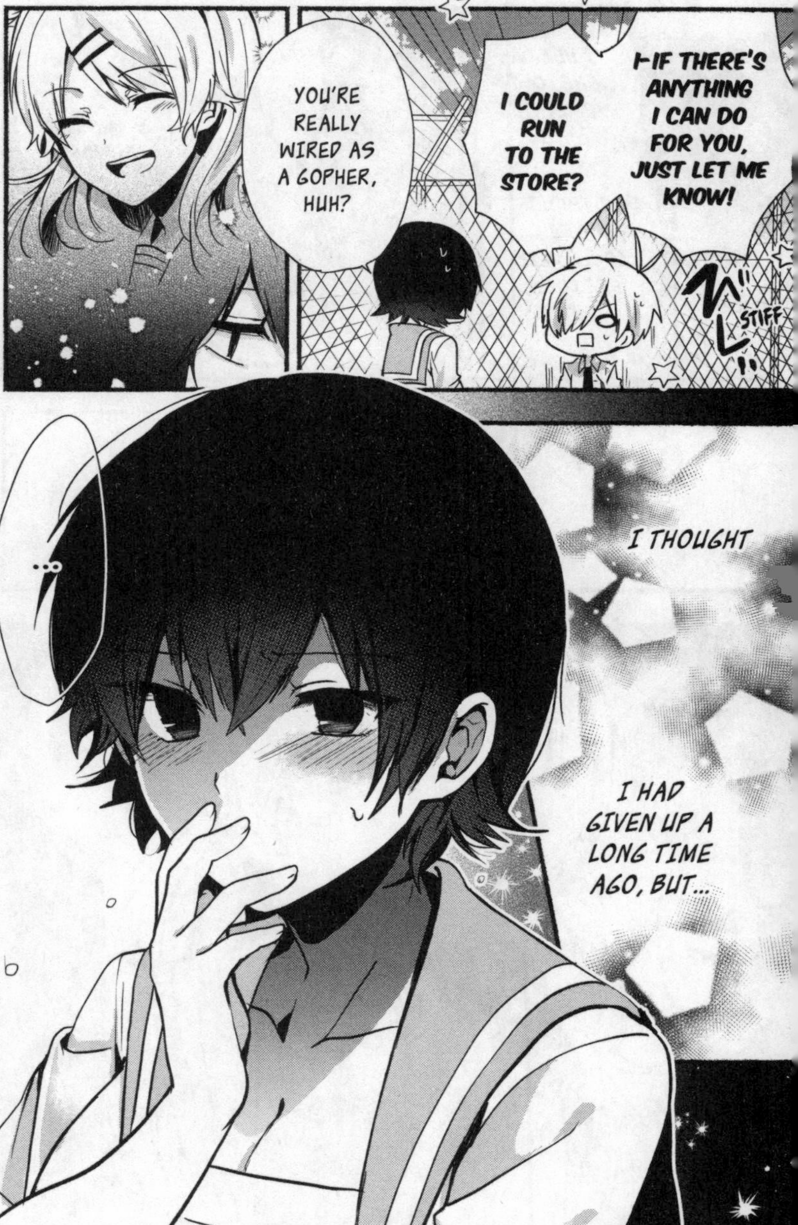
I-IF THERE'S ANYTHING I CAN DO FOR YOU, JUST LET ME KNOW!
I COULD RUN TO THE STORE?
STIFF
YOU'RE REALLY WIRED AS A GOPHER, HUH?
I THOUGHT
I HAD GIVEN UP A LONG TIME AGO, BUT...
...

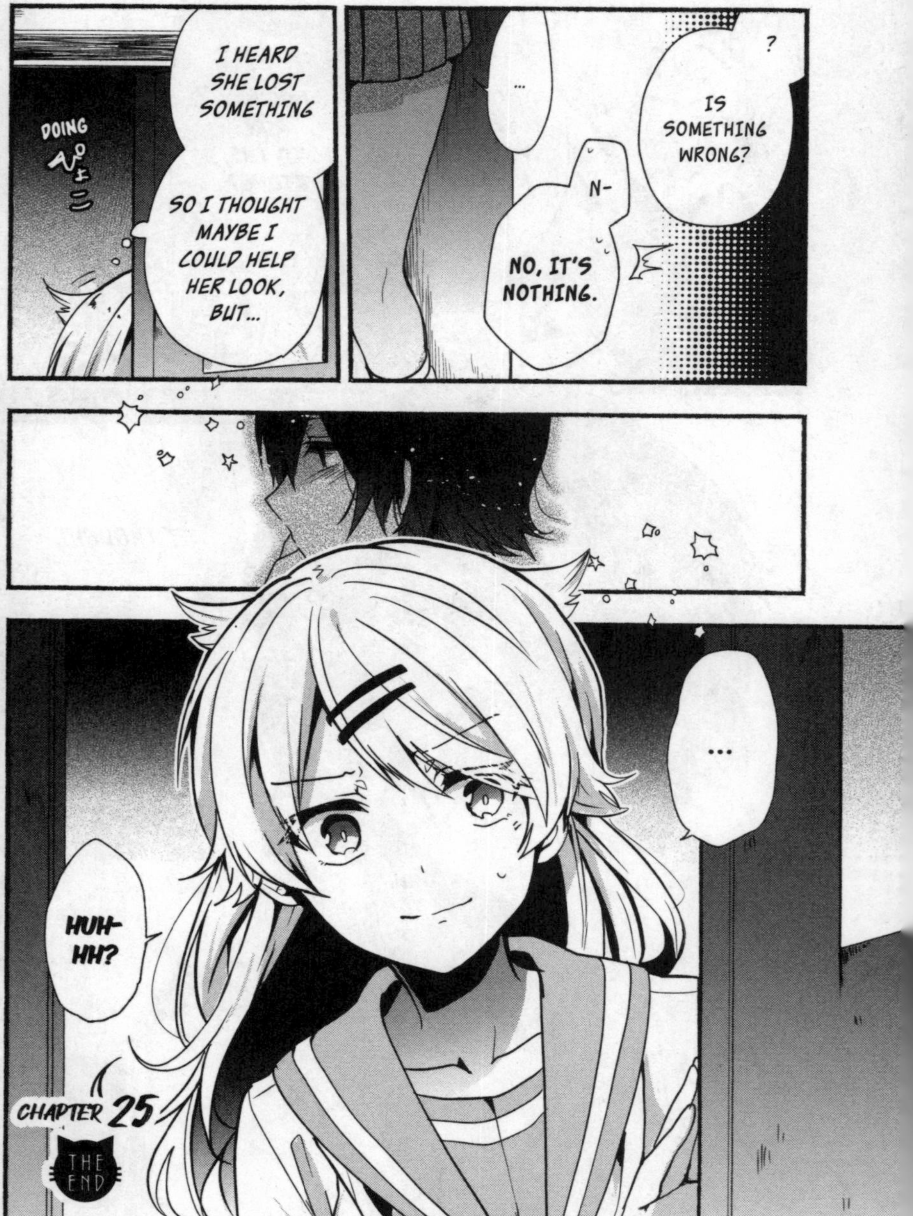
?
IS SOMETHING WRONG?
...
N-
NO, IT'S NOTHING.
I HEARD SHE LOST SOMETHING
SO I THOUGHT MAYBE I COULD HELP HER LOOK, BUT...
DOING
...
HUH-HH?
CHAPTER 25
THE END

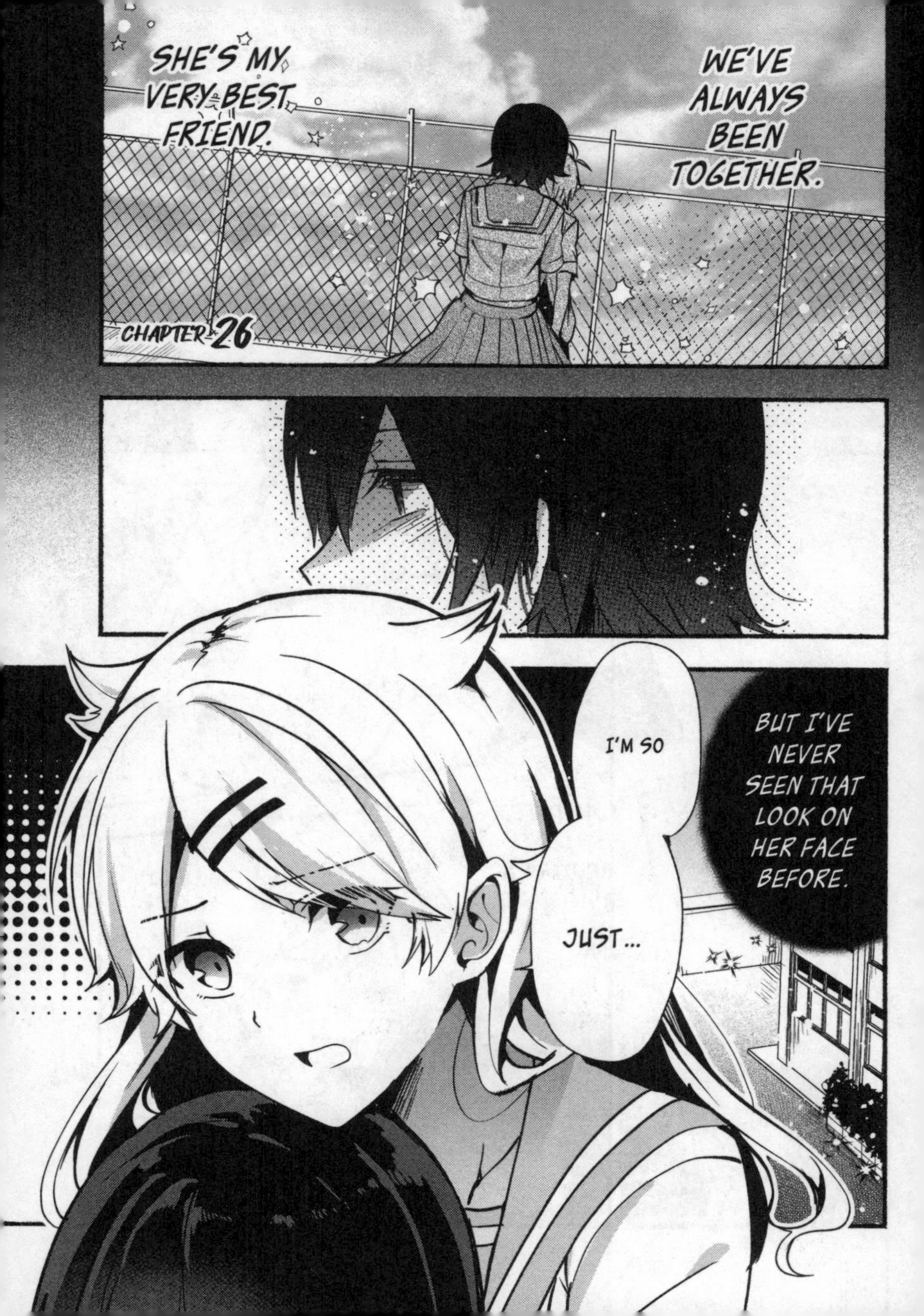
WE'VE ALWAYS BEEN TOGETHER.
SHE'S MY VERY BEST FRIEND.
CHAPTER 26
BUT I'VE NEVER SEEN THAT LOOK ON HER FACE BEFORE.
I'M SO
JUST...

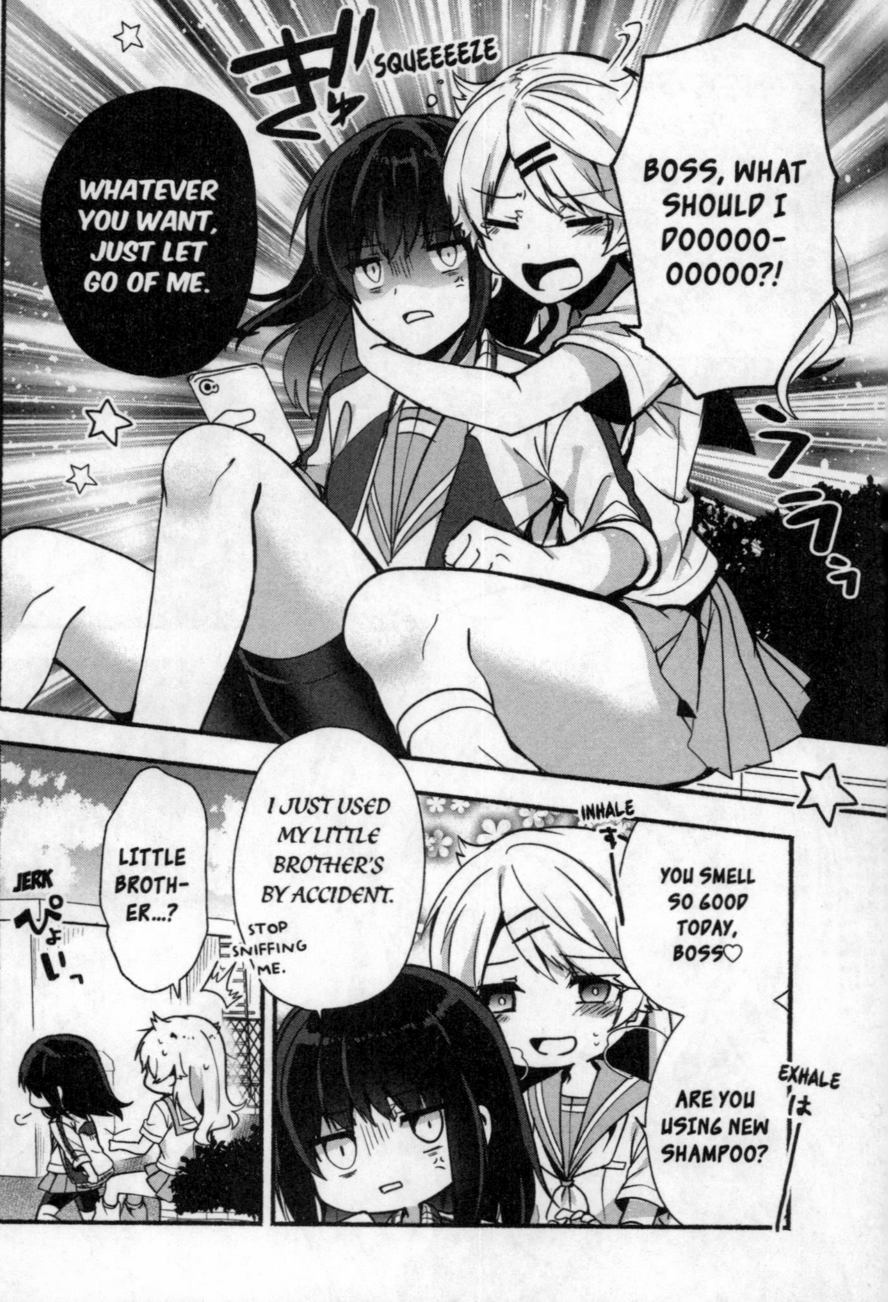
SQUEEEEZE
BOSS, WHAT SHOULD I DOOOOO-OOOOO?!
WHATEVER YOU WANT, JUST LET GO OF ME.
INHALE
YOU SMELL SO GOOD TODAY, BOSS♡
EXHALE
ARE YOU USING NEW SHAMPOO?
STOP SNIFFING ME.
I JUST USED MY LITTLE BROTHER'S BY ACCIDENT.
LITTLE BROTH-ER...?
JERK

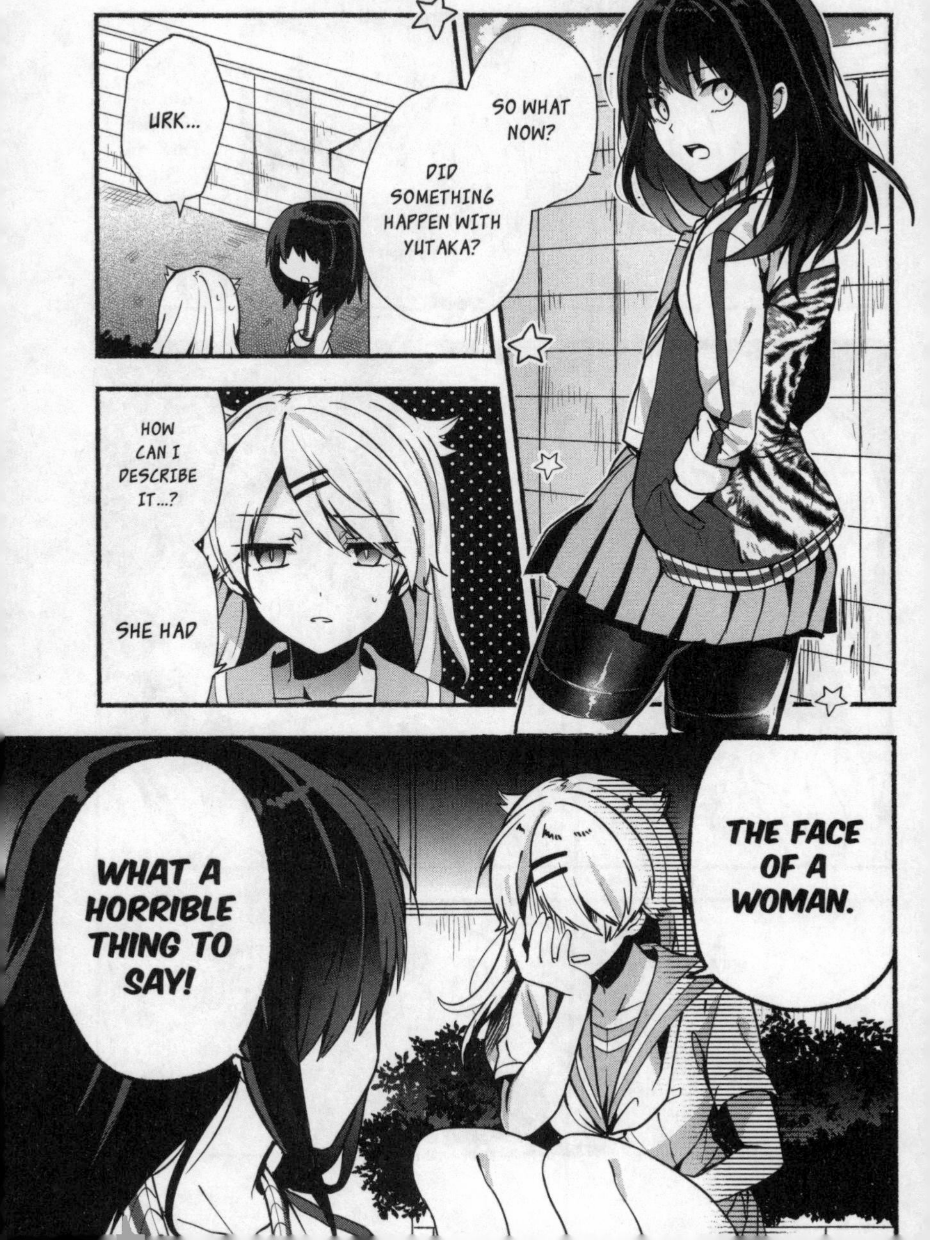
SO WHAT NOW?
DID SOMETHING HAPPEN WITH YUTAKA?
URK...
HOW CAN I DESCRIBE IT...?
SHE HAD
THE FACE OF A WOMAN.
WHAT A HORRIBLE THING TO SAY!

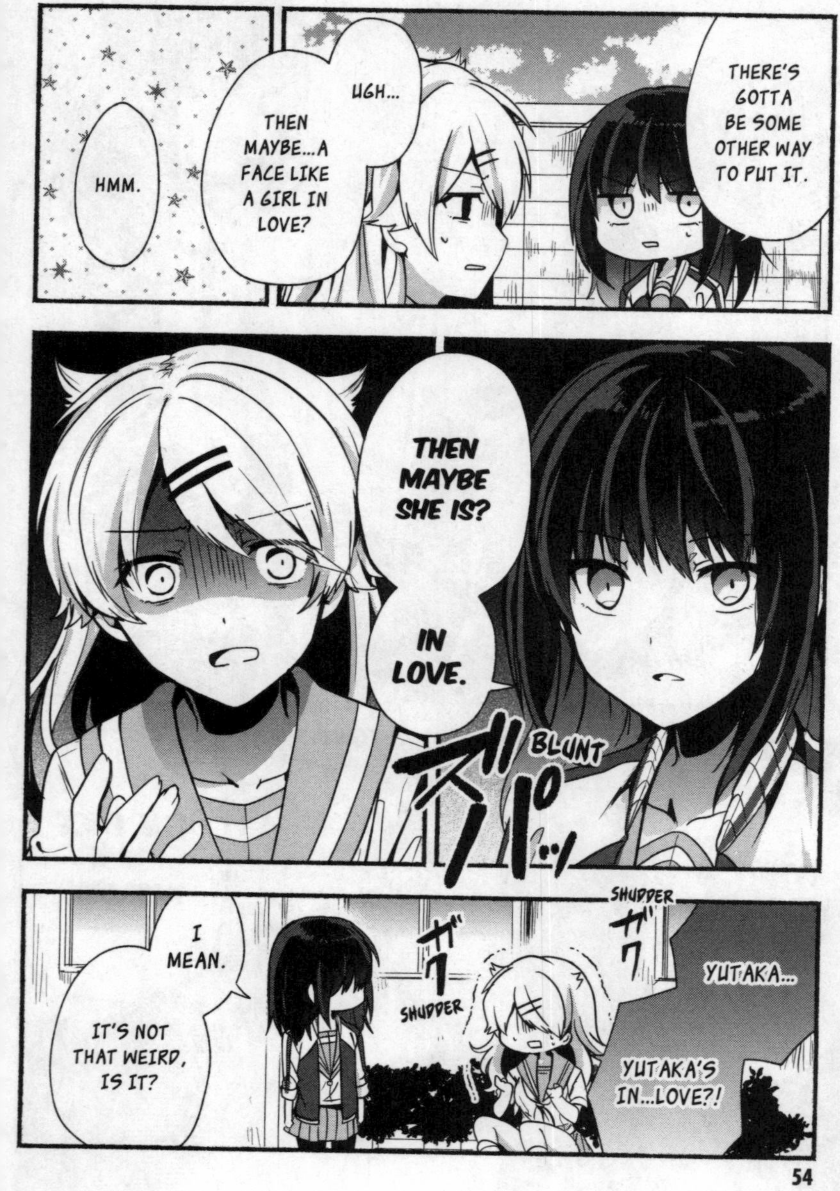
THERE'S GOTTA BE SOME OTHER WAY TO PUT IT.
UGH...
THEN MAYBE...A FACE LIKE A GIRL IN LOVE?
HMM.
THEN MAYBE SHE IS?
IN LOVE.
BLUNT
SHUDDER
YUTAKA...
YUTAKA'S IN...LOVE?!
SHUDDER
I MEAN.
IT'S NOT THAT WEIRD, IS IT?

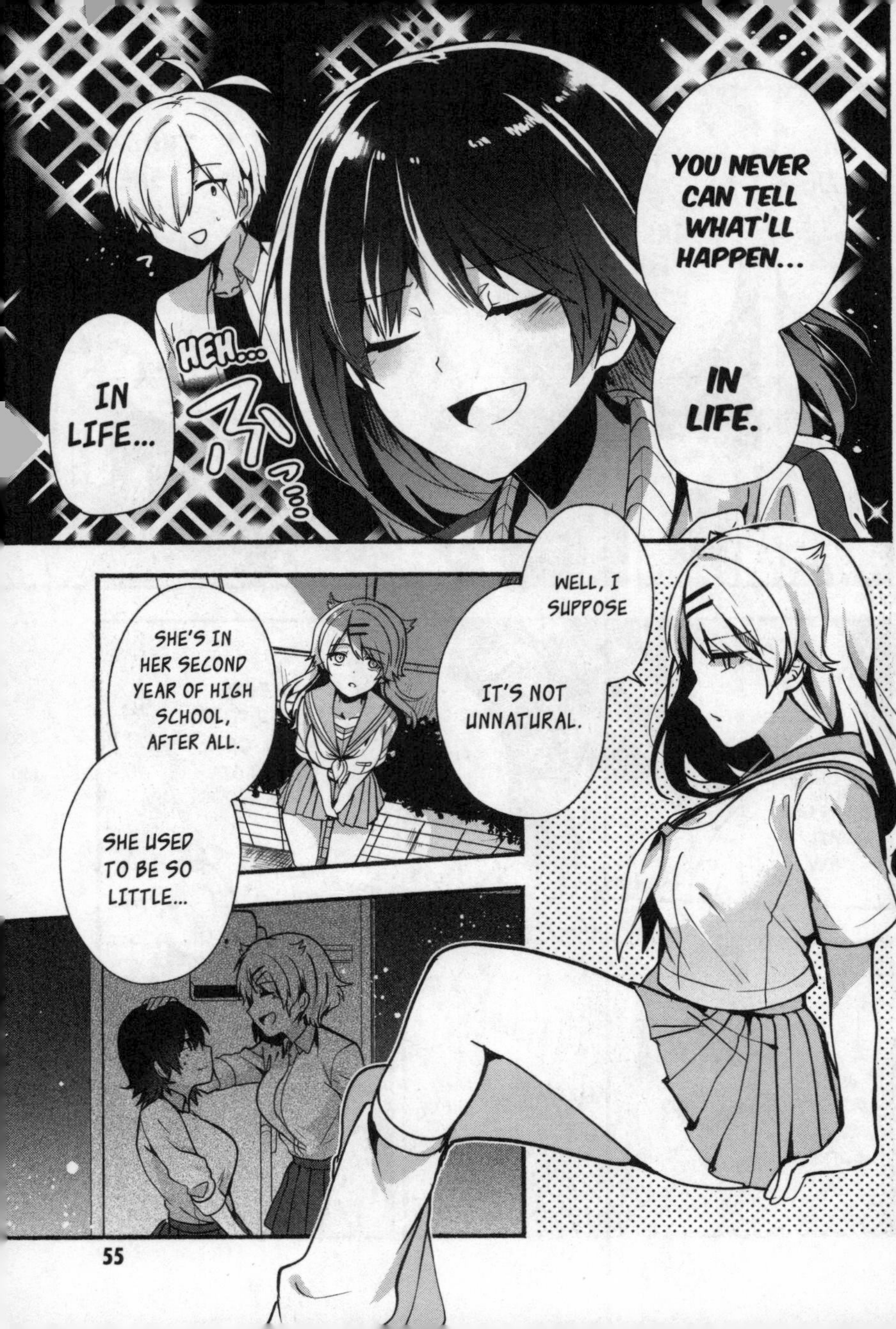
YOU NEVER CAN TELL WHAT'LL HAPPEN...
IN LIFE.
HEH...
IN LIFE...
WELL, I SUPPOSE
IT'S NOT UNNATURAL.
SHE'S IN HER SECOND YEAR OF HIGH SCHOOL, AFTER ALL.
SHE USED TO BE SO LITTLE...

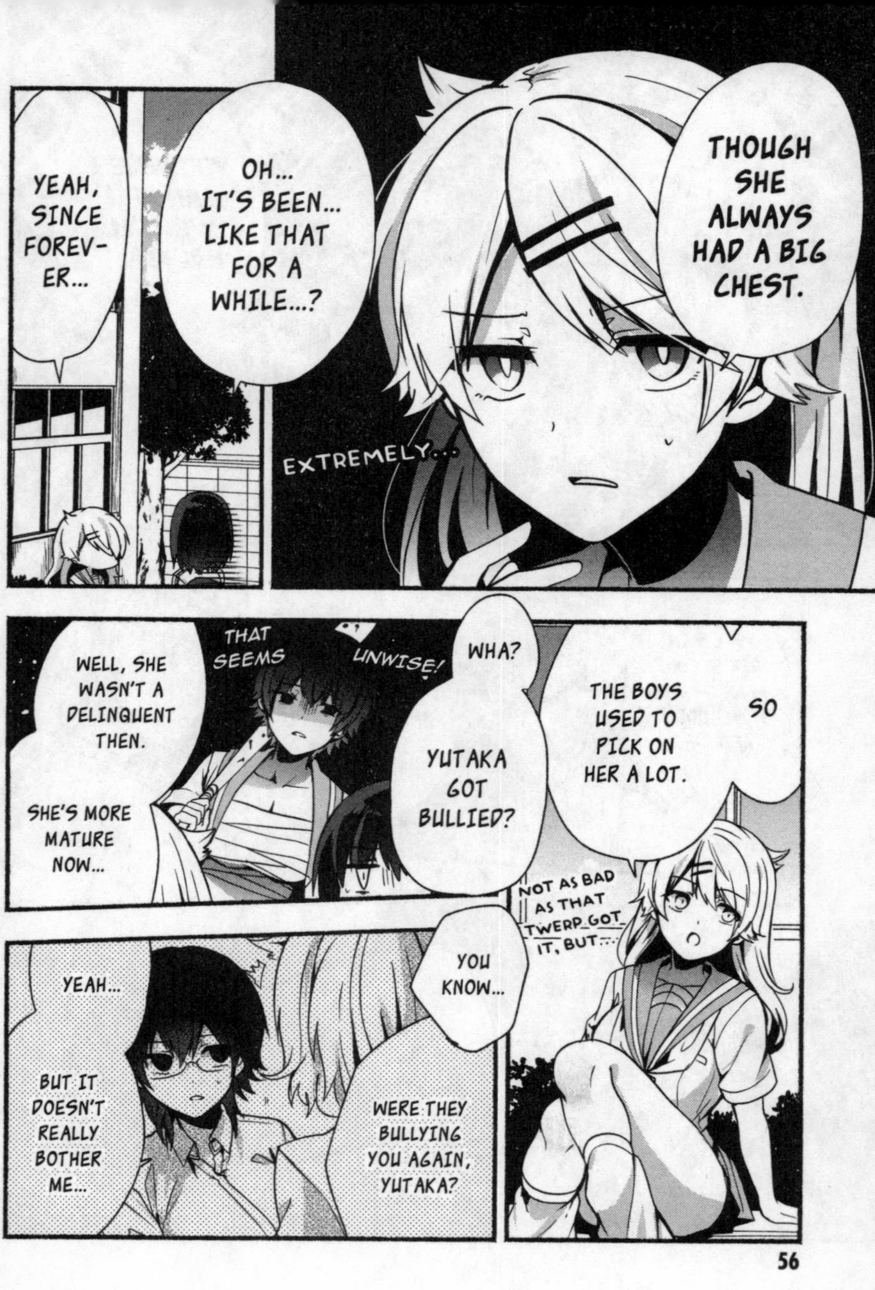
THOUGH SHE ALWAYS HAD A BIG CHEST.
EXTREMELY...
OH... IT'S BEEN... LIKE THAT FOR A WHILE...?
YEAH, SINCE FOREV-ER...
SO
THE BOYS USED TO PICK ON HER A LOT.
NOT AS BAD AS THAT TWERP GOT IT, BUT...
WHA?
YUTAKA GOT BULLIED?
THAT SEEMS UNWISE!
WELL, SHE WASN'T A DELINQUENT THEN.
SHE'S MORE MATURE NOW...
YOU KNOW...
WERE THEY BULLYING YOU AGAIN, YUTAKA?
YEAH...
BUT IT DOESN'T REALLY BOTHER ME...

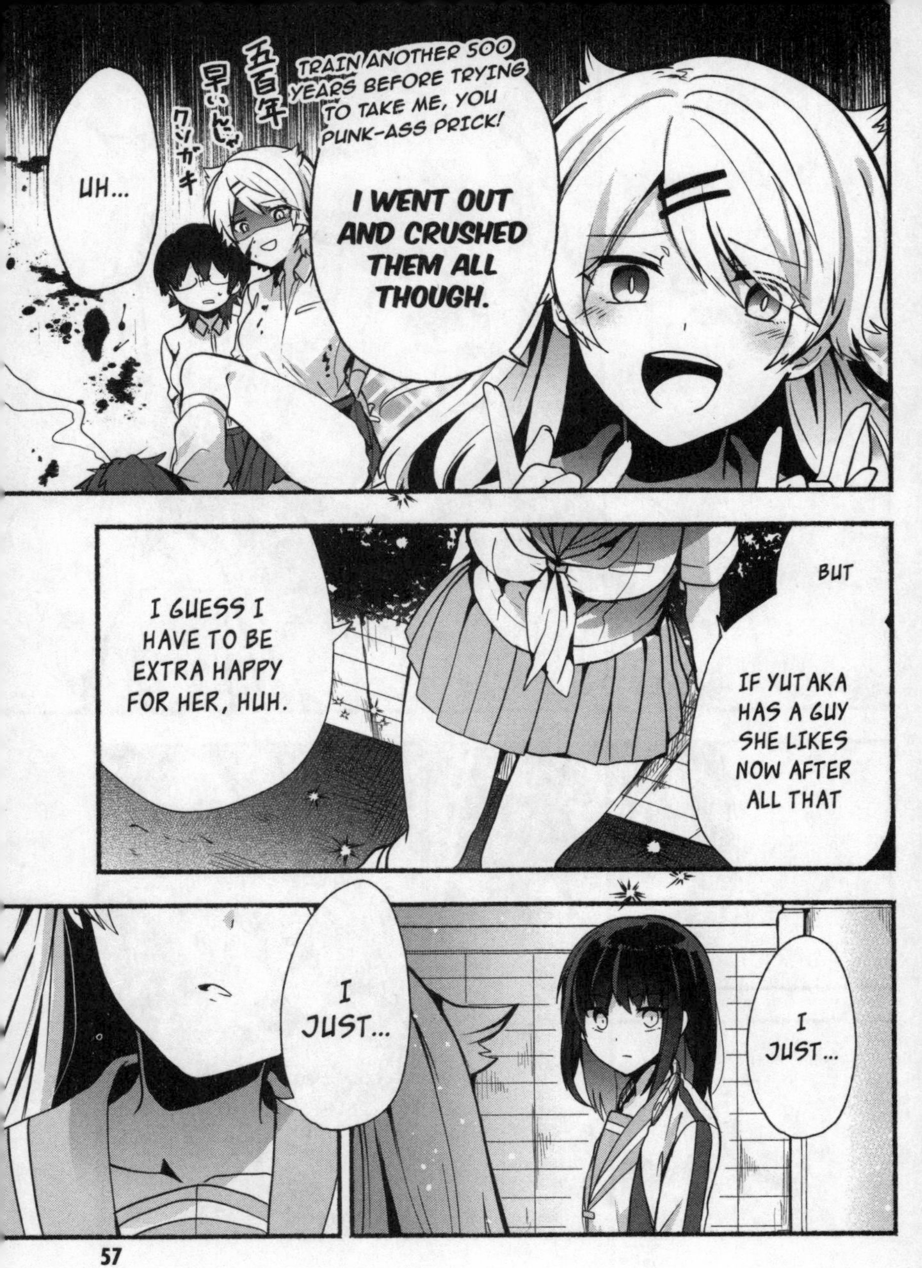
I WENT OUT AND CRUSHED THEM ALL THOUGH.
五百年早いんじゃクソガキ
TRAIN ANOTHER 500 YEARS BEFORE TRYING TO TAKE ME, YOU PUNK-ASS PRICK!
UH...
BUT
IF YUTAKA HAS A GUY SHE LIKES NOW AFTER ALL THAT
I GUESS I HAVE TO BE EXTRA HAPPY FOR HER, HUH.
I JUST...
I JUST...

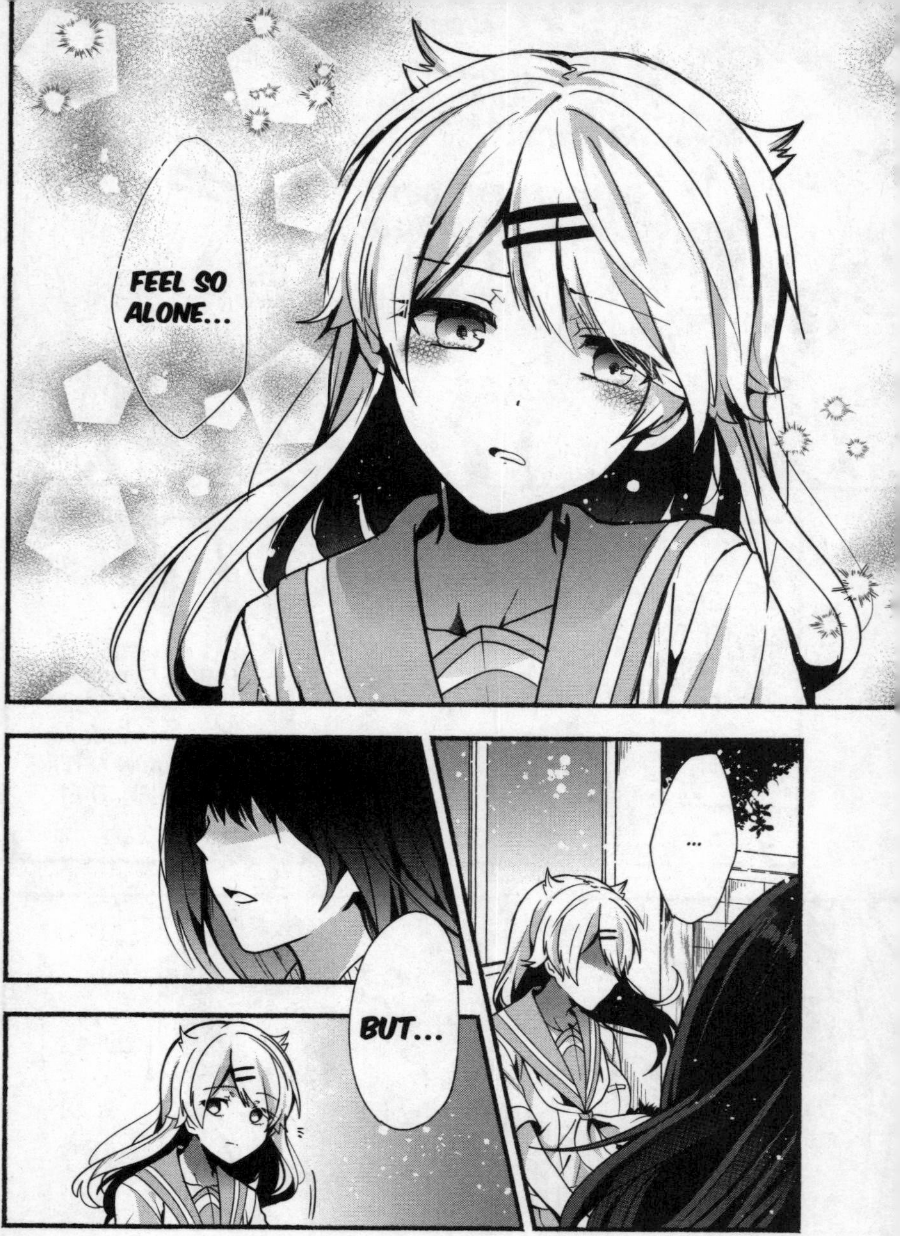
FEEL SO ALONE...
...
BUT...

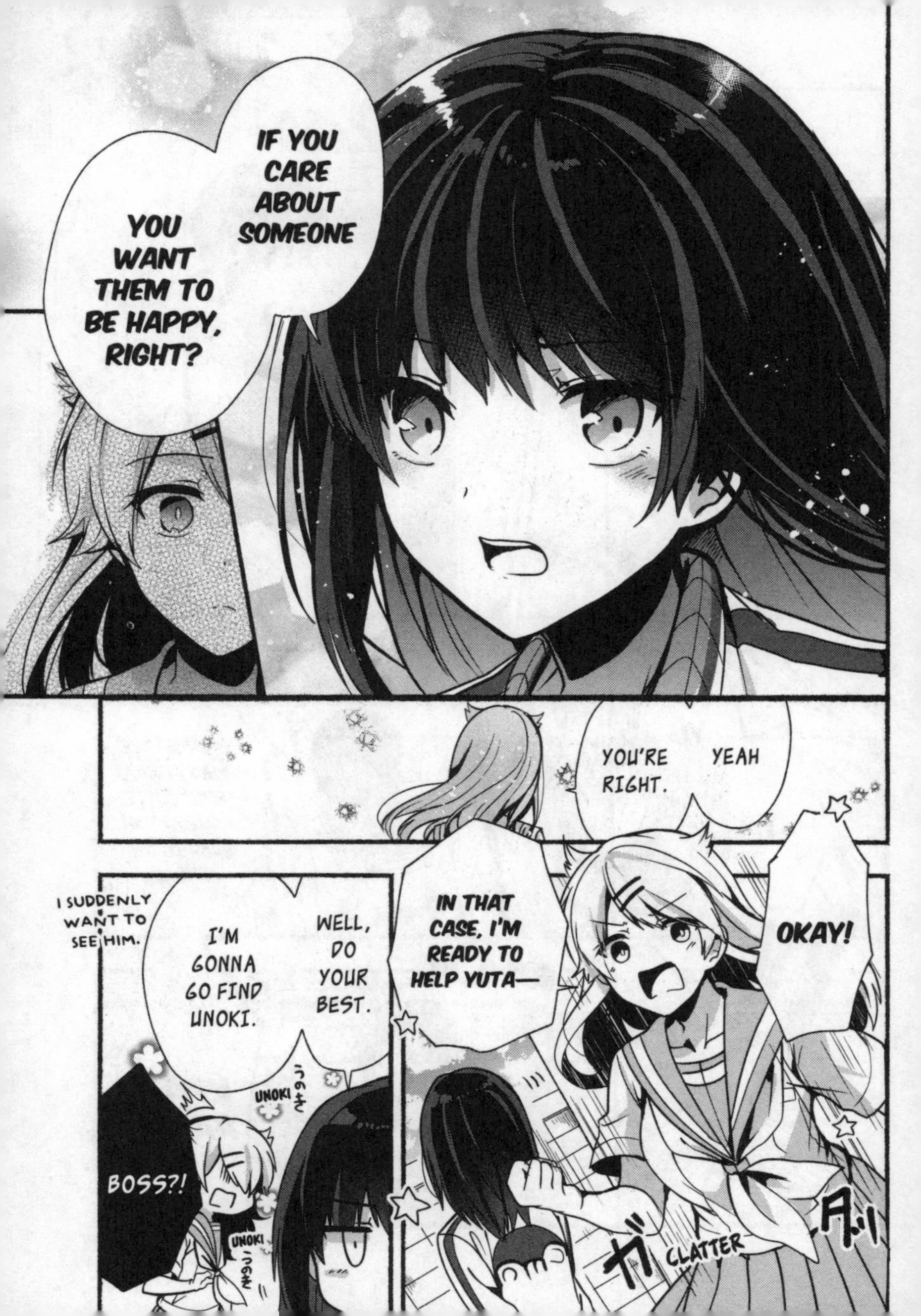
IF YOU CARE ABOUT SOMEONE
YOU WANT THEM TO BE HAPPY, RIGHT?
YEAH
YOU'RE RIGHT.
OKAY!
IN THAT CASE, I'M READY TO HELP YUTA—
CLATTER
WELL, DO YOUR BEST.
I'M GONNA GO FIND UNOKI.
I SUDDENLY WANT TO SEE HIM.
UNOKI
BOSS?!
UNOKI

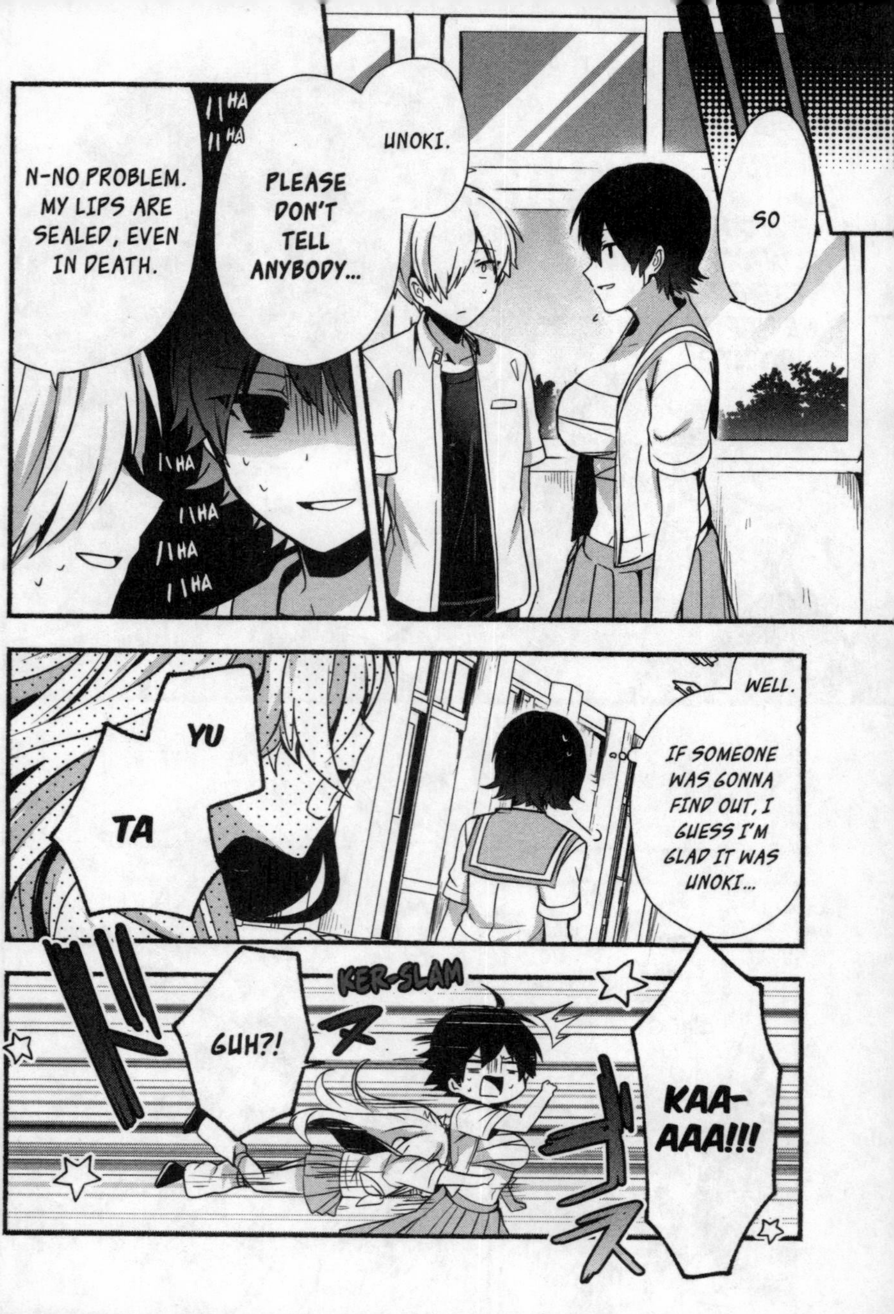
SO
UNOKI.
PLEASE DON'T TELL ANYBODY...
HA
HA
N-NO PROBLEM. MY LIPS ARE SEALED, EVEN IN DEATH.
HA
HA
HA
HA
WELL.
IF SOMEONE WAS GONNA FIND OUT, I GUESS I'M GLAD IT WAS UNOKI...
YU
TA
KAA-AAA!!!
KER-SLAM
GUH?!

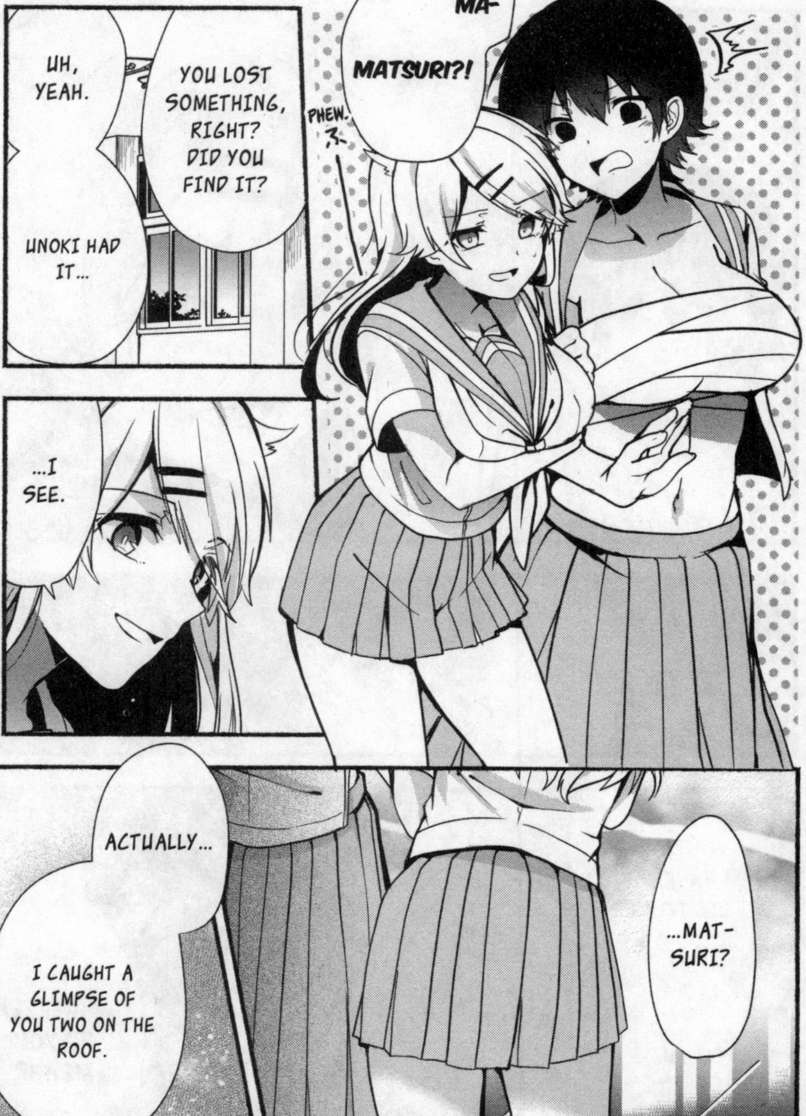
MA-
MATSURI?!
PHEW.
YOU LOST SOMETHING, RIGHT? DID YOU FIND IT?
UH, YEAH.
UNOKI HAD IT...
...I SEE.
...MAT-SURI?
ACTUALLY...
I CAUGHT A GLIMPSE OF YOU TWO ON THE ROOF.

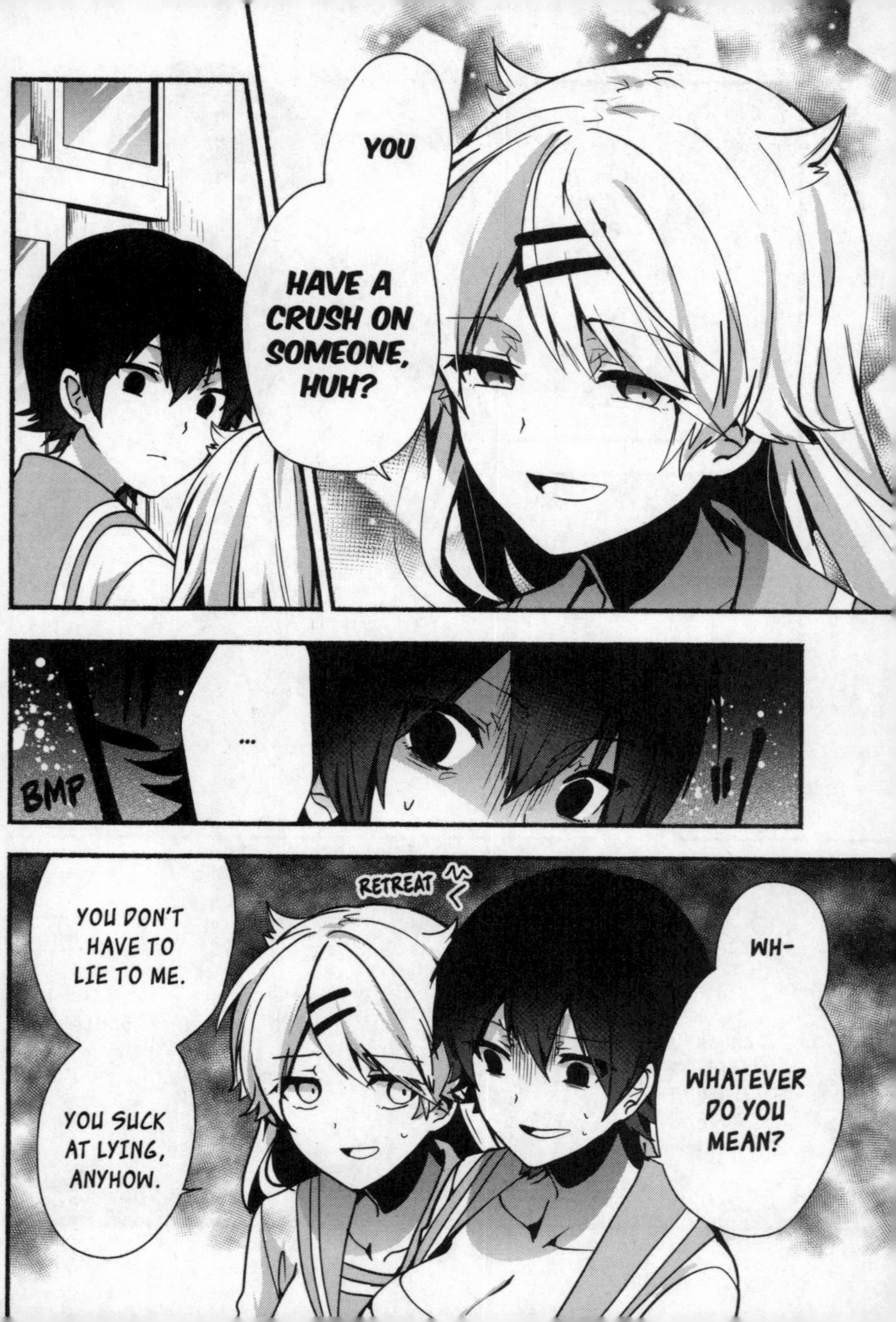
YOU
HAVE A CRUSH ON SOMEONE, HUH?
...
BMP
WH-
WHATEVER DO YOU MEAN?
RETREAT
YOU DON'T HAVE TO LIE TO ME.
YOU SUCK AT LYING, ANYHOW.

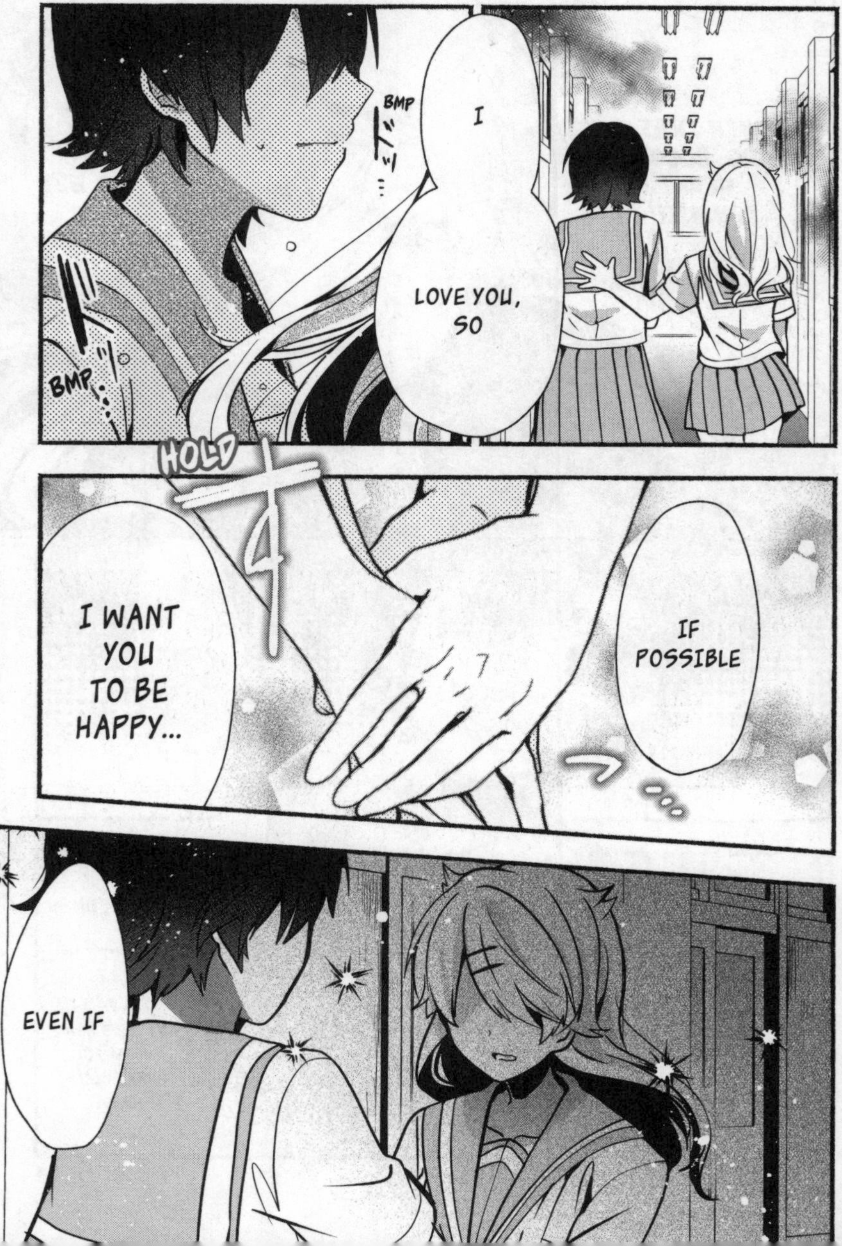
I
LOVE YOU, SO
BMP
BMP
IF POSSIBLE
HOLD
I WANT YOU TO BE HAPPY...
EVEN IF

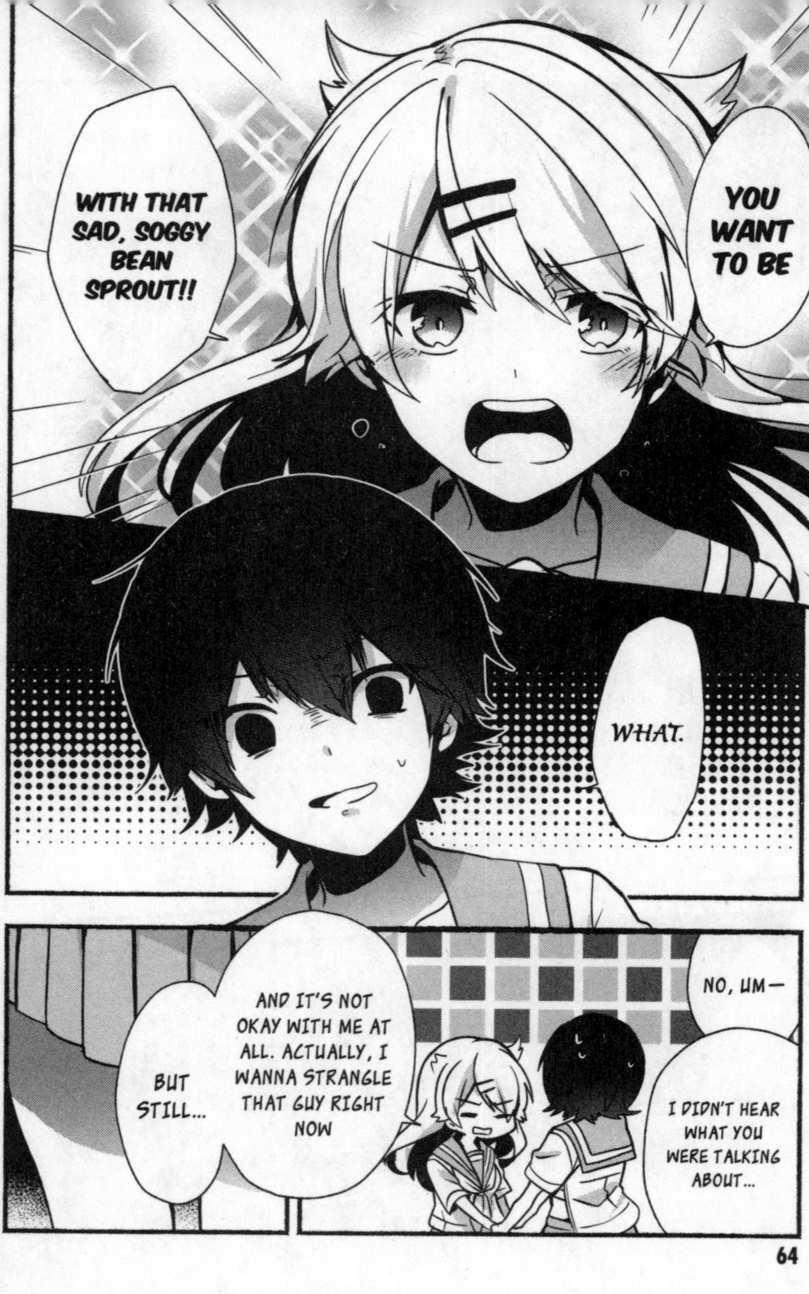
YOU WANT TO BE
WITH THAT SAD, SOGGY BEAN SPROUT!!
WHAT.
NO, UM—
I DIDN'T HEAR WHAT YOU WERE TALKING ABOUT...
AND IT'S NOT OKAY WITH ME AT ALL. ACTUALLY, I WANNA STRANGLE THAT GUY RIGHT NOW
BUT STILL...

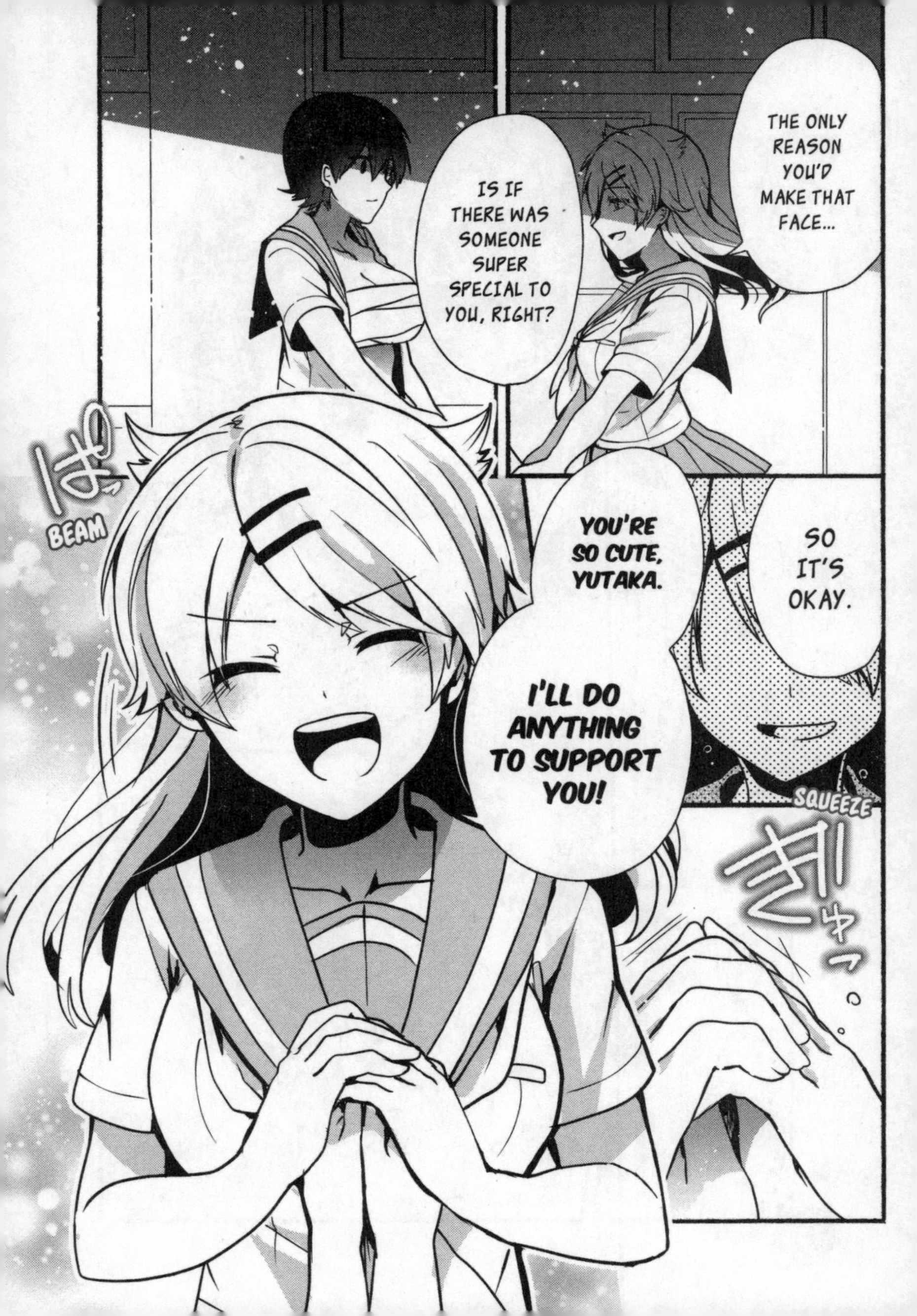
THE ONLY REASON YOU'D MAKE THAT FACE...
IS IF THERE WAS SOMEONE SUPER SPECIAL TO YOU, RIGHT?
SO IT'S OKAY.
SQUEEZE
BEAM
YOU'RE SO CUTE, YUTAKA.
I'LL DO ANYTHING TO SUPPORT YOU!

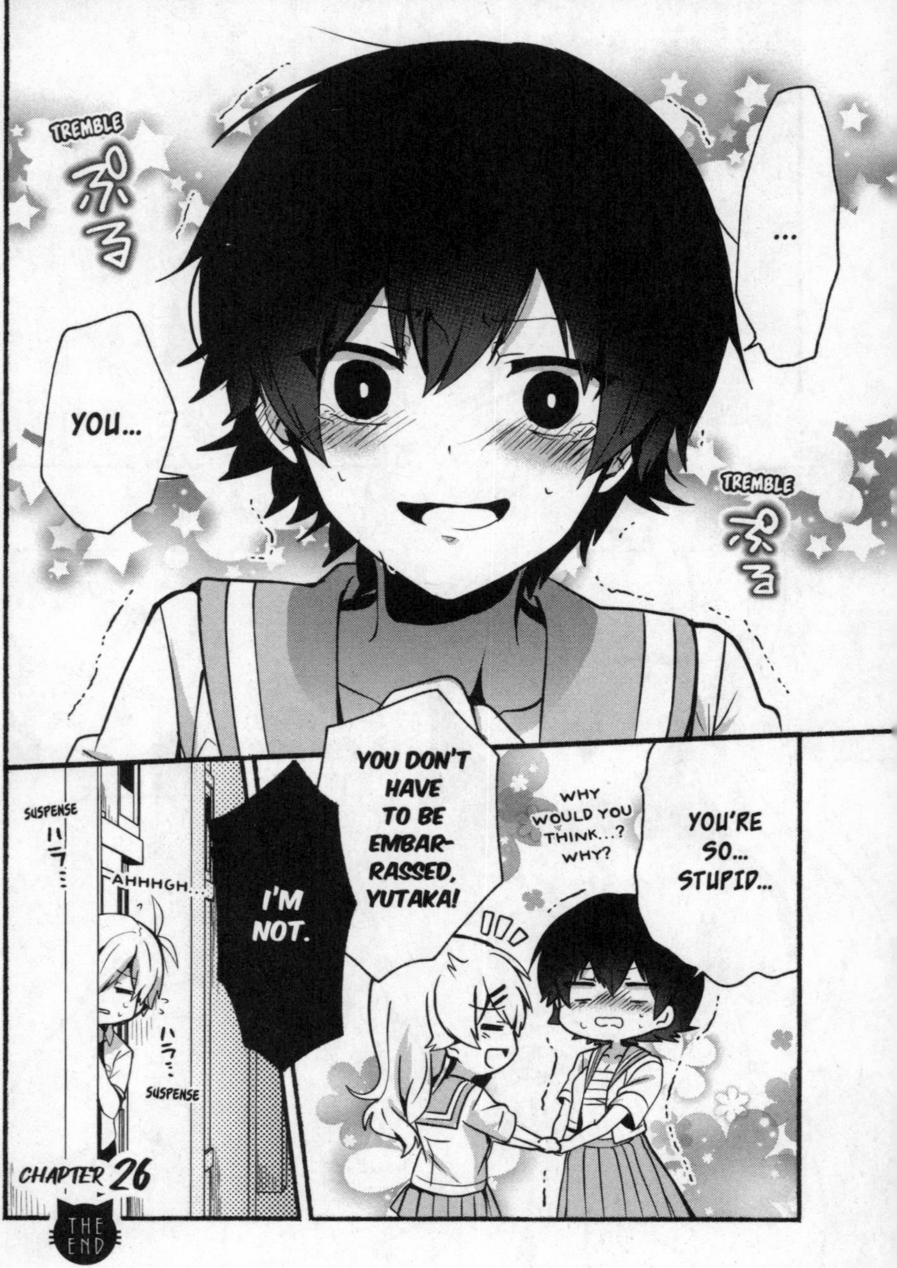
...
TREMBLE
ぷる
YOU...
TREMBLE
ぷる
YOU'RE SO... STUPID...
WHY WOULD YOU THINK...? WHY?
YOU DON'T HAVE TO BE EMBARRASSED, YUTAKA!
I'M NOT.
AHHHGH...
SUSPENSE
ハラ
ハラ
SUSPENSE
CHAPTER 26
THE END

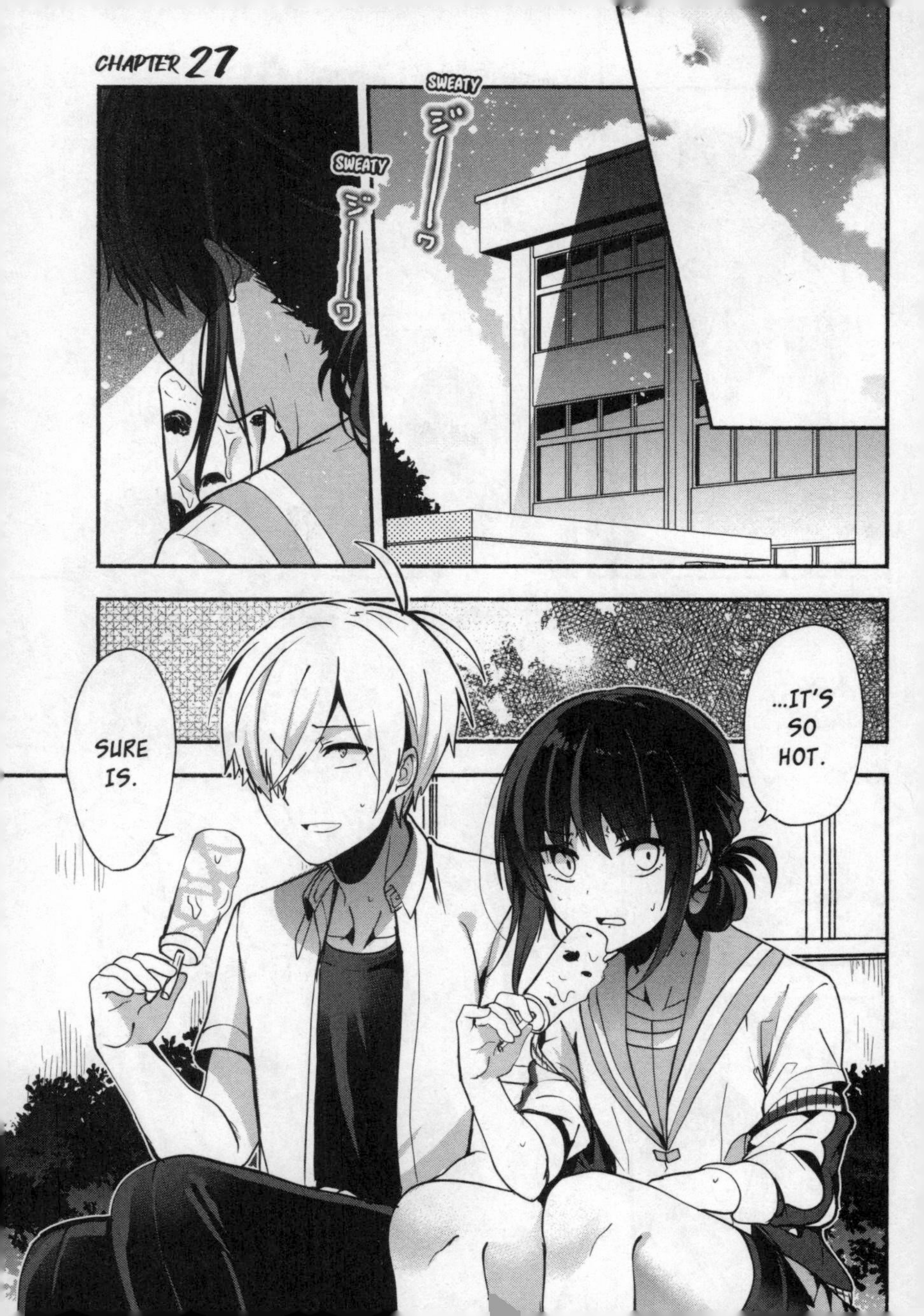
CHAPTER 27
SWEATY
SWEATY
...IT'S SO HOT.
SURE IS.

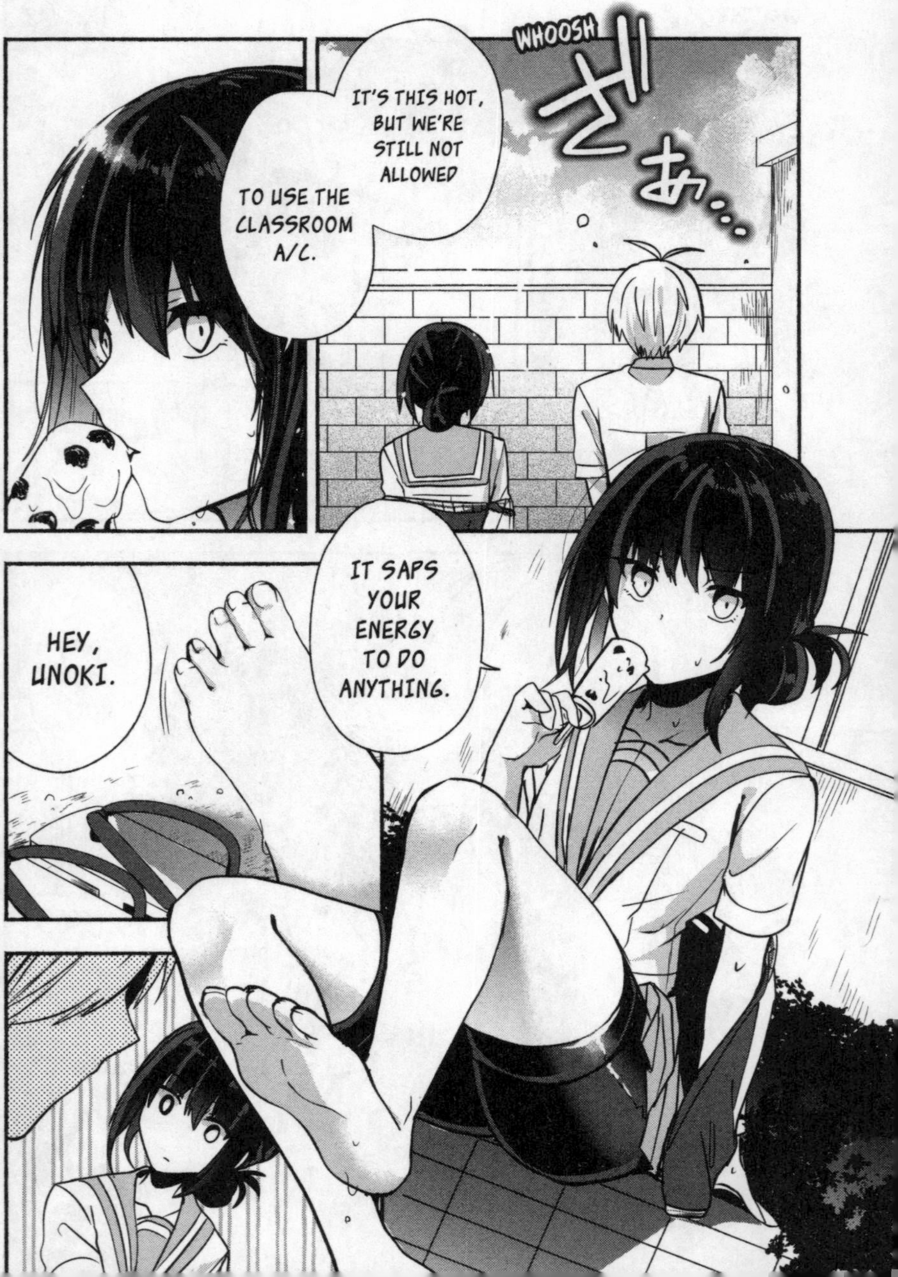
WHOOSH
ざぁ…
IT'S THIS HOT, BUT WE'RE STILL NOT ALLOWED
TO USE THE CLASSROOM A/C.
IT SAPS YOUR ENERGY TO DO ANYTHING.
HEY, UNOKI.

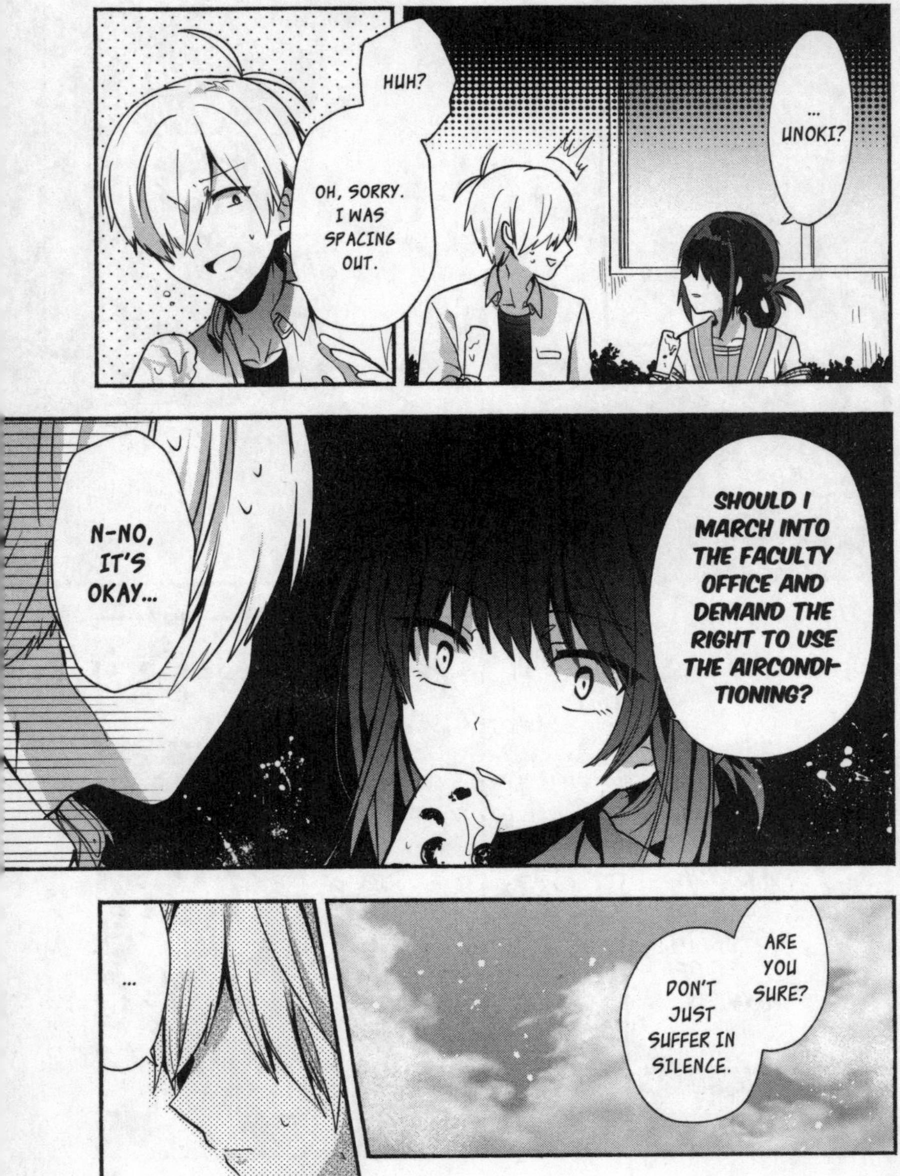
...UNOKI?
HUH?
OH, SORRY. I WAS SPACING OUT.
SHOULD I MARCH INTO THE FACULTY OFFICE AND DEMAND THE RIGHT TO USE THE AIRCONDITIONING?
N-NO, IT'S OKAY...
ARE YOU SURE?
DON'T JUST SUFFER IN SILENCE.
...

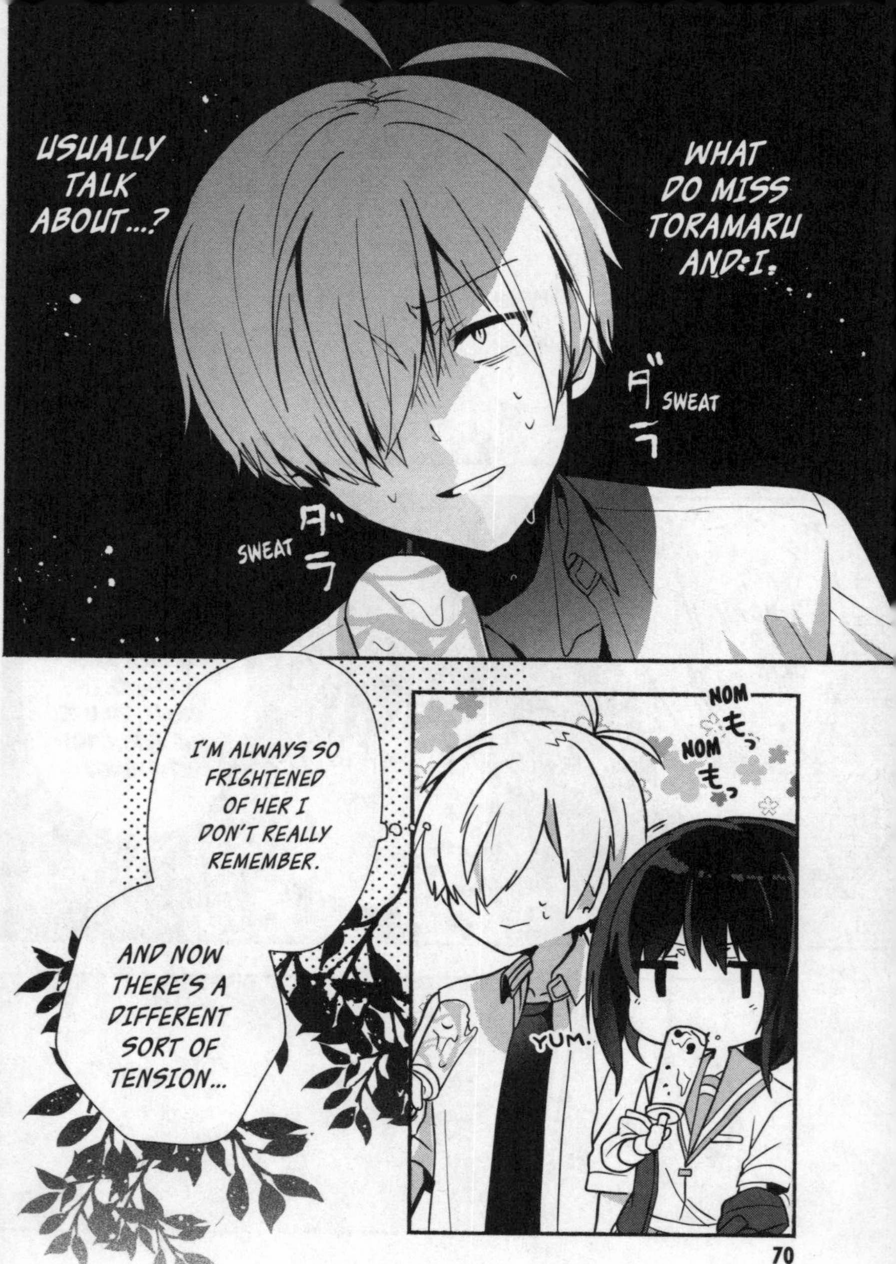
WHAT DO MISS TORAMARU AND I...
USUALLY TALK ABOUT...?
ダラ SWEAT
ダラ SWEAT
NOM もっ
NOM もっ
YUM.
I'M ALWAYS SO FRIGHTENED OF HER I DON'T REALLY REMEMBER.
AND NOW THERE'S A DIFFERENT SORT OF TENSION...

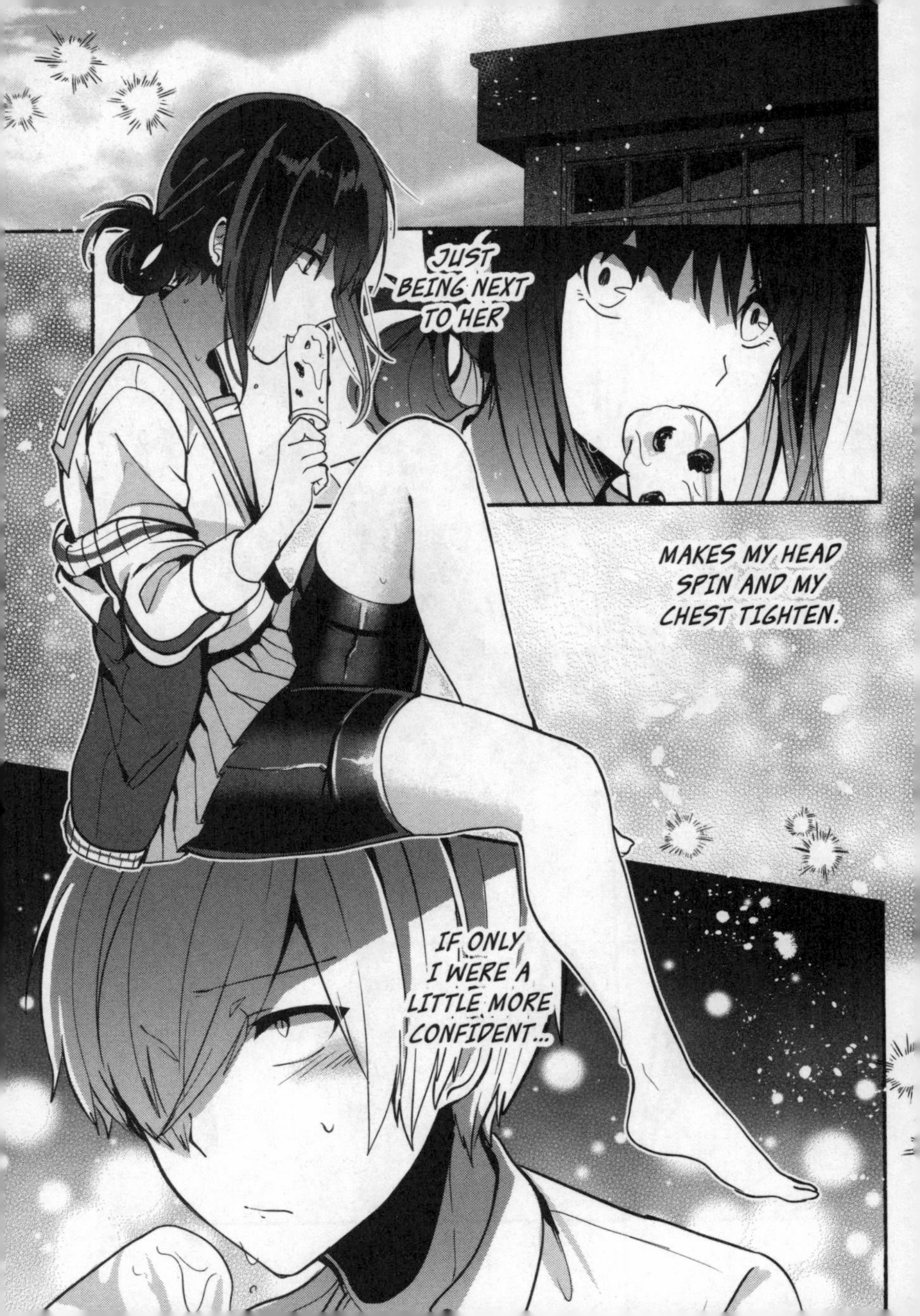
JUST BEING NEXT TO HER
MAKES MY HEAD SPIN AND MY CHEST TIGHTEN.
IF ONLY I WERE A LITTLE MORE CONFIDENT...

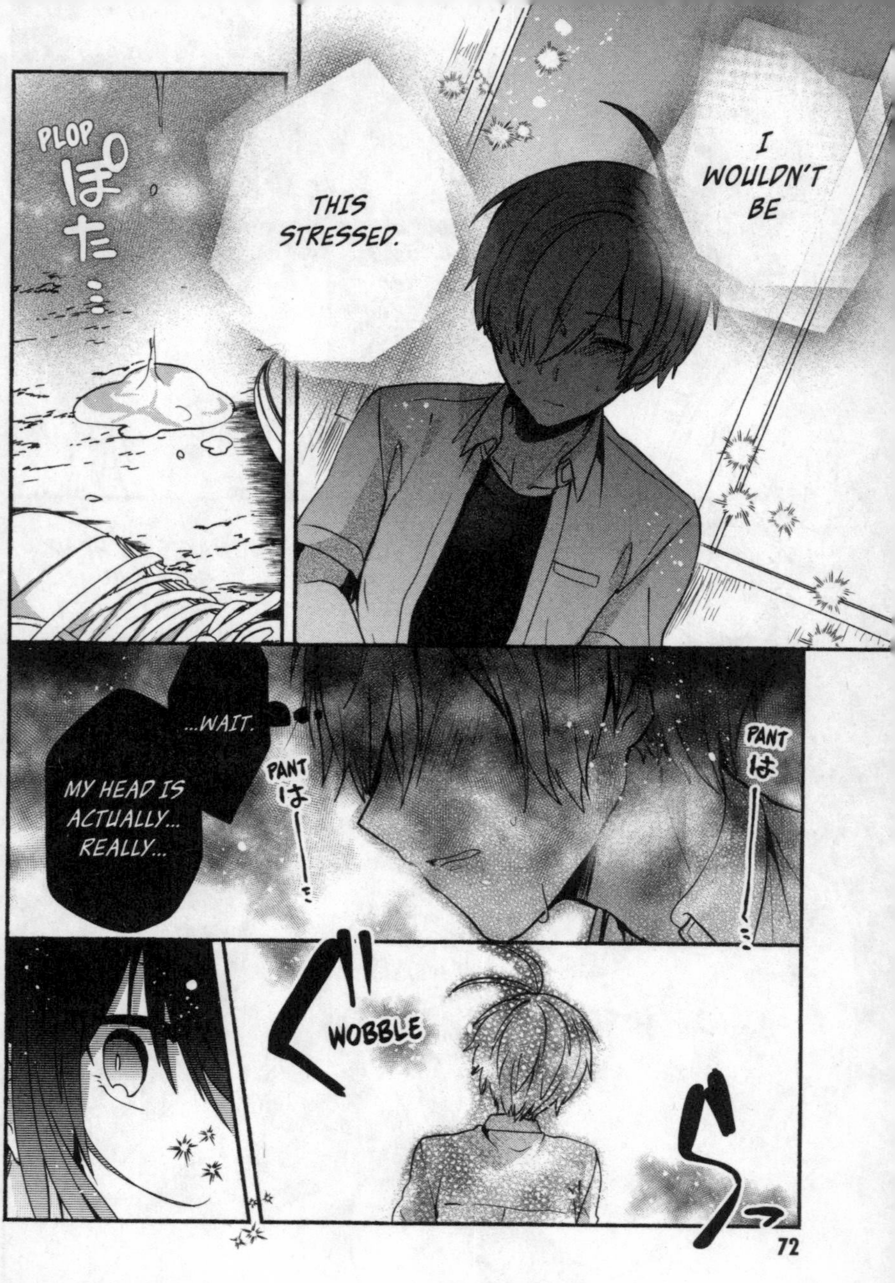
I WOULDN'T BE
THIS STRESSED.
PLOP
ぽた…
PANT
は—…
PANT
は—…
...WAIT.
MY HEAD IS ACTUALLY... REALLY...
ら
ぐ
WOBBLE

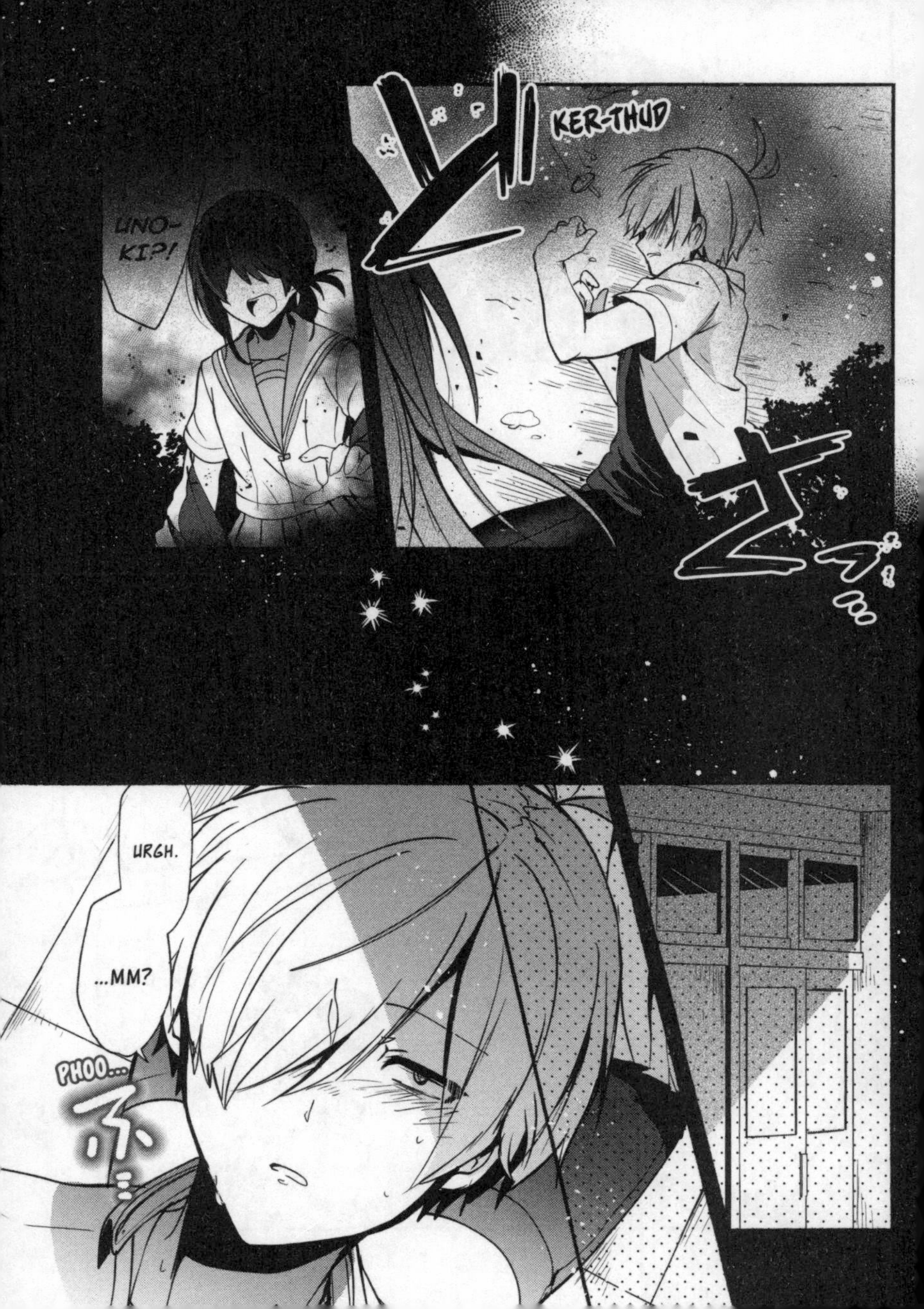
KER-THUD
UNO-KI?!
URGH.
...MM?
PHOO...

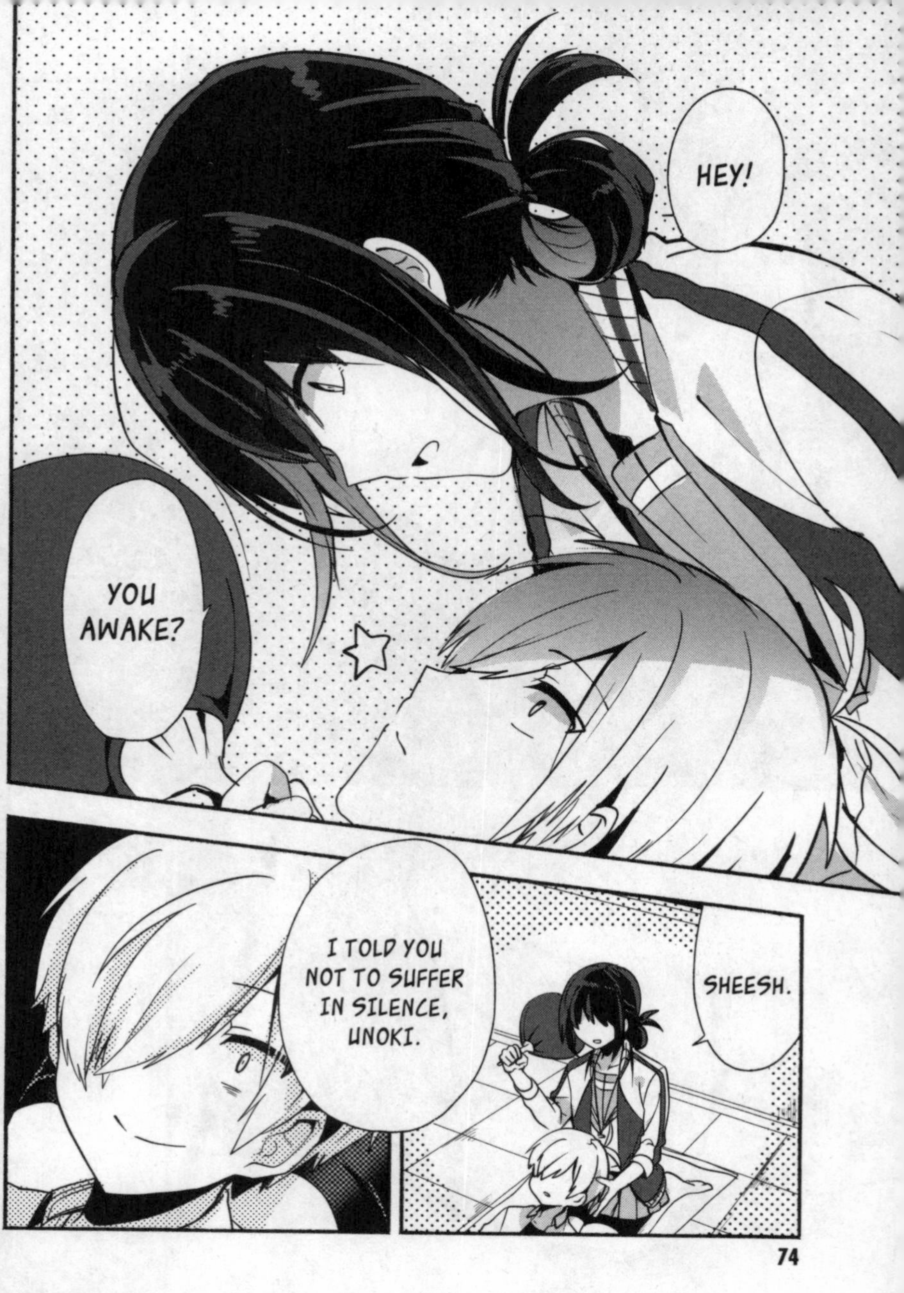
HEY!
YOU AWAKE?
SHEESH.
I TOLD YOU NOT TO SUFFER IN SILENCE, UNOKI.

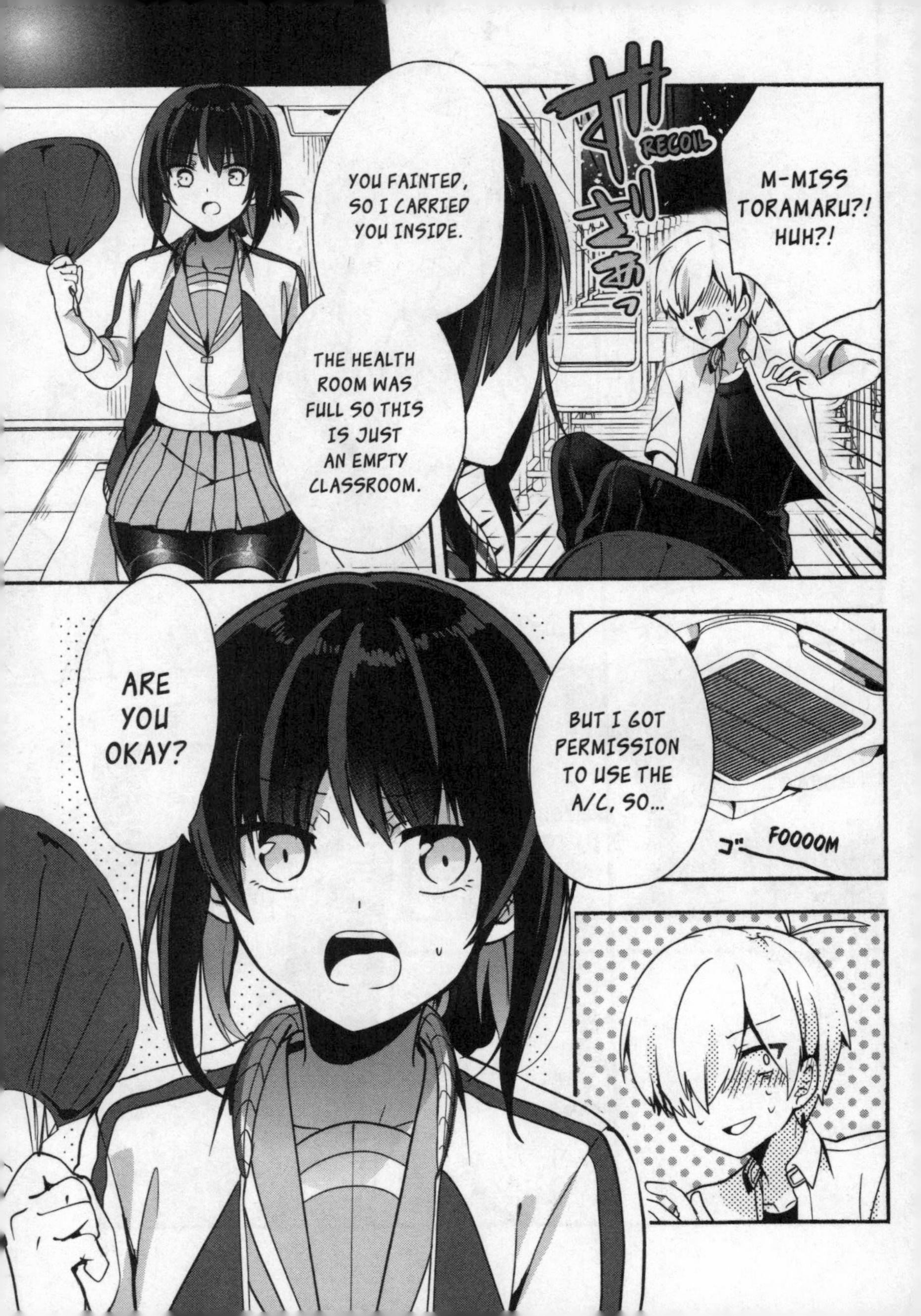
RECOIL
M-MISS TORAMARU?! HUH?!
YOU FAINTED, SO I CARRIED YOU INSIDE.
THE HEALTH ROOM WAS FULL SO THIS IS JUST AN EMPTY CLASSROOM.
BUT I GOT PERMISSION TO USE THE A/C, SO...
FOOOOM
ARE YOU OKAY?

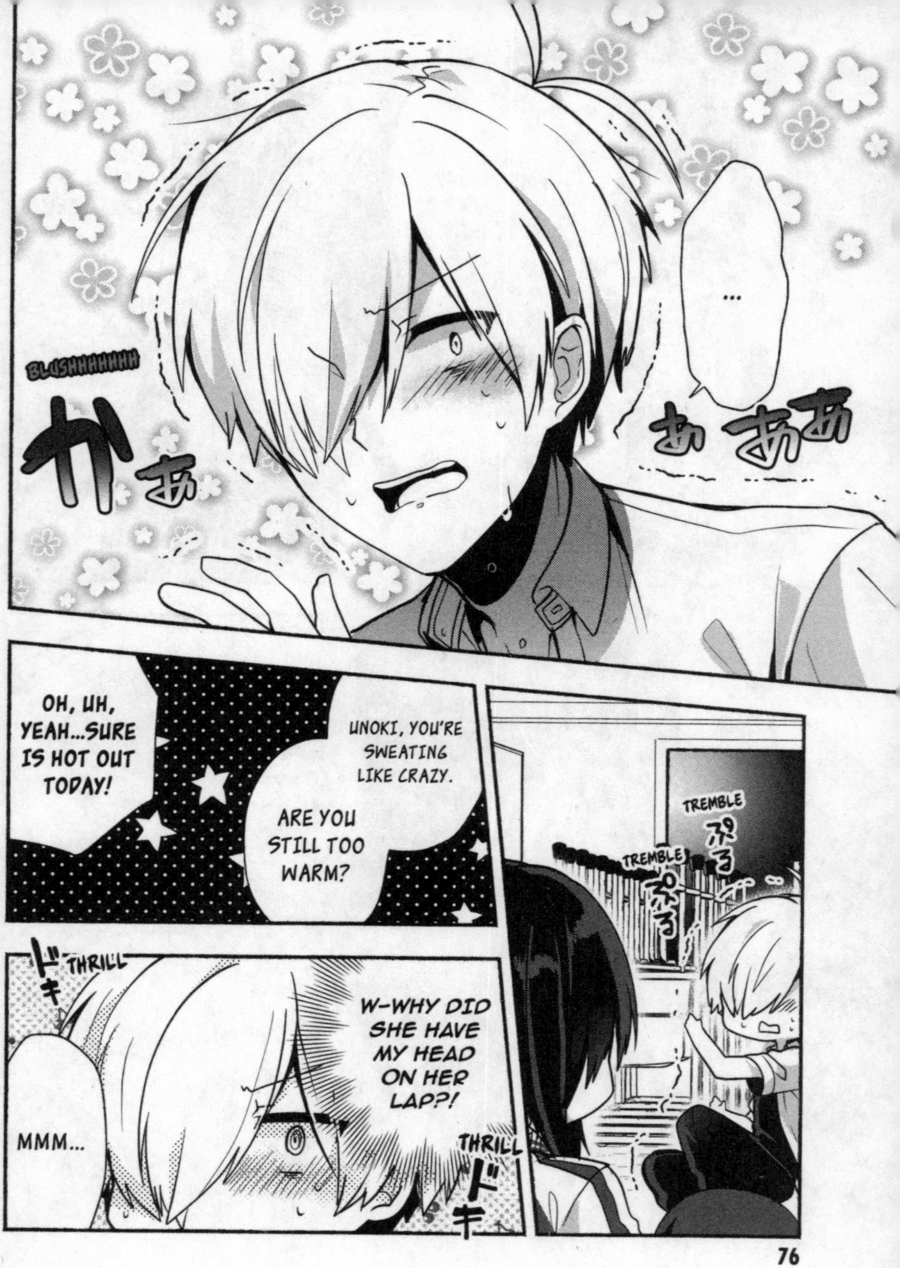
...
あぁぁ
BLUSHHHHHHH
かぁ
TREMBLE
ぷる
TREMBLE
ぷる
UNOKI, YOU'RE SWEATING LIKE CRAZY.
ARE YOU STILL TOO WARM?
OH, UH, YEAH...SURE IS HOT OUT TODAY!
W-WHY DID SHE HAVE MY HEAD ON HER LAP?!
THRILL
ドキ
MMM...
ドキ
THRILL

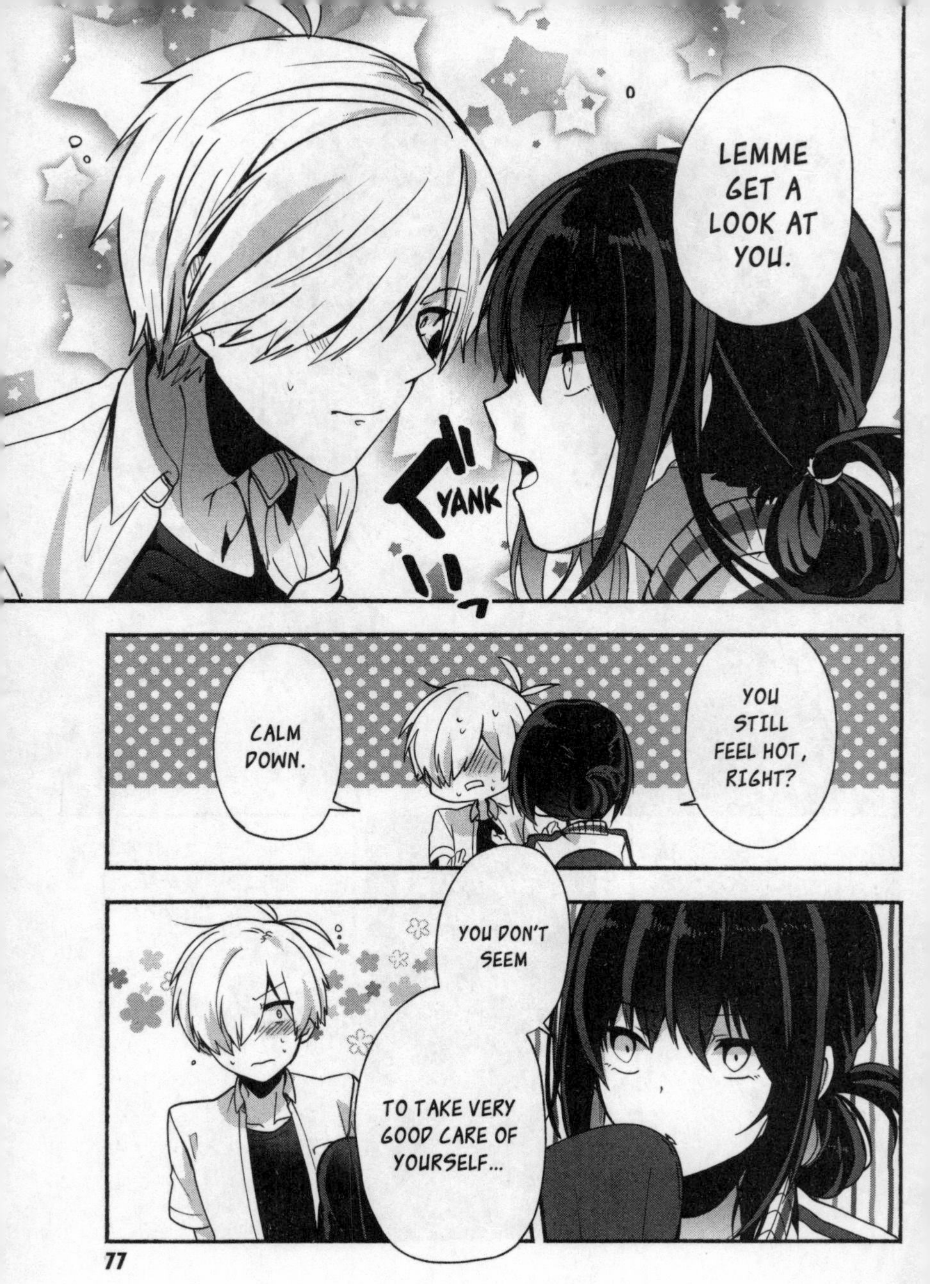
LEMME GET A LOOK AT YOU.
YANK
YOU STILL FEEL HOT, RIGHT?
CALM DOWN.
YOU DON'T SEEM
TO TAKE VERY GOOD CARE OF YOURSELF...

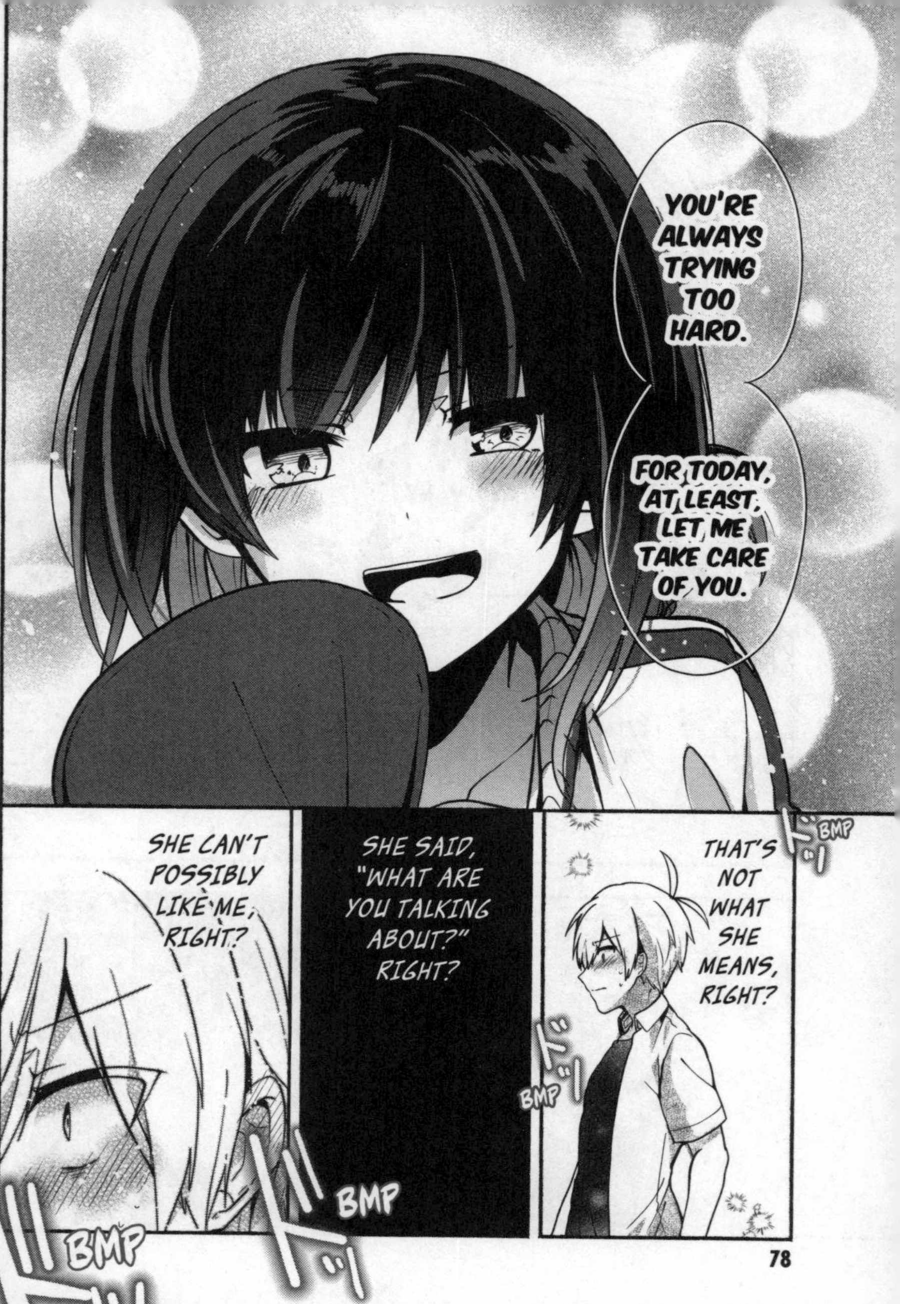
YOU'RE ALWAYS TRYING TOO HARD.
FOR TODAY, AT LEAST, LET ME TAKE CARE OF YOU.
BMP
THAT'S NOT WHAT SHE MEANS, RIGHT?
BMP
SHE SAID, "WHAT ARE YOU TALKING ABOUT?" RIGHT?
SHE CAN'T POSSIBLY LIKE ME, RIGHT?
BMP
BMP

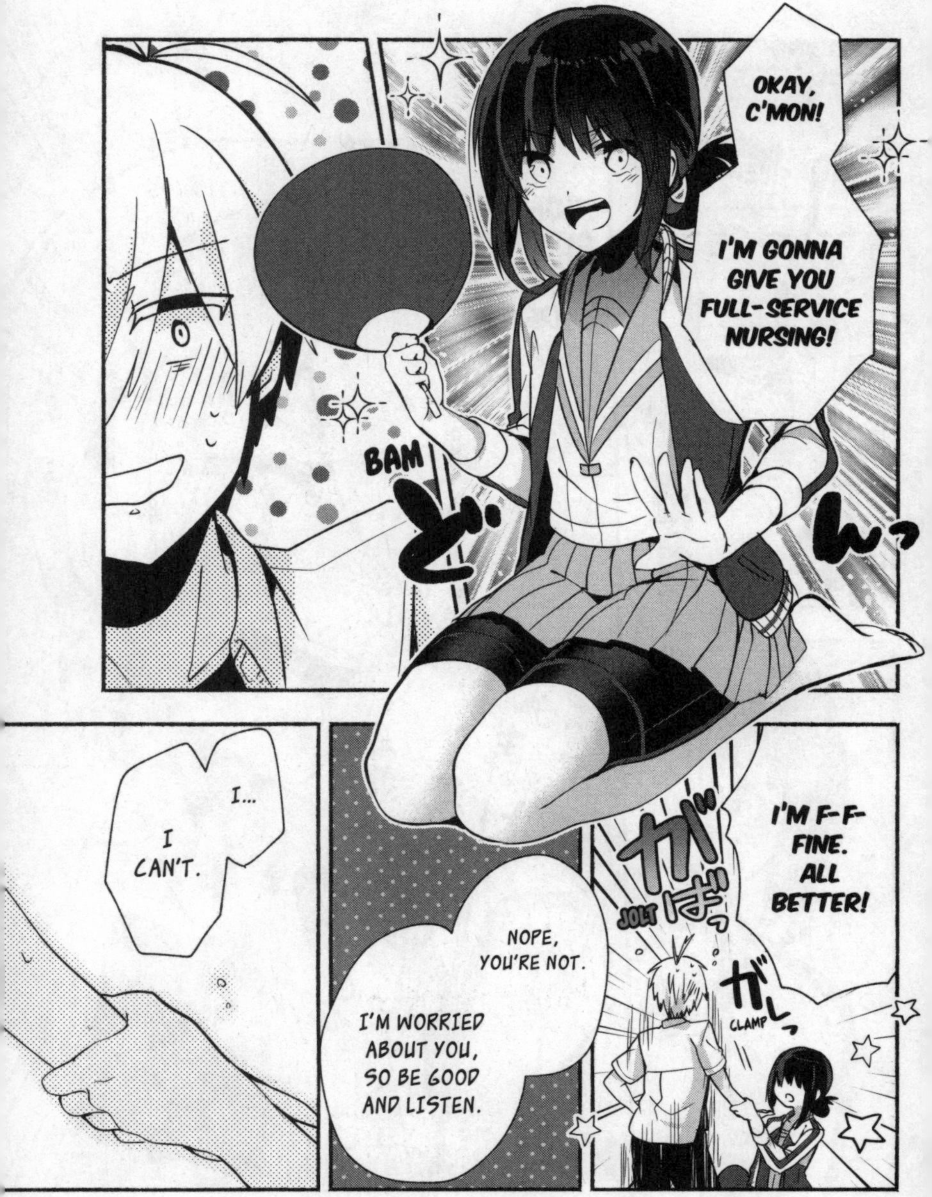
OKAY, C'MON!
I'M GONNA GIVE YOU FULL-SERVICE NURSING!
BAM
どんっ
I'M F-F-FINE. ALL BETTER!
がばっ
JOLT
がしっ
CLAMP
NOPE, YOU'RE NOT.
I'M WORRIED ABOUT YOU, SO BE GOOD AND LISTEN.
I...
I CAN'T.

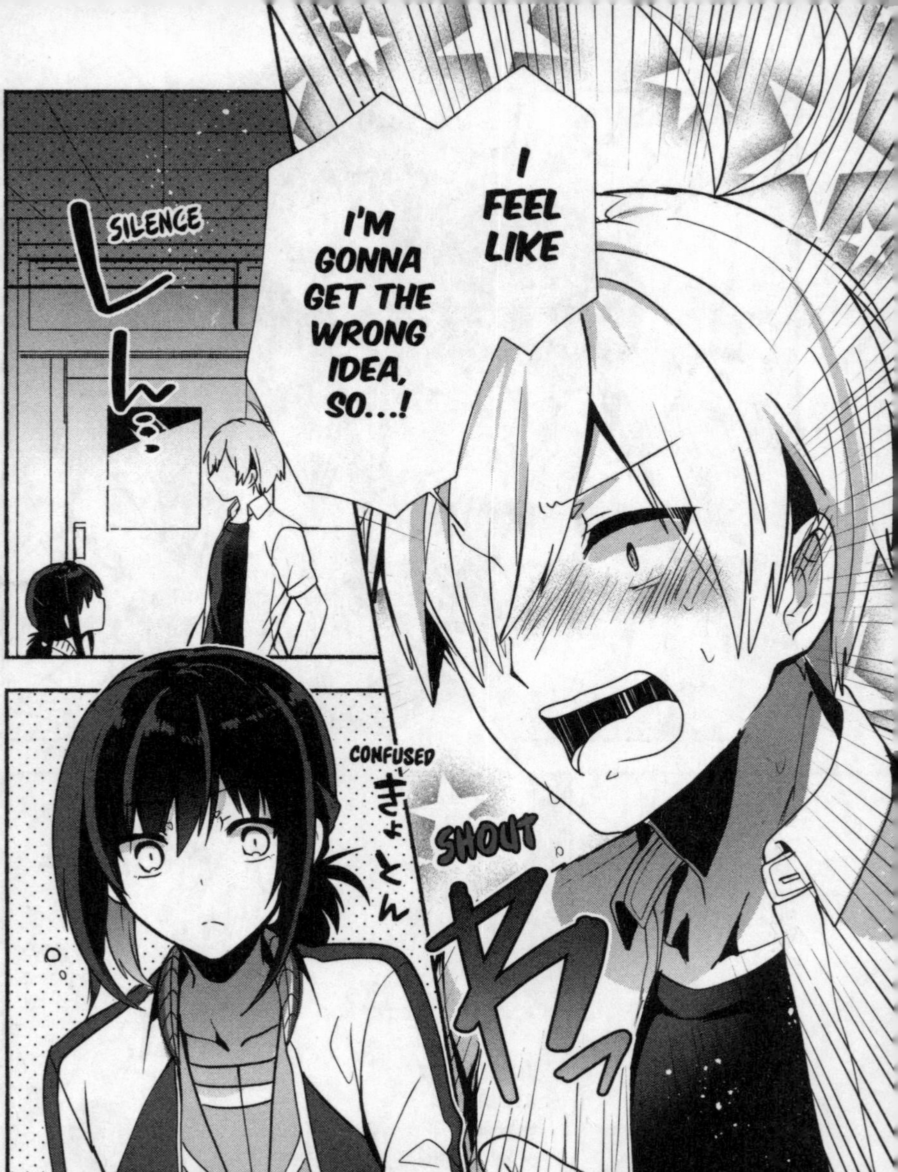
I FEEL LIKE I'M GONNA GET THE WRONG IDEA, SO...!
SHOUT
SILENCE
CONFUSED

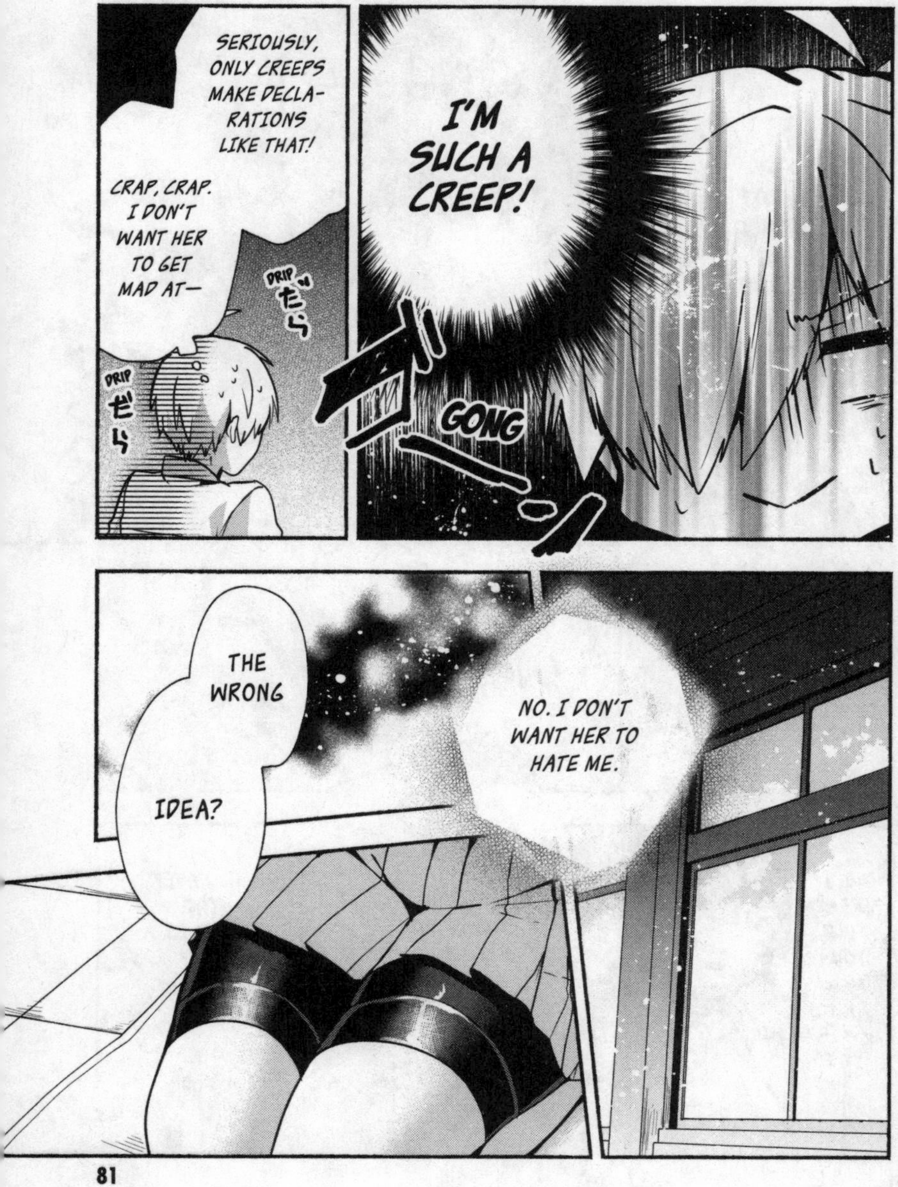
I'M SUCH A CREEP!
GONG
SERIOUSLY, ONLY CREEPS MAKE DECLARATIONS LIKE THAT!
CRAP, CRAP. I DON'T WANT HER TO GET MAD AT—
DRIP だら
DRIP だら
NO. I DON'T WANT HER TO HATE ME.
THE WRONG IDEA?

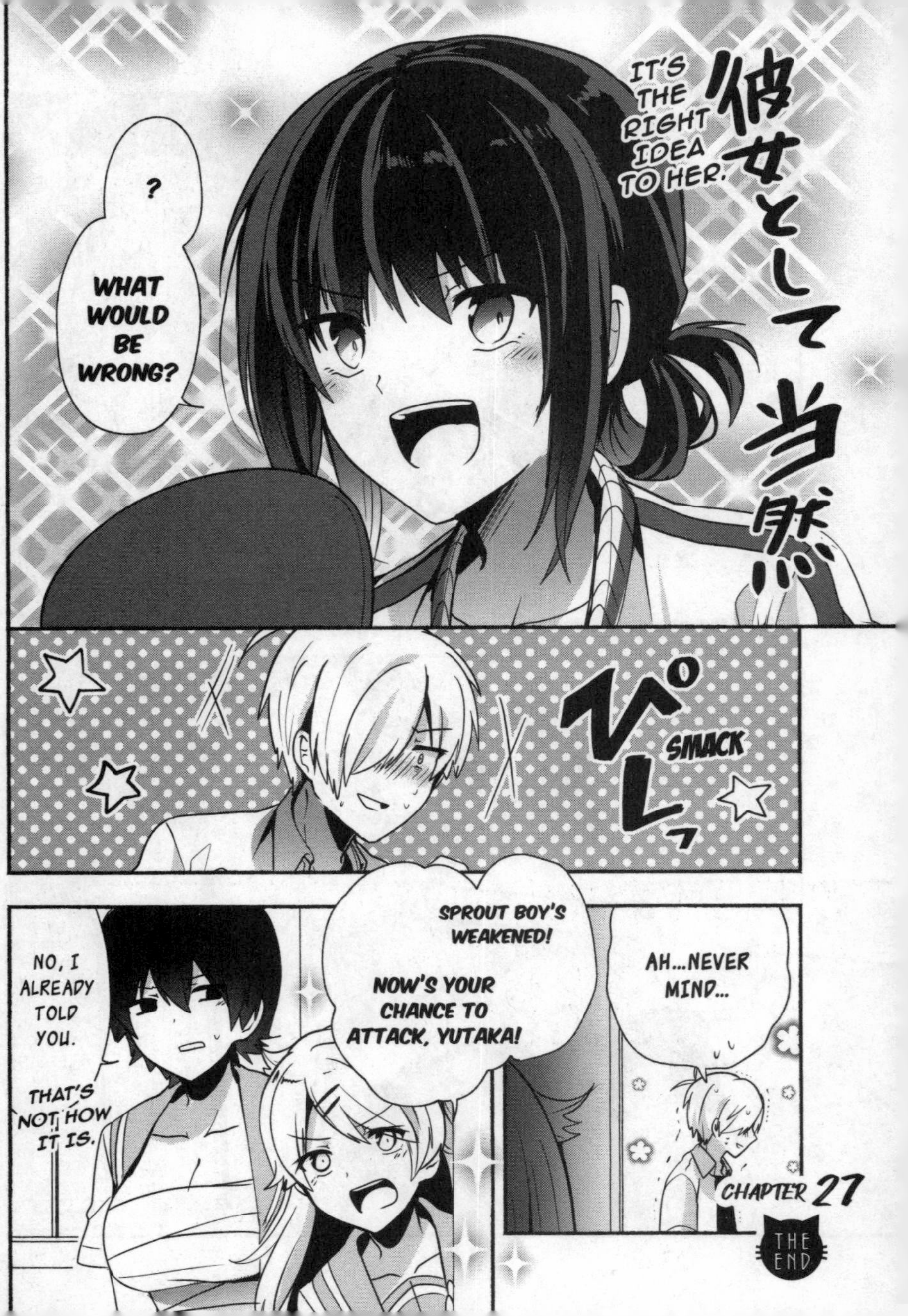
彼女として当然
IT'S THE RIGHT IDEA TO HER.
?
WHAT WOULD BE WRONG?
ぴしっ
SMACK
AH...NEVER MIND...
SPROUT BOY'S WEAKENED!
NOW'S YOUR CHANCE TO ATTACK, YUTAKA!
NO, I ALREADY TOLD YOU.
THAT'S NOT HOW IT IS.
CHAPTER 27
THE END

CHAPTER 28

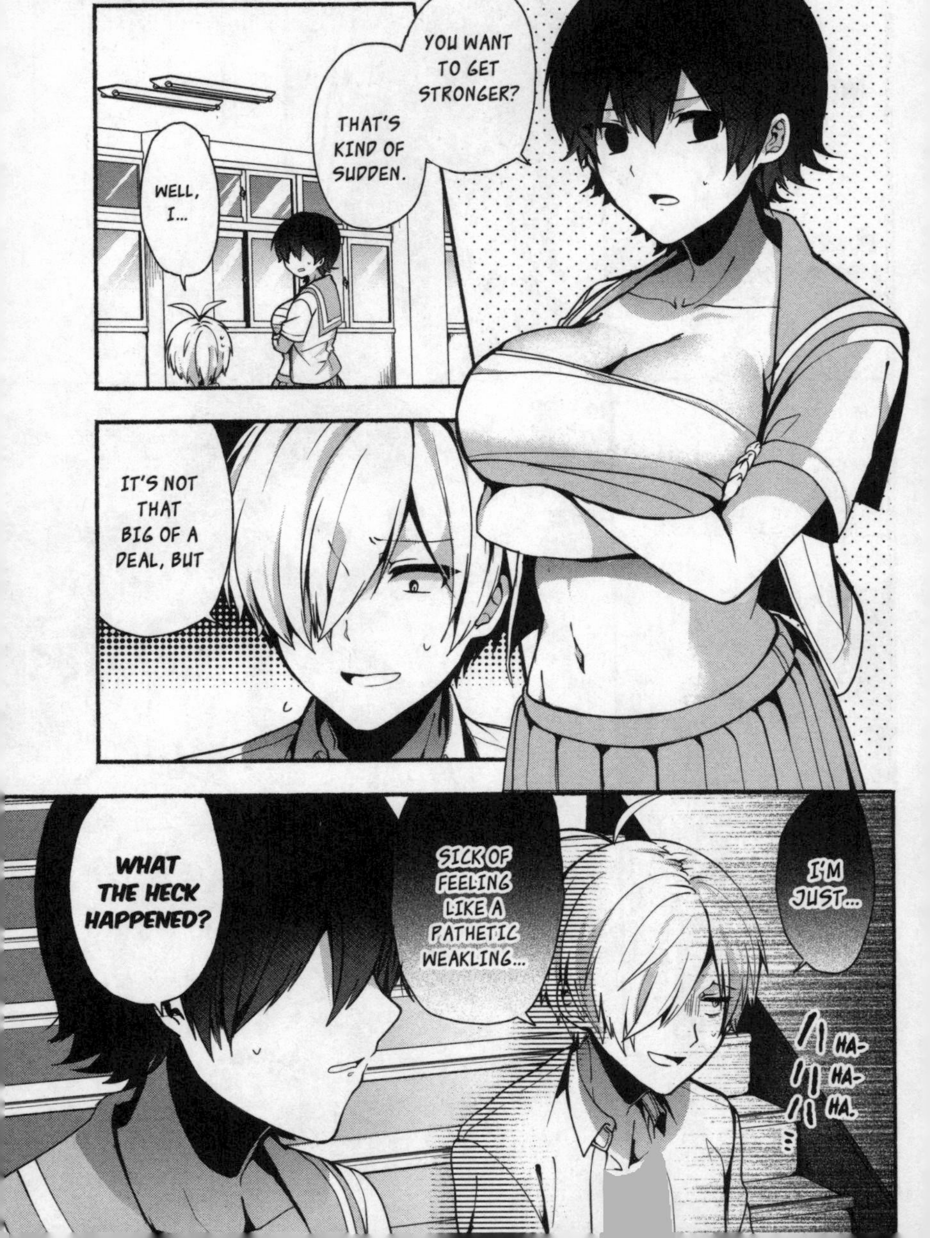

YOU WANT TO GET STRONGER?
THAT'S KIND OF SUDDEN.
WELL, I...
IT'S NOT THAT BIG OF A DEAL, BUT
I'M JUST...
HA-HA-HA.
SICK OF FEELING LIKE A PATHETIC WEAKLING...
WHAT THE HECK HAPPENED?

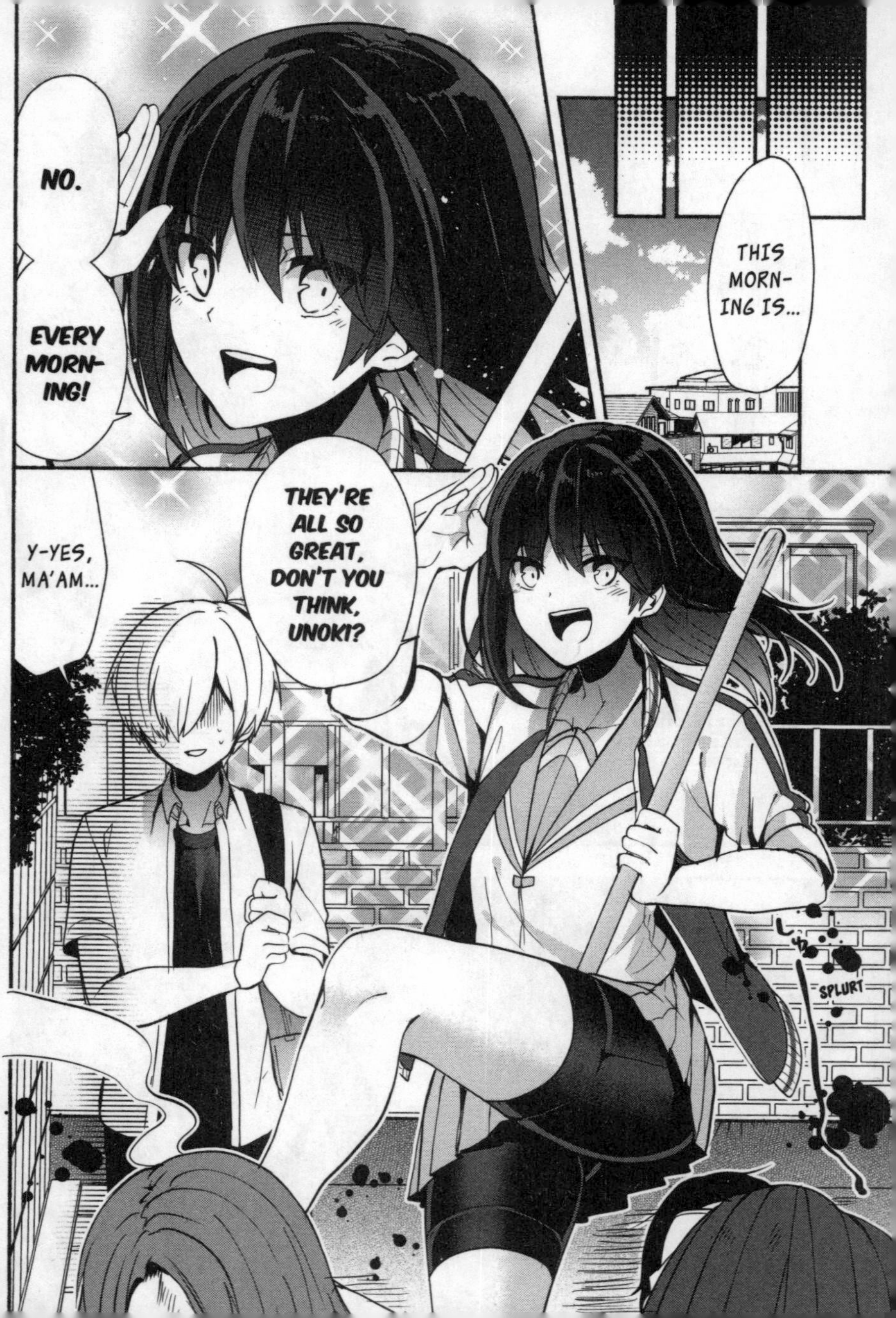
THIS MORNING IS...
NO.
EVERY MORNING!
THEY'RE ALL SO GREAT, DON'T YOU THINK, UNOKI?
Y-YES, MA'AM...
SPLURT

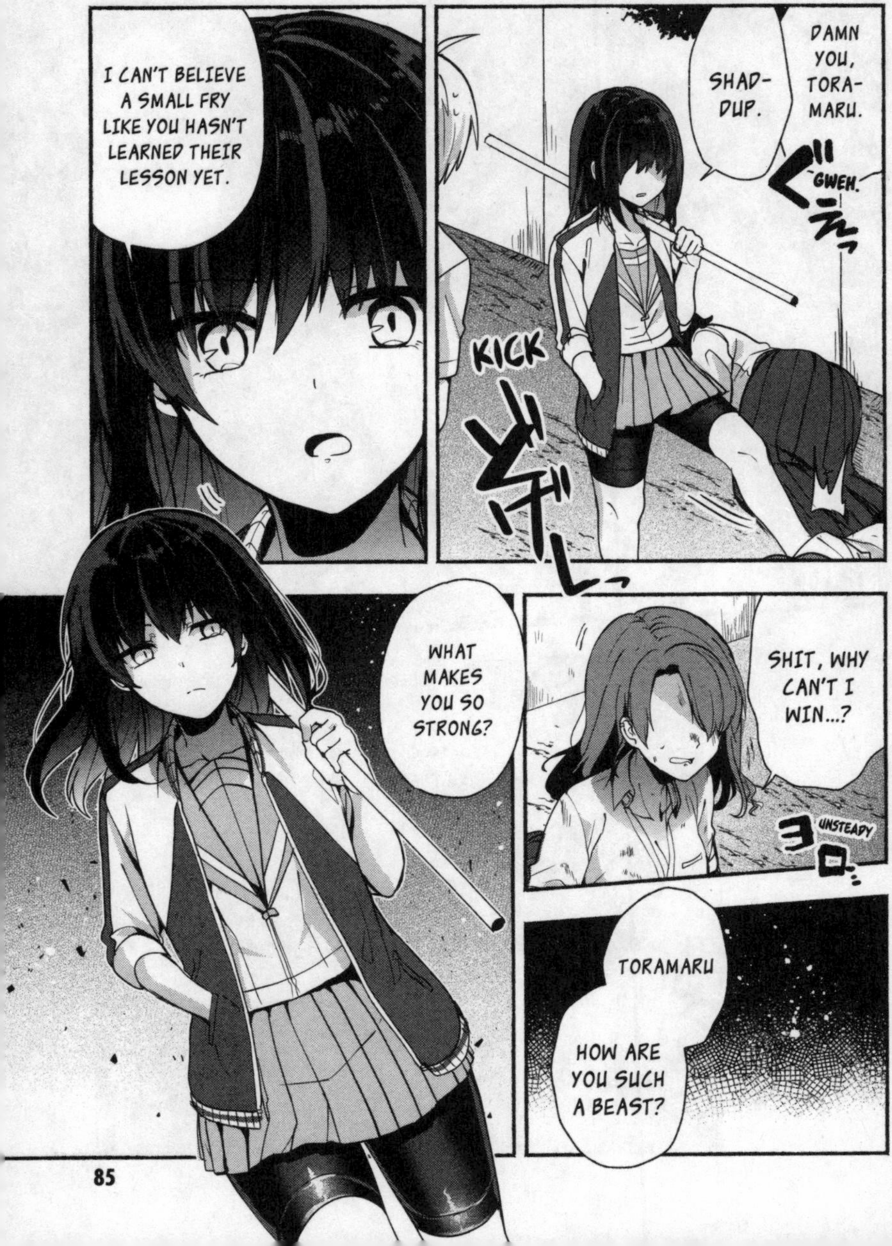
DAMN YOU, TORA-MARU.
SHAD-DUP.
GWEH.
KICK
I CAN'T BELIEVE A SMALL FRY LIKE YOU HASN'T LEARNED THEIR LESSON YET.
SHIT, WHY CAN'T I WIN...?
UNSTEADY
TORAMARU
HOW ARE YOU SUCH A BEAST?
WHAT MAKES YOU SO STRONG?

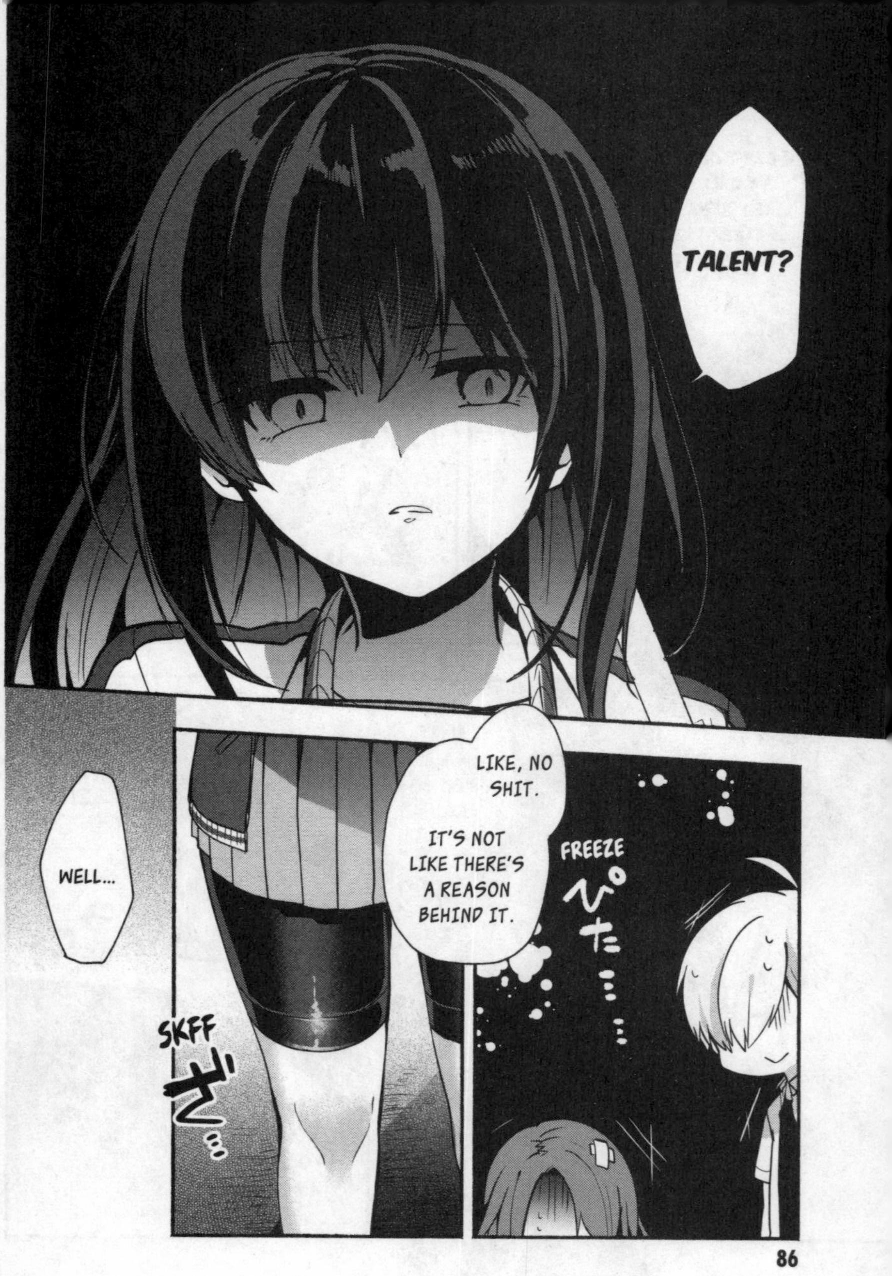
TALENT?
LIKE, NO SHIT.
IT'S NOT LIKE THERE'S A REASON BEHIND IT.
FREEZE
WELL...
SKFF

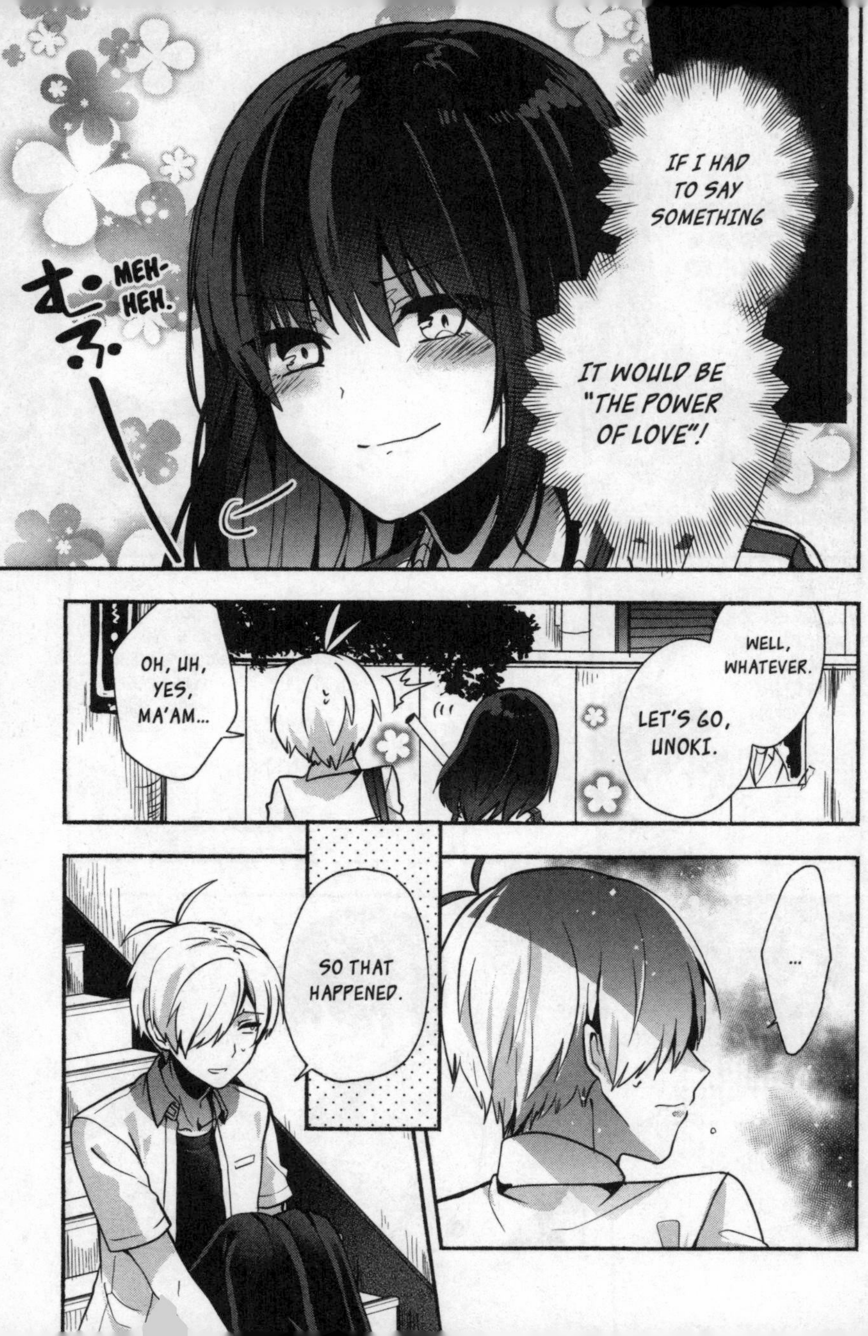
IF I HAD TO SAY SOMETHING
IT WOULD BE "THE POWER OF LOVE"!
むふ
MEH-HEH.
WELL, WHATEVER.
LET'S GO, UNOKI.
OH, UH, YES, MA'AM...
...
SO THAT HAPPENED.

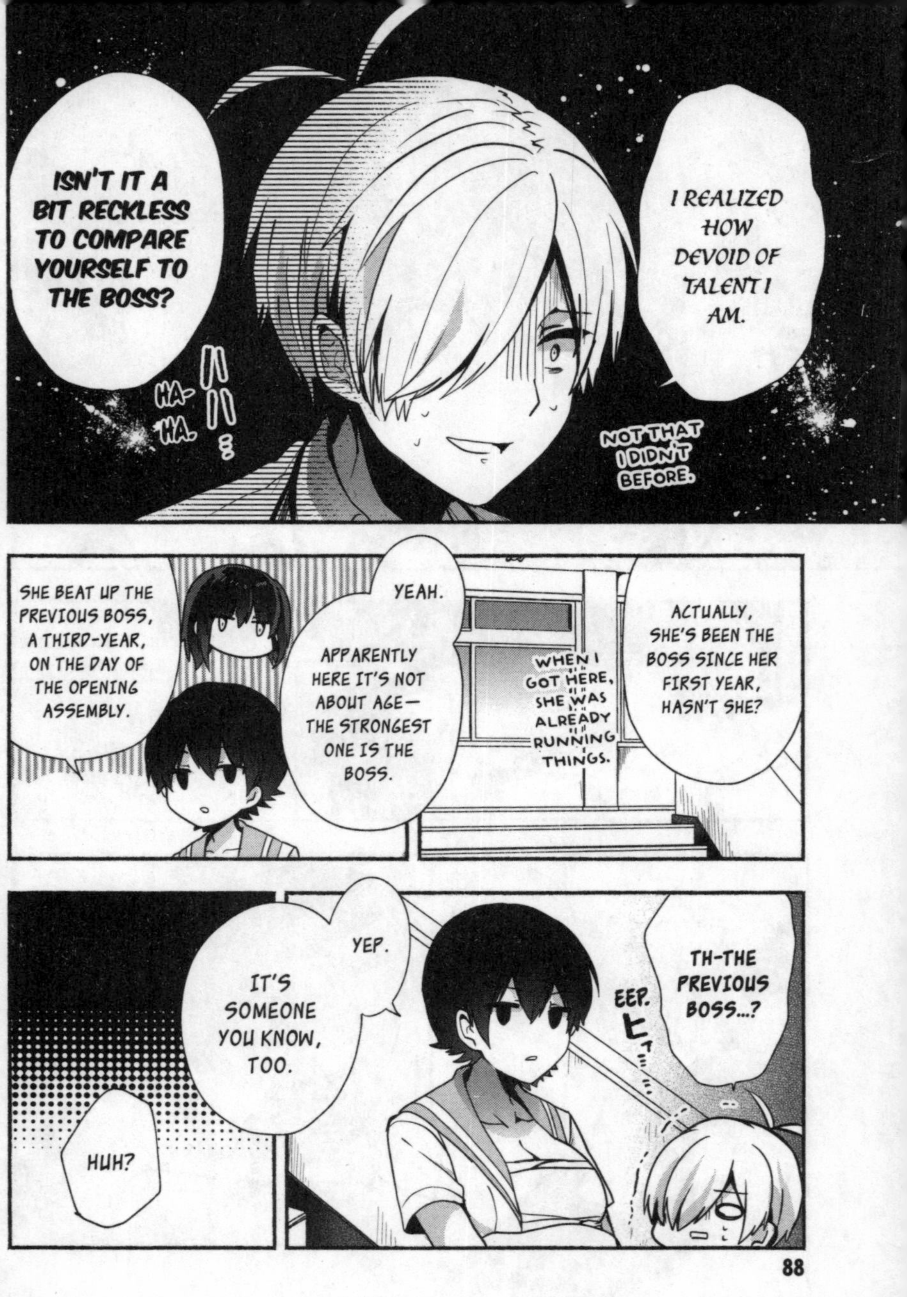
I REALIZED HOW DEVOID OF TALENT I AM.
ISN'T IT A BIT RECKLESS TO COMPARE YOURSELF TO THE BOSS?
HA-HA.
NOT THAT I DIDN'T BEFORE.
ACTUALLY, SHE'S BEEN THE BOSS SINCE HER FIRST YEAR, HASN'T SHE?
WHEN I GOT HERE, SHE WAS ALREADY RUNNING THINGS.
YEAH.
APPARENTLY HERE IT'S NOT ABOUT AGE—THE STRONGEST ONE IS THE BOSS.
SHE BEAT UP THE PREVIOUS BOSS, A THIRD-YEAR, ON THE DAY OF THE OPENING ASSEMBLY.
TH-THE PREVIOUS BOSS...?
EEP.
YEP.
IT'S SOMEONE YOU KNOW, TOO.
HUH?

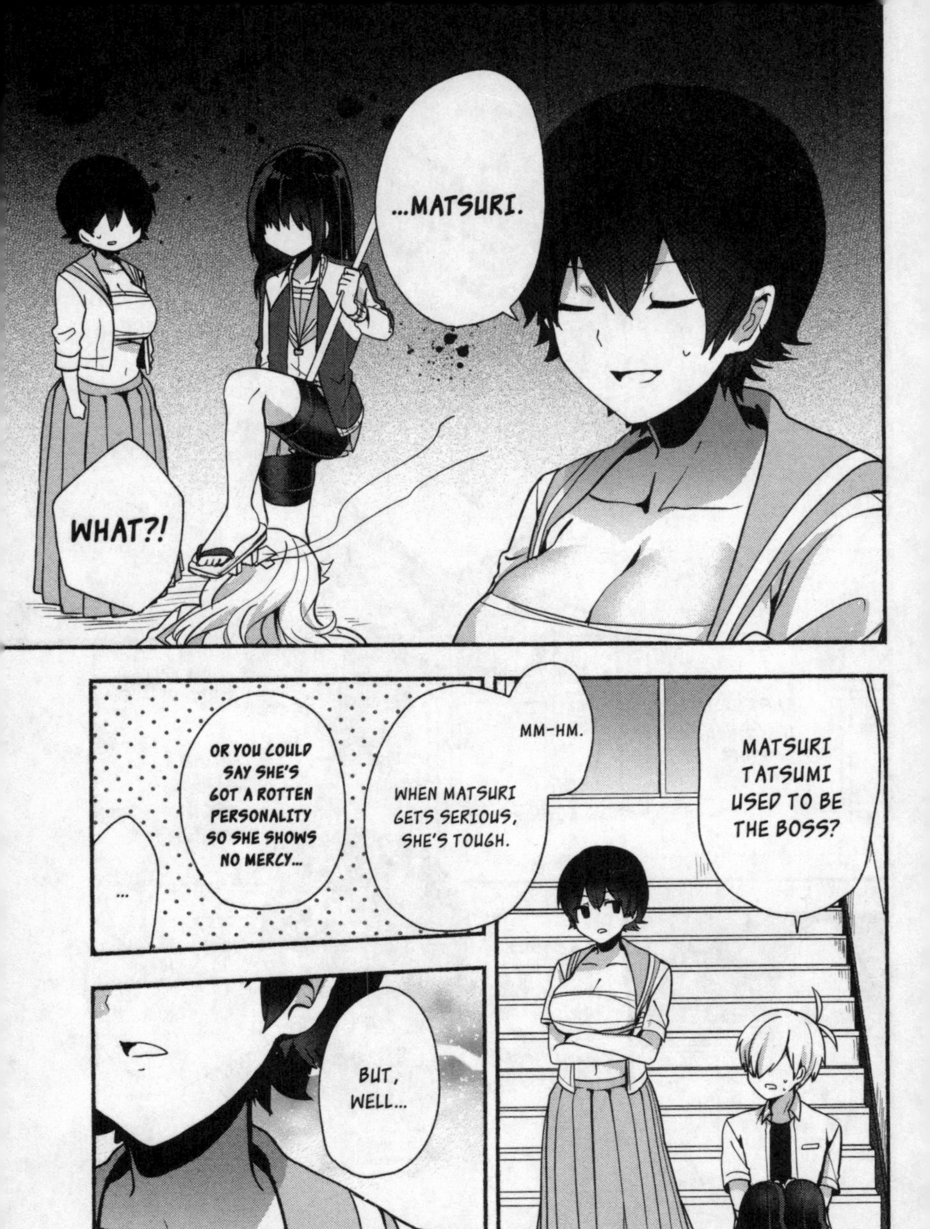
...MATSURI.
WHAT?!
MATSURI TATSUMI USED TO BE THE BOSS?
MM-HM.
WHEN MATSURI GETS SERIOUS, SHE'S TOUGH.
OR YOU COULD SAY SHE'S GOT A ROTTEN PERSONALITY SO SHE SHOWS NO MERCY...
...
BUT, WELL...

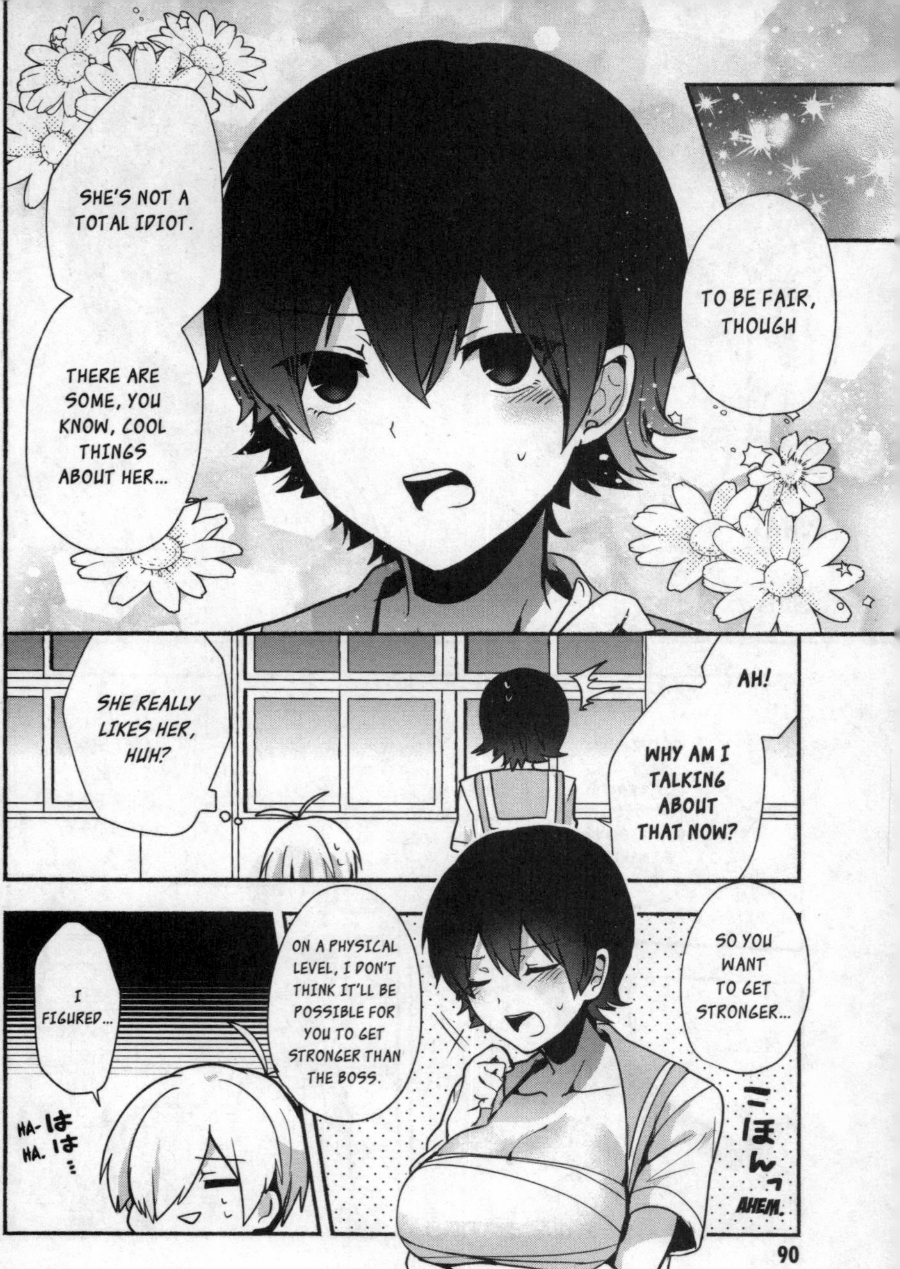
TO BE FAIR, THOUGH
SHE'S NOT A TOTAL IDIOT.
THERE ARE SOME, YOU KNOW, COOL THINGS ABOUT HER...
AH!
WHY AM I TALKING ABOUT THAT NOW?
SHE REALLY LIKES HER, HUH?
SO YOU WANT TO GET STRONGER...
こほんっ
AHEM.
ON A PHYSICAL LEVEL, I DON'T THINK IT'LL BE POSSIBLE FOR YOU TO GET STRONGER THAN THE BOSS.
I FIGURED...
はは…
HA-HA.

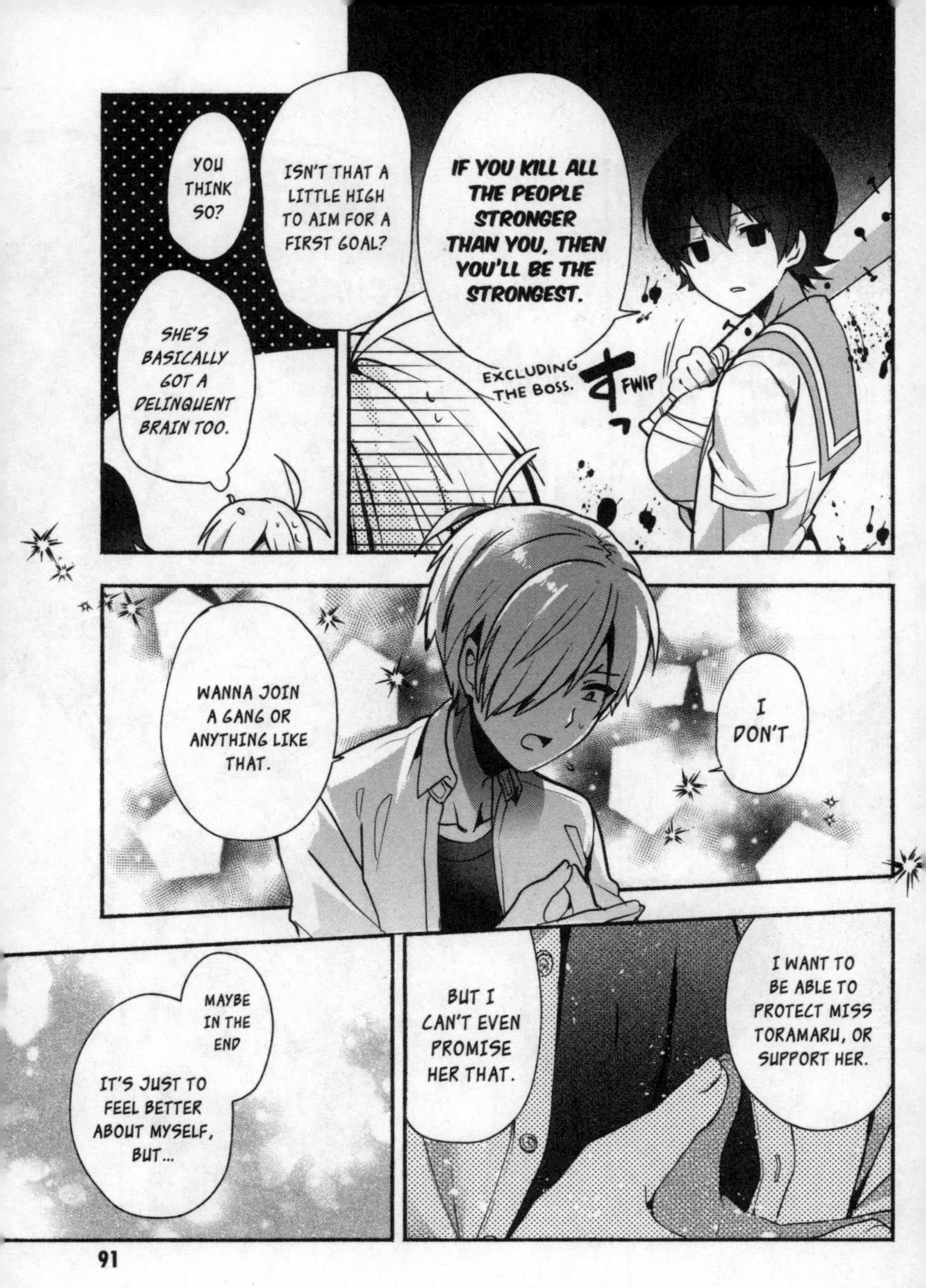
IF YOU KILL ALL THE PEOPLE STRONGER THAN YOU, THEN YOU'LL BE THE STRONGEST.
EXCLUDING THE BOSS.
FWIP
ISN'T THAT A LITTLE HIGH TO AIM FOR A FIRST GOAL?
YOU THINK SO?
SHE'S BASICALLY GOT A DELINQUENT BRAIN TOO.
I DON'T
WANNA JOIN A GANG OR ANYTHING LIKE THAT.
I WANT TO BE ABLE TO PROTECT MISS TORAMARU, OR SUPPORT HER.
BUT I CAN'T EVEN PROMISE HER THAT.
MAYBE IN THE END
IT'S JUST TO FEEL BETTER ABOUT MYSELF, BUT...

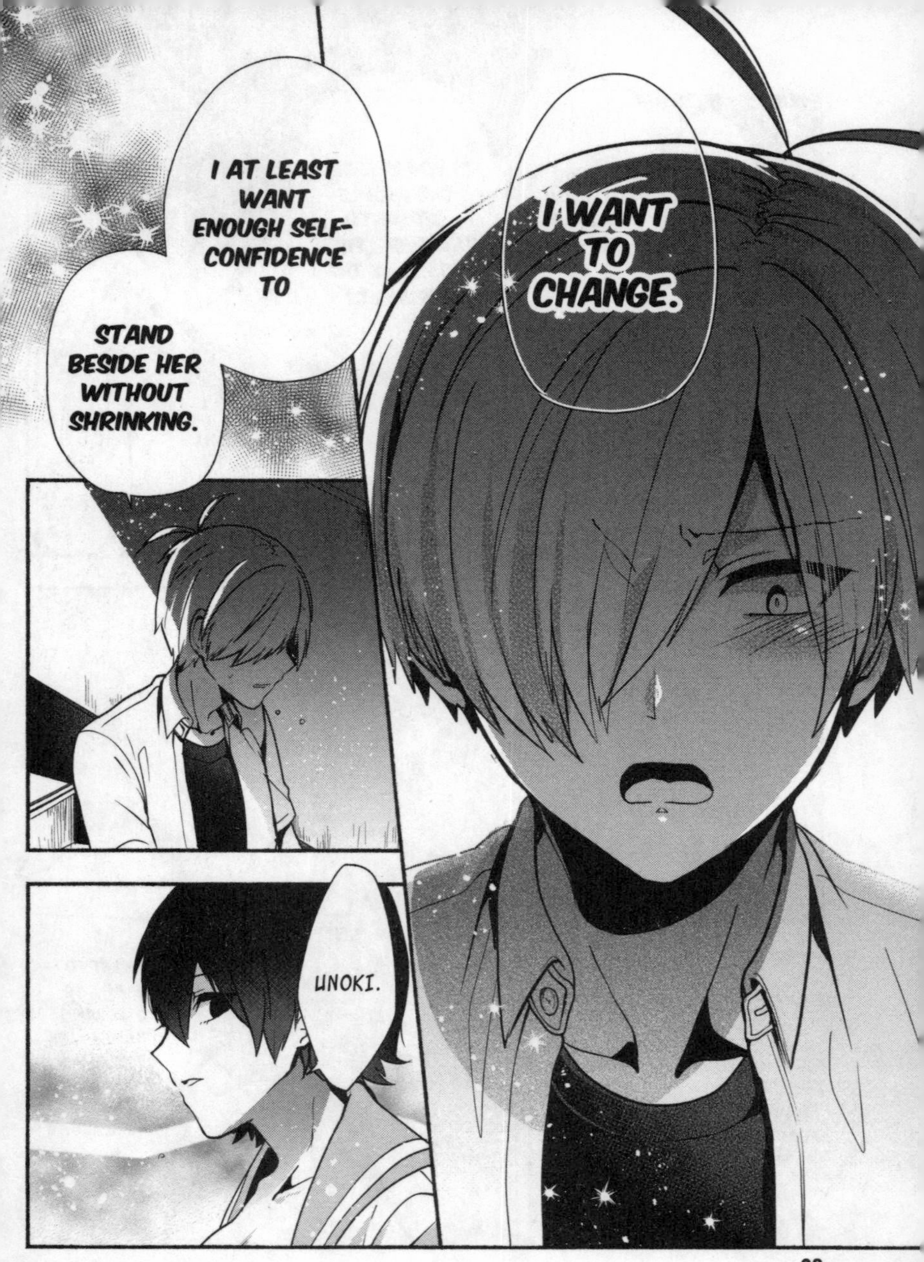
I WANT TO CHANGE.
I AT LEAST WANT ENOUGH SELF-CONFIDENCE TO
STAND BESIDE HER WITHOUT SHRINKING.
UNOKI.

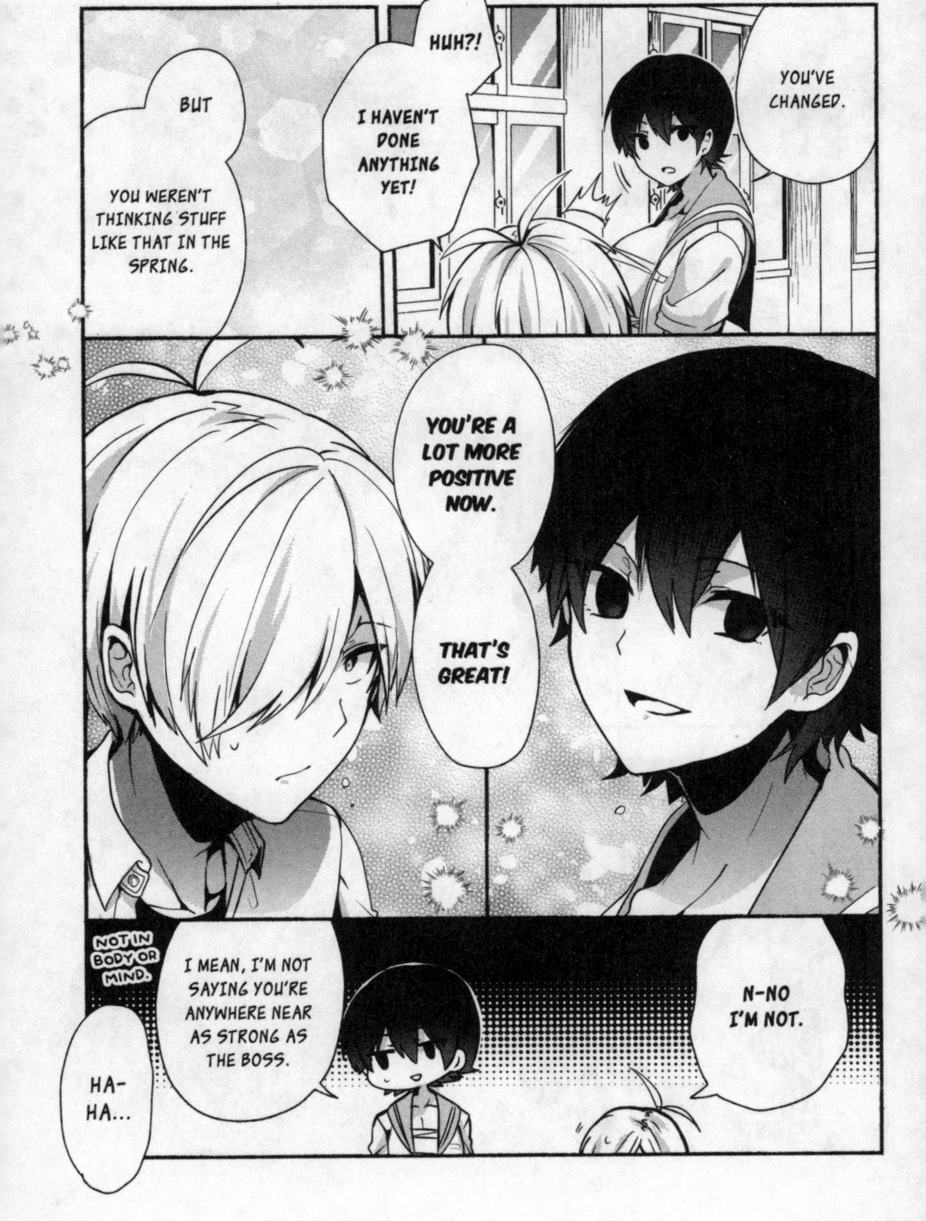

YOU'VE CHANGED.
HUH?!
I HAVEN'T DONE ANYTHING YET!
BUT
YOU WEREN'T THINKING STUFF LIKE THAT IN THE SPRING.
YOU'RE A LOT MORE POSITIVE NOW.
THAT'S GREAT!
N-NO I'M NOT.
I MEAN, I'M NOT SAYING YOU'RE ANYWHERE NEAR AS STRONG AS THE BOSS.
HA-HA...
NOT IN BODY OR MIND.

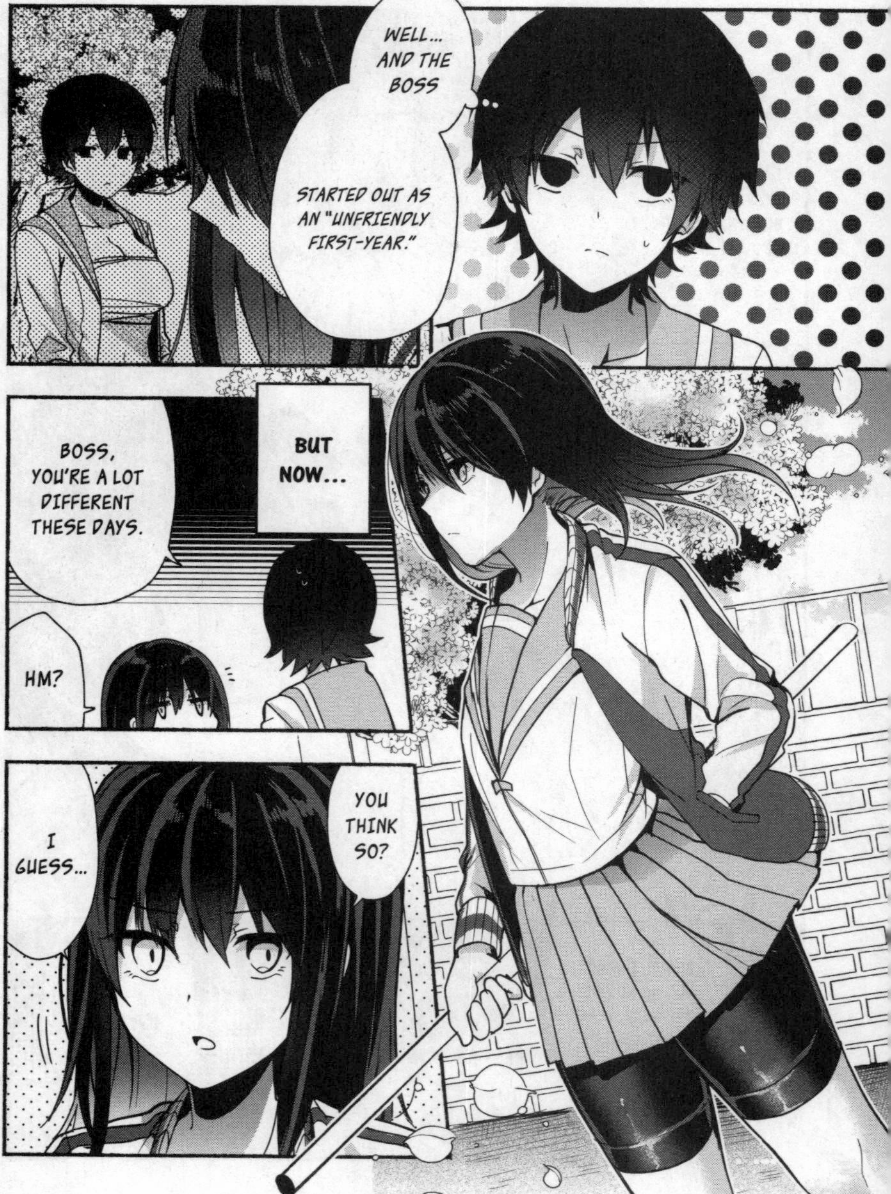
WELL... AND THE BOSS
STARTED OUT AS AN "UNFRIENDLY FIRST-YEAR."
BUT NOW...
BOSS, YOU'RE A LOT DIFFERENT THESE DAYS.
HM?
YOU THINK SO?
I GUESS...

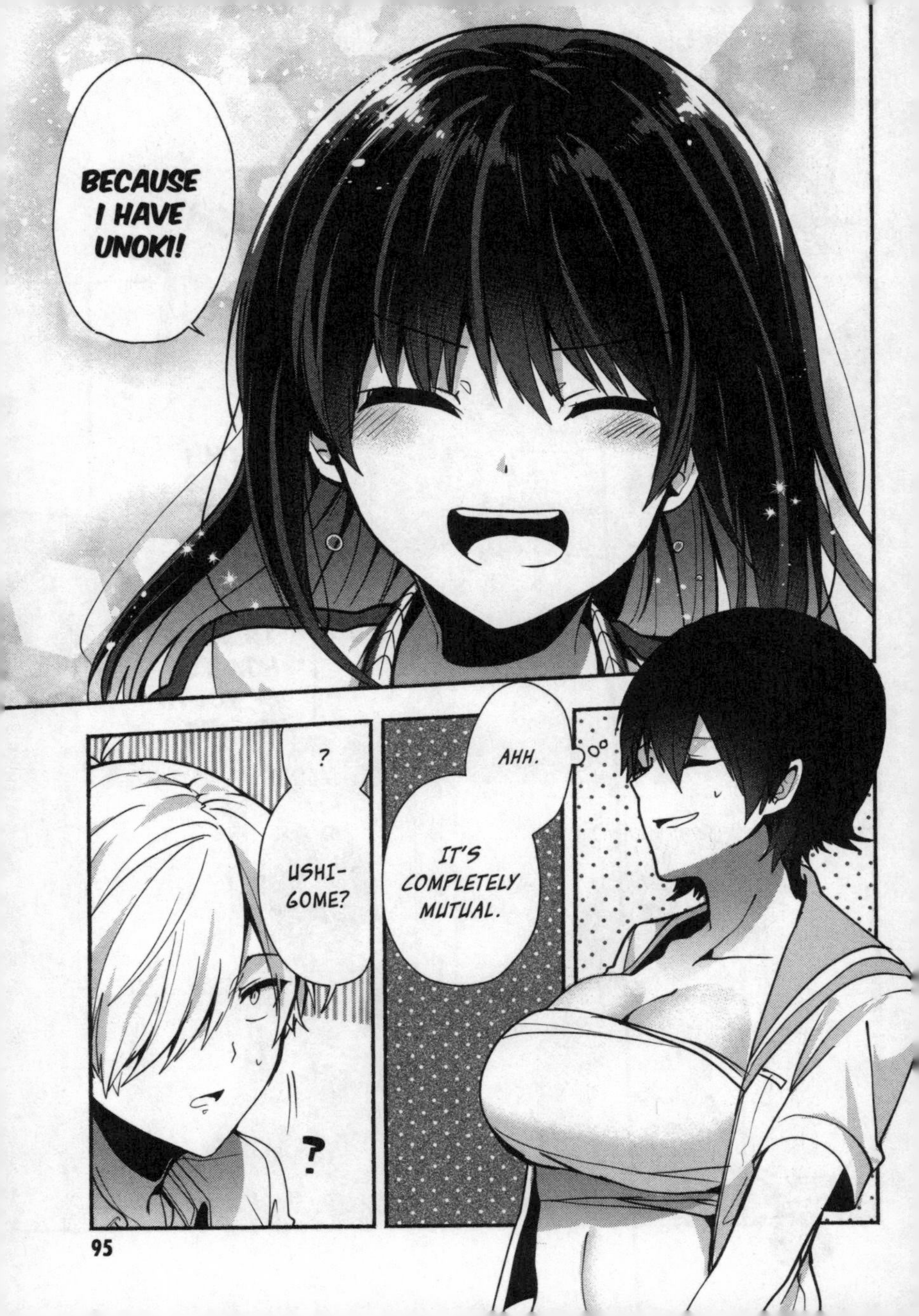
BECAUSE I HAVE UNOKI!
AHH.
IT'S COMPLETELY MUTUAL.
?
USHI-GOME?
?

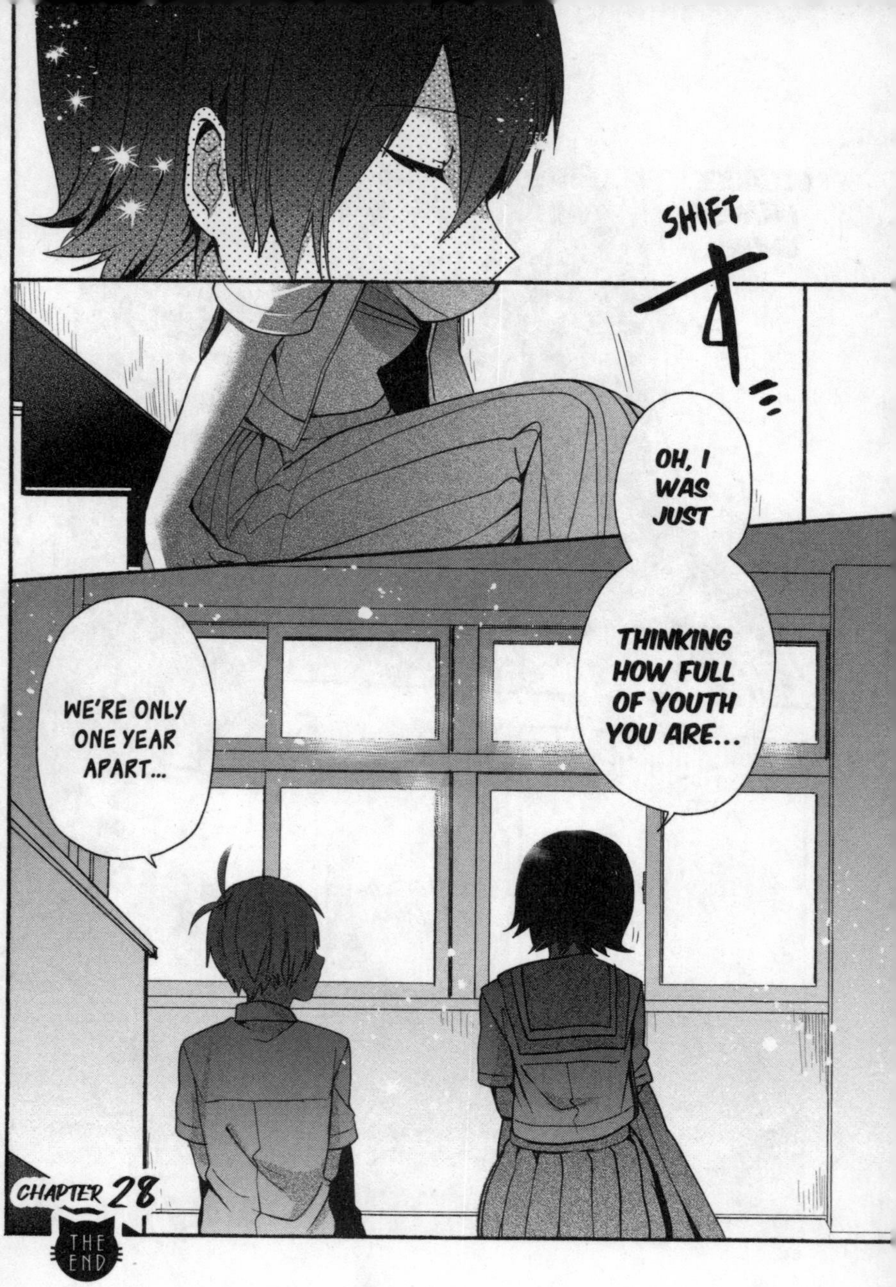
SHIFT
OH, I WAS JUST THINKING HOW FULL OF YOUTH YOU ARE...
WE'RE ONLY ONE YEAR APART...
CHAPTER 28
THE END

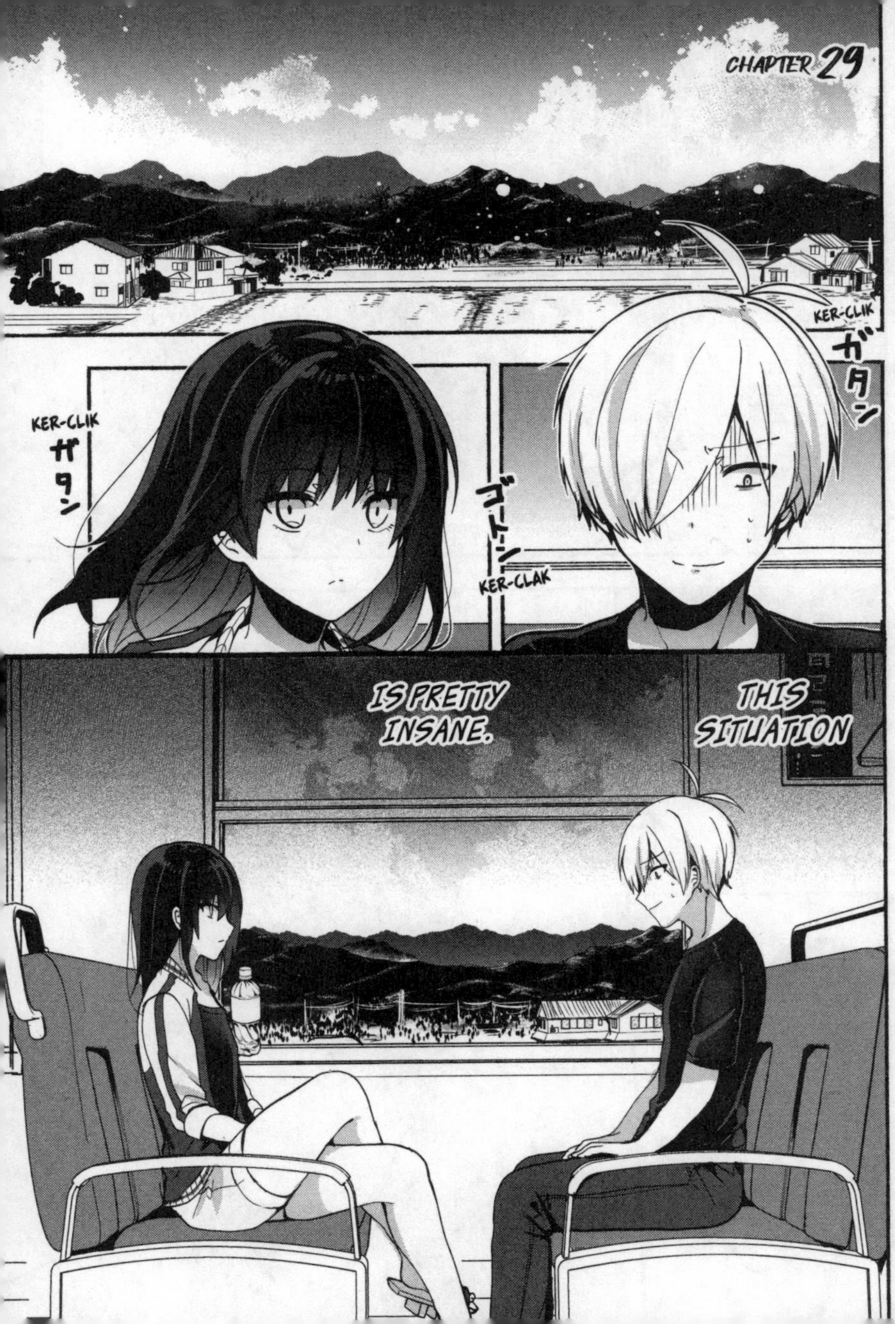
CHAPTER 29
KER-CLIK
ガタン
ゴトン
KER-CLAK
KER-CLIK
ガタン
THIS SITUATION
IS PRETTY INSANE.

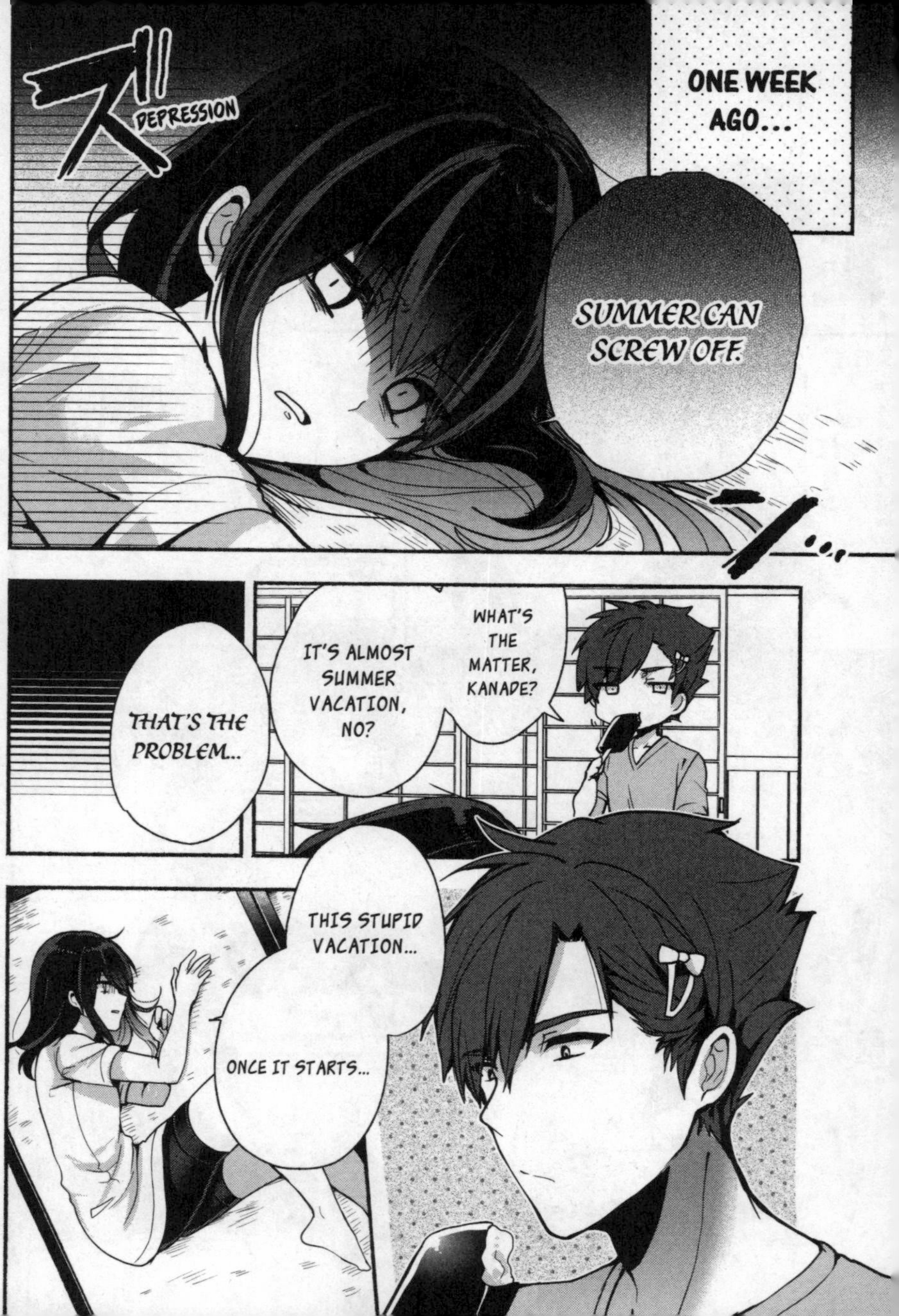
ONE WEEK AGO...
DEPRESSION
SUMMER CAN SCREW OFF.
...
WHAT'S THE MATTER, KANADE?
IT'S ALMOST SUMMER VACATION, NO?
THAT'S THE PROBLEM...
THIS STUPID VACATION...
ONCE IT STARTS...

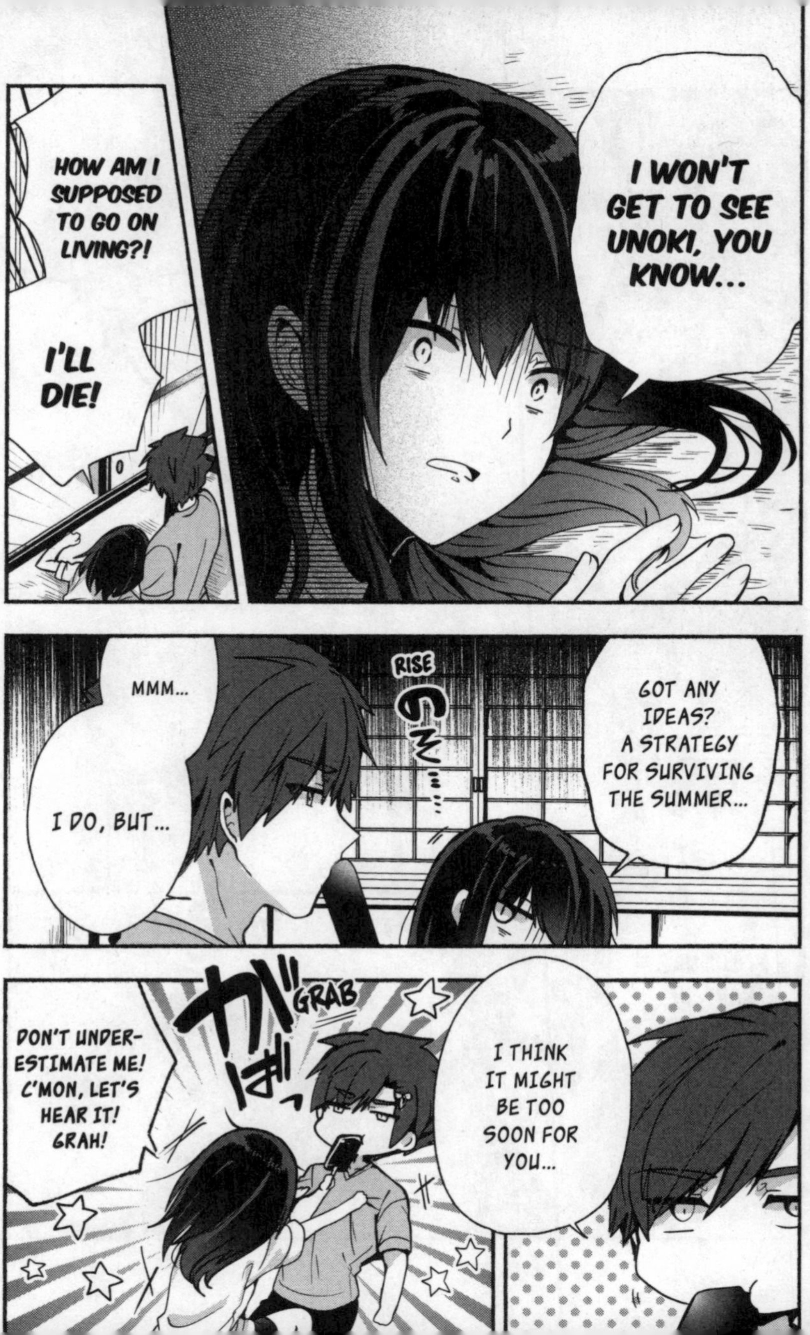
I WON'T GET TO SEE UNOKI, YOU KNOW...
HOW AM I SUPPOSED TO GO ON LIVING?!
I'LL DIE!
GOT ANY IDEAS? A STRATEGY FOR SURVIVING THE SUMMER...
RISE
MMM...
I DO, BUT...
I THINK IT MIGHT BE TOO SOON FOR YOU...
GRAB
DON'T UNDER-ESTIMATE ME! C'MON, LET'S HEAR IT! GRAH!

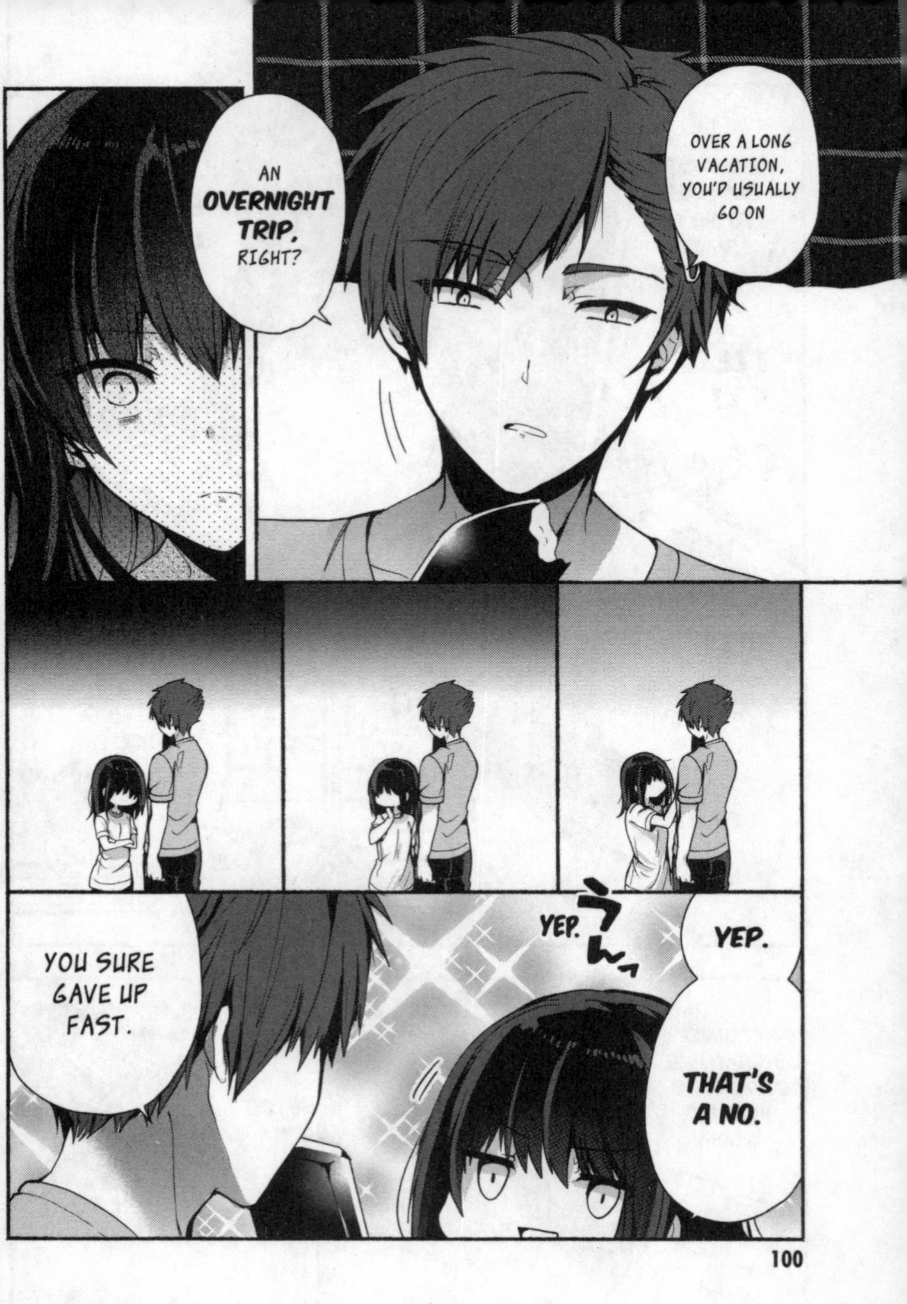
OVER A LONG VACATION, YOU'D USUALLY GO ON
AN **OVERNIGHT TRIP,** RIGHT?
YEP.
THAT'S A NO.
うん、
YEP.
YOU SURE GAVE UP FAST.

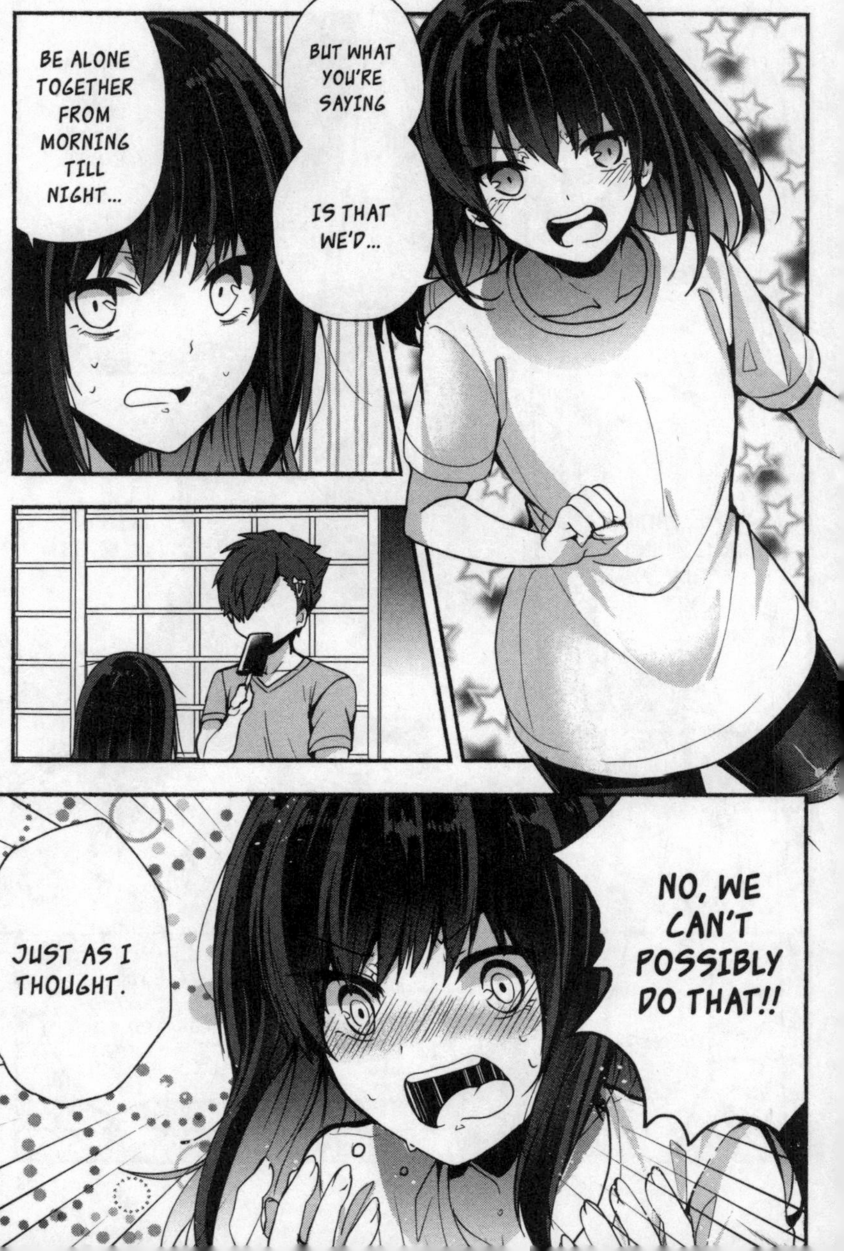
BUT WHAT YOU'RE SAYING
IS THAT WE'D...
BE ALONE TOGETHER FROM MORNING TILL NIGHT...
NO, WE CAN'T POSSIBLY DO THAT!!
JUST AS I THOUGHT.

NOT THAT I THINK ANYTHING WOULD HAPPEN.
IT COULD JUST BE A TRIP...
B-BUT
EVEN IF I INVITED HIM
DO YOU THINK UNOKI WOULD ACTUALLY COME?!
UH...
YOU'LL HAVE TO ASK HIM YOURSELF...
DAMMIT!
I KNOW...

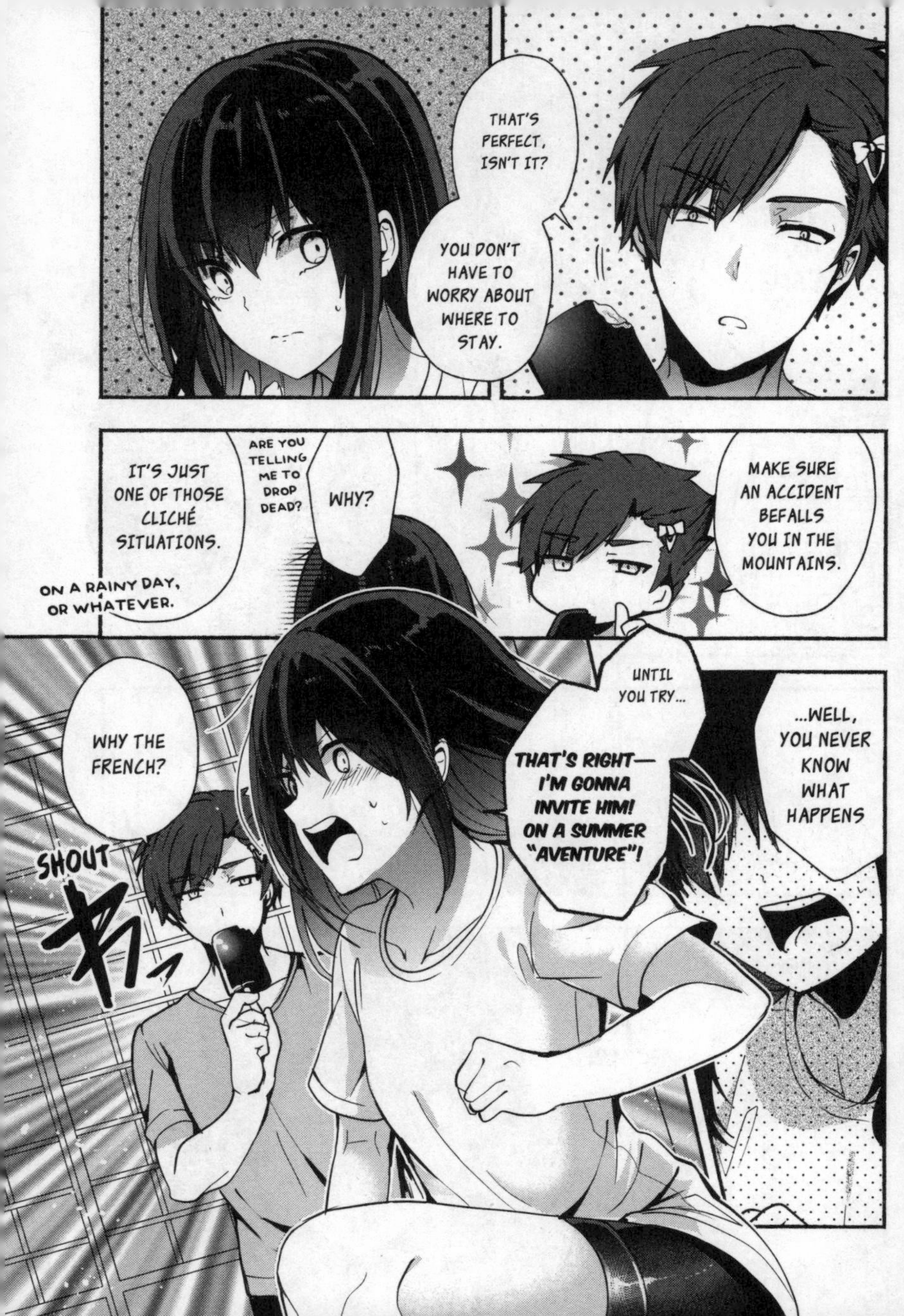
THAT'S PERFECT, ISN'T IT?
YOU DON'T HAVE TO WORRY ABOUT WHERE TO STAY.
MAKE SURE AN ACCIDENT BEFALLS YOU IN THE MOUNTAINS.
WHY?
ARE YOU TELLING ME TO DROP DEAD?
IT'S JUST ONE OF THOSE CLICHÉ SITUATIONS.
ON A RAINY DAY, OR WHATEVER.
...WELL, YOU NEVER KNOW WHAT HAPPENS
UNTIL YOU TRY...
THAT'S RIGHT— I'M GONNA INVITE HIM! ON A SUMMER "AVENTURE"!
SHOUT
WHY THE FRENCH?

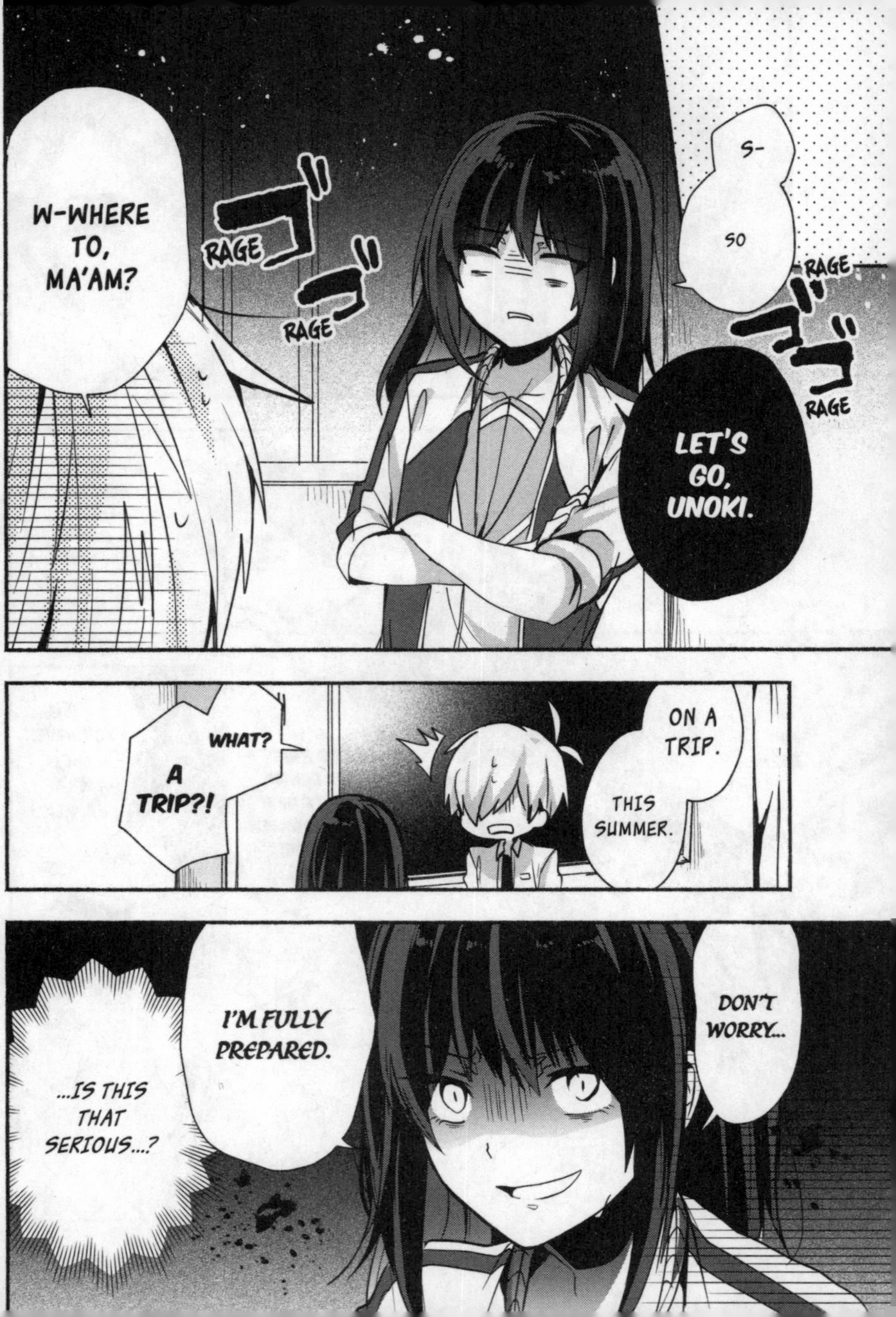
S- SO
RAGE ゴゴ RAGE
LET'S GO, UNOKI.
RAGE ゴゴ RAGE
W-WHERE TO, MA'AM?
ON A TRIP. THIS SUMMER.
WHAT? A TRIP?!
DON'T WORRY...
I'M FULLY PREPARED.
...IS THIS THAT SERIOUS...?

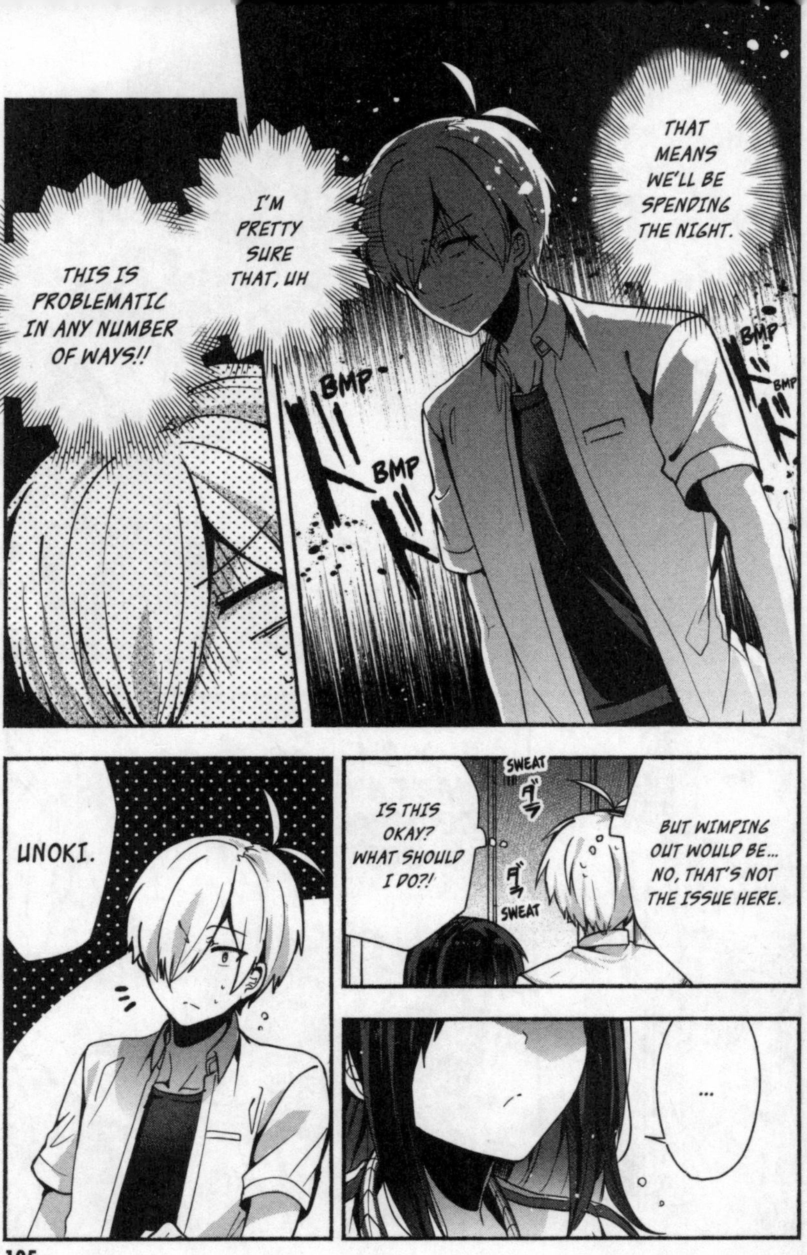
THAT MEANS WE'LL BE SPENDING THE NIGHT.
I'M PRETTY SURE THAT, UH
THIS IS PROBLEMATIC IN ANY NUMBER OF WAYS!!
BMP
BMP
BMP
BMP
BUT WIMPING OUT WOULD BE... NO, THAT'S NOT THE ISSUE HERE.
SWEAT
SWEAT
IS THIS OKAY? WHAT SHOULD I DO?!
...
UNOKI.

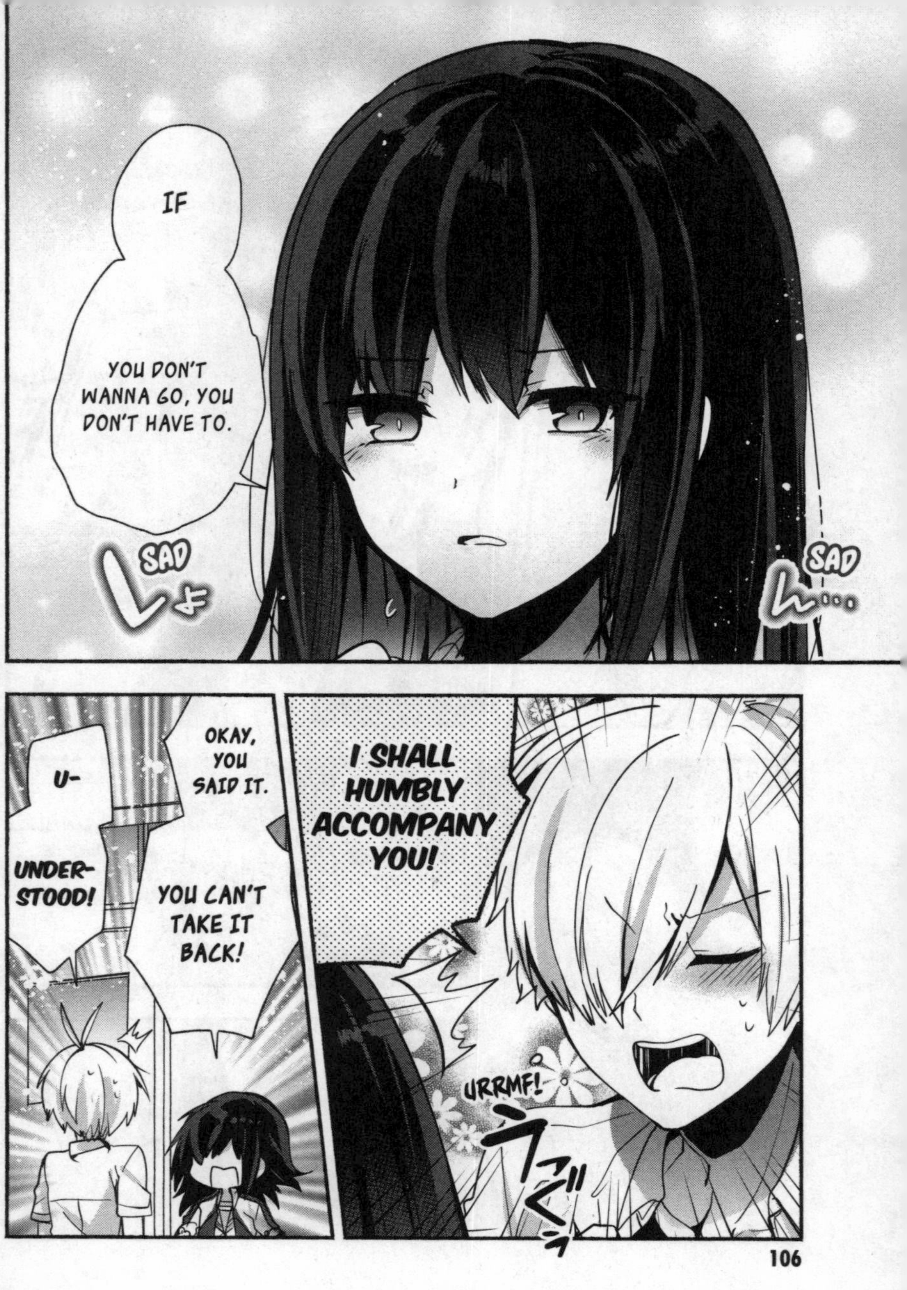
IF
YOU DON'T WANNA GO, YOU DON'T HAVE TO.
SAD ん...
SAD しょ
I SHALL HUMBLY ACCOMPANY YOU!
URRMF!
うぐぐ
OKAY, YOU SAID IT.
YOU CAN'T TAKE IT BACK!
U-
UNDER-STOOD!

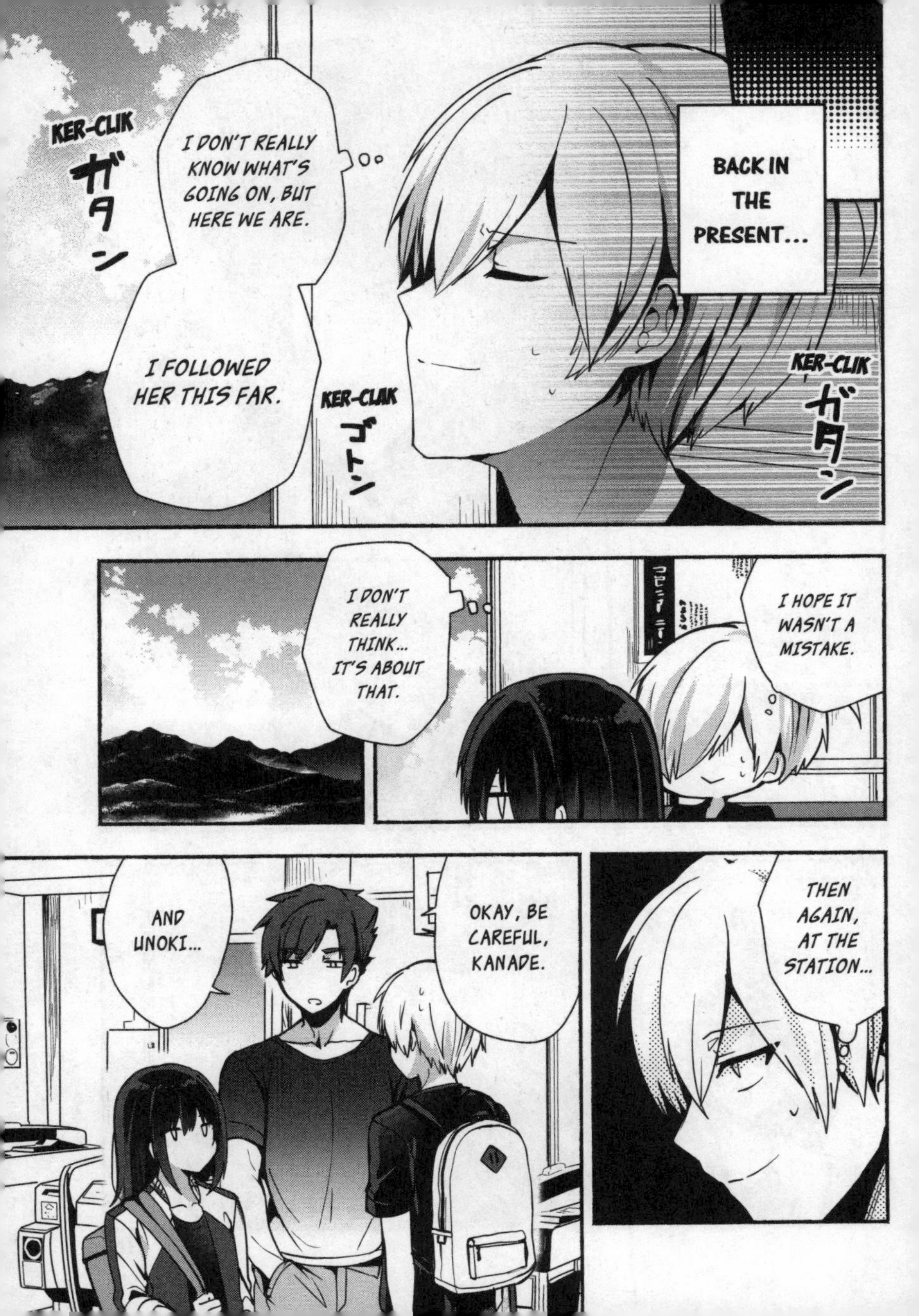
BACK IN THE PRESENT...
KER-CLIK
ガタン
I DON'T REALLY KNOW WHAT'S GOING ON, BUT HERE WE ARE.
I FOLLOWED HER THIS FAR.
KER-CLAK
ゴトン
KER-CLIK
ガタン
I HOPE IT WASN'T A MISTAKE.
I DON'T REALLY THINK... IT'S ABOUT THAT.
THEN AGAIN, AT THE STATION...
OKAY, BE CAREFUL, KANADE.
AND UNOKI...

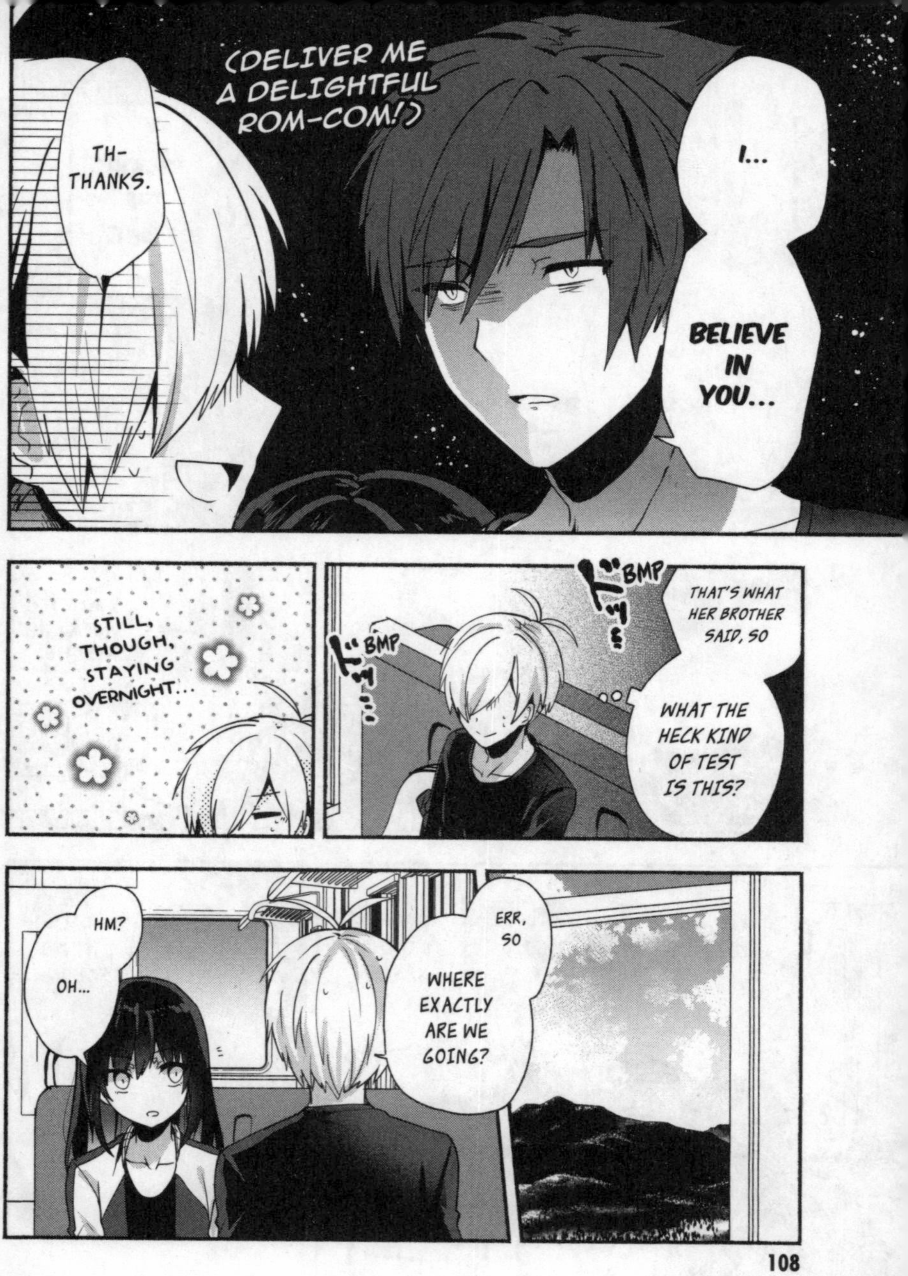
I...
BELIEVE IN YOU...
(DELIVER ME A DELIGHTFUL ROM-COM!)
TH- THANKS.
BMP
BMP
THAT'S WHAT HER BROTHER SAID, SO
WHAT THE HECK KIND OF TEST IS THIS?
STILL, THOUGH, STAYING OVERNIGHT...
ERR, SO
WHERE EXACTLY ARE WE GOING?
HM?
OH...

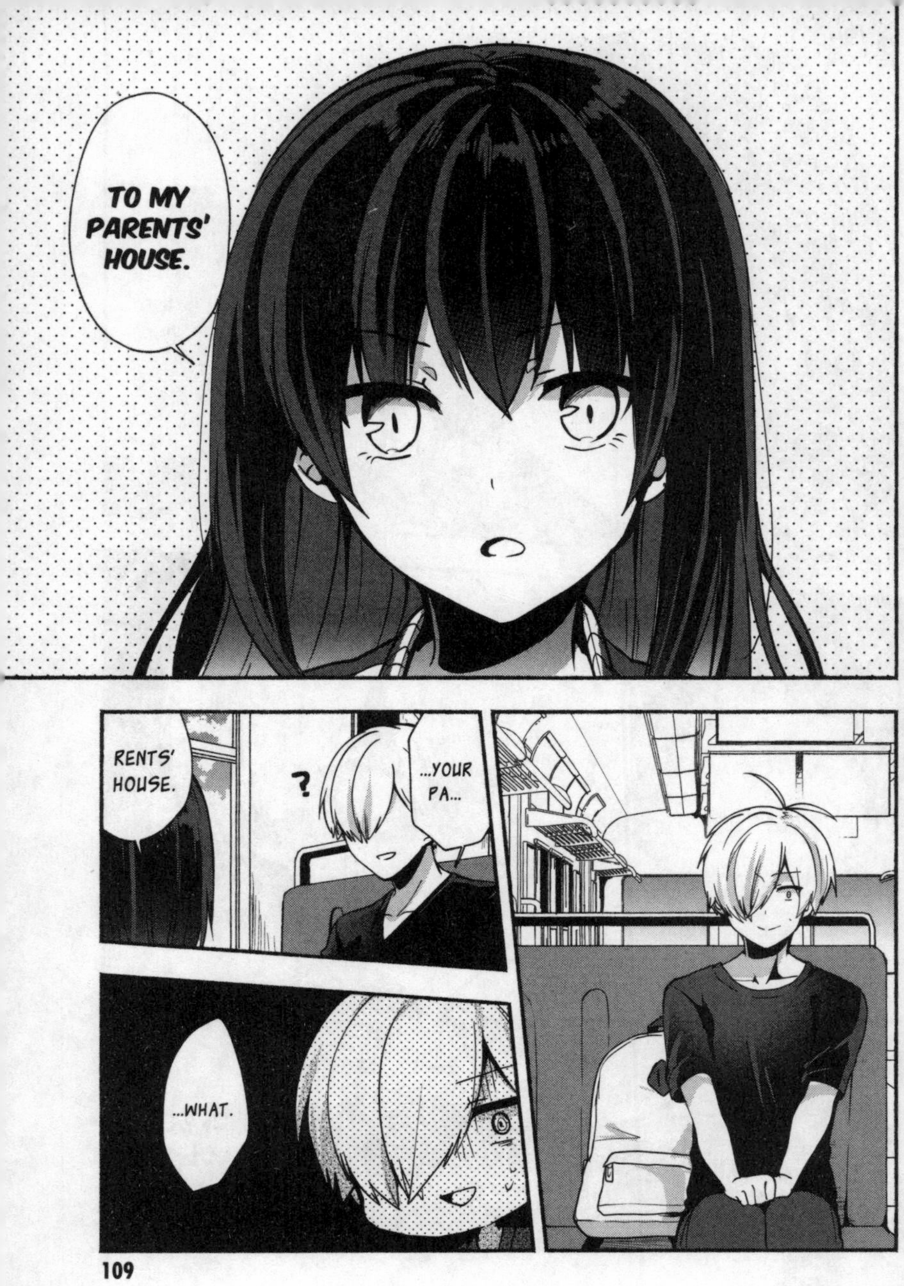
TO MY PARENTS' HOUSE.
...YOUR PA...
?
RENTS' HOUSE.
...WHAT.

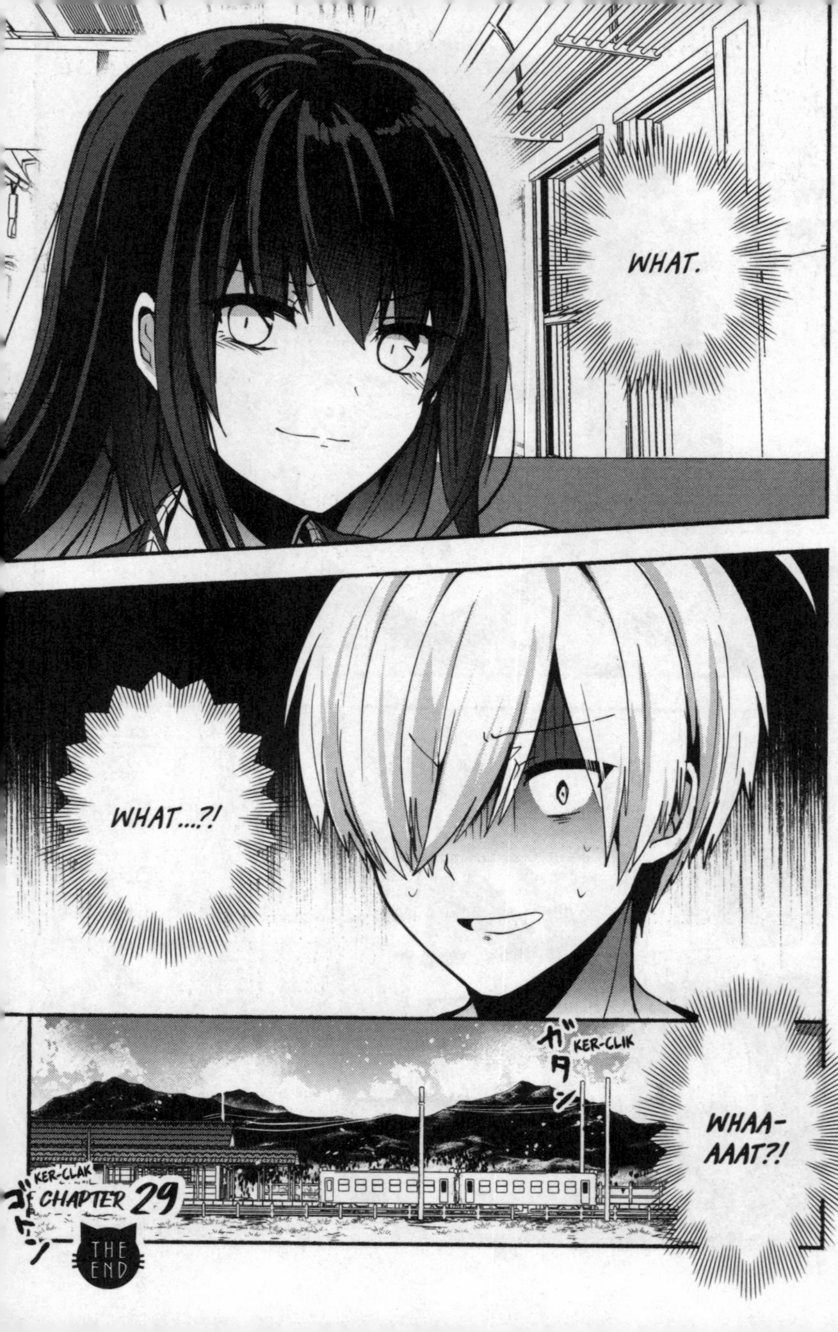
WHAT.
WHAT...?!
WHAA-
AAAT?!
ガタン
KER-CLIK
ゴトン
KER-CLAK
CHAPTER 29
THE END

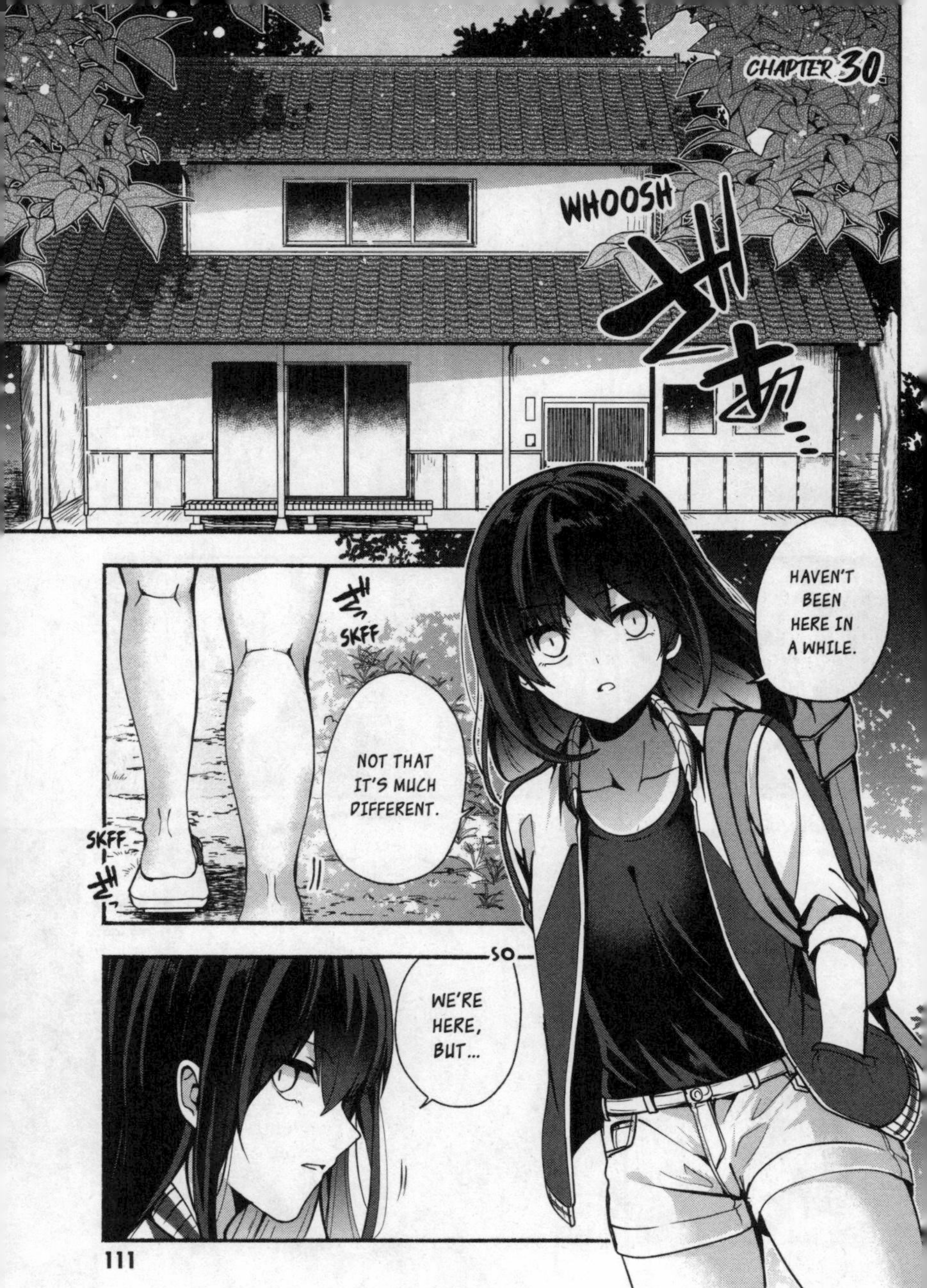
CHAPTER 30
WHOOSH
HAVEN'T BEEN HERE IN A WHILE.
SKFF
SKFF
NOT THAT IT'S MUCH DIFFERENT.
SO
WE'RE HERE, BUT...

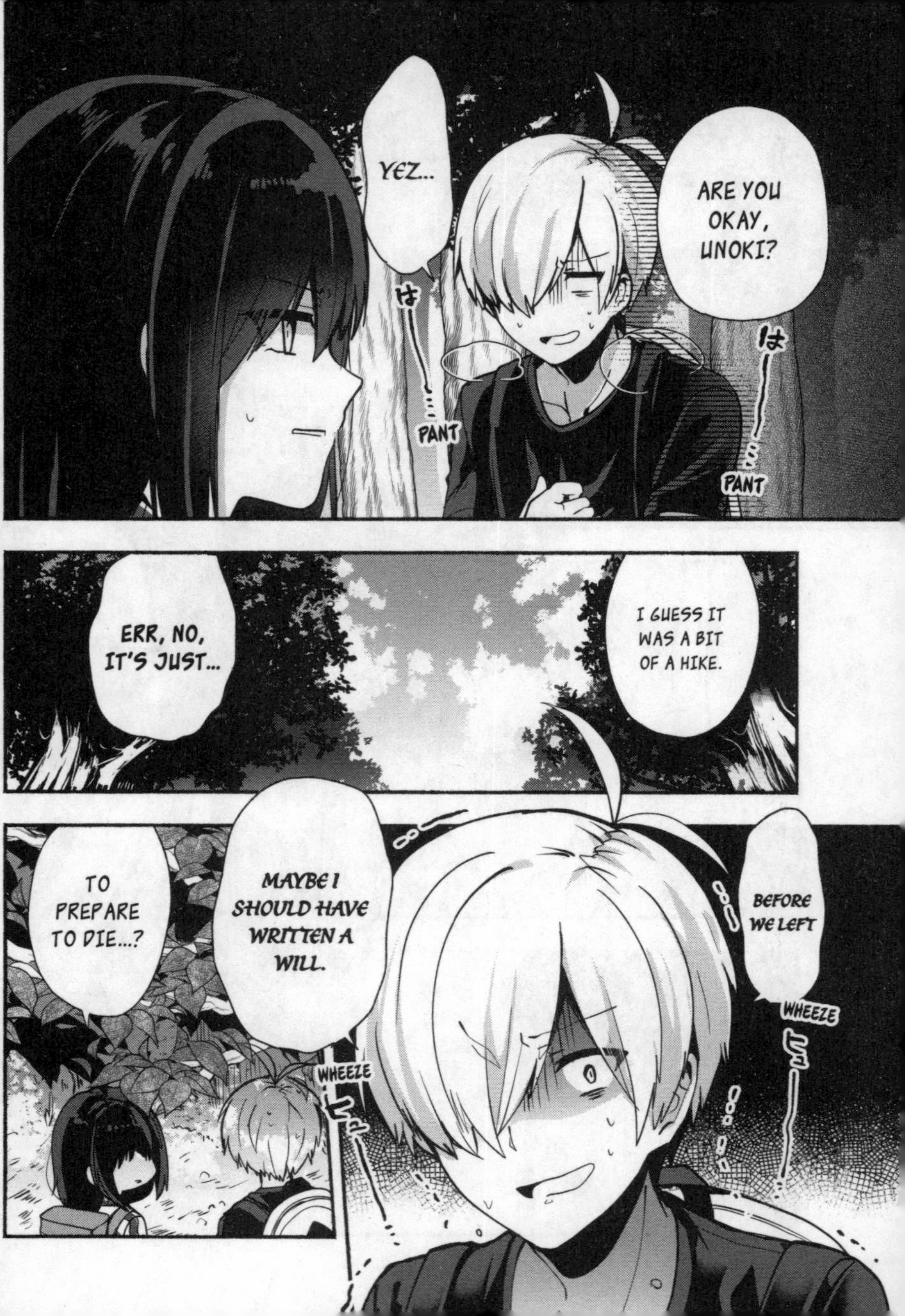
ARE YOU OKAY, UNOKI?
は
PANT
YEZ...
は
PANT
I GUESS IT WAS A BIT OF A HIKE.
ERR, NO, IT'S JUST...
BEFORE WE LEFT
WHEEZE
MAYBE I SHOULD HAVE WRITTEN A WILL.
WHEEZE
TO PREPARE TO DIE...?

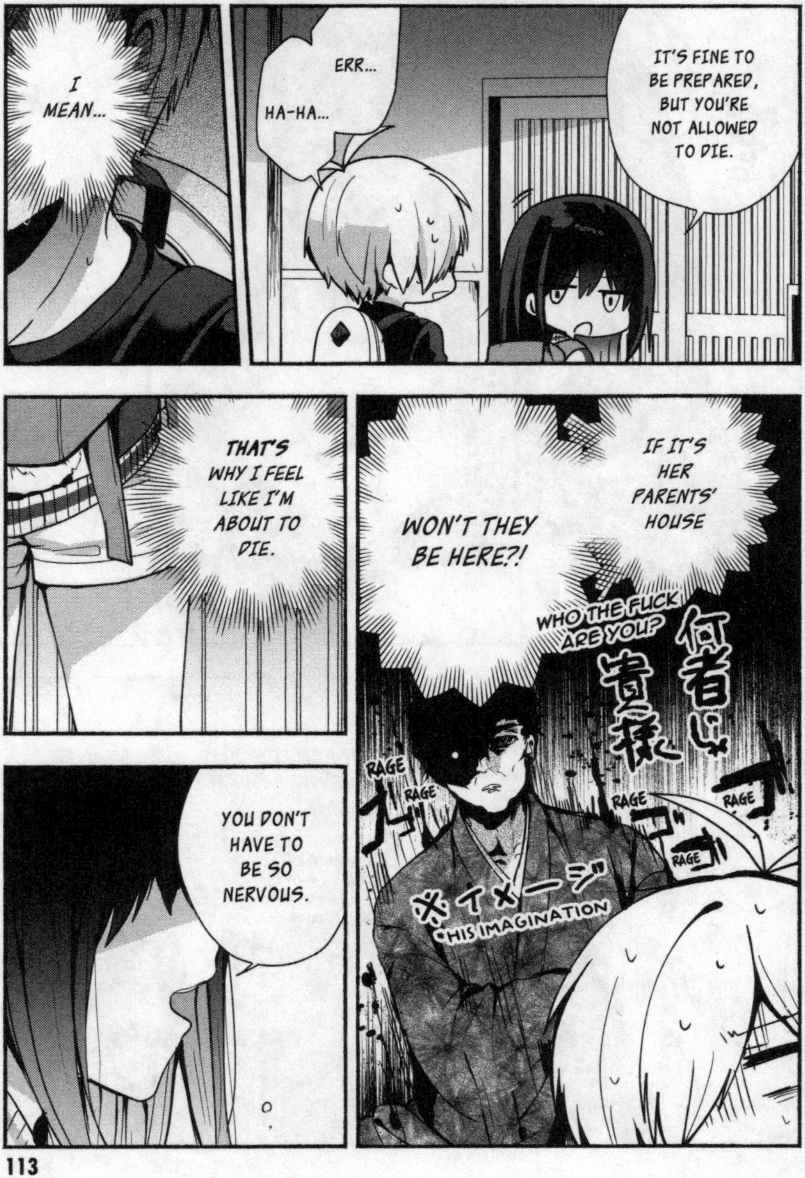
IT'S FINE TO BE PREPARED, BUT YOU'RE NOT ALLOWED TO DIE.
ERR...
HA-HA...
I MEAN...
IF IT'S HER PARENTS' HOUSE
WON'T THEY BE HERE?!
WHO THE FUCK ARE YOU?
何者じゃ貴様
RAGE
RAGE
RAGE
RAGE
RAGE
※イメージ
*HIS IMAGINATION
THAT'S WHY I FEEL LIKE I'M ABOUT TO DIE.
YOU DON'T HAVE TO BE SO NERVOUS.

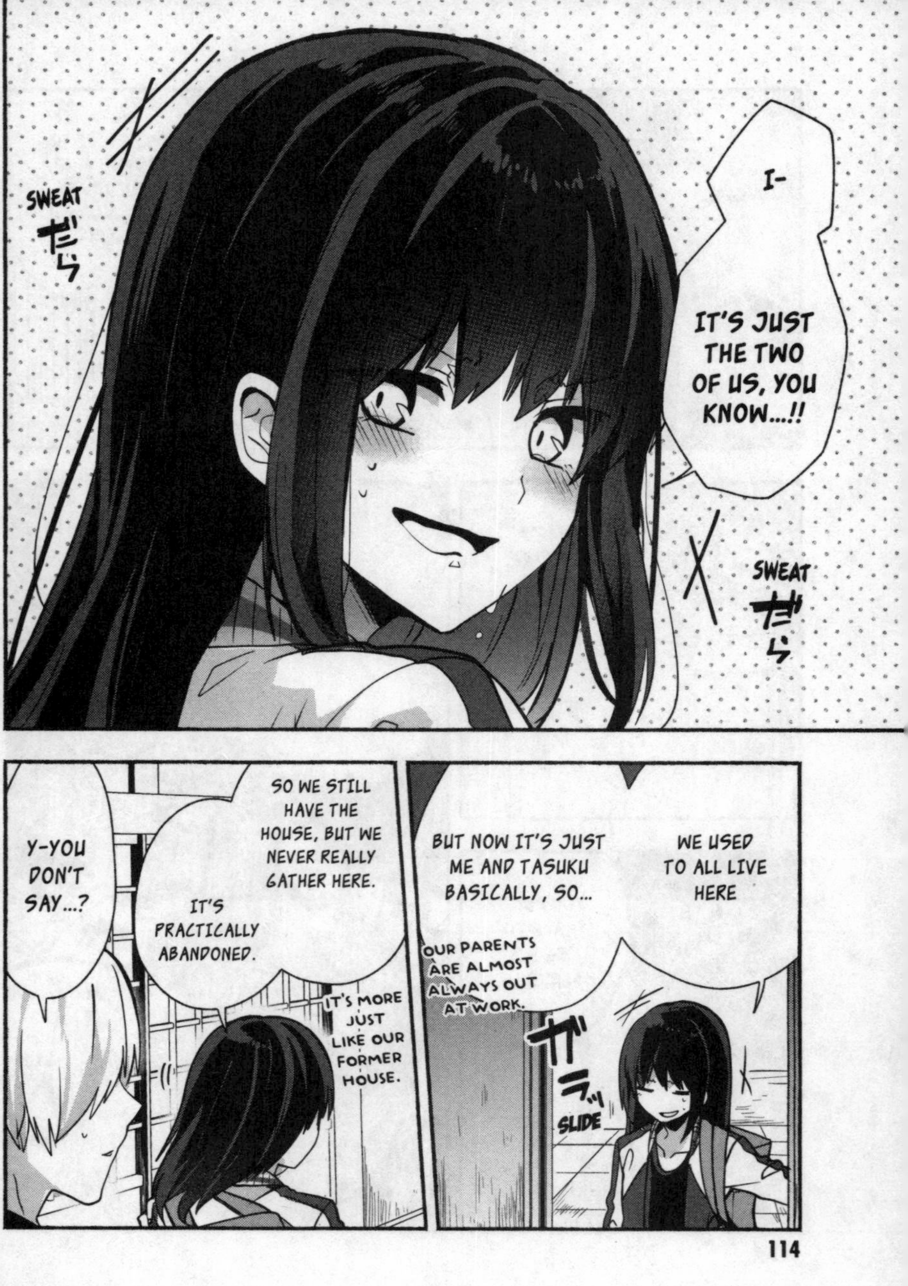
I-
IT'S JUST THE TWO OF US, YOU KNOW...!!
SWEAT
だら
SWEAT
だら
WE USED TO ALL LIVE HERE
BUT NOW IT'S JUST ME AND TASUKU BASICALLY, SO...
OUR PARENTS ARE ALMOST ALWAYS OUT AT WORK.
ガラッ
SLIDE
SO WE STILL HAVE THE HOUSE, BUT WE NEVER REALLY GATHER HERE.
IT'S PRACTICALLY ABANDONED.
IT'S MORE JUST LIKE OUR FORMER HOUSE.
Y-YOU DON'T SAY...?

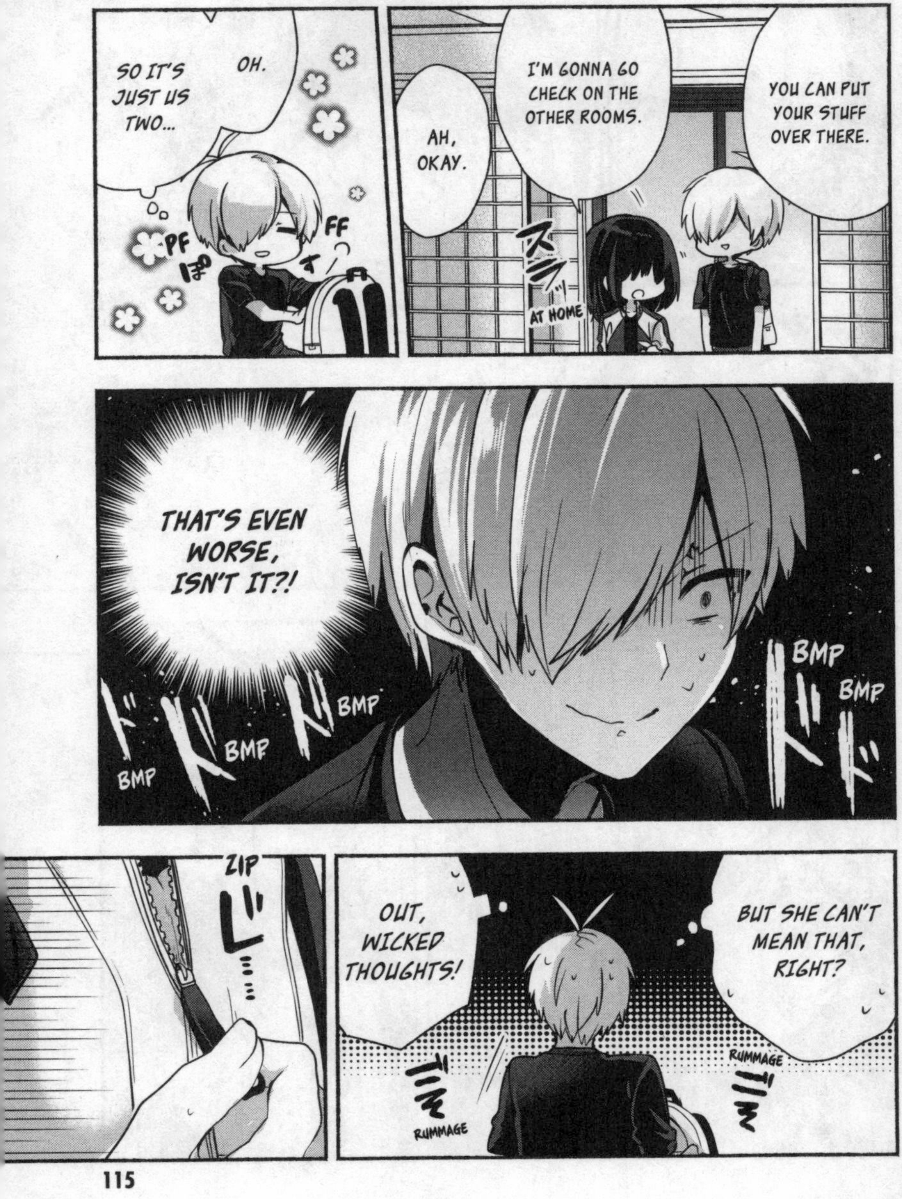
YOU CAN PUT YOUR STUFF OVER THERE.
I'M GONNA GO CHECK ON THE OTHER ROOMS.
AH, OKAY.
AT HOME
OH.
SO IT'S JUST US TWO...
FF
PF
THAT'S EVEN WORSE, ISN'T IT?!
BMP
BMP
BMP
BMP
BMP
BUT SHE CAN'T MEAN THAT, RIGHT?
OUT, WICKED THOUGHTS!
RUMMAGE
RUMMAGE
ZIP

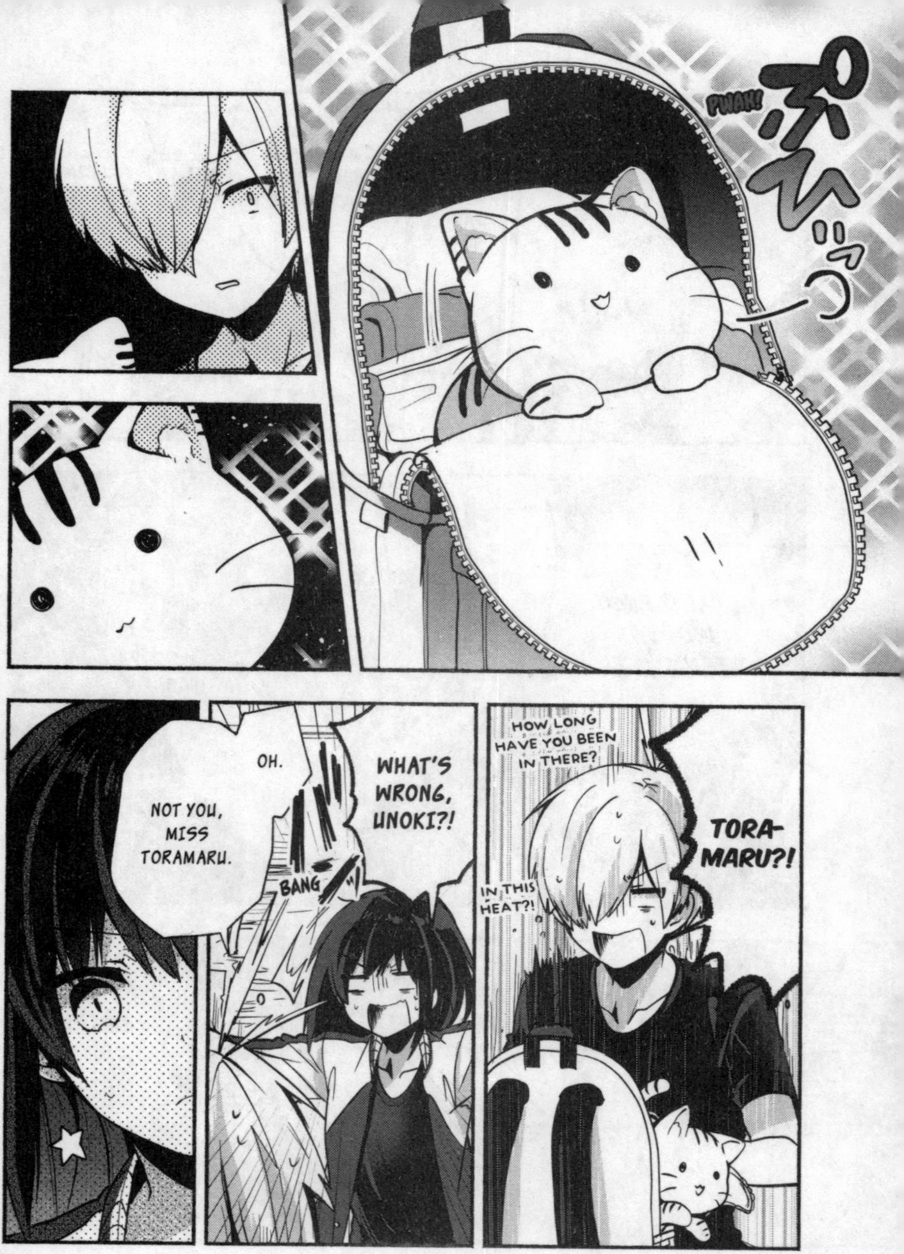
PWAH!
TORA-MARU?!
HOW LONG HAVE YOU BEEN IN THERE?
IN THIS HEAT?!
WHAT'S WRONG, UNOKI?!
OH.
BANG
NOT YOU, MISS TORAMARU.

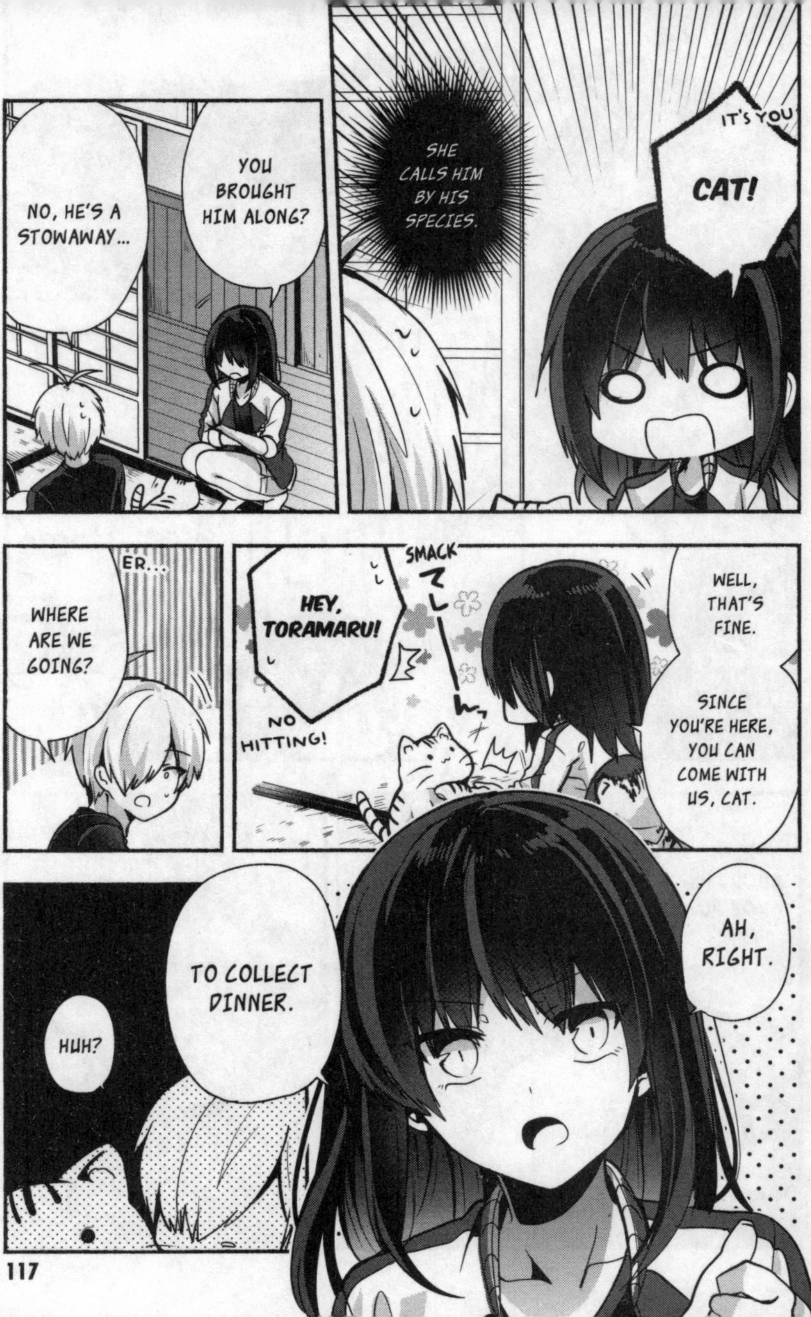
IT'S YOU
CAT!
SHE CALLS HIM BY HIS SPECIES.
YOU BROUGHT HIM ALONG?
NO, HE'S A STOWAWAY...
WELL, THAT'S FINE.
SINCE YOU'RE HERE, YOU CAN COME WITH US, CAT.
SMACK
HEY, TORAMARU!
NO HITTING!
ER...
WHERE ARE WE GOING?
AH, RIGHT.
TO COLLECT DINNER.
HUH?

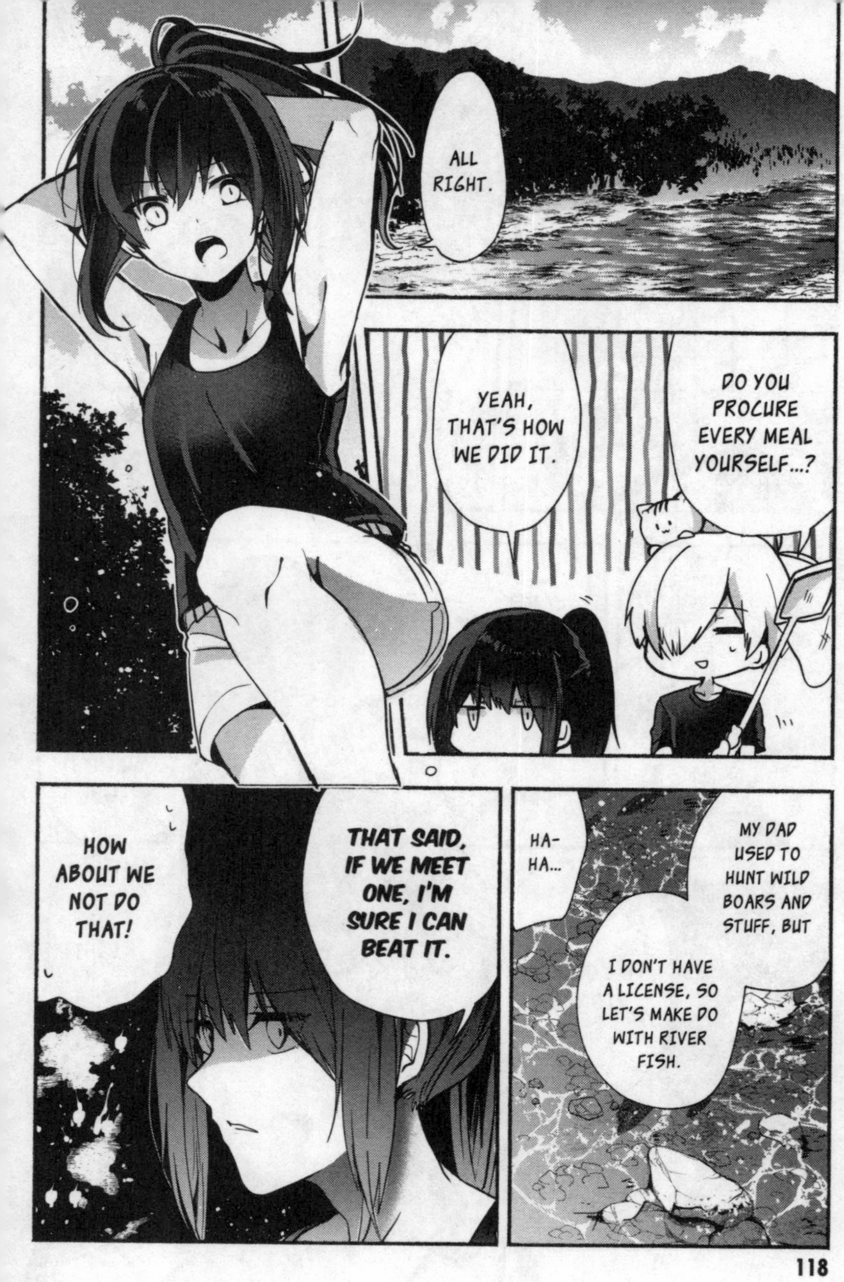
ALL RIGHT.
DO YOU PROCURE EVERY MEAL YOURSELF...?
YEAH, THAT'S HOW WE DID IT.
MY DAD USED TO HUNT WILD BOARS AND STUFF, BUT
I DON'T HAVE A LICENSE, SO LET'S MAKE DO WITH RIVER FISH.
HA-HA...
THAT SAID, IF WE MEET ONE, I'M SURE I CAN BEAT IT.
HOW ABOUT WE NOT DO THAT!

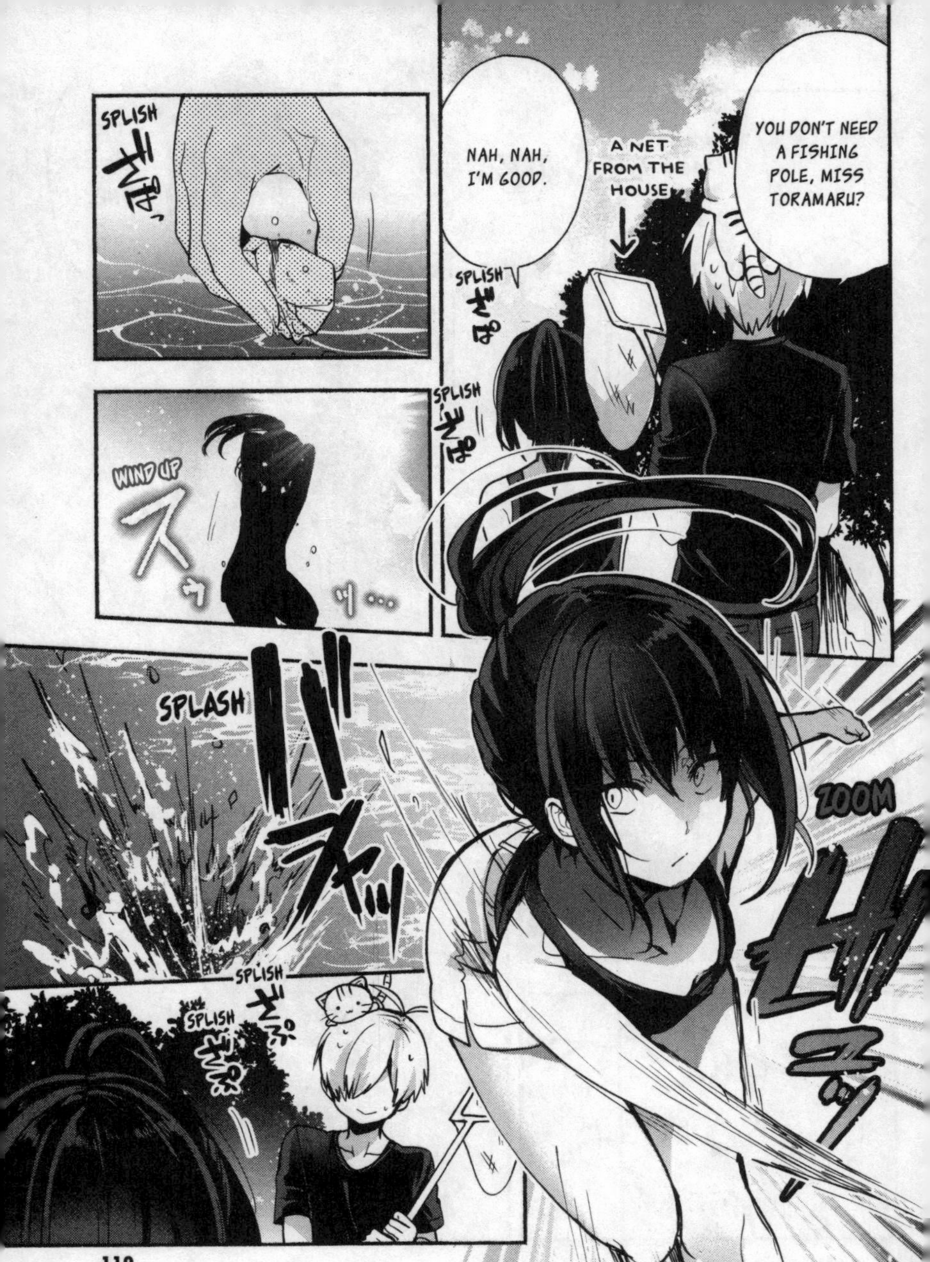
YOU DON'T NEED A FISHING POLE, MISS TORAMARU?
A NET FROM THE HOUSE
NAH, NAH, I'M GOOD.
SPLISH
SPLISH
SPLISH
WIND UP
ZOOM
SPLASH
SPLISH
SPLISH

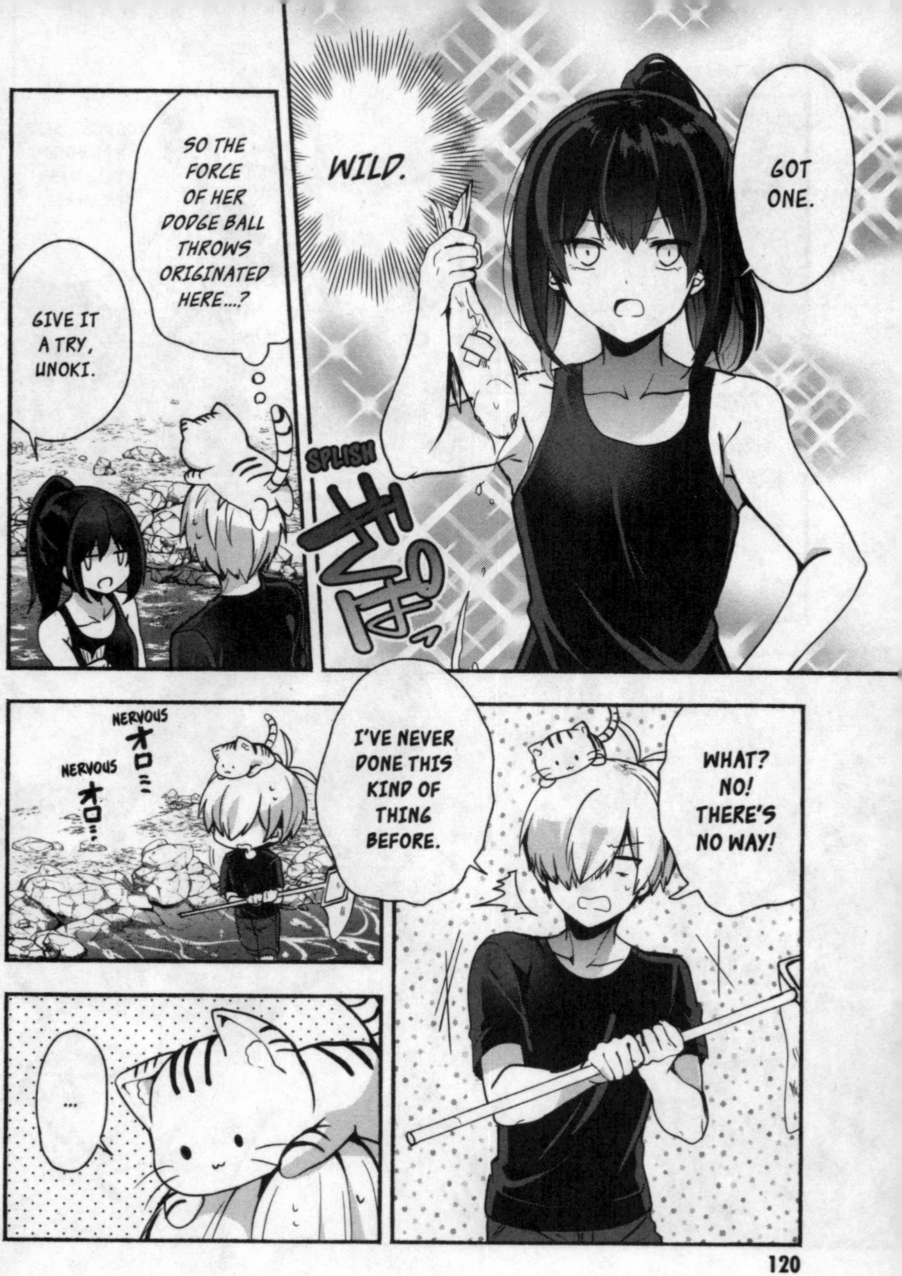
GOT ONE.
WILD.
SPLISH
SO THE FORCE OF HER DODGE BALL THROWS ORIGINATED HERE...?
GIVE IT A TRY, UNOKI.
WHAT? NO! THERE'S NO WAY!
I'VE NEVER DONE THIS KIND OF THING BEFORE.
NERVOUS
オロ
NERVOUS
オロ
...

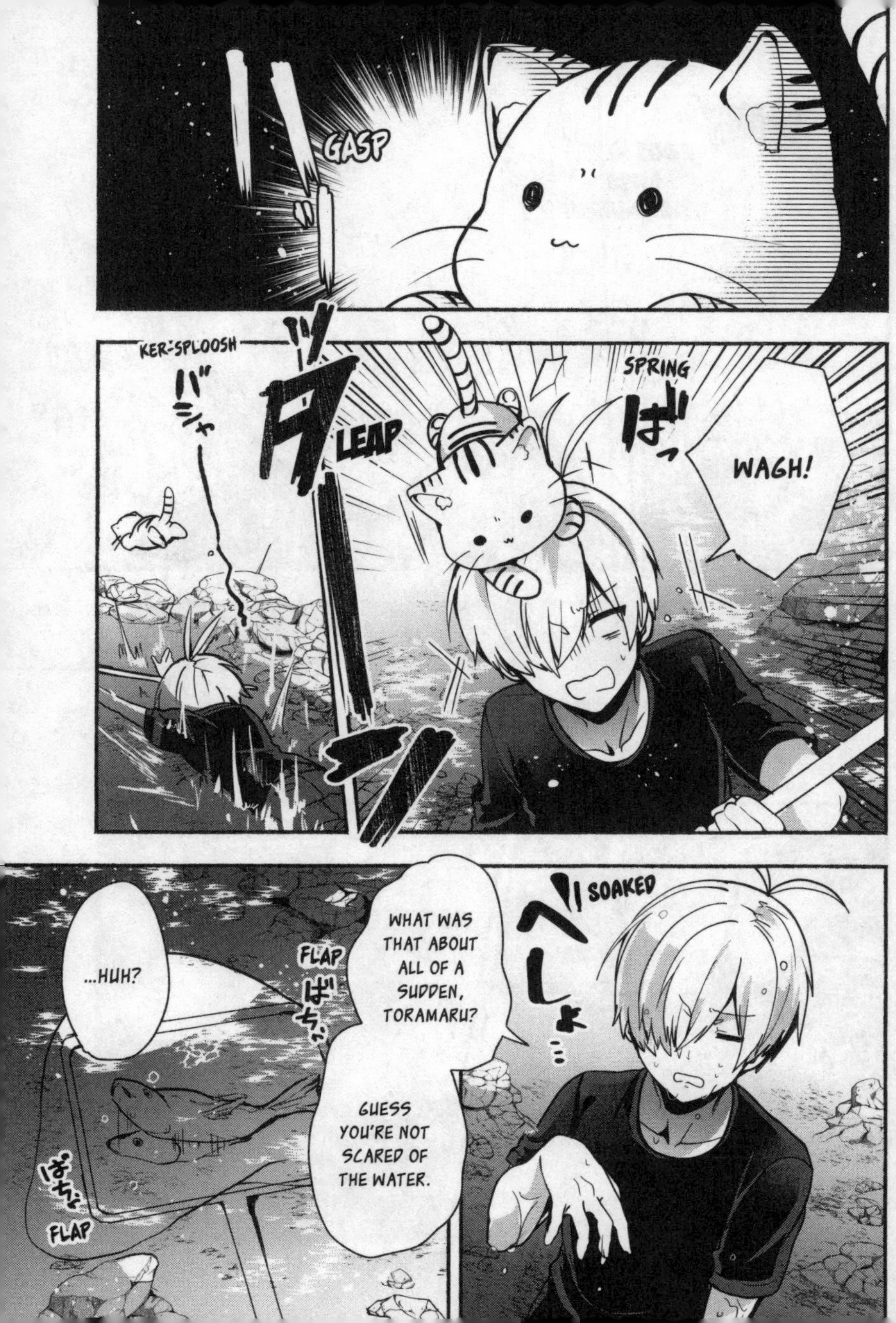
GASP
WAGH!
SPRING
ばっ
LEAP
KER-SPLOOSH
バシャ
SOAKED
WHAT WAS THAT ABOUT ALL OF A SUDDEN, TORAMARU?
GUESS YOU'RE NOT SCARED OF THE WATER.
FLAP
...HUH?
FLAP

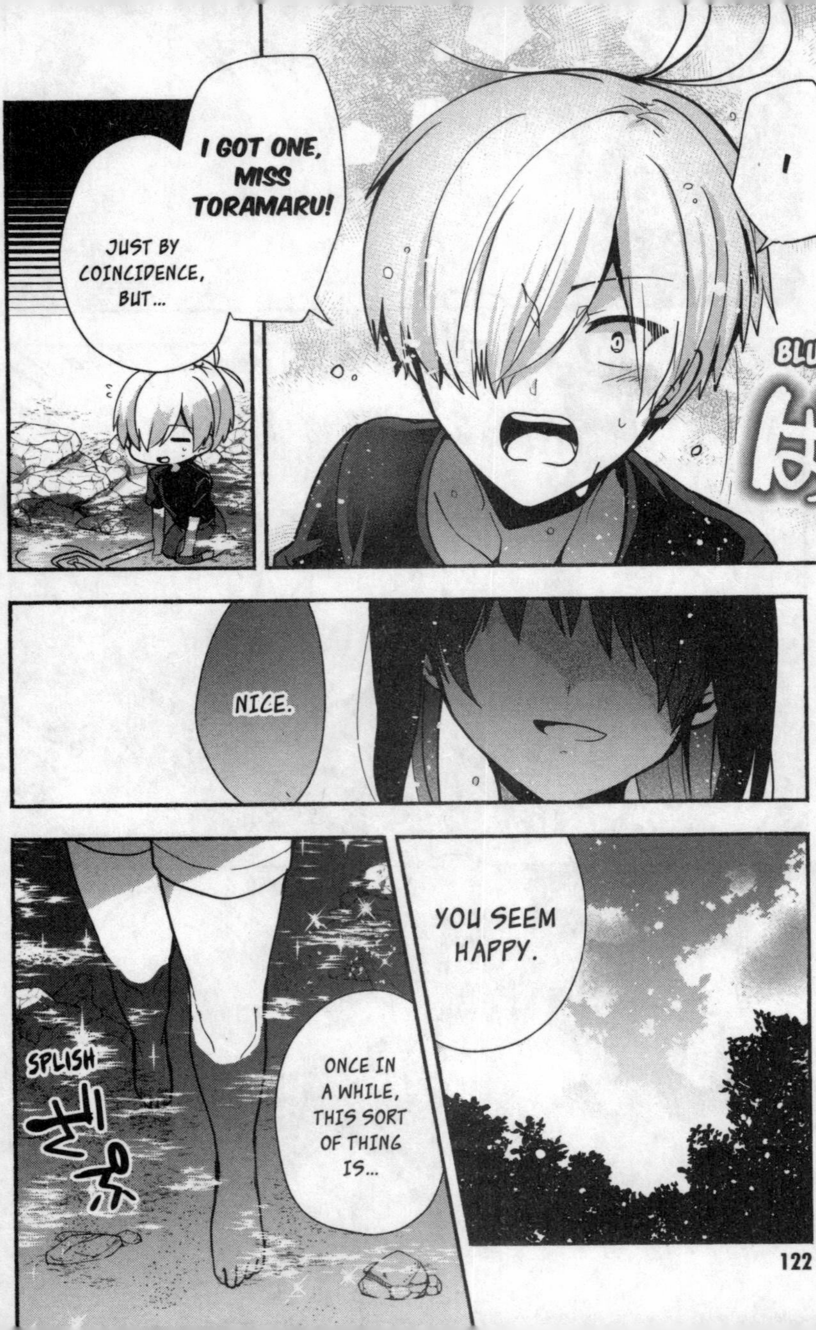
!
BLUSH
ぱっ
I GOT ONE, MISS TORAMARU!
JUST BY COINCIDENCE, BUT...
NICE.
YOU SEEM HAPPY.
ONCE IN A WHILE, THIS SORT OF THING IS...
SPLISH

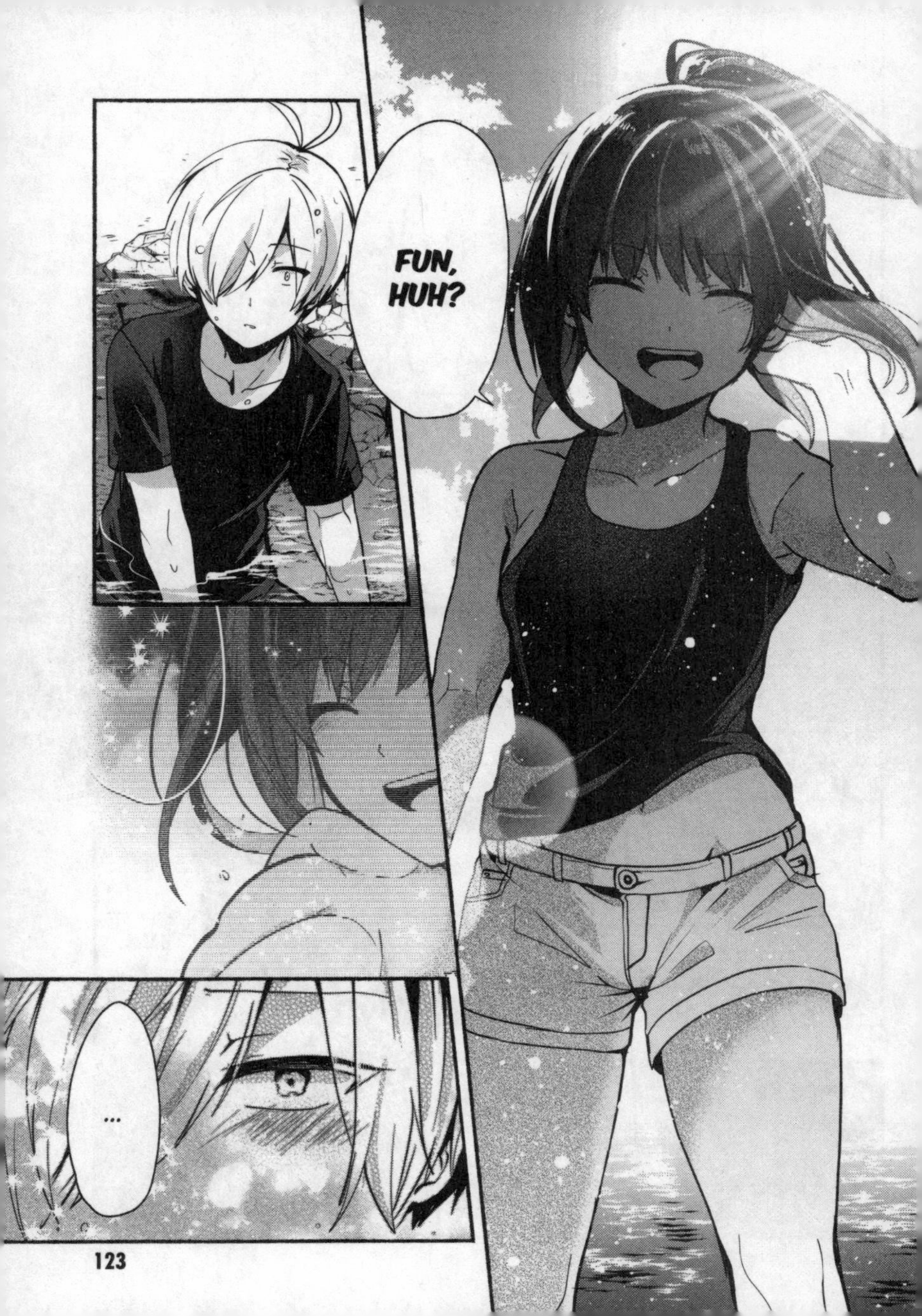
FUN, HUH?
...

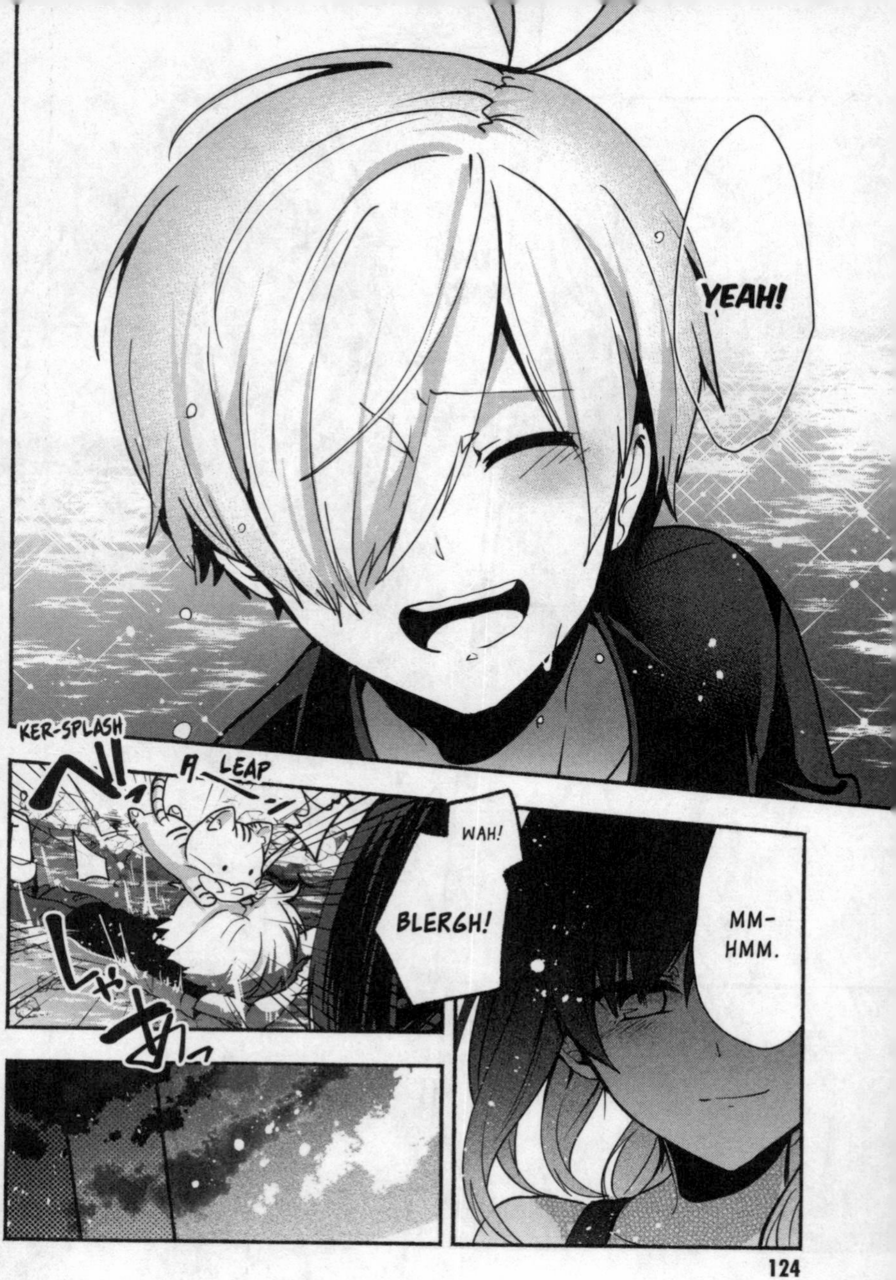
YEAH!
WAH!
BLERGH!
MM-HMM.
KER-SPLASH
LEAP

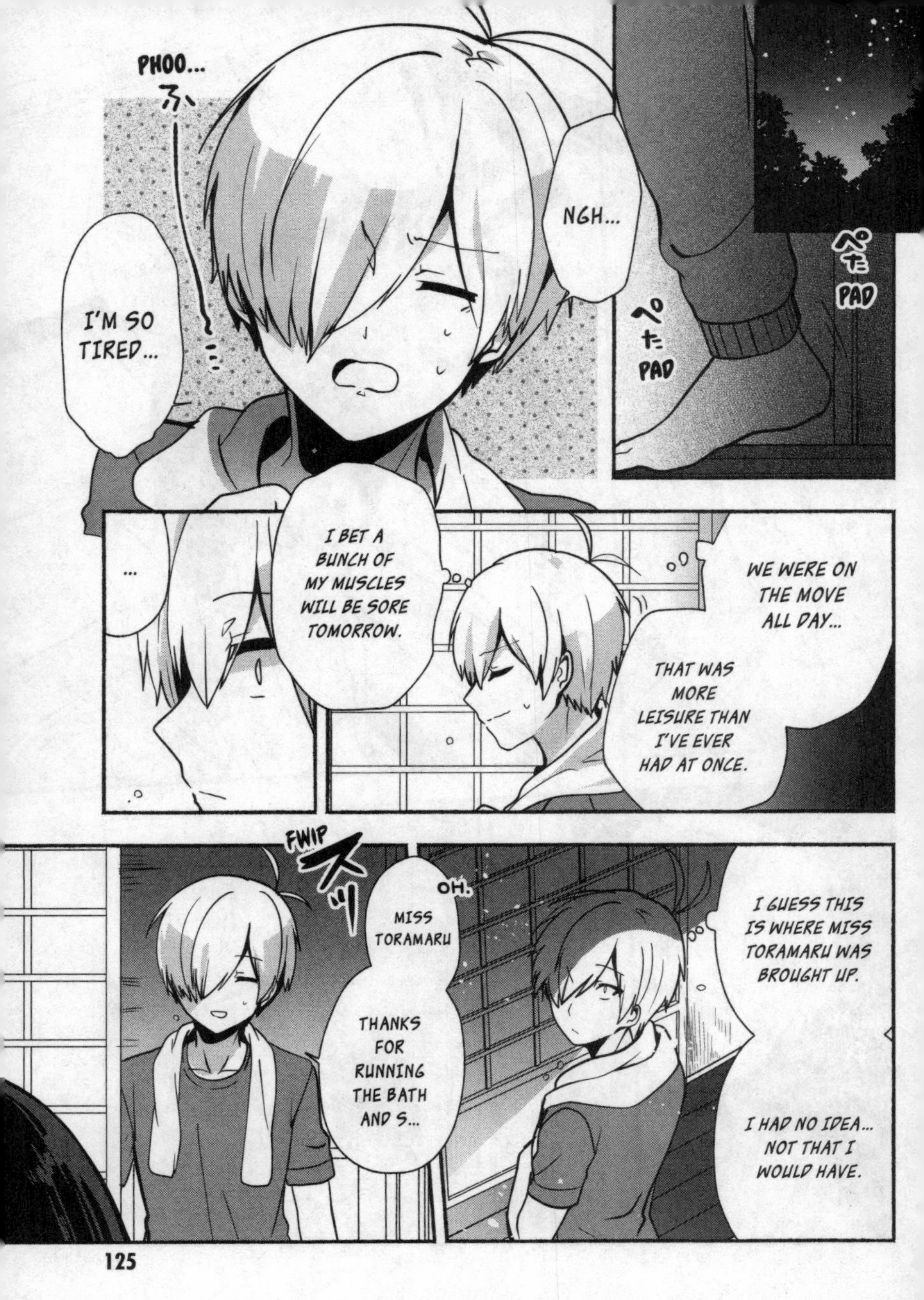
ぺた PAD
ぺた PAD
NGH...
PHOO... ふぅ
I'M SO TIRED...
WE WERE ON THE MOVE ALL DAY...
THAT WAS MORE LEISURE THAN I'VE EVER HAD AT ONCE.
I BET A BUNCH OF MY MUSCLES WILL BE SORE TOMORROW.
...
I GUESS THIS IS WHERE MISS TORAMARU WAS BROUGHT UP.
I HAD NO IDEA... NOT THAT I WOULD HAVE.
FWIP スッ
OH. MISS TORAMARU
THANKS FOR RUNNING THE BATH AND S...

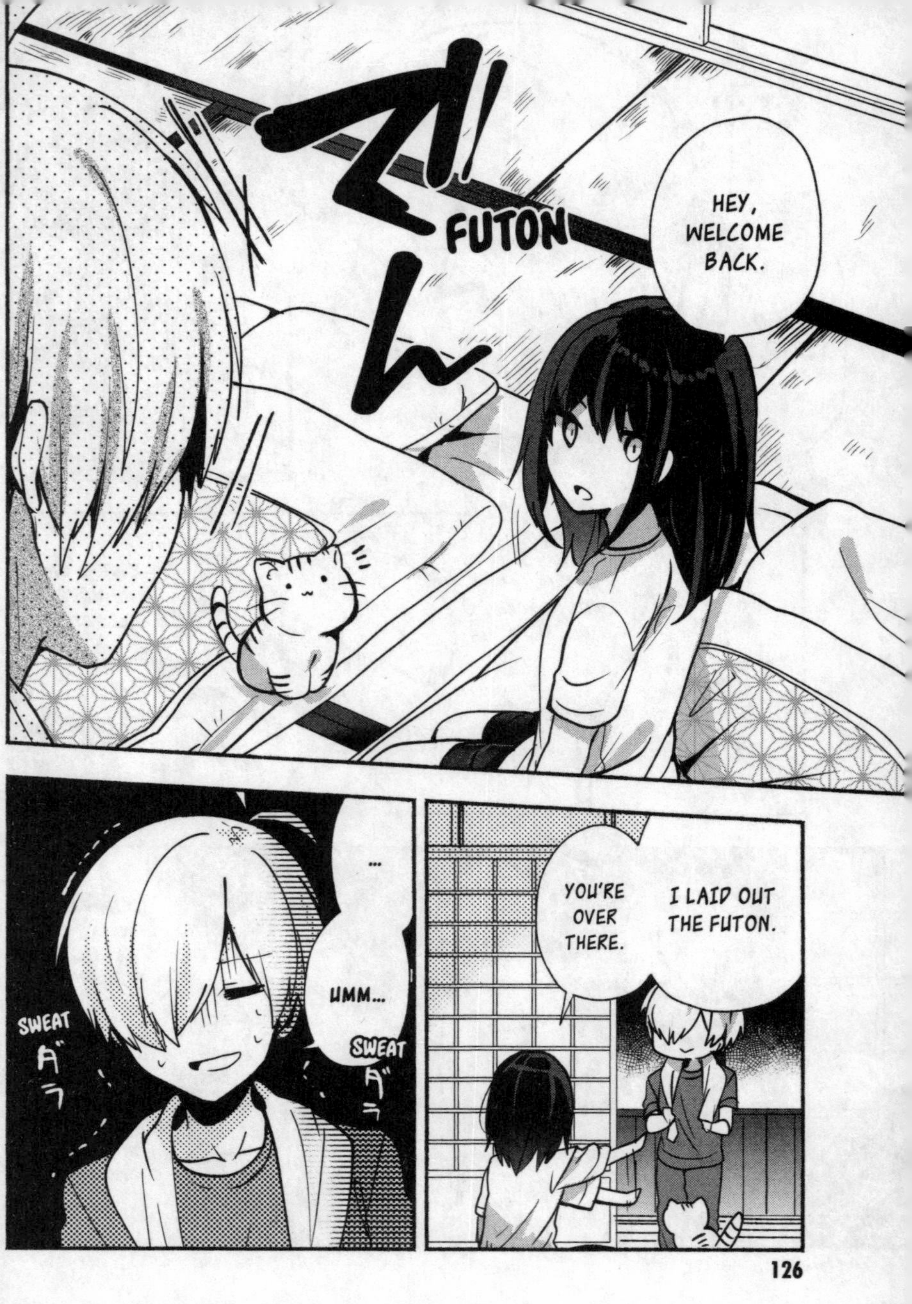
FUTON
HEY, WELCOME BACK.
I LAID OUT THE FUTON.
YOU'RE OVER THERE.
...
UMM...
SWEAT
SWEAT

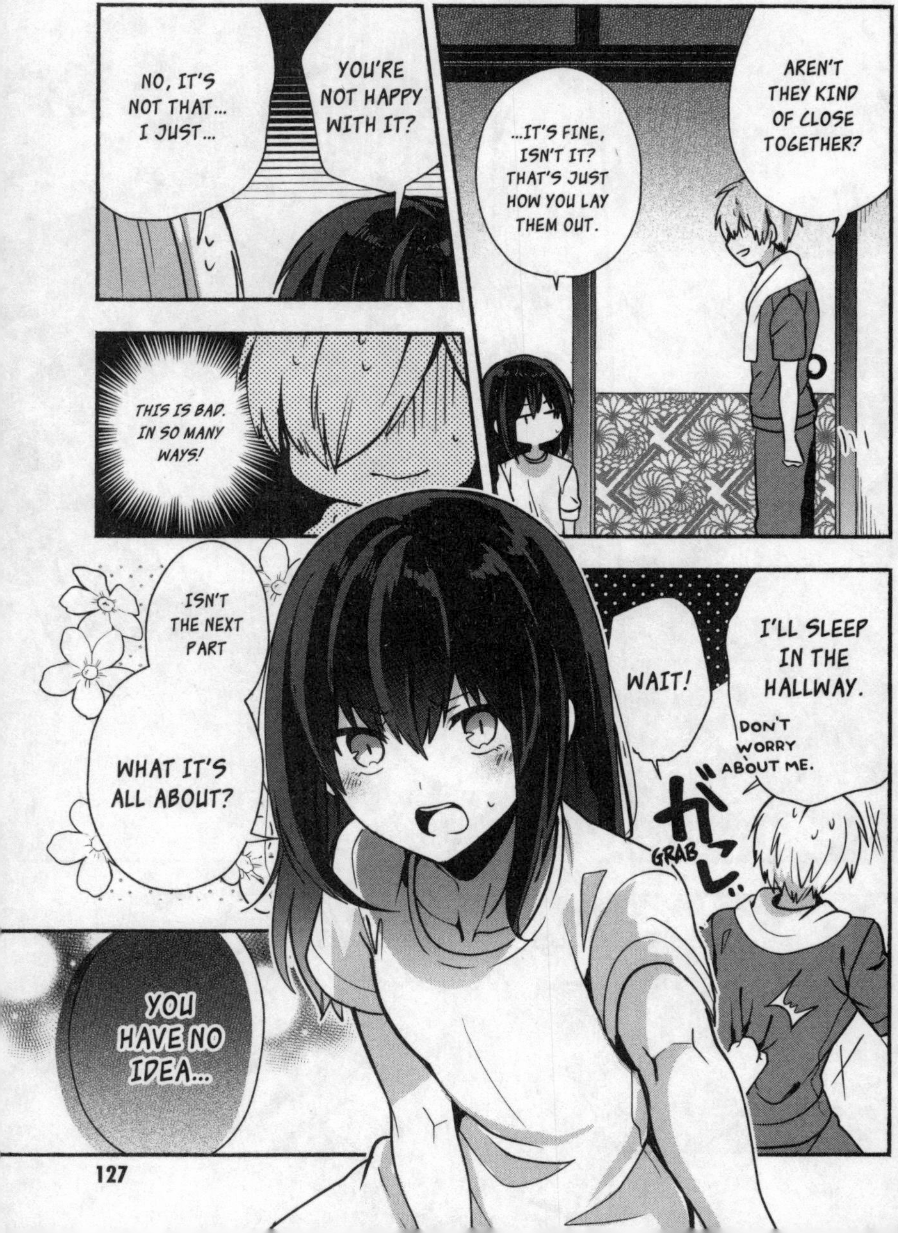
AREN'T THEY KIND OF CLOSE TOGETHER?
...IT'S FINE, ISN'T IT? THAT'S JUST HOW YOU LAY THEM OUT.
YOU'RE NOT HAPPY WITH IT?
NO, IT'S NOT THAT... I JUST...
THIS IS BAD. IN SO MANY WAYS!
I'LL SLEEP IN THE HALLWAY.
DON'T WORRY ABOUT ME.
WAIT!
GRAB
ISN'T THE NEXT PART
WHAT IT'S ALL ABOUT?
YOU HAVE NO IDEA...

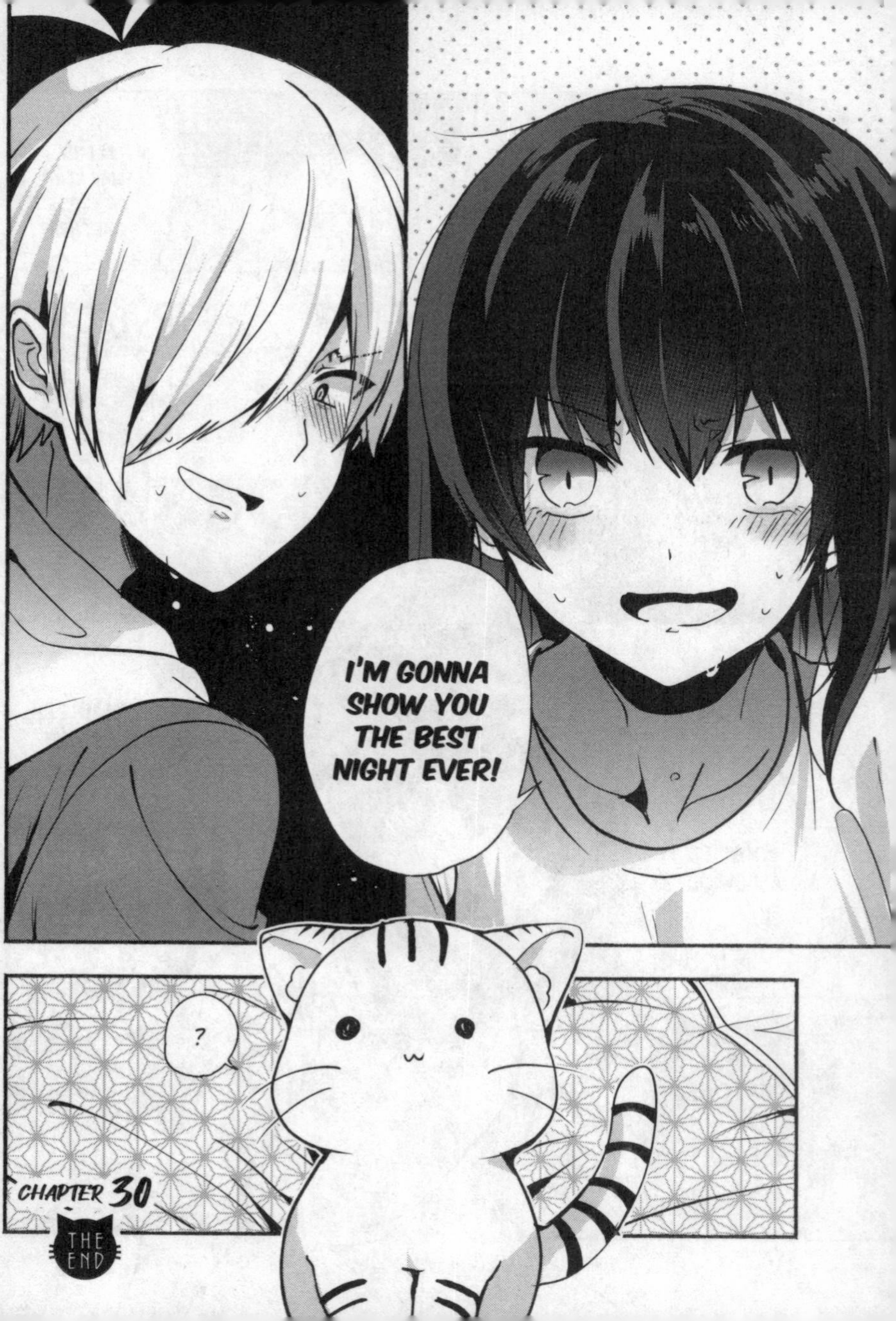
I'M GONNA SHOW YOU THE BEST NIGHT EVER!
?
CHAPTER 30
THE END

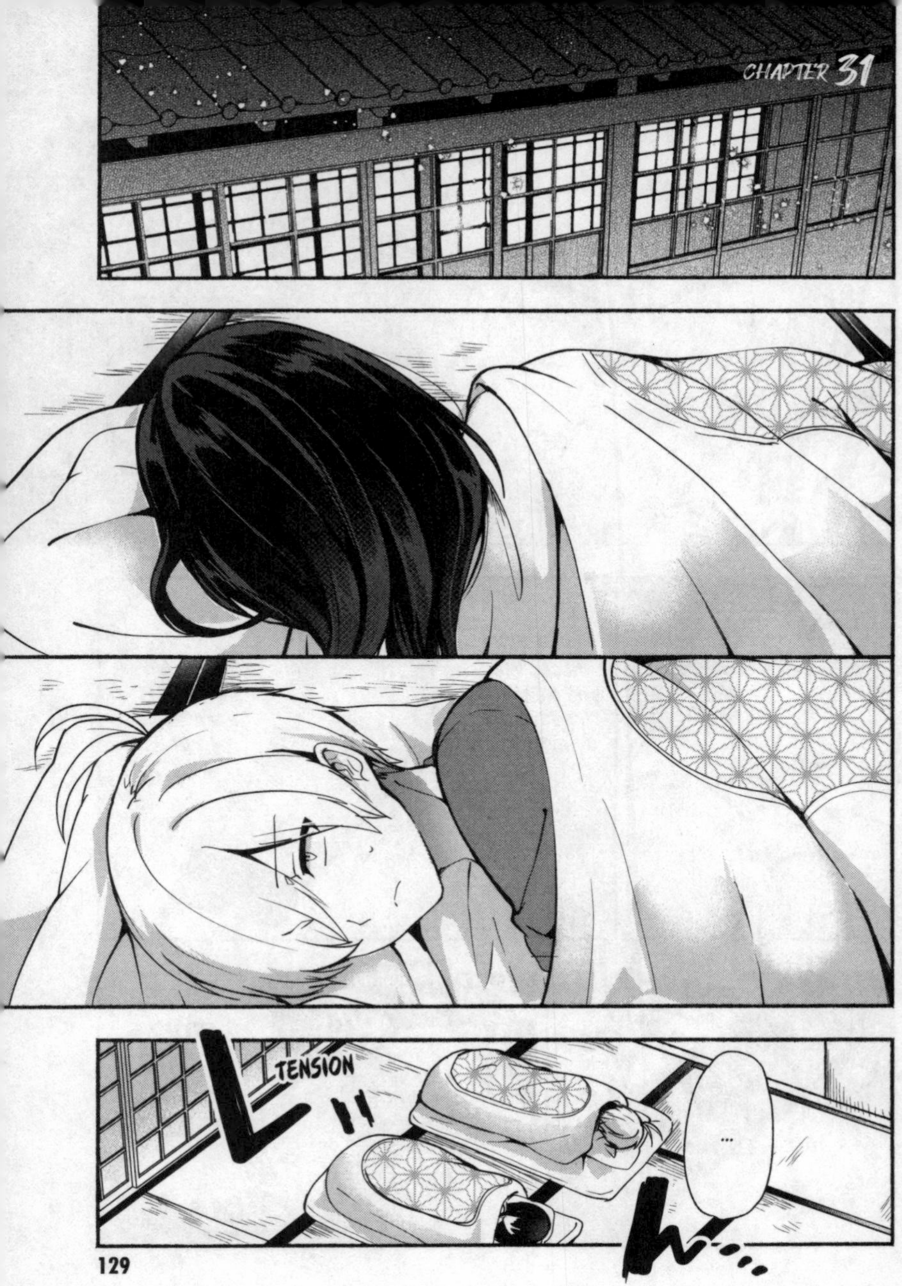
CHAPTER 31
TENSION
...

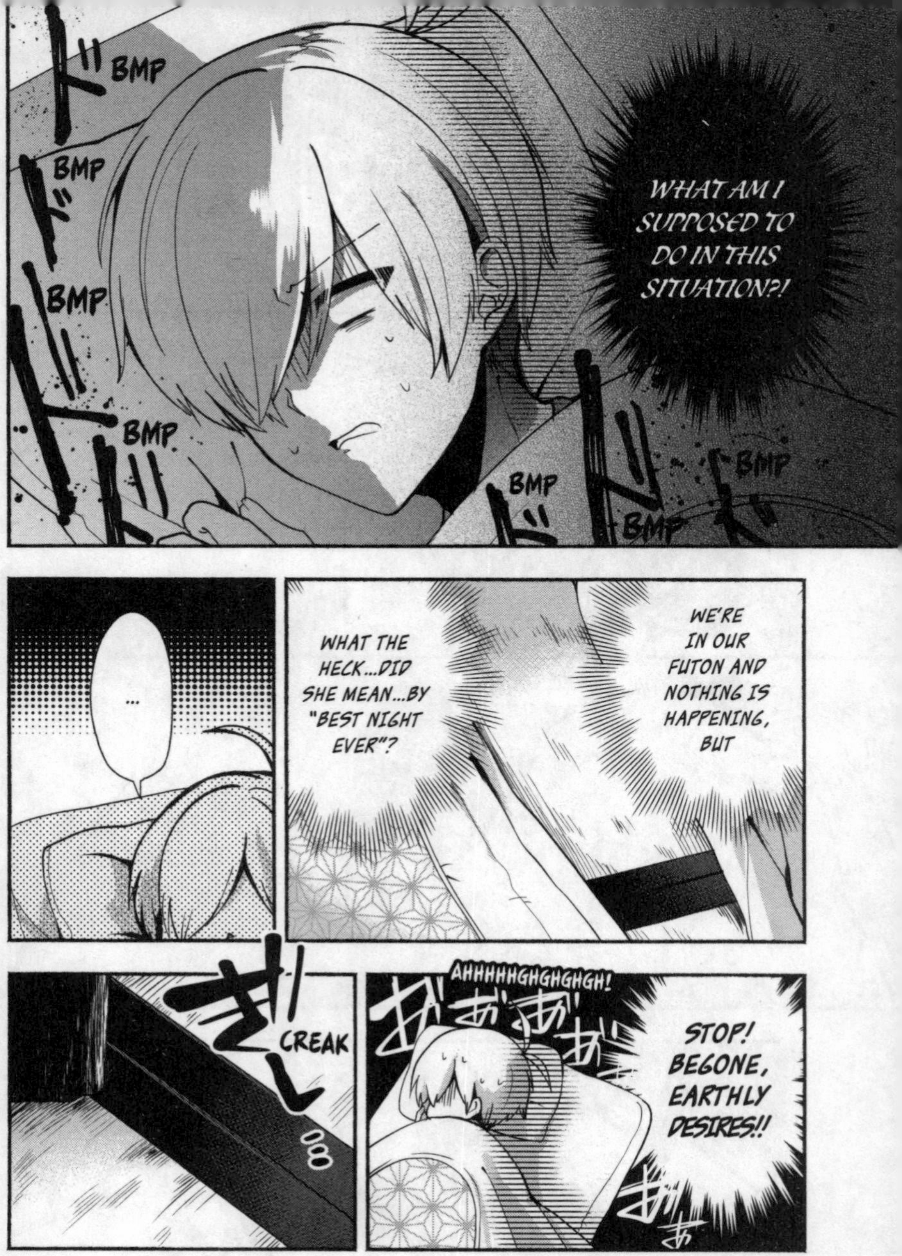
BMP
BMP
BMP
BMP
WHAT AM I SUPPOSED TO DO IN THIS SITUATION?!
BMP
BMP
BMP
WE'RE IN OUR FUTON AND NOTHING IS HAPPENING, BUT
WHAT THE HECK...DID SHE MEAN...BY "BEST NIGHT EVER"?
...
AHHHHHGHGHGHGH!
STOP! BEGONE, EARTHLY DESIRES!!
CREAK

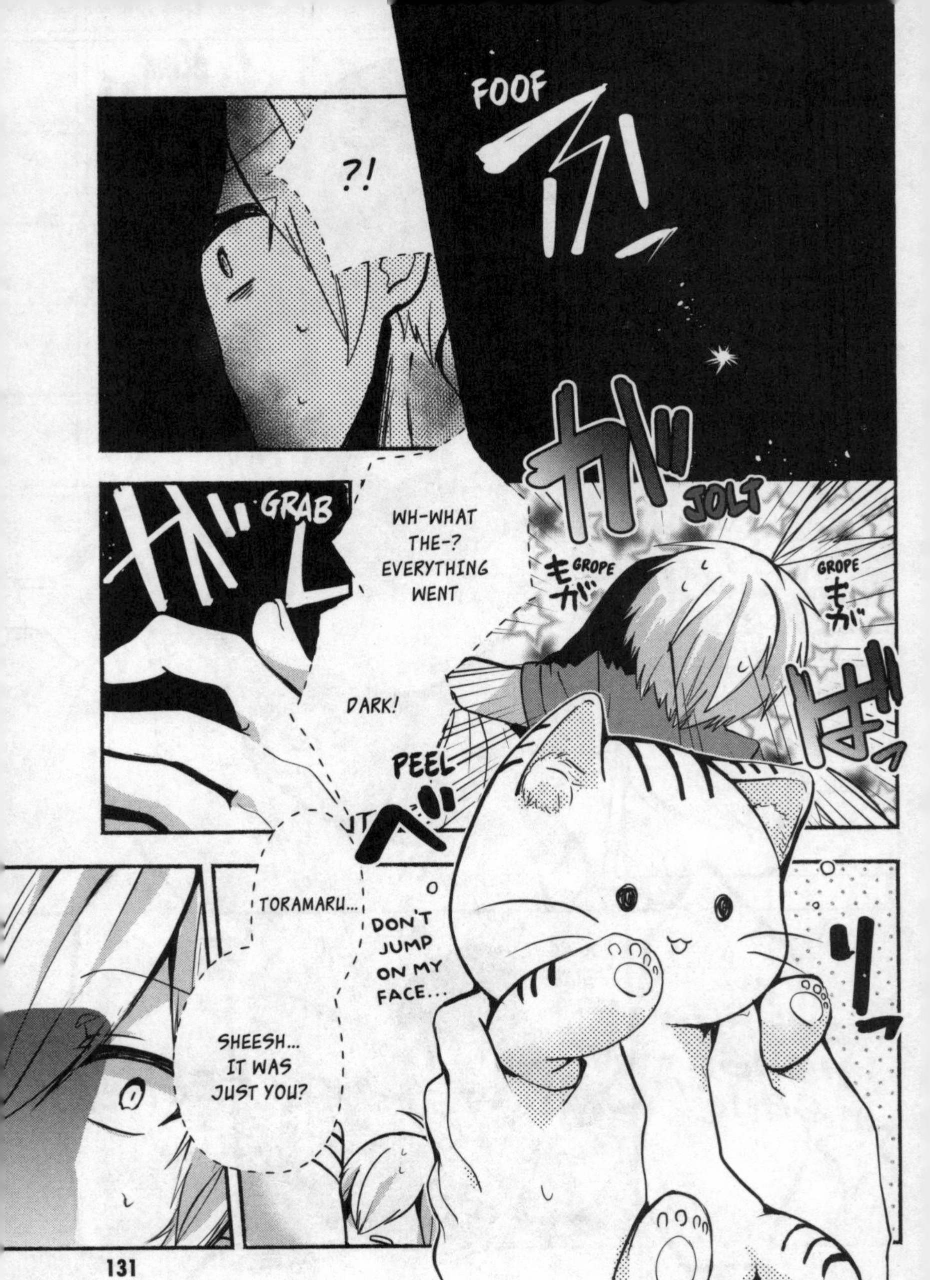
FOOF
?!
JOLT
GROPE
GROPE
WH-WHAT THE-? EVERYTHING WENT
DARK!
GRAB
PEEL
TORAMARU...
DON'T JUMP ON MY FACE...
SHEESH... IT WAS JUST YOU?

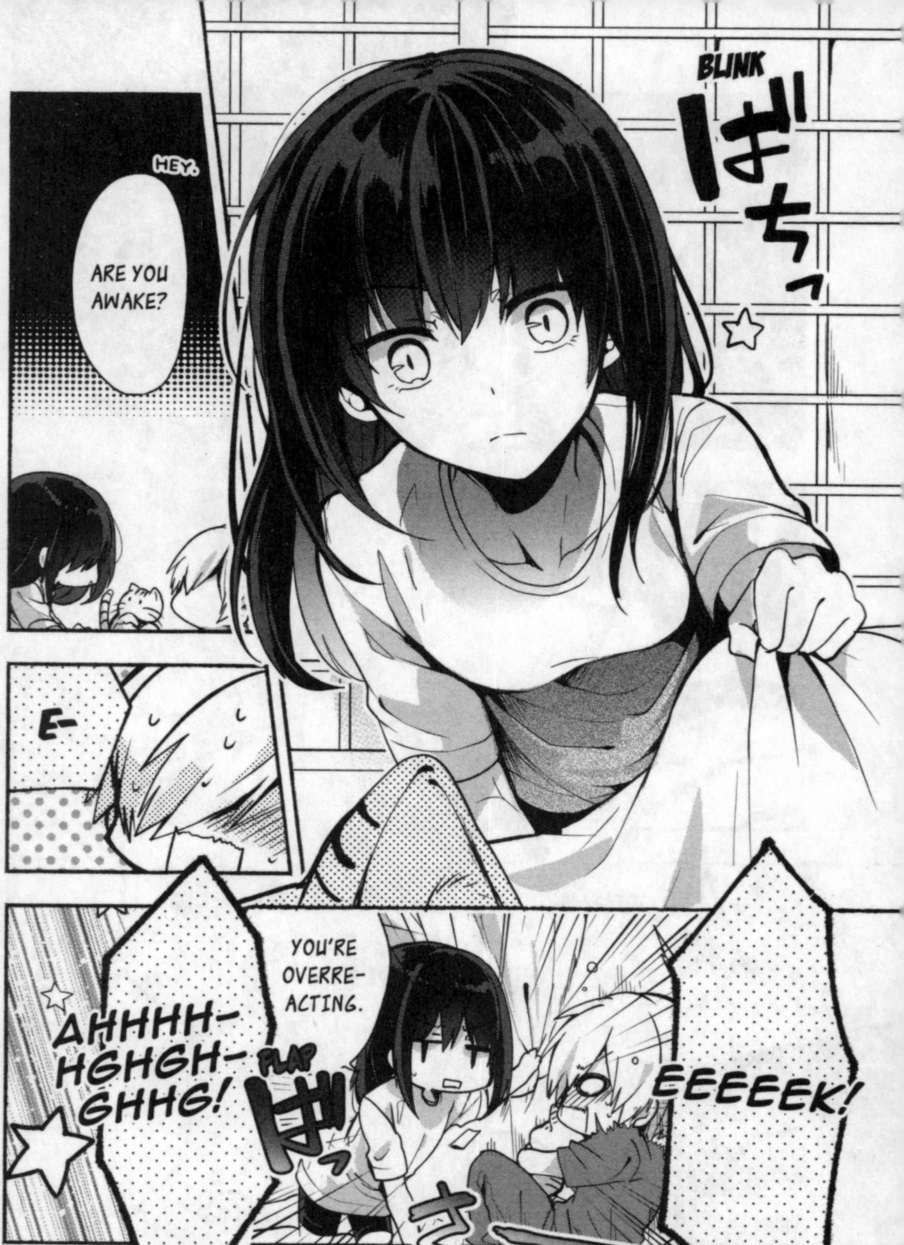
BLINK
ぱちっ
HEY.
ARE YOU AWAKE?
E-
EEEEEEK!
YOU'RE OVERRE-ACTING.
FLAP
ばっ
AHHHH-HGHGH-GHHG!
さー

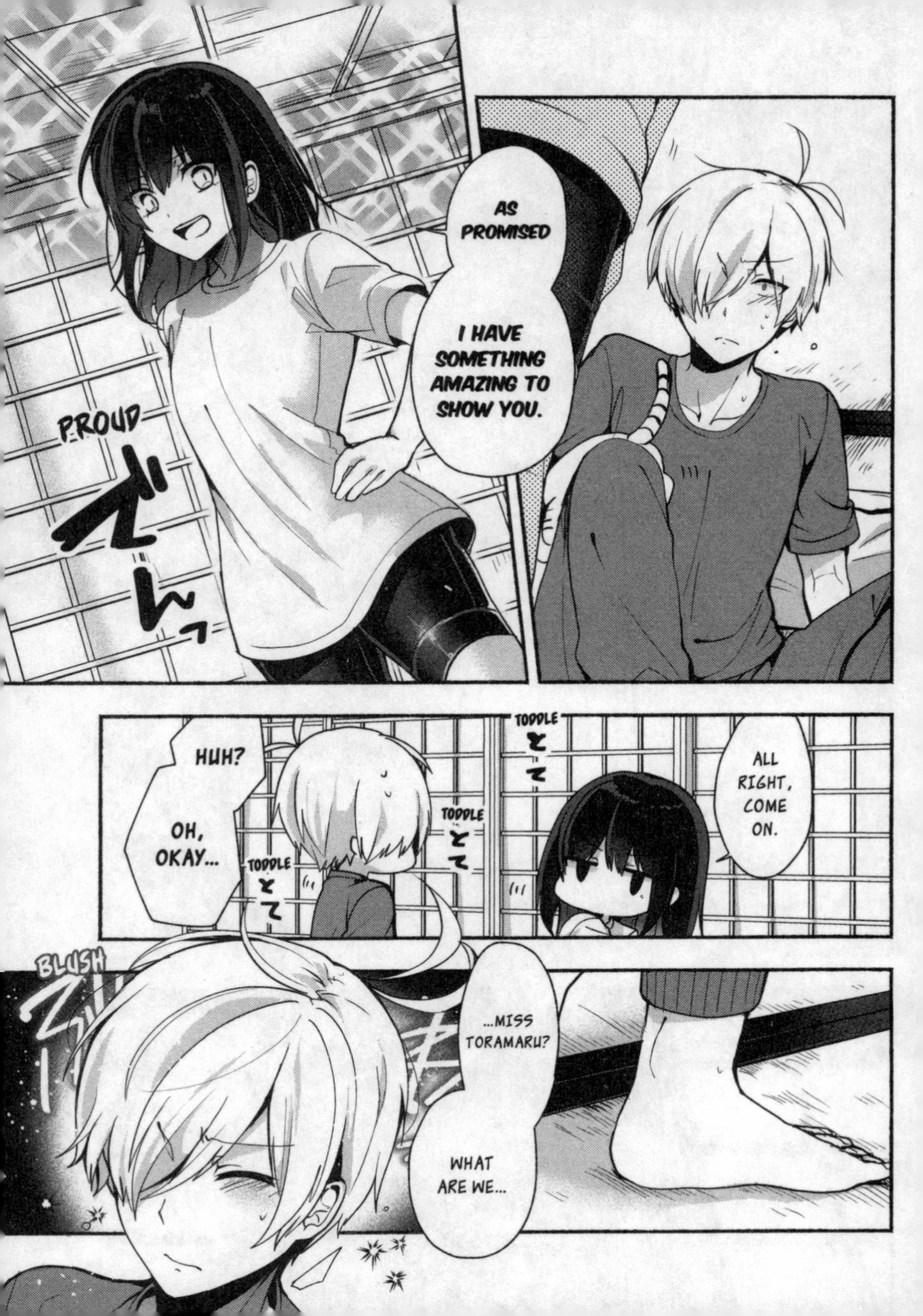
AS PROMISED
I HAVE SOMETHING AMAZING TO SHOW YOU.
PROUD
ALL RIGHT, COME ON.
TODDLE
TODDLE
TODDLE
HUH?
OH, OKAY...
...MISS TORAMARU?
WHAT ARE WE...
BLUSH

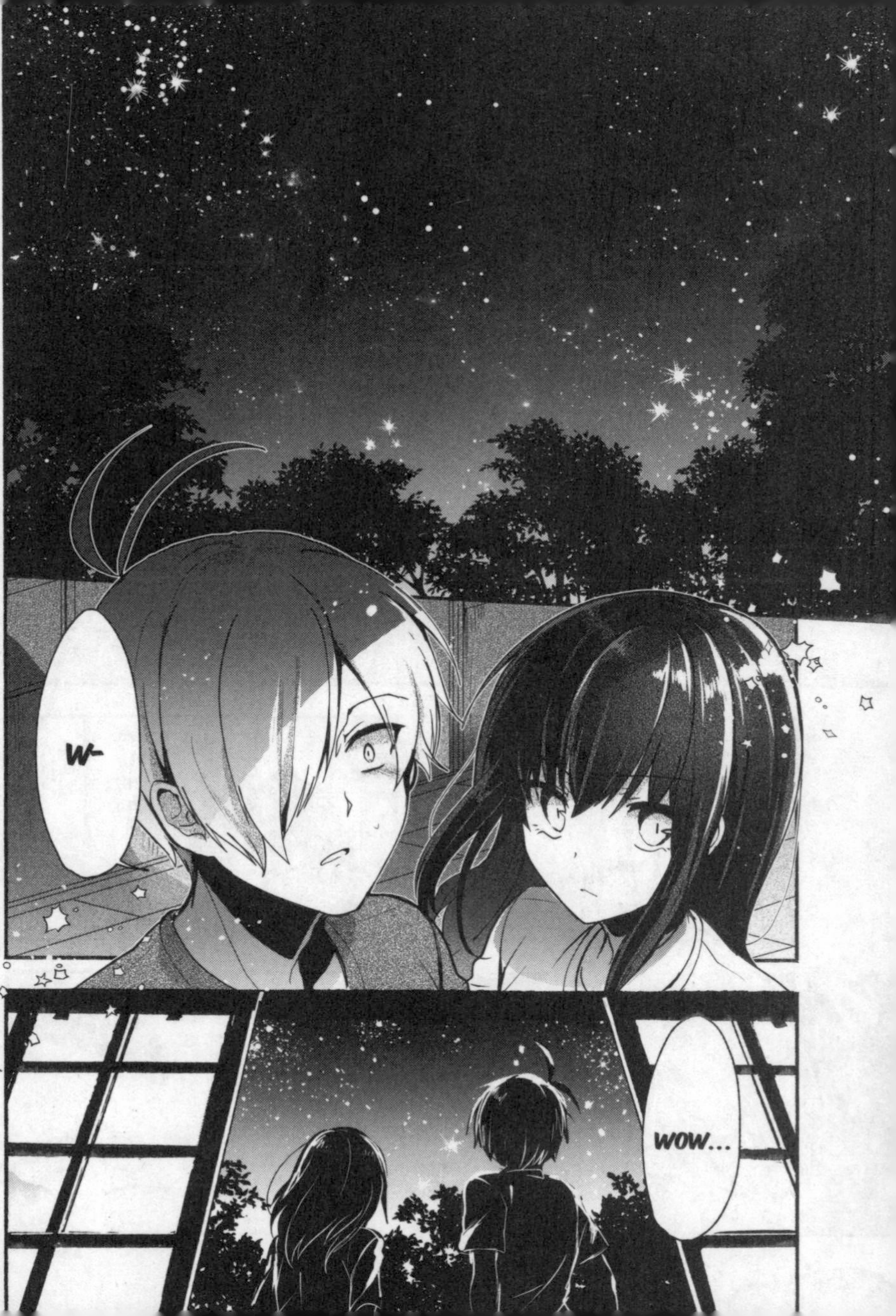
W-
WOW...

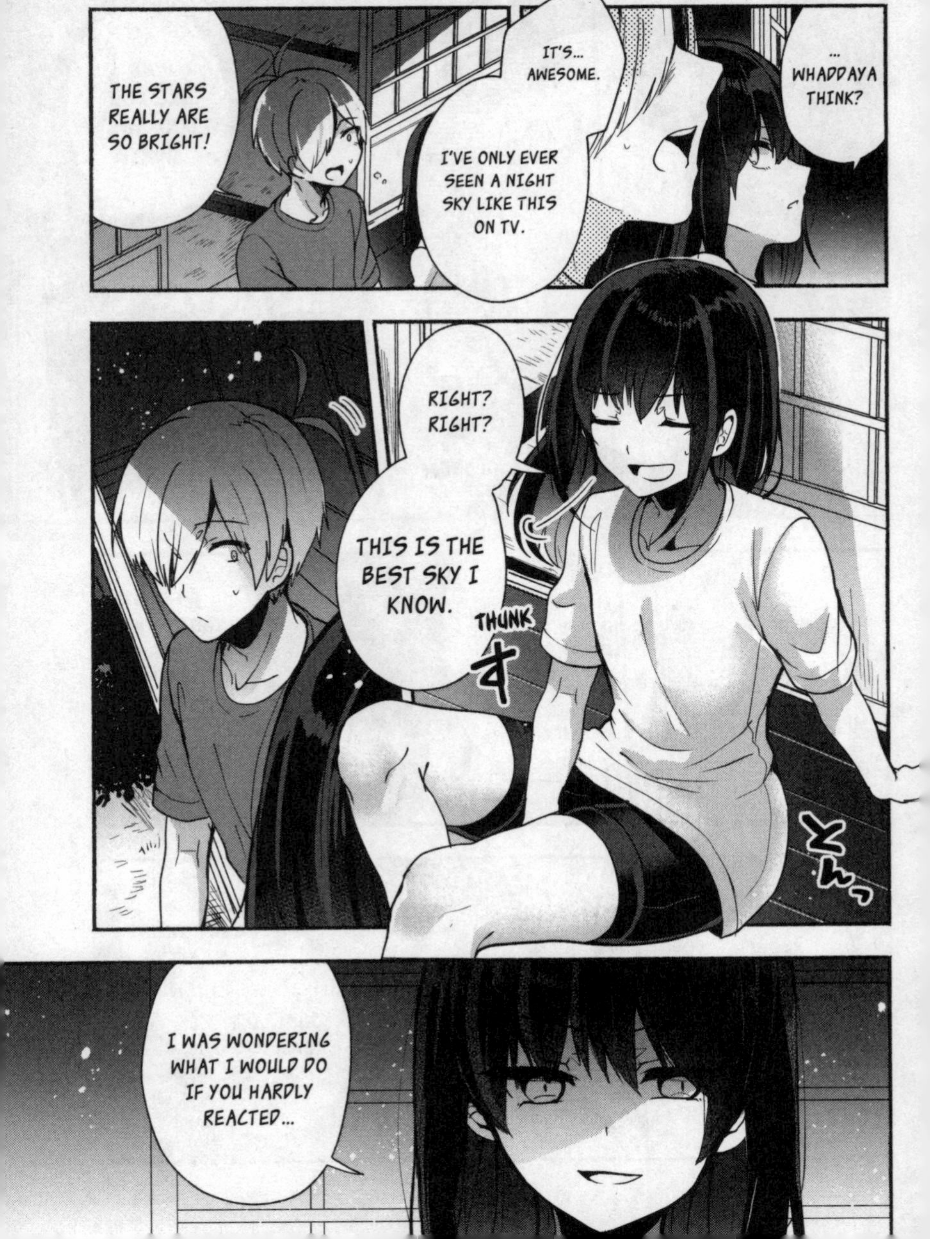
... WHADDAYA THINK?
IT'S... AWESOME.
I'VE ONLY EVER SEEN A NIGHT SKY LIKE THIS ON TV.
THE STARS REALLY ARE SO BRIGHT!
RIGHT? RIGHT?
THIS IS THE BEST SKY I KNOW.
とんっ
THUNK
す
I WAS WONDERING WHAT I WOULD DO IF YOU HARDLY REACTED...

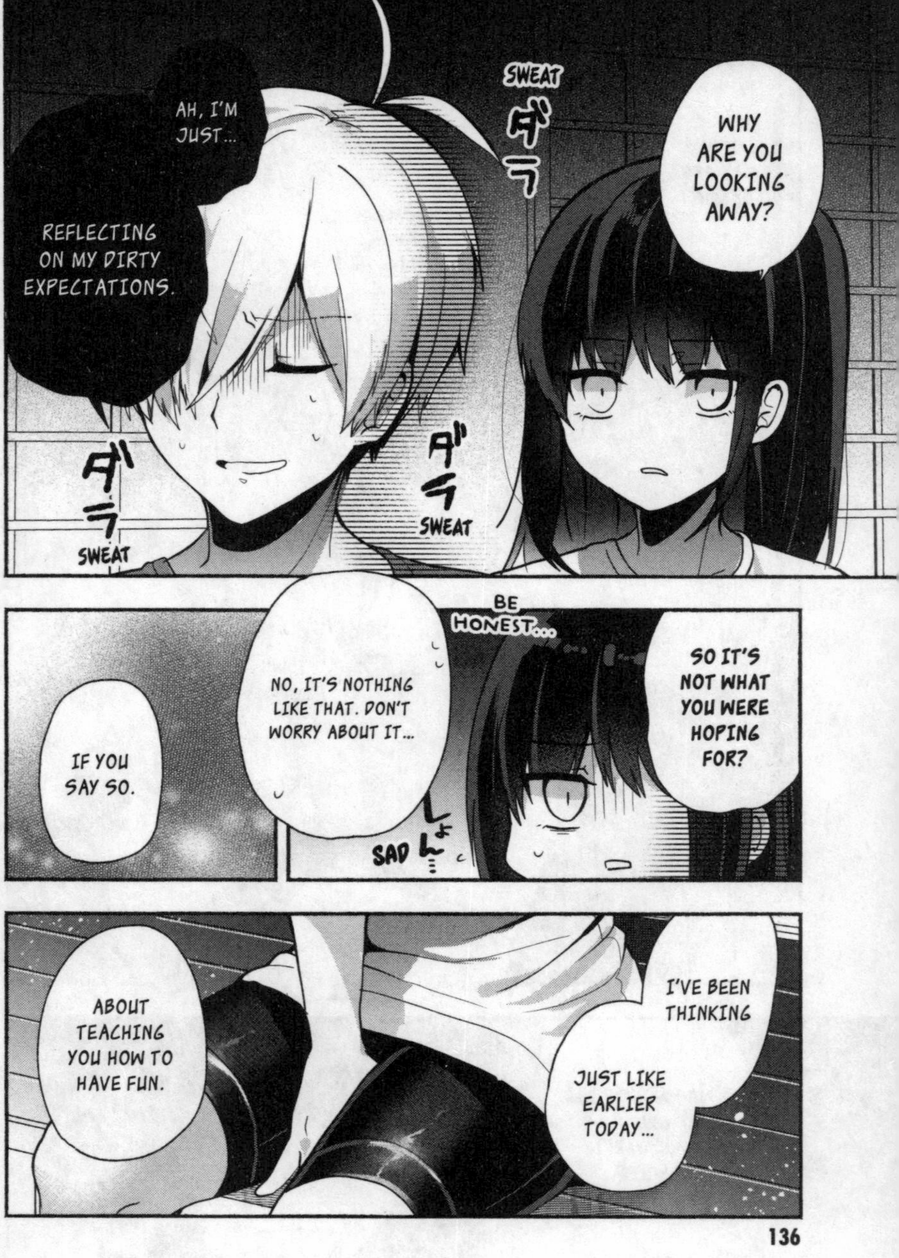
WHY ARE YOU LOOKING AWAY?
SWEAT
ダラ
AH, I'M JUST...
REFLECTING ON MY DIRTY EXPECTATIONS.
ダラ
SWEAT
ダラ
SWEAT
BE HONEST...
SO IT'S NOT WHAT YOU WERE HOPING FOR?
NO, IT'S NOTHING LIKE THAT. DON'T WORRY ABOUT IT...
しょん...
SAD
IF YOU SAY SO.
I'VE BEEN THINKING
JUST LIKE EARLIER TODAY...
ABOUT TEACHING YOU HOW TO HAVE FUN.

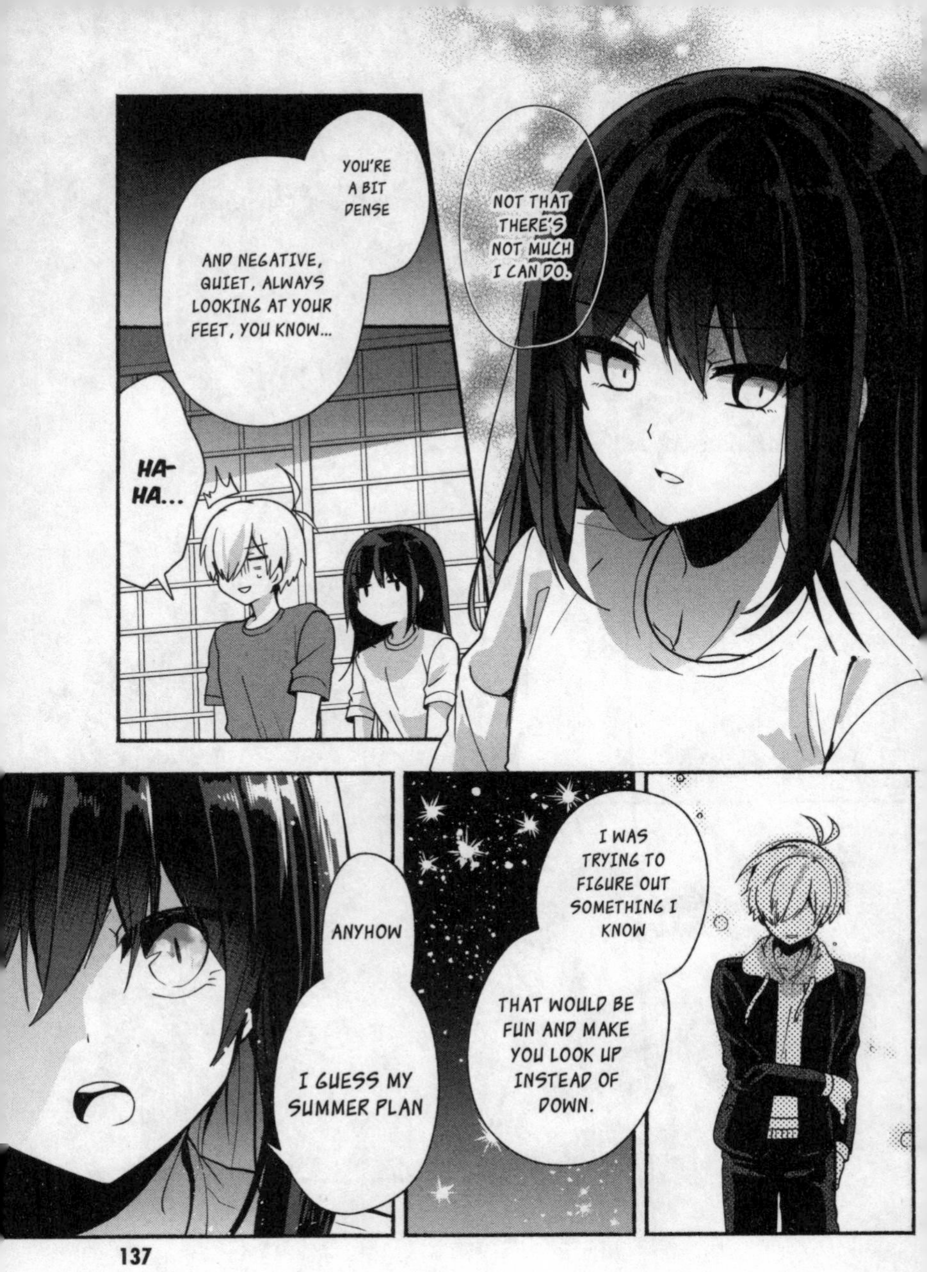
NOT THAT THERE'S NOT MUCH I CAN DO.
YOU'RE A BIT DENSE
AND NEGATIVE, QUIET, ALWAYS LOOKING AT YOUR FEET, YOU KNOW...
HA-HA...
I WAS TRYING TO FIGURE OUT SOMETHING I KNOW
THAT WOULD BE FUN AND MAKE YOU LOOK UP INSTEAD OF DOWN.
ANYHOW
I GUESS MY SUMMER PLAN

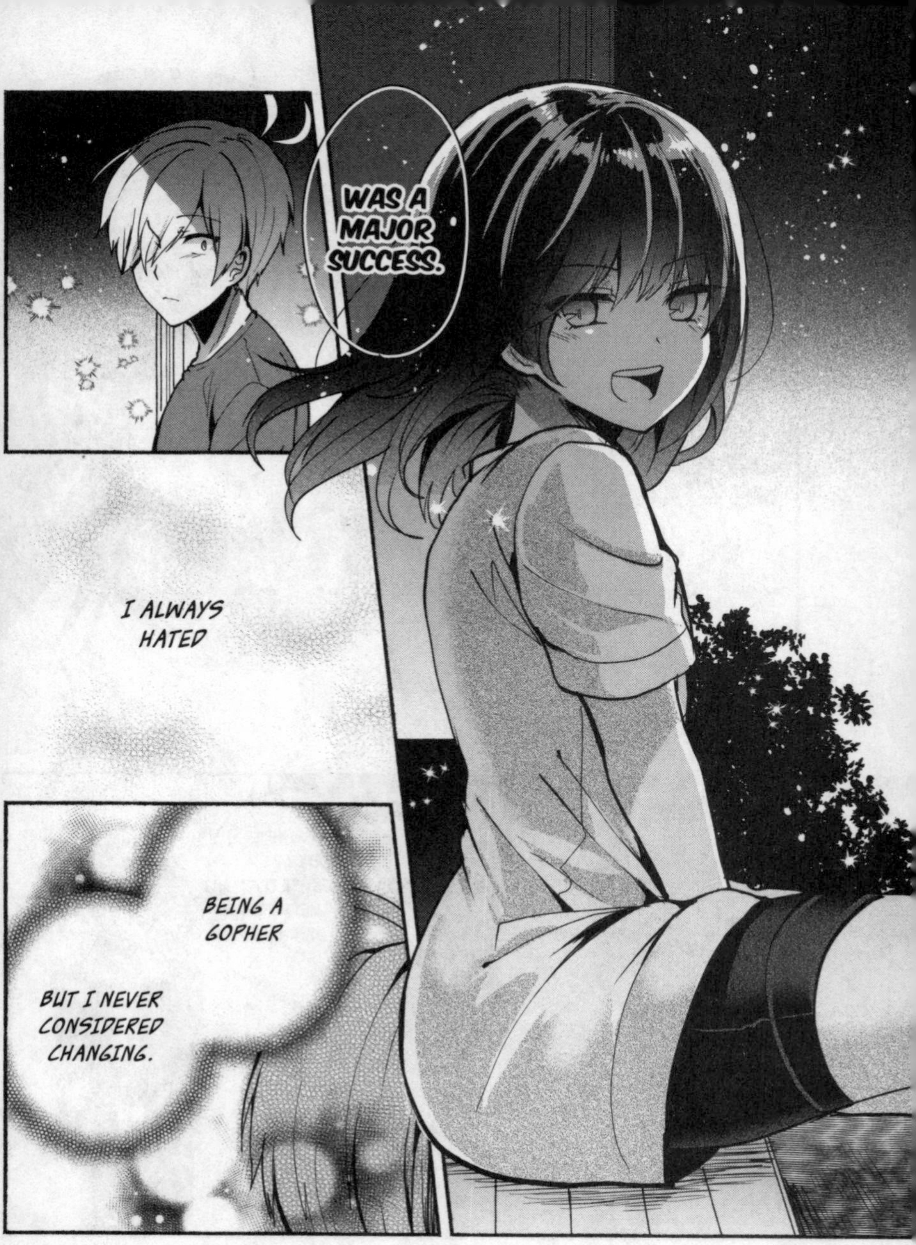
WAS A MAJOR SUCCESS.
I ALWAYS HATED
BEING A GOPHER
BUT I NEVER CONSIDERED CHANGING.

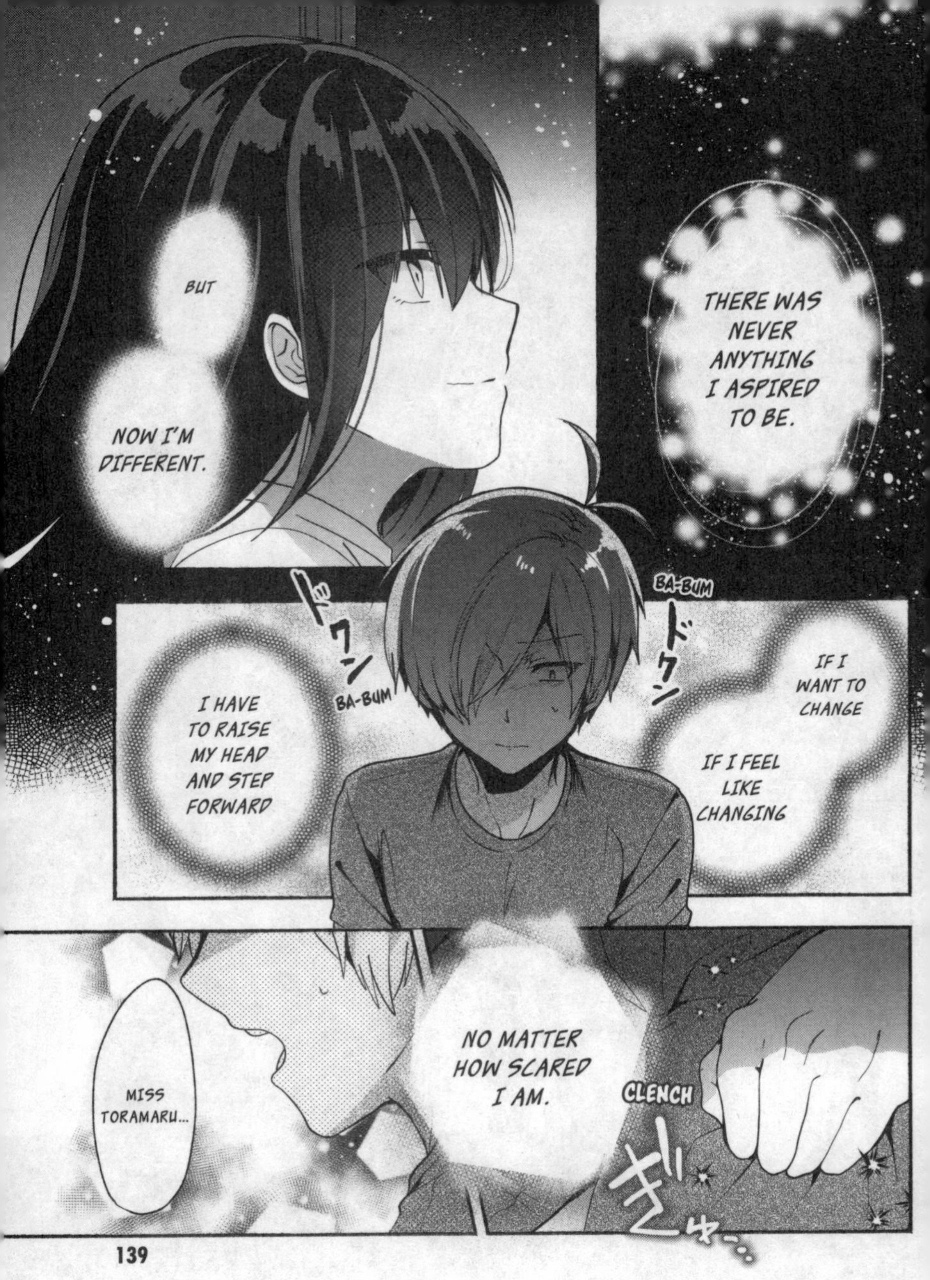
THERE WAS NEVER ANYTHING I ASPIRED TO BE.
BUT
NOW I'M DIFFERENT.
BA-BUM
IF I WANT TO CHANGE
IF I FEEL LIKE CHANGING
BA-BUM
I HAVE TO RAISE MY HEAD AND STEP FORWARD
CLENCH
NO MATTER HOW SCARED I AM.
MISS TORAMARU...

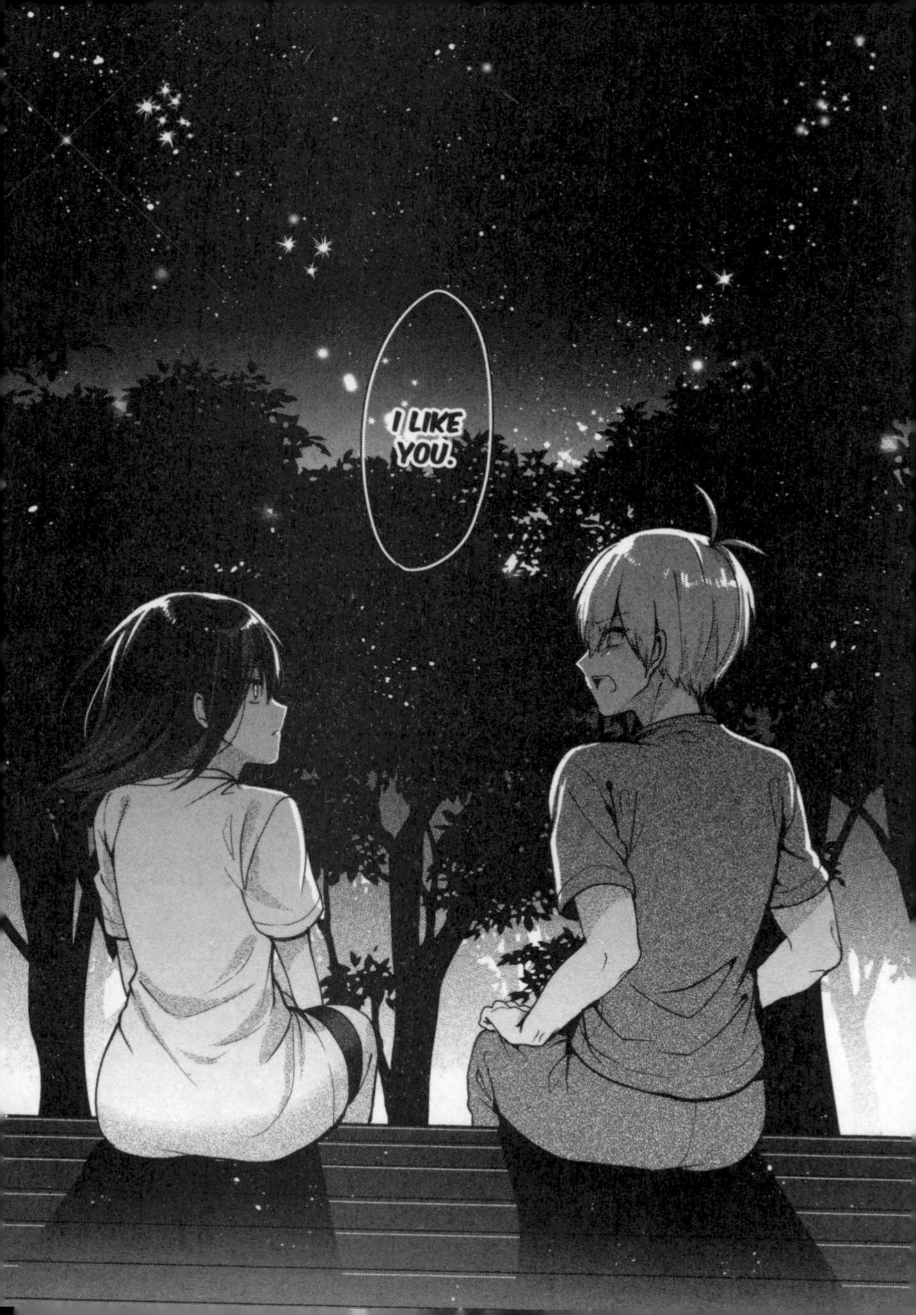
I LIKE YOU.

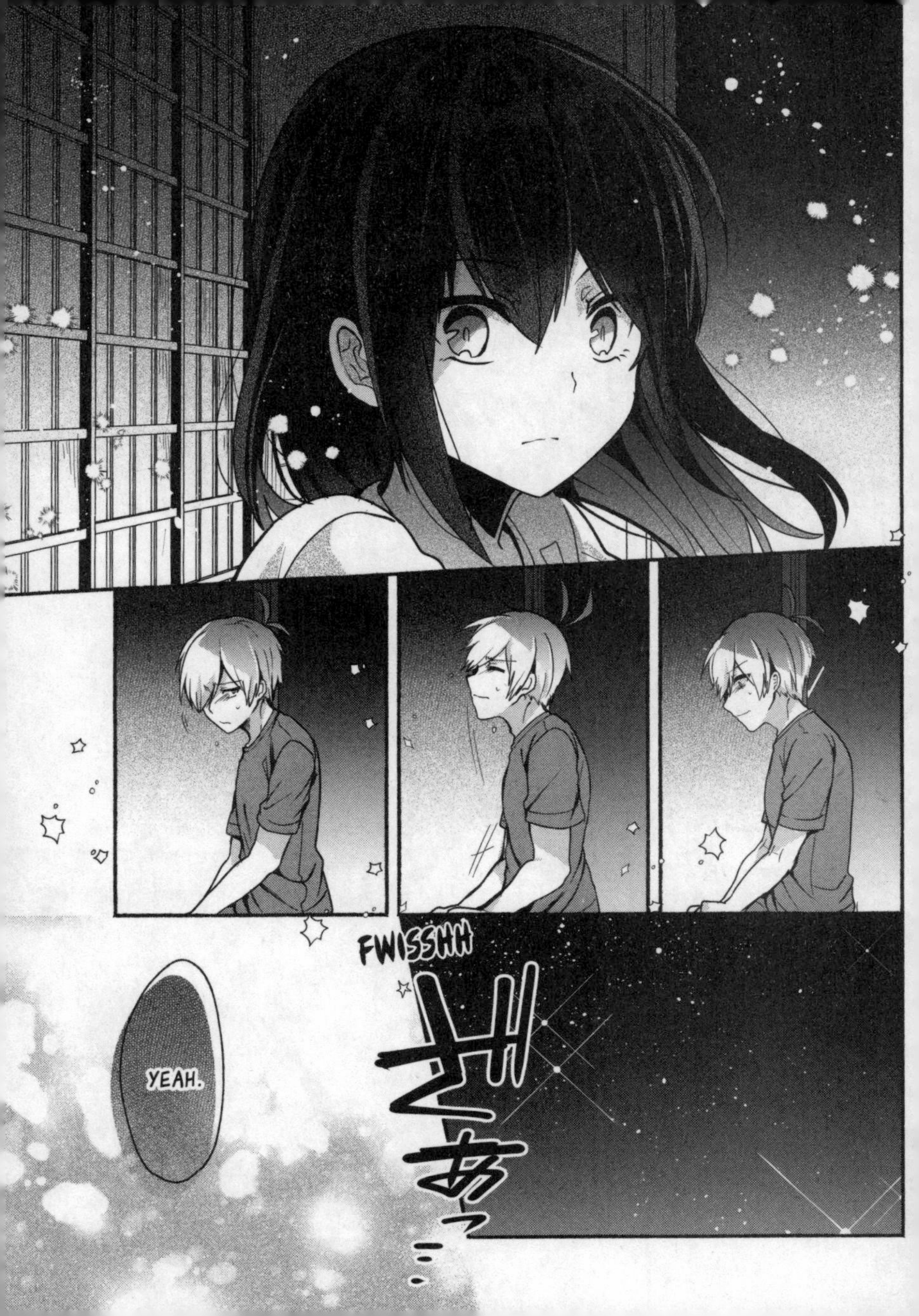

FWISSHH
ざあっ…
YEAH.

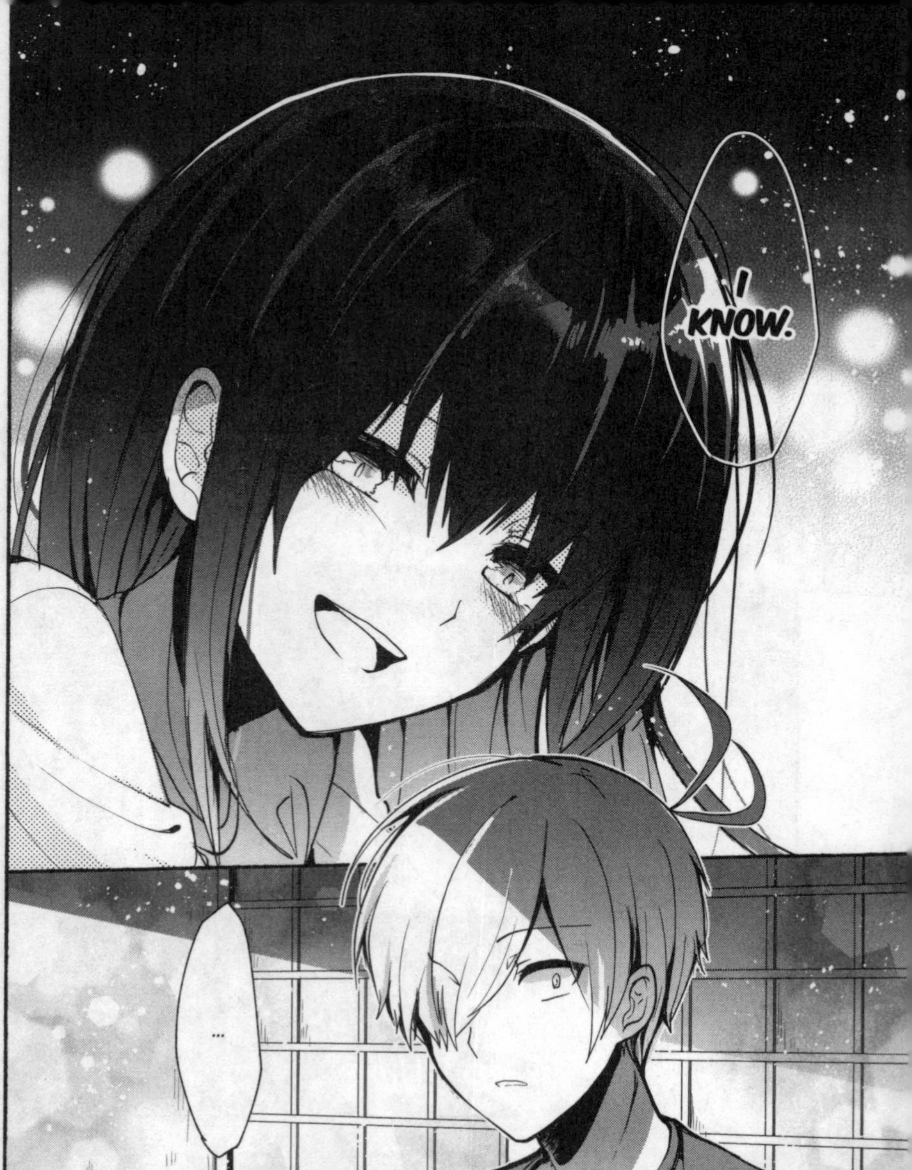
I KNOW.
...

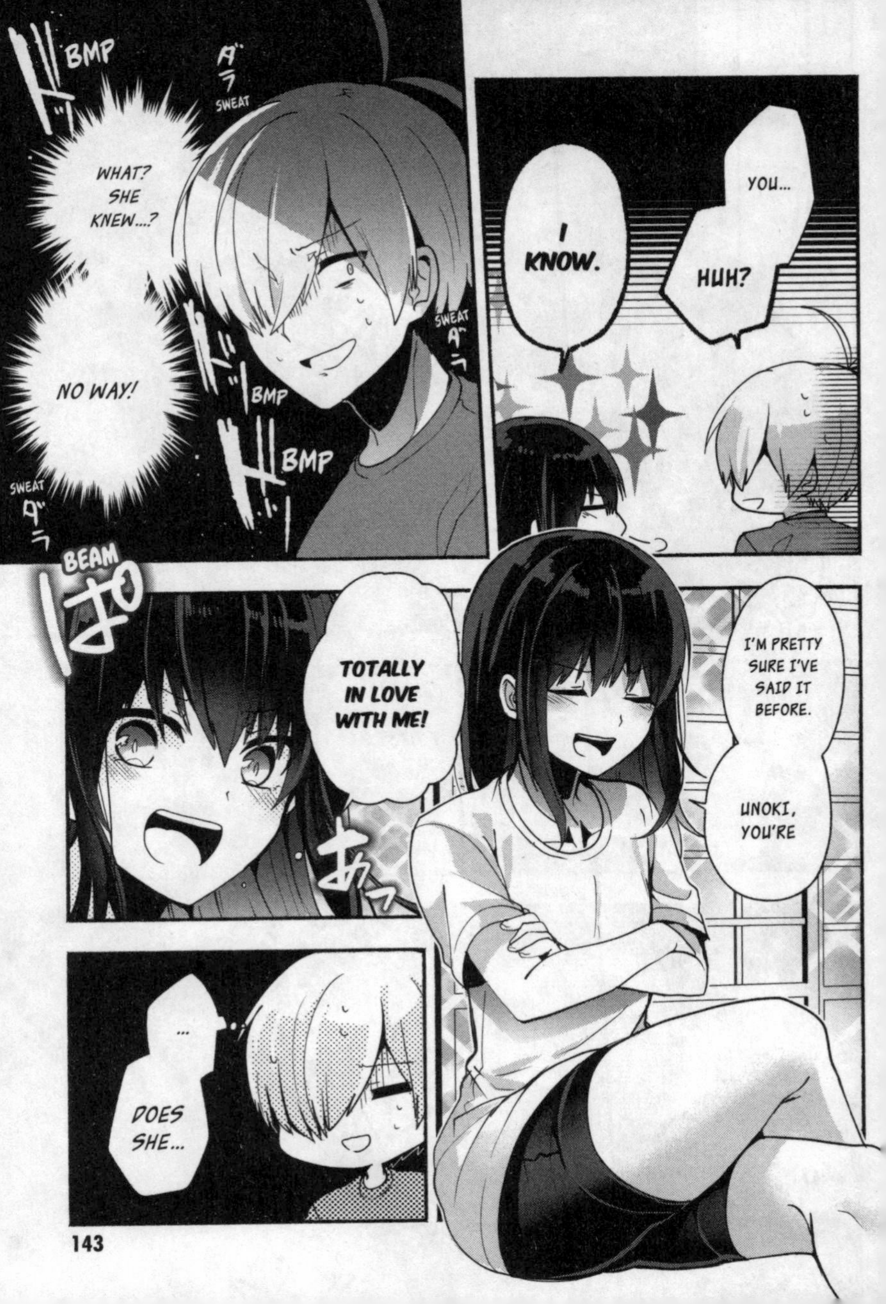
YOU... HUH?
I KNOW.
BMP
SWEAT
WHAT? SHE KNEW...?
NO WAY!
SWEAT
BMP
BMP
SWEAT
I'M PRETTY SURE I'VE SAID IT BEFORE.
UNOKI, YOU'RE
TOTALLY IN LOVE WITH ME!
BEAM
...
DOES SHE...

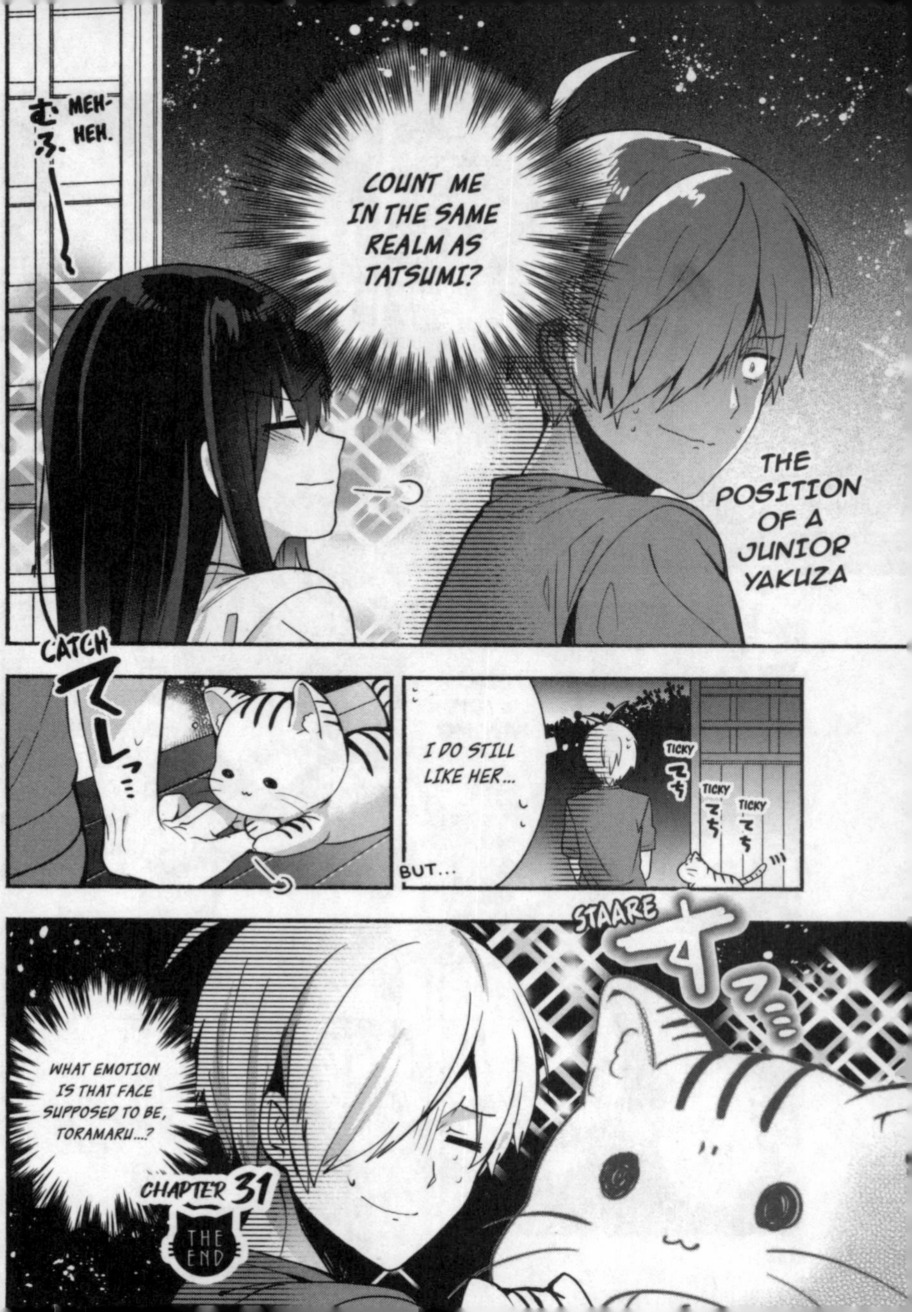
COUNT ME IN THE SAME REALM AS TATSUMI?
THE POSITION OF A JUNIOR YAKUZA
むふ〜
MEH-HEH.
I DO STILL LIKE HER...
TICKY
てち
TICKY
てち
TICKY
てち
BUT...
CATCH
STAARE
WHAT EMOTION IS THAT FACE SUPPOSED TO BE, TORAMARU...?
CHAPTER 31
THE END

CHAPTER 32

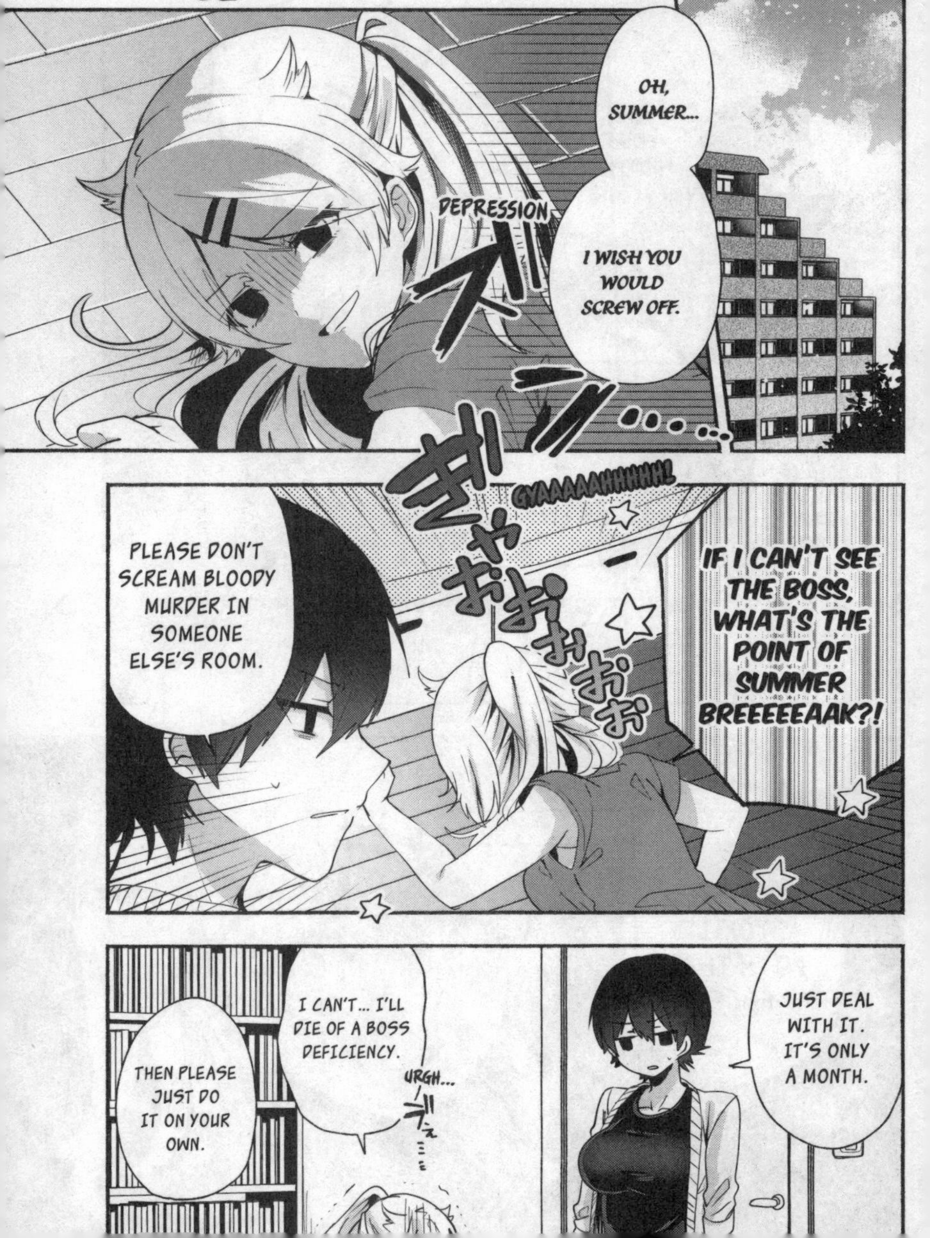
OH, SUMMER...
I WISH YOU WOULD SCREW OFF.
DEPRESSION
GYAAAAHHHHH!
IF I CAN'T SEE THE BOSS, WHAT'S THE POINT OF SUMMER BREEEEEAAK?!
PLEASE DON'T SCREAM BLOODY MURDER IN SOMEONE ELSE'S ROOM.
JUST DEAL WITH IT. IT'S ONLY A MONTH.
I CAN'T... I'LL DIE OF A BOSS DEFICIENCY.
URGH...
THEN PLEASE JUST DO IT ON YOUR OWN.

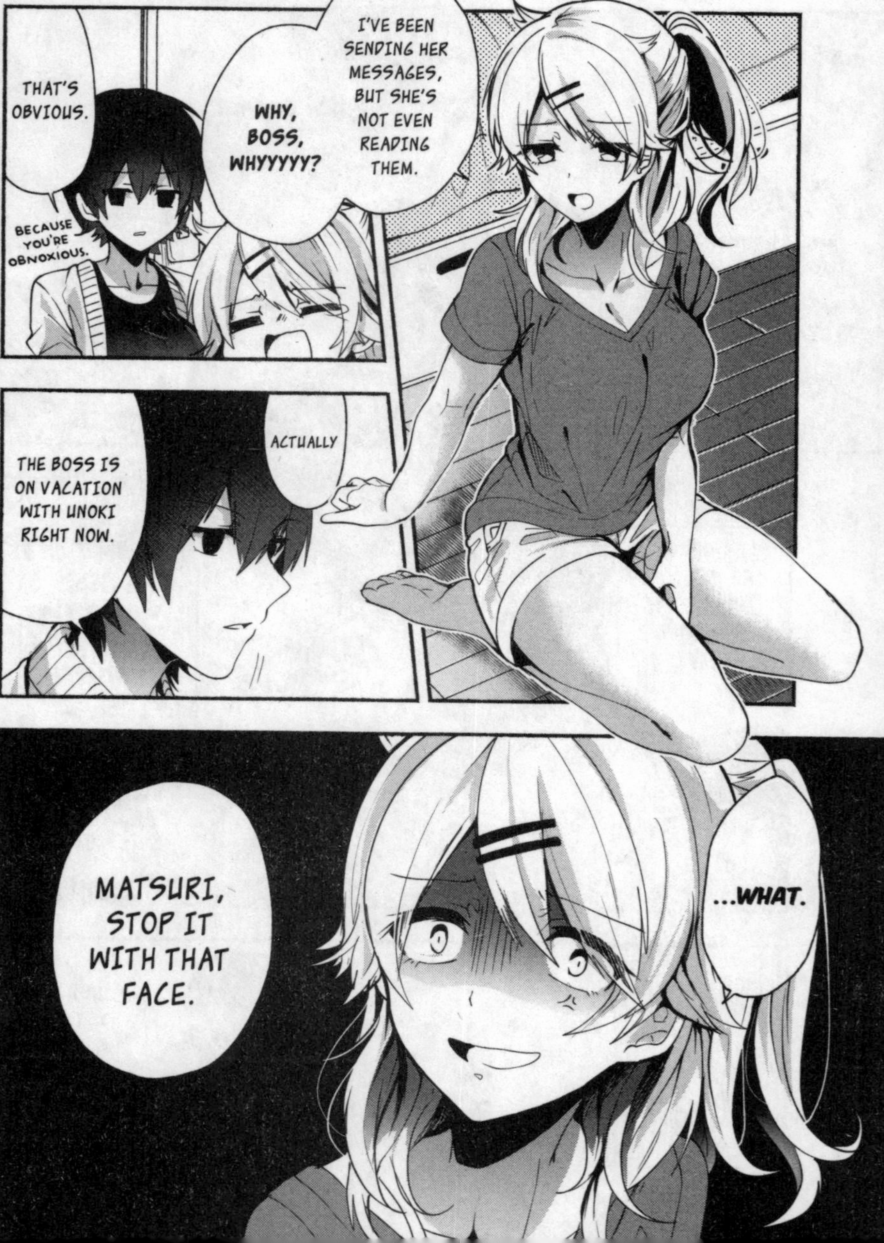
I'VE BEEN SENDING HER MESSAGES, BUT SHE'S NOT EVEN READING THEM.
WHY, BOSS, WHYYYYY?
THAT'S OBVIOUS.
BECAUSE YOU'RE OBNOXIOUS.
ACTUALLY
THE BOSS IS ON VACATION WITH UNOKI RIGHT NOW.
...WHAT.
MATSURI, STOP IT WITH THAT FACE.

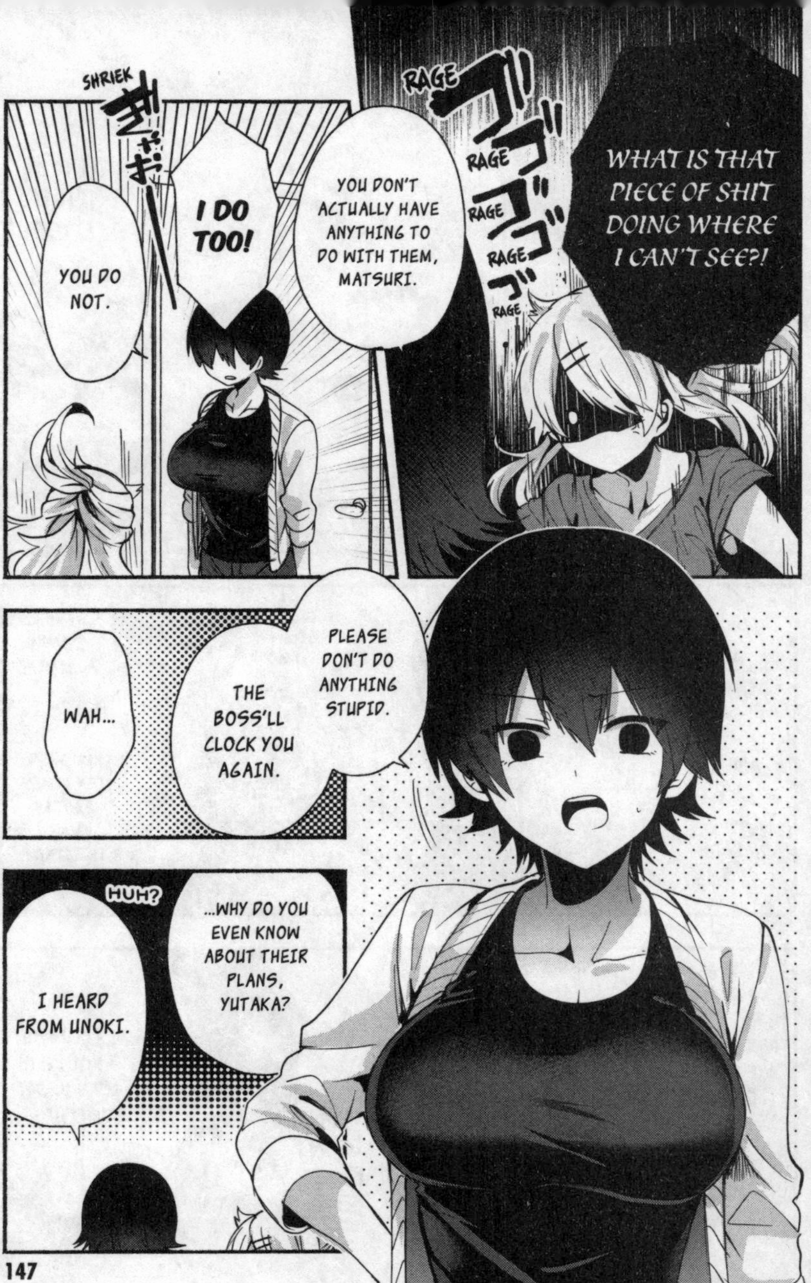
RAGE
RAGE
RAGE
RAGE
RAGE
WHAT IS THAT PIECE OF SHIT DOING WHERE I CAN'T SEE?!
YOU DON'T ACTUALLY HAVE ANYTHING TO DO WITH THEM, MATSURI.
SHRIEK
I DO TOO!
YOU DO NOT.
PLEASE DON'T DO ANYTHING STUPID.
THE BOSS'LL CLOCK YOU AGAIN.
WAH...
HUH?
...WHY DO YOU EVEN KNOW ABOUT THEIR PLANS, YUTAKA?
I HEARD FROM UNOKI.

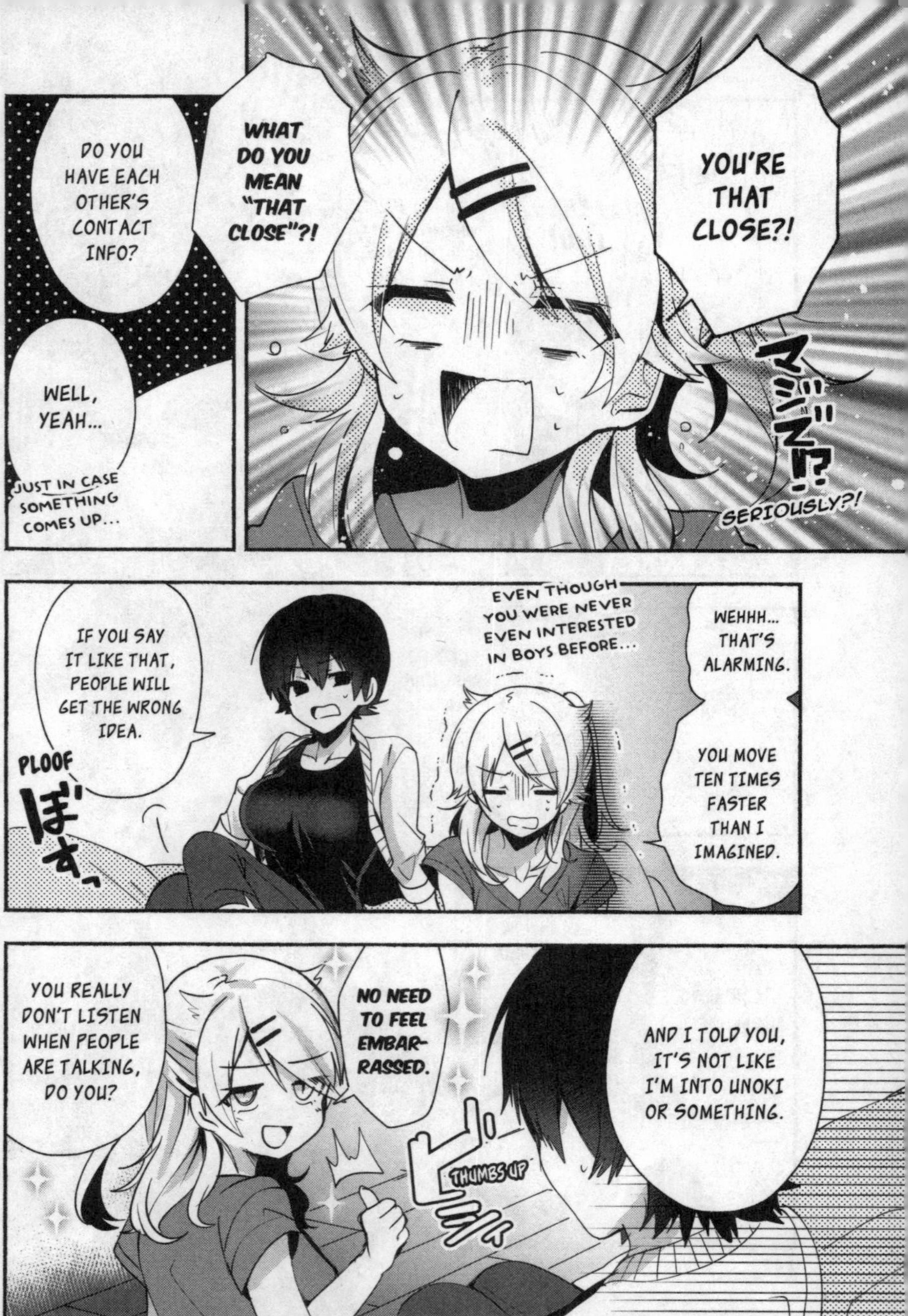
YOU'RE THAT CLOSE?!
マジで!?
SERIOUSLY?!
WHAT DO YOU MEAN "THAT CLOSE"?!
DO YOU HAVE EACH OTHER'S CONTACT INFO?
WELL, YEAH...
JUST IN CASE SOMETHING COMES UP...
WEHHH... THAT'S ALARMING.
YOU MOVE TEN TIMES FASTER THAN I IMAGINED.
EVEN THOUGH YOU WERE NEVER EVEN INTERESTED IN BOYS BEFORE...
IF YOU SAY IT LIKE THAT, PEOPLE WILL GET THE WRONG IDEA.
ぼすっ
PLOOF
AND I TOLD YOU, IT'S NOT LIKE I'M INTO UNOKI OR SOMETHING.
NO NEED TO FEEL EMBARRASSED.
THUMBS UP
YOU REALLY DON'T LISTEN WHEN PEOPLE ARE TALKING, DO YOU?

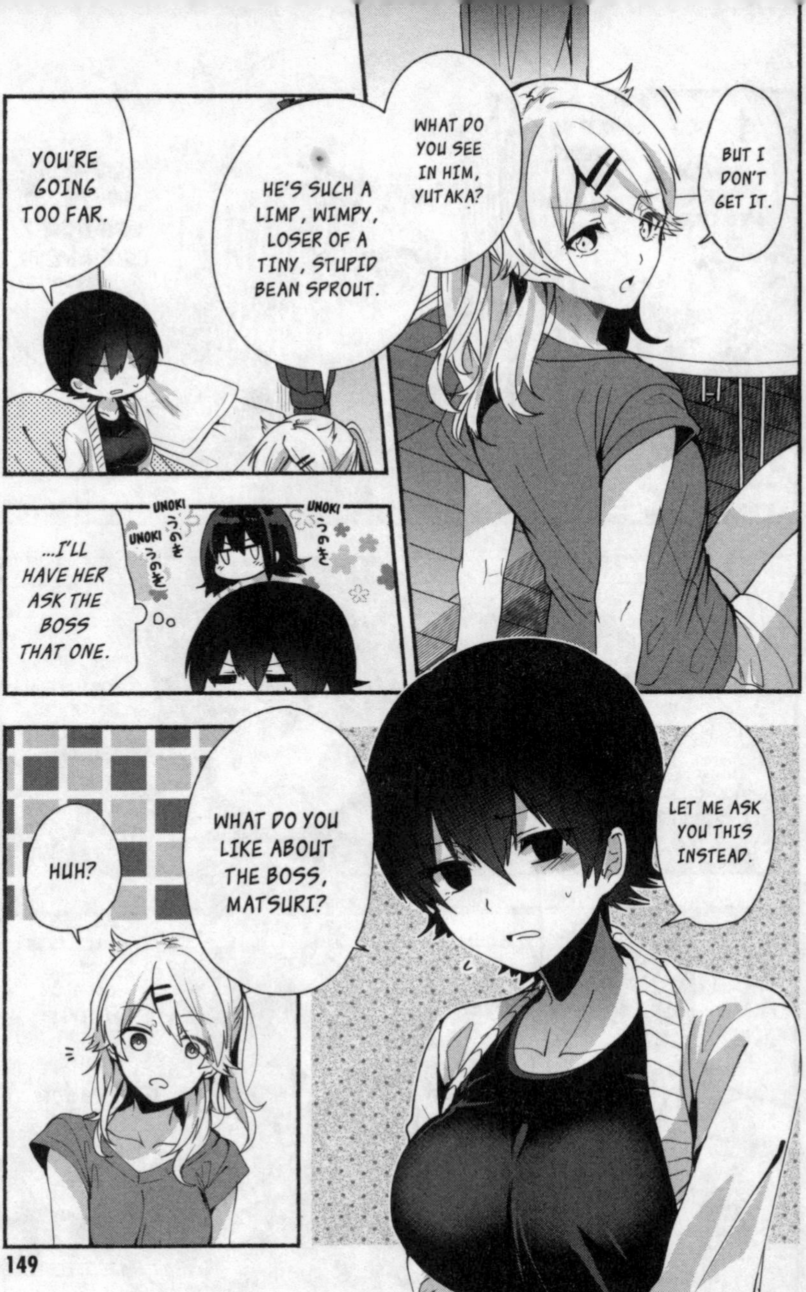
BUT I DON'T GET IT.
WHAT DO YOU SEE IN HIM, YUTAKA?
HE'S SUCH A LIMP, WIMPY, LOSER OF A TINY, STUPID BEAN SPROUT.
YOU'RE GOING TOO FAR.
UNOKI うのき
UNOKI うのき
UNOKI うのき
...I'LL HAVE HER ASK THE BOSS THAT ONE.
LET ME ASK YOU THIS INSTEAD.
WHAT DO YOU LIKE ABOUT THE BOSS, MATSURI?
HUH?

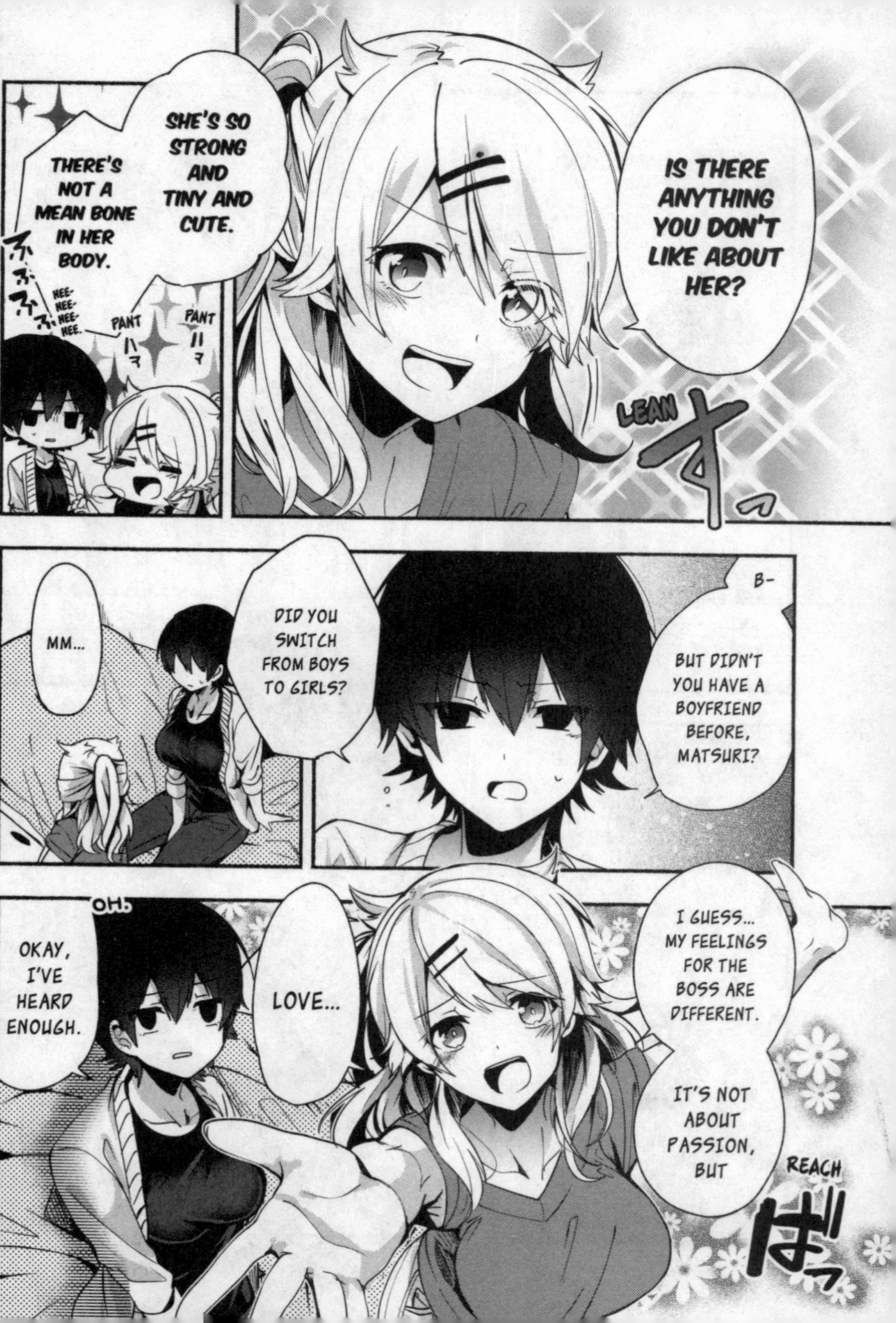
IS THERE ANYTHING YOU DON'T LIKE ABOUT HER?
LEAN
すっ
SHE'S SO STRONG AND TINY AND CUTE.
THERE'S NOT A MEAN BONE IN HER BODY.
ふふふふ
HEE-HEE-HEE-HEE.
PANT
ハァ
PANT
ハァ
B-
BUT DIDN'T YOU HAVE A BOYFRIEND BEFORE, MATSURI?
DID YOU SWITCH FROM BOYS TO GIRLS?
MM...
I GUESS... MY FEELINGS FOR THE BOSS ARE DIFFERENT.
IT'S NOT ABOUT PASSION, BUT
REACH
ばっ
LOVE...
OH.
OKAY, I'VE HEARD ENOUGH.

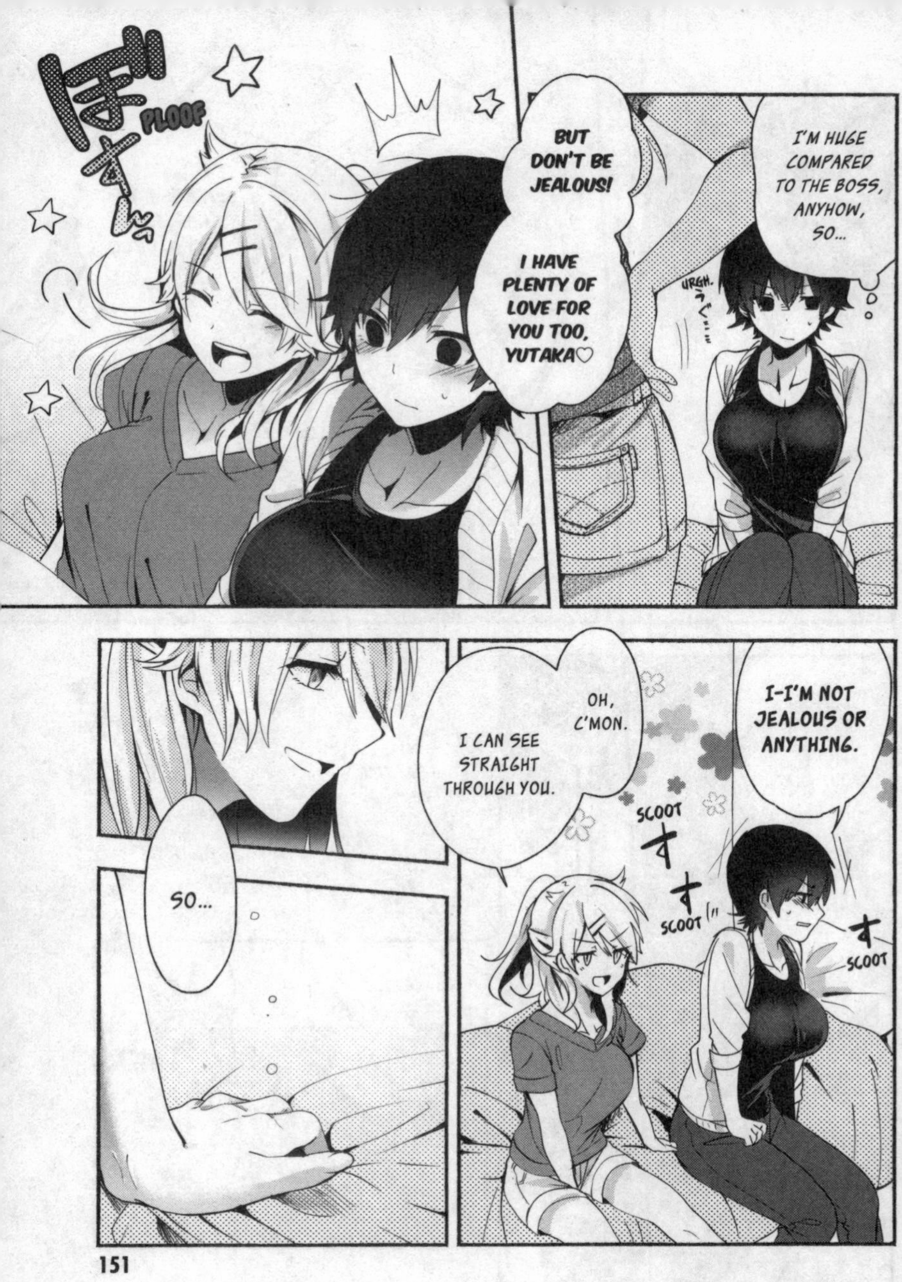

I'M HUGE COMPARED TO THE BOSS, ANYHOW, SO...
URGH.
BUT DON'T BE JEALOUS!
I HAVE PLENTY OF LOVE FOR YOU TOO, YUTAKA♡
ぽすん
PLOOF
I-I'M NOT JEALOUS OR ANYTHING.
OH, C'MON.
I CAN SEE STRAIGHT THROUGH YOU.
す
SCOOT
す
SCOOT
す
SCOOT
SO...

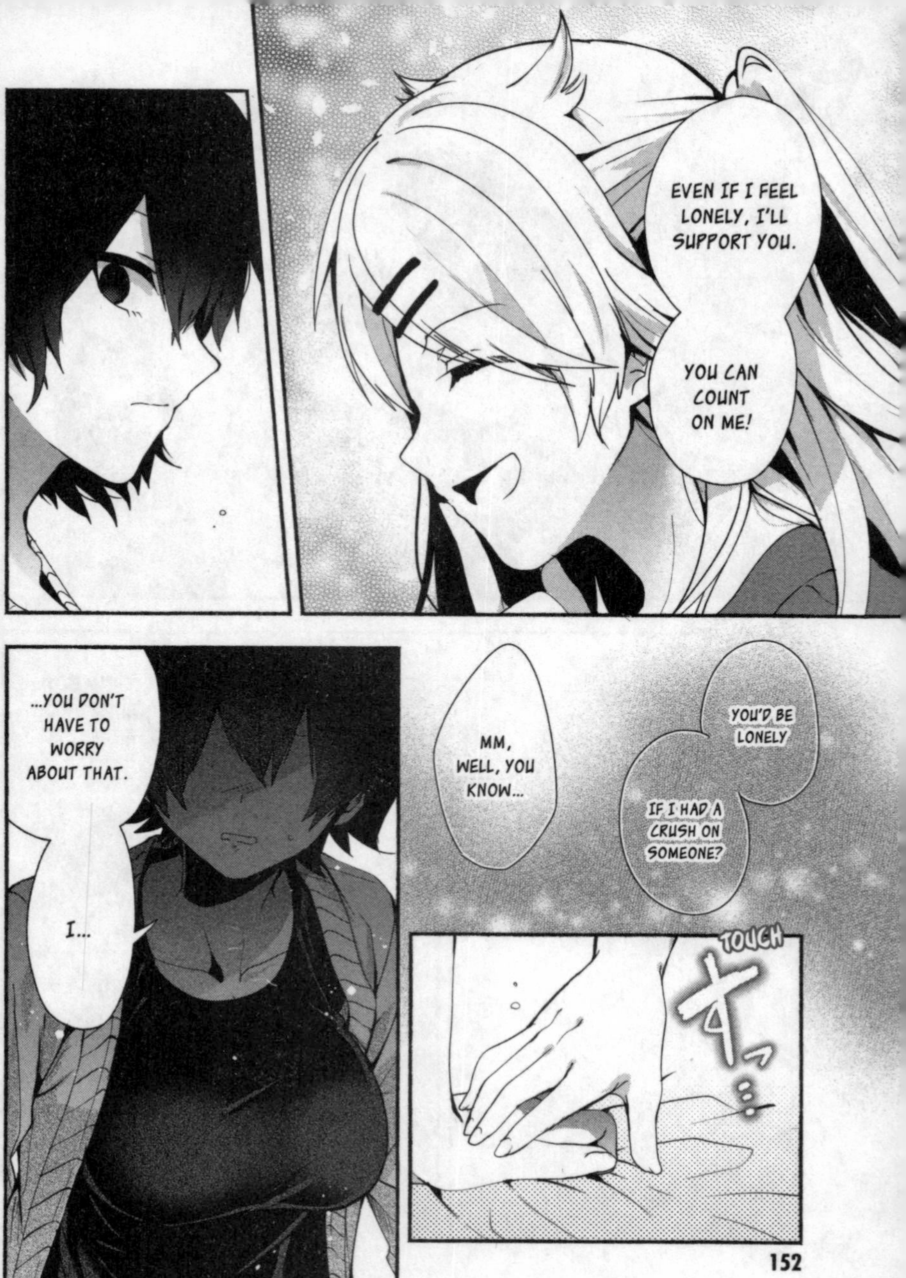
EVEN IF I FEEL LONELY, I'LL SUPPORT YOU.
YOU CAN COUNT ON ME!
YOU'D BE LONELY
IF I HAD A CRUSH ON SOMEONE?
MM, WELL, YOU KNOW...
TOUCH
...YOU DON'T HAVE TO WORRY ABOUT THAT.
I...

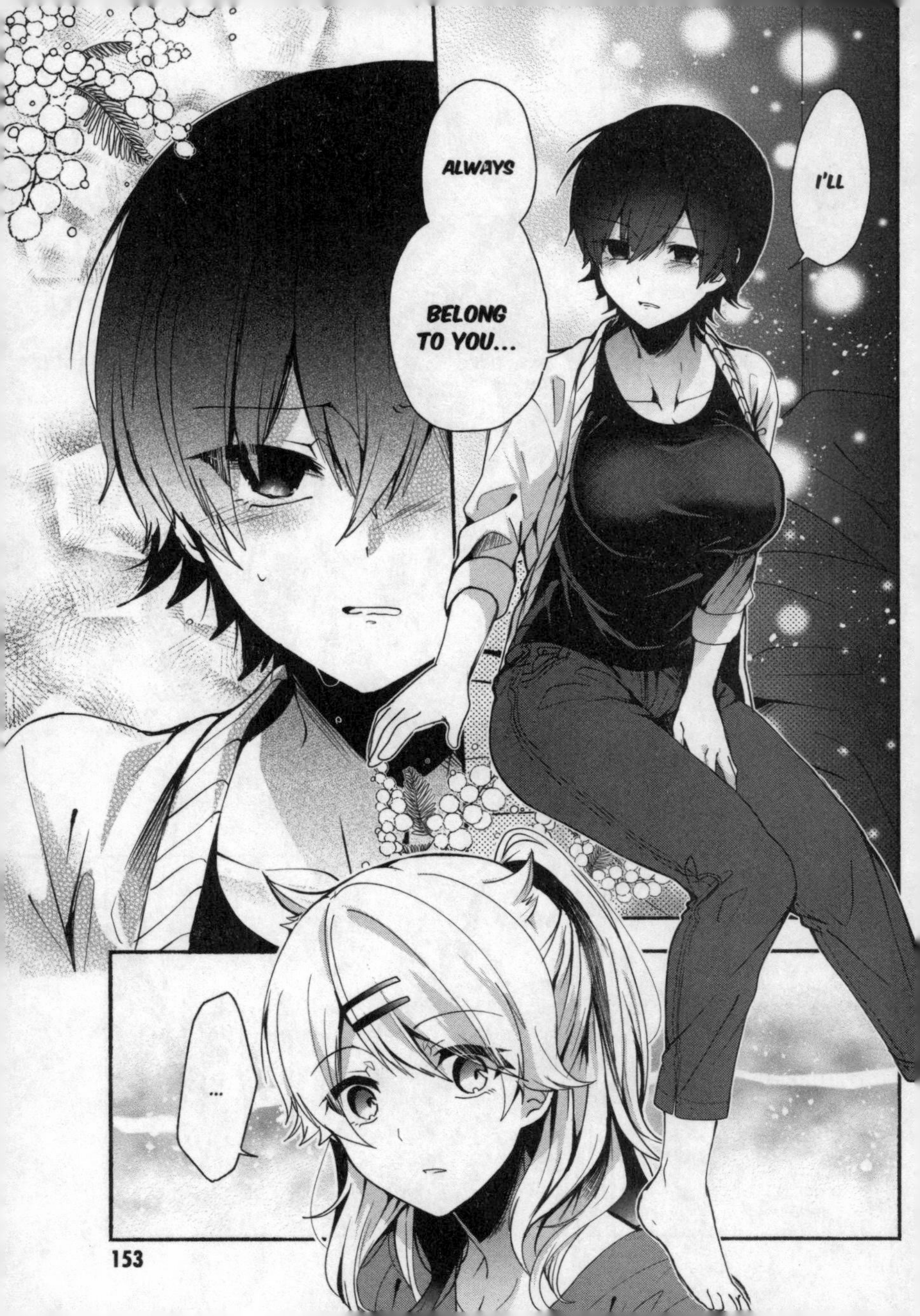
I'LL
ALWAYS
BELONG TO YOU...
...

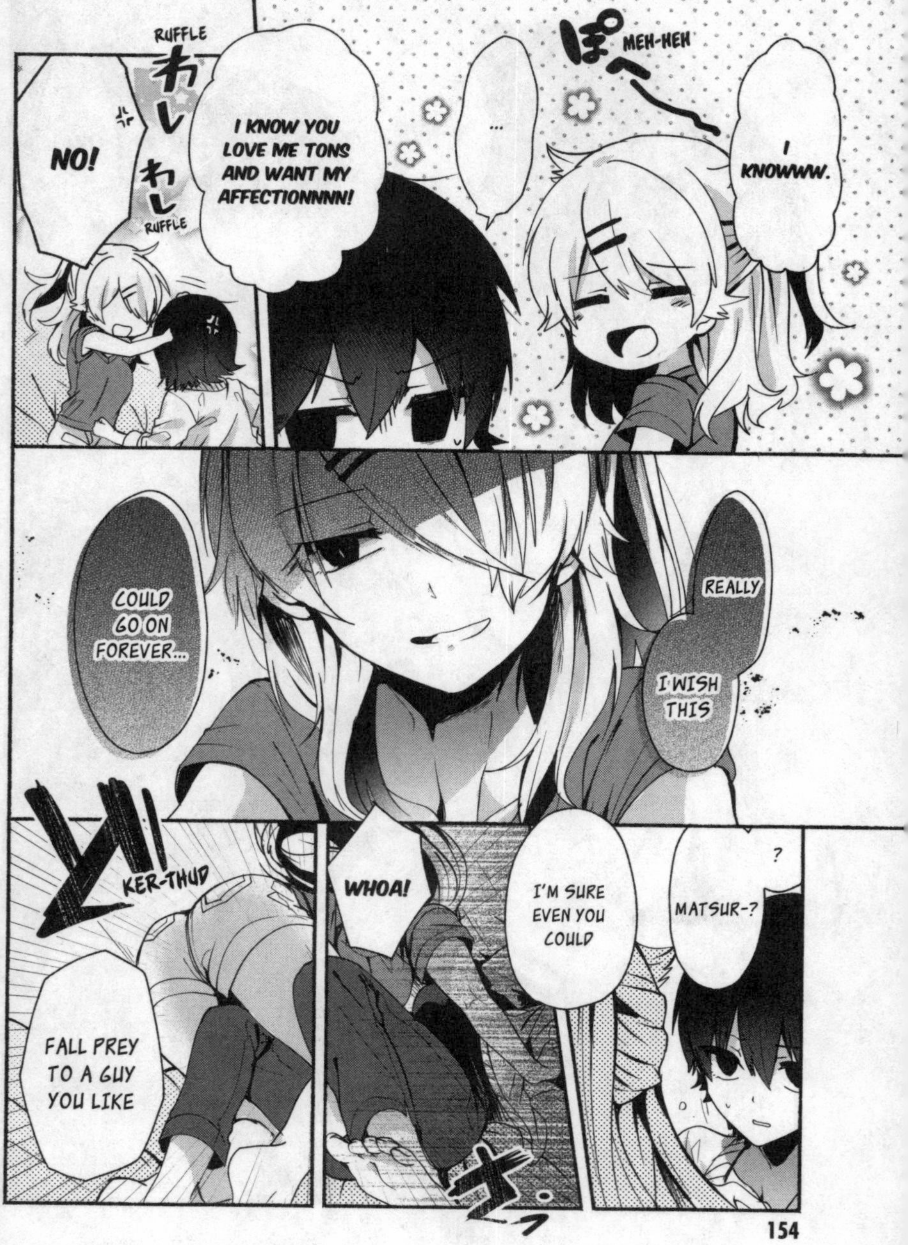

ぽへ~
MEH-HEH
I KNOWWW.
...
I KNOW YOU LOVE ME TONS AND WANT MY AFFECTIONNNN!
RUFFLE
わしわし
RUFFLE
NO!
REALLY I WISH THIS
COULD GO ON FOREVER...
?
MATSUR-?
I'M SURE EVEN YOU COULD
WHOA!
KER-THUD
FALL PREY TO A GUY YOU LIKE

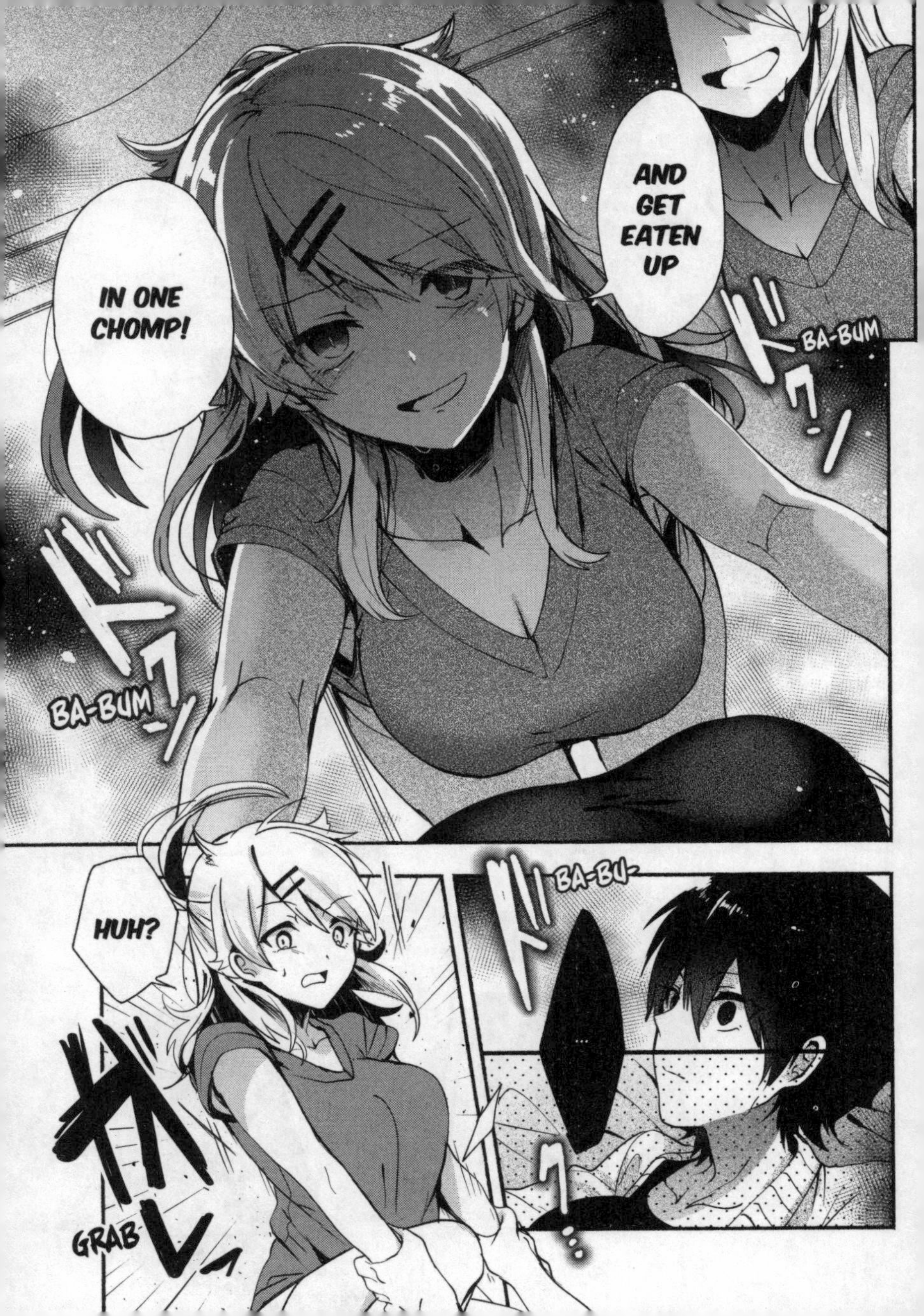
AND GET EATEN UP
IN ONE CHOMP!
BA-BUM
BA-BUM
BA-BU-
...
HUH?
GRAB

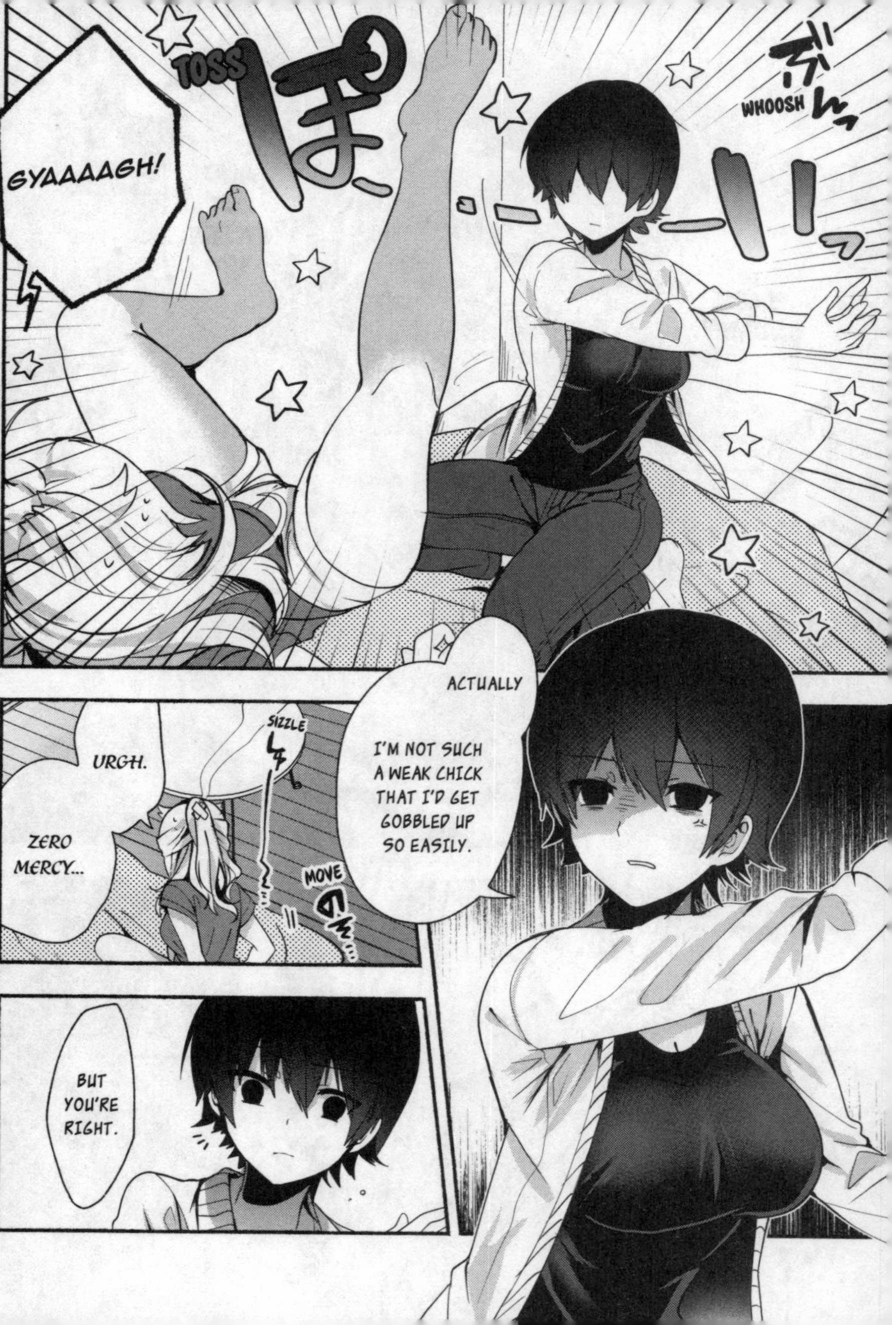

WHOOSH
TOSS
ぽ
GYAAAAGH!
ACTUALLY
I'M NOT SUCH A WEAK CHICK THAT I'D GET GOBBLED UP SO EASILY.
SIZZLE
URGH.
ZERO MERCY...
MOVE
BUT YOU'RE RIGHT.

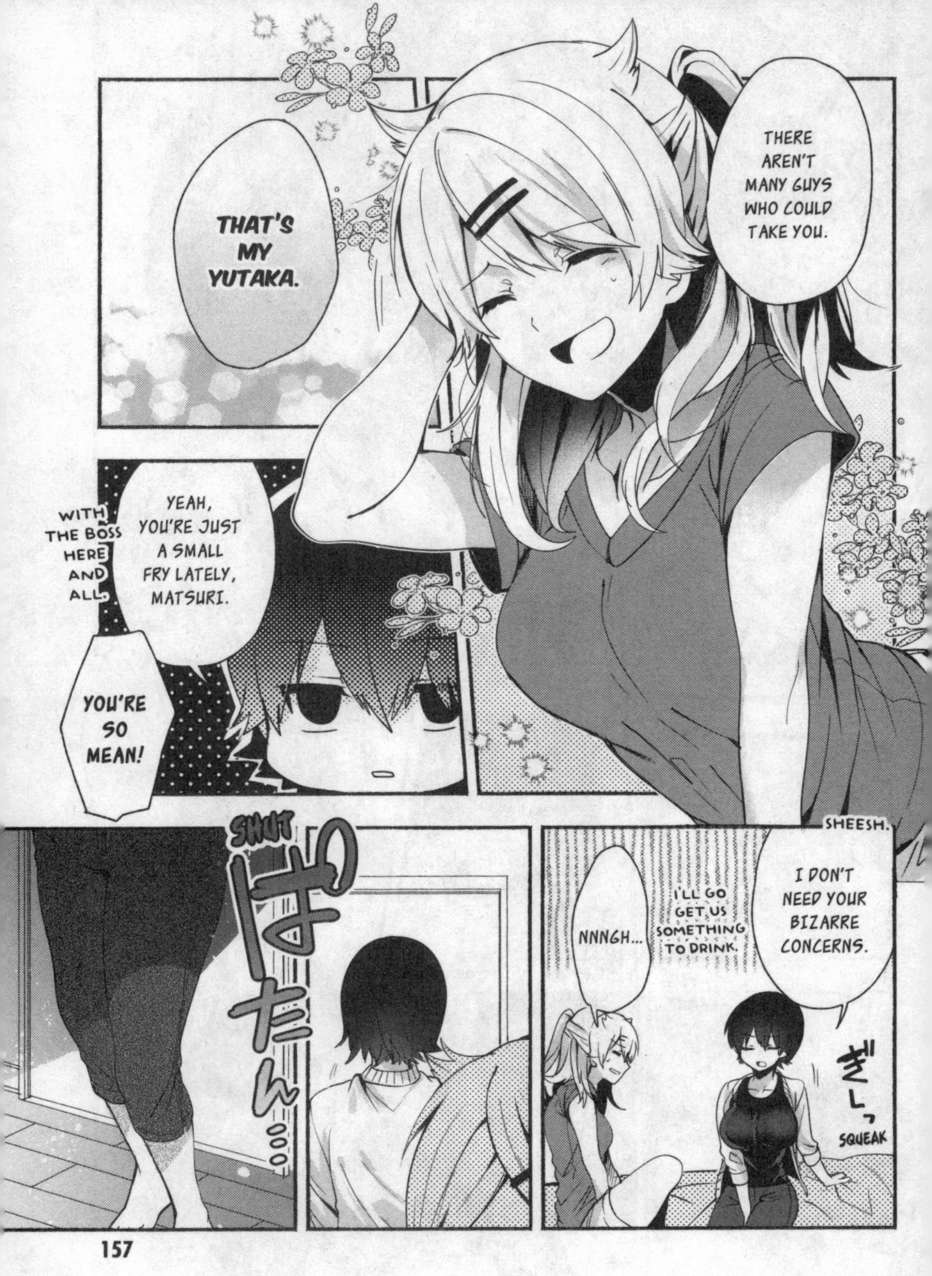
THERE AREN'T MANY GUYS WHO COULD TAKE YOU.
THAT'S MY YUTAKA.
YEAH, YOU'RE JUST A SMALL FRY LATELY, MATSURI.
WITH THE BOSS HERE AND ALL.
YOU'RE SO MEAN!
SHEESH.
I DON'T NEED YOUR BIZARRE CONCERNS.
I'LL GO GET US SOMETHING TO DRINK.
NNNGH...
ぎしっ
SQUEAK
SHUT
ばたん。。。

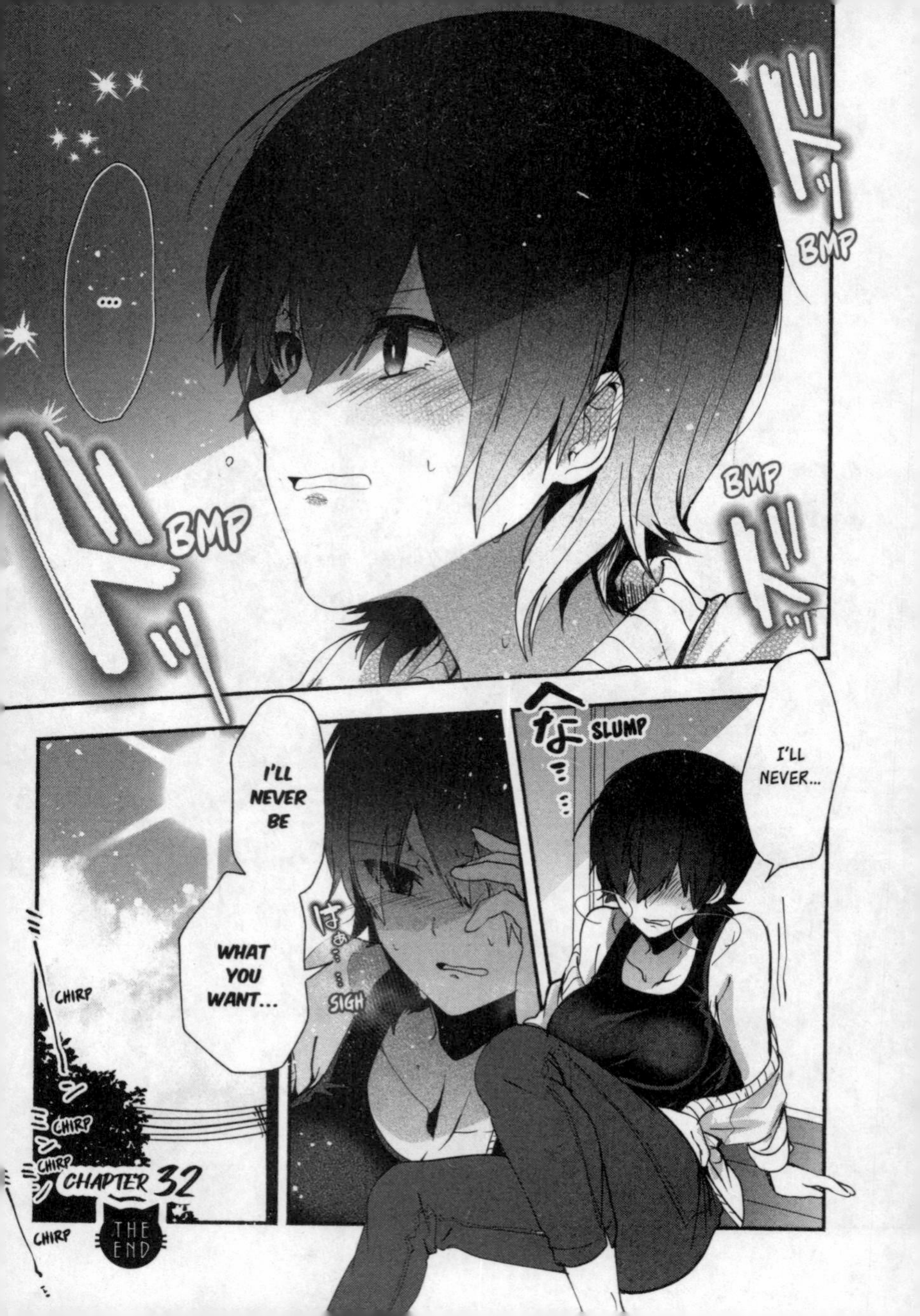
BMP
...
BMP
BMP
SLUMP
I'LL NEVER...
I'LL NEVER BE WHAT YOU WANT...
SIGH
CHIRP
CHIRP
CHIRP
CHAPTER 32
THE END
CHIRP

CHAPTER 33

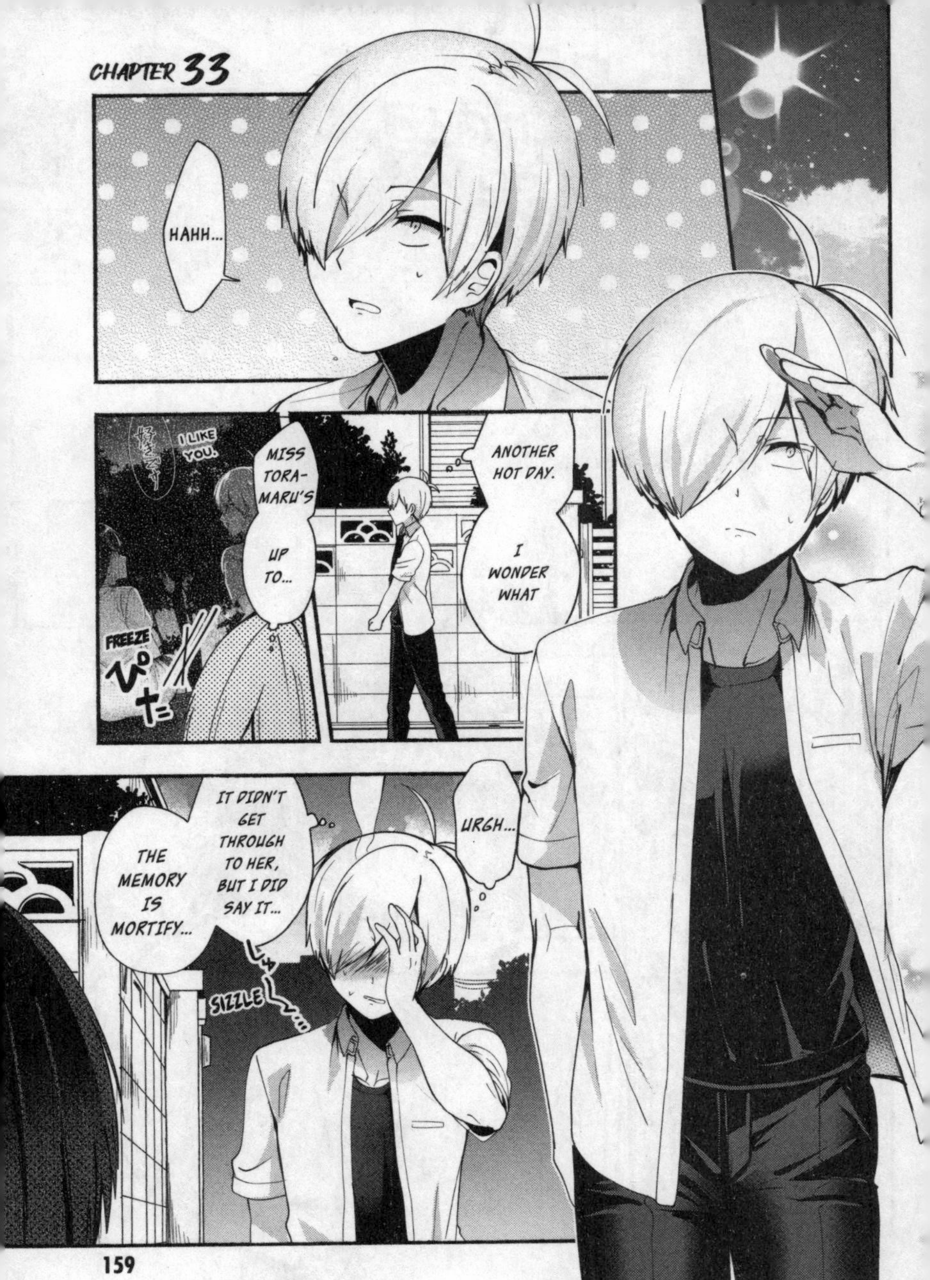
HAHH...
ANOTHER HOT DAY.
I WONDER WHAT
MISS TORA-MARU'S
UP TO...
I LIKE YOU.
FREEZE
URGH...
IT DIDN'T GET THROUGH TO HER, BUT I DID SAY IT...
THE MEMORY IS MORTIFY...
SIZZLE

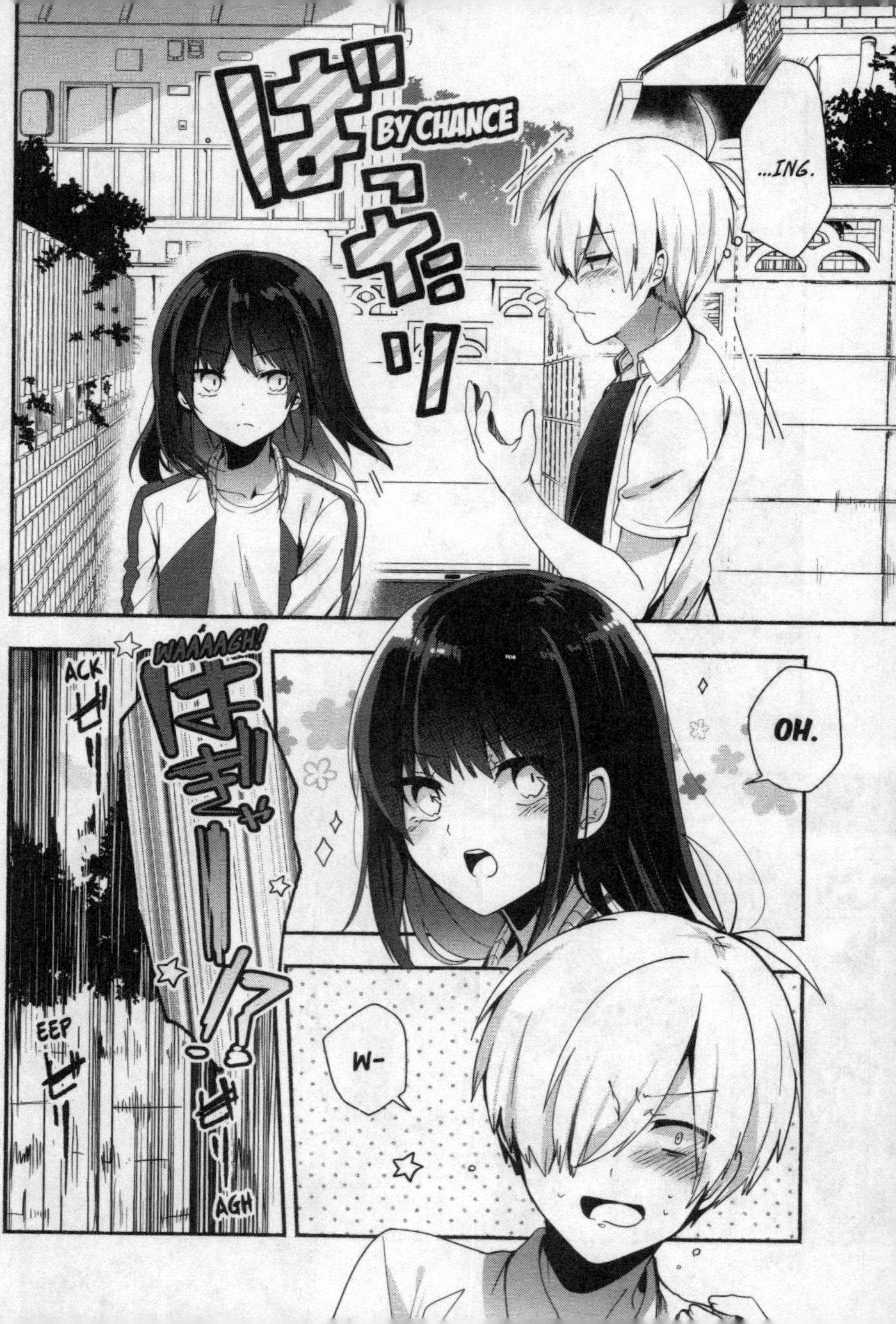

...ING.
BY CHANCE
OH.
W-
WAAAAGH!
ACK
EEP
AGH

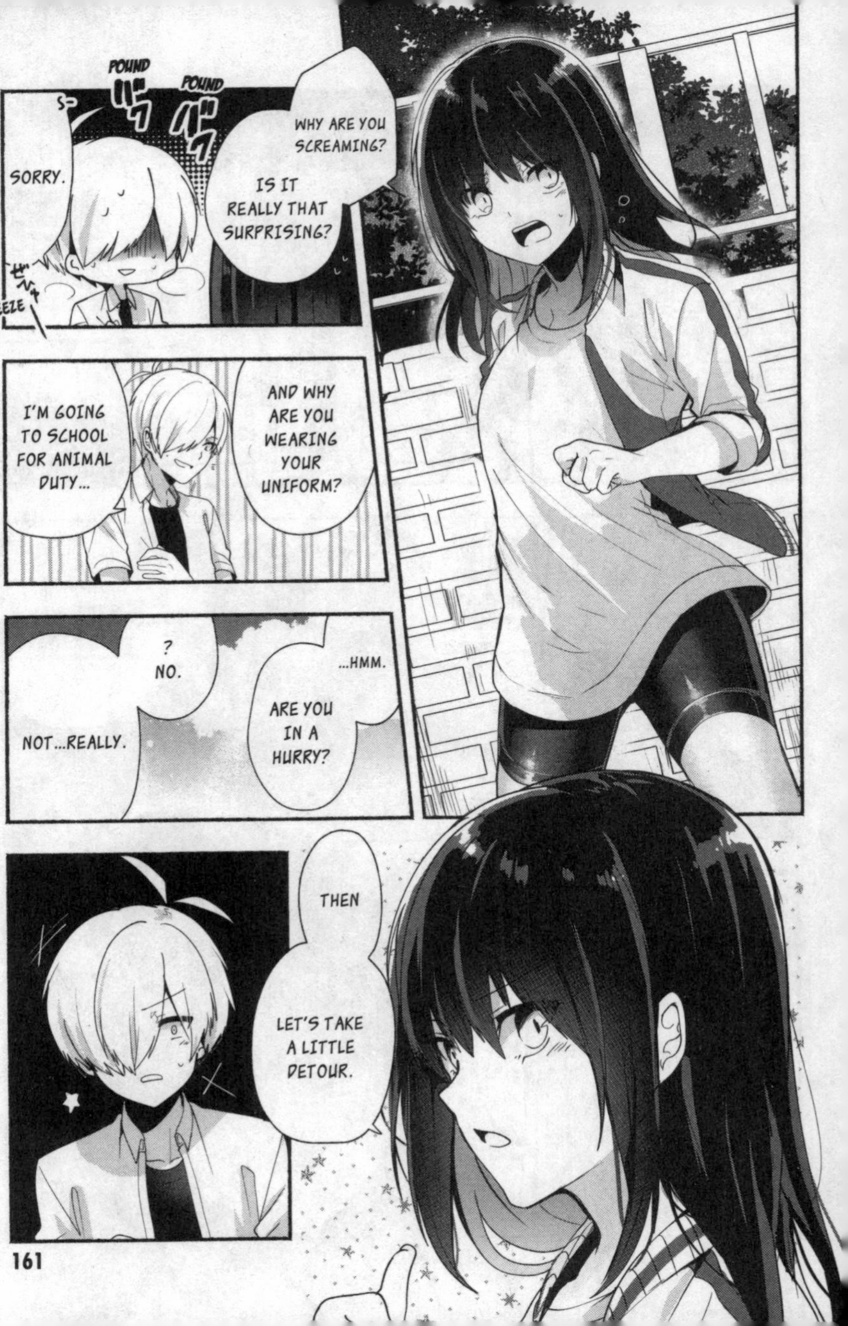
WHY ARE YOU SCREAMING?
IS IT REALLY THAT SURPRISING?
POUND
POUND
SORRY.
WHEEZE
AND WHY ARE YOU WEARING YOUR UNIFORM?
I'M GOING TO SCHOOL FOR ANIMAL DUTY...
...HMM.
ARE YOU IN A HURRY?
? NO.
NOT...REALLY.
THEN
LET'S TAKE A LITTLE DETOUR.

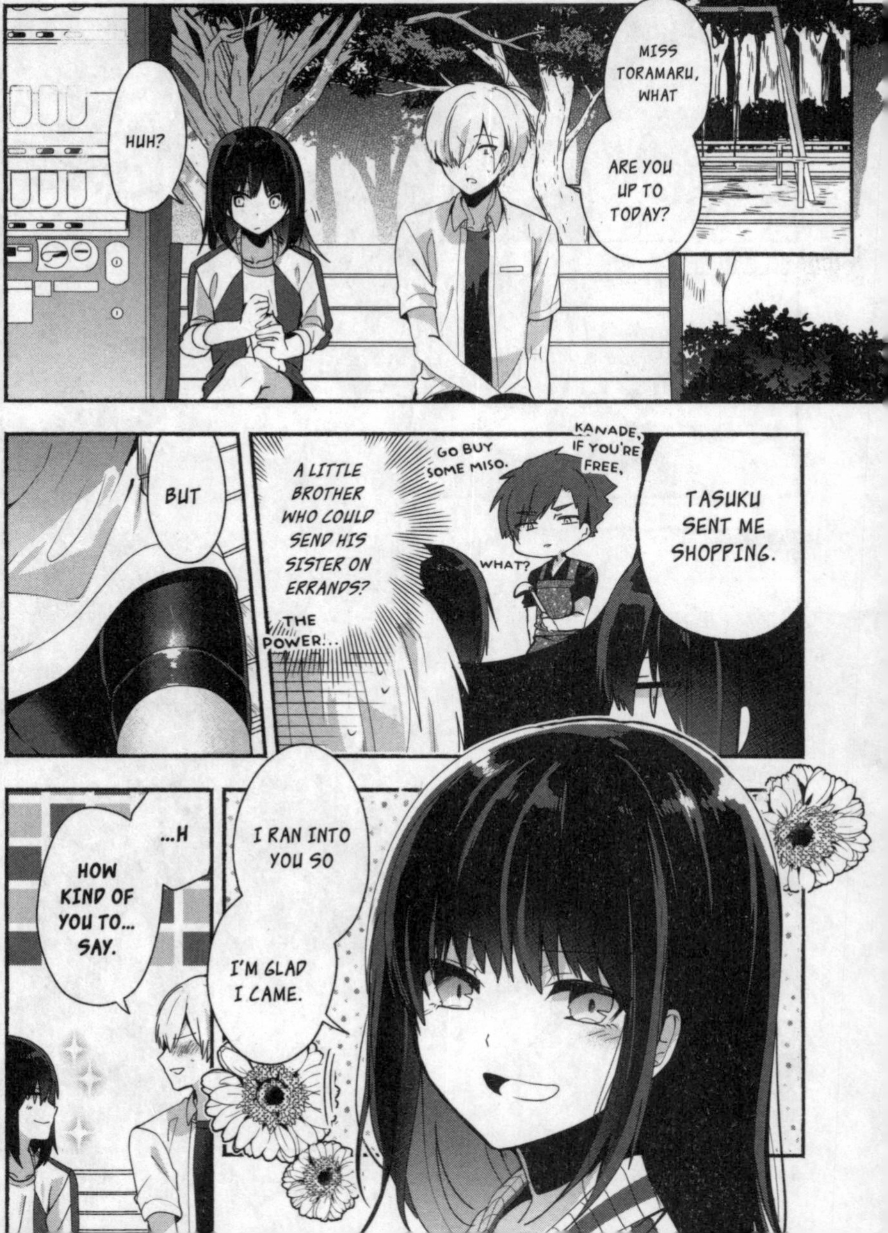
MISS TORAMARU, WHAT
ARE YOU UP TO TODAY?
HUH?
TASUKU SENT ME SHOPPING.
KANADE, IF YOU'RE FREE,
GO BUY SOME MISO.
WHAT?
A LITTLE BROTHER WHO COULD SEND HIS SISTER ON ERRANDS?
THE POWER...
BUT
I RAN INTO YOU SO
I'M GLAD I CAME.
...H
HOW KIND OF YOU TO... SAY.

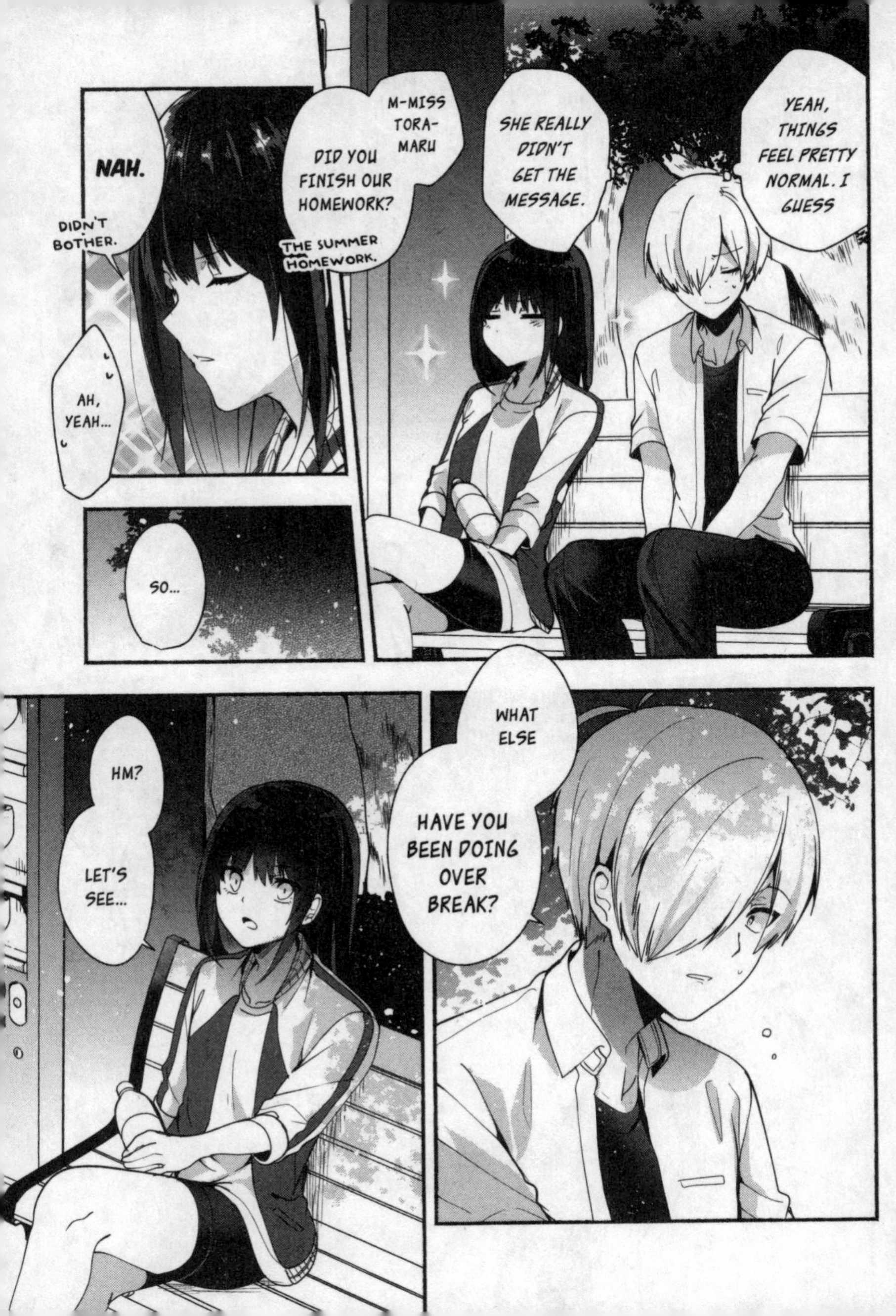
YEAH, THINGS FEEL PRETTY NORMAL. I GUESS
SHE REALLY DIDN'T GET THE MESSAGE.
M-MISS TORA-MARU
DID YOU FINISH OUR HOMEWORK?
THE SUMMER HOMEWORK.
NAH.
DIDN'T BOTHER.
AH, YEAH...
SO...
WHAT ELSE
HAVE YOU BEEN DOING OVER BREAK?
HM?
LET'S SEE...

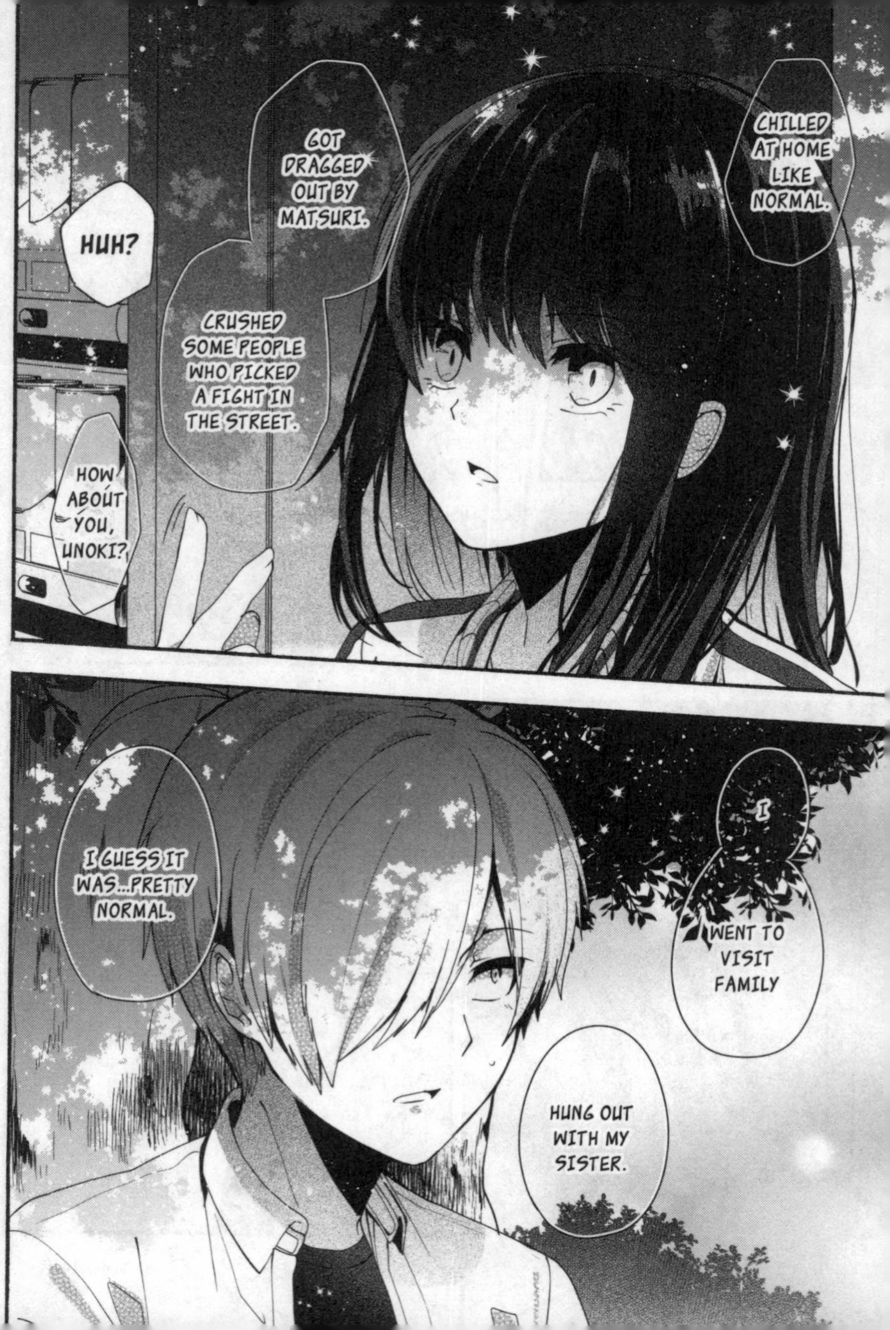
CHILLED AT HOME LIKE NORMAL.
GOT DRAGGED OUT BY MATSURI.
HUH?
CRUSHED SOME PEOPLE WHO PICKED A FIGHT IN THE STREET.
HOW ABOUT YOU, UNOKI?
I WENT TO VISIT FAMILY
HUNG OUT WITH MY SISTER.
I GUESS IT WAS...PRETTY NORMAL.

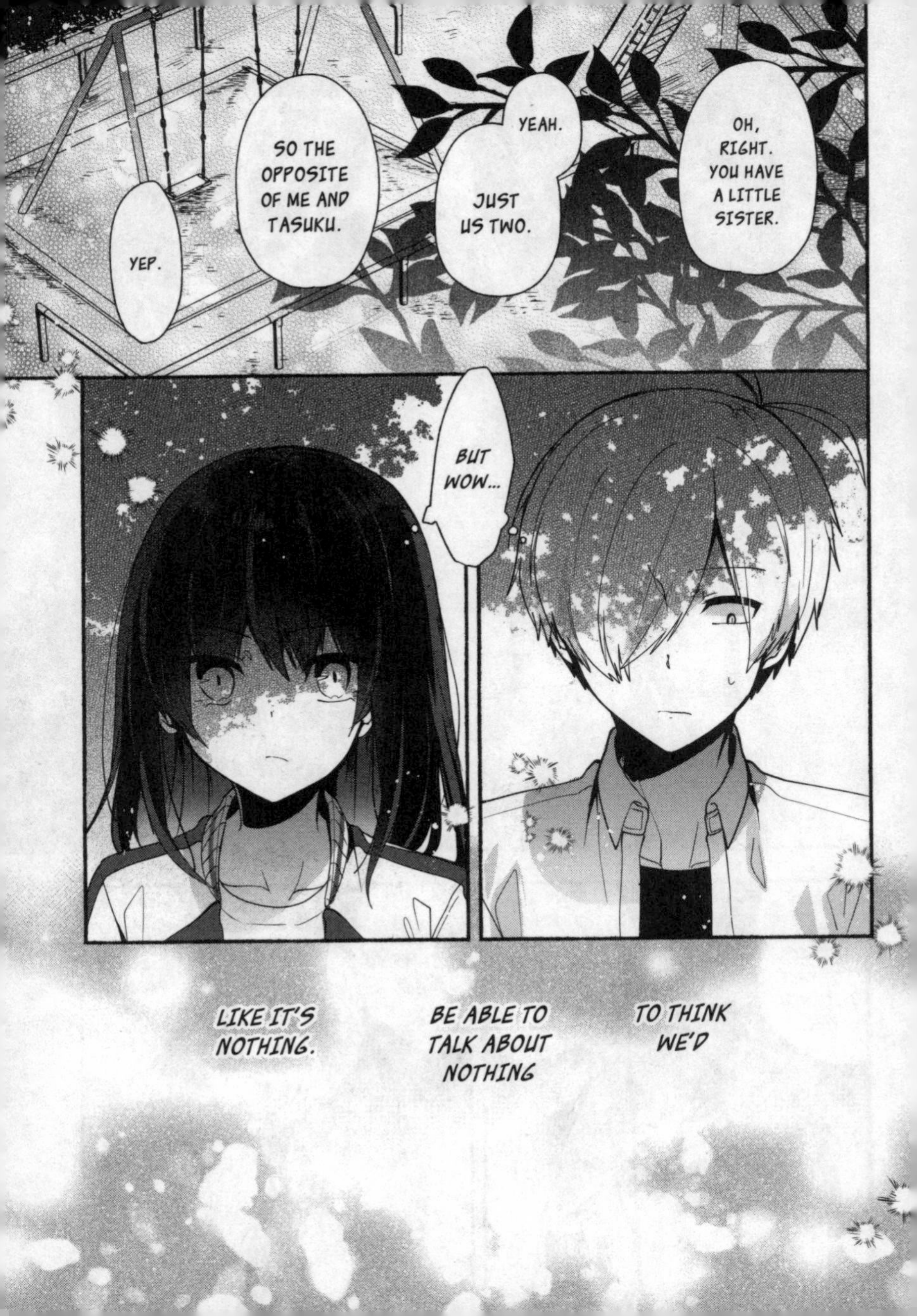
OH, RIGHT. YOU HAVE A LITTLE SISTER.
YEAH.
JUST US TWO.
SO THE OPPOSITE OF ME AND TASUKU.
YEP.
BUT WOW...
TO THINK WE'D
BE ABLE TO TALK ABOUT NOTHING
LIKE IT'S NOTHING.

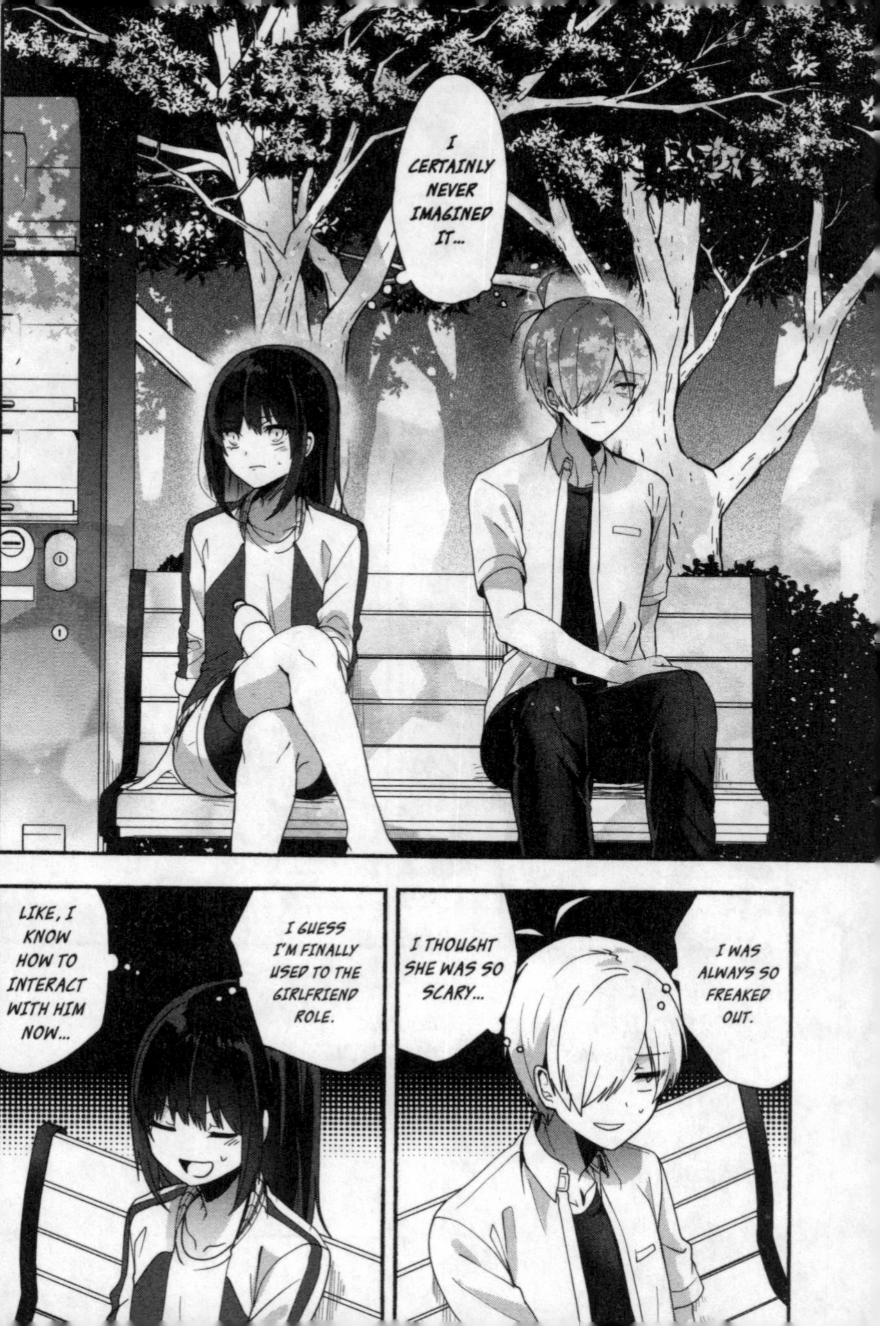
I CERTAINLY NEVER IMAGINED IT...
I WAS ALWAYS SO FREAKED OUT.
I THOUGHT SHE WAS SO SCARY...
I GUESS I'M FINALLY USED TO THE GIRLFRIEND ROLE.
LIKE, I KNOW HOW TO INTERACT WITH HIM NOW...

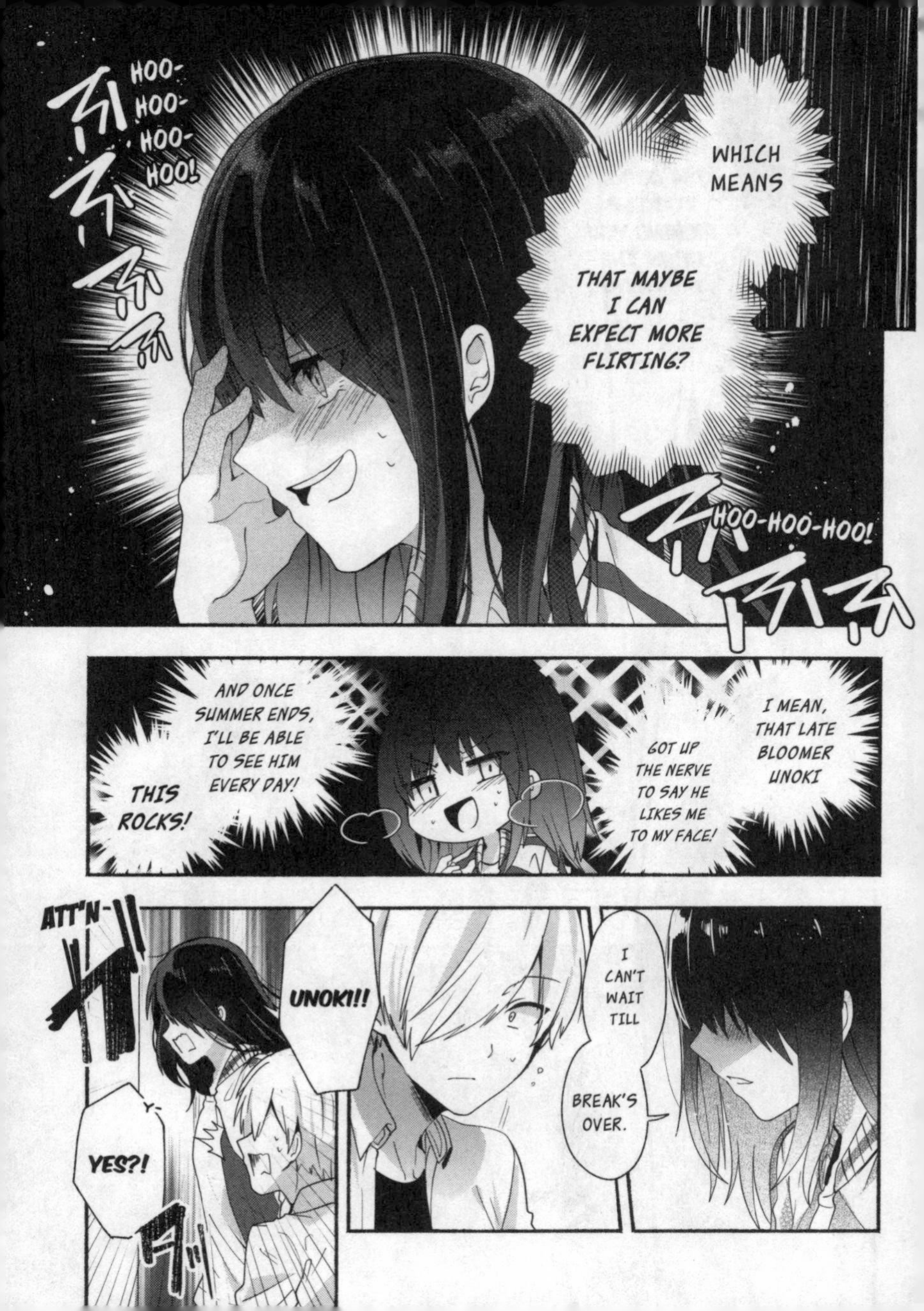
WHICH MEANS
THAT MAYBE I CAN EXPECT MORE FLIRTING?
HOO-HOO-HOO-HOO!
HOO-HOO-HOO!
I MEAN, THAT LATE BLOOMER UNOKI
GOT UP THE NERVE TO SAY HE LIKES ME TO MY FACE!
AND ONCE SUMMER ENDS, I'LL BE ABLE TO SEE HIM EVERY DAY!
THIS ROCKS!
I CAN'T WAIT TILL
BREAK'S OVER.
UNOKI!!
ATT'N-
Y-
YES?!

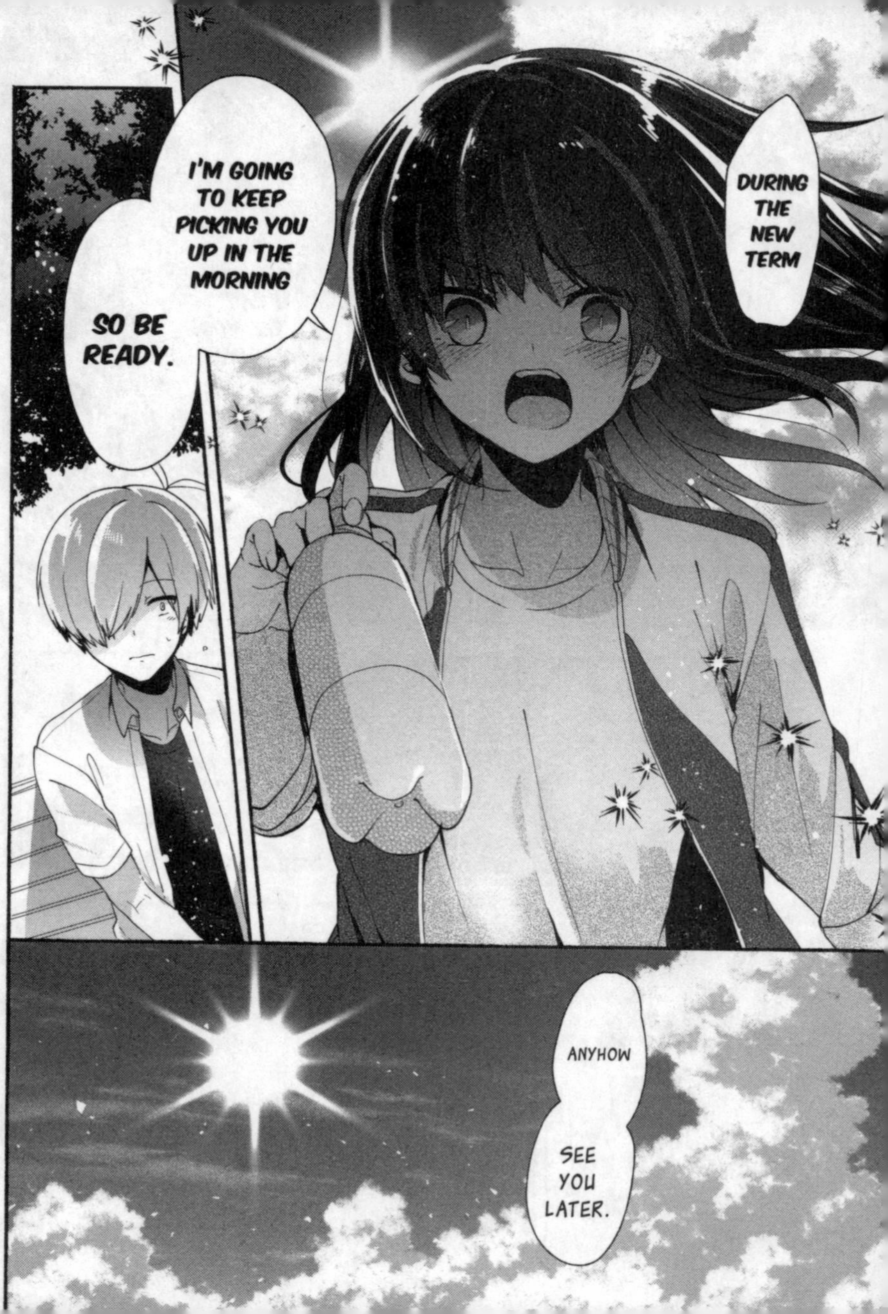
DURING THE NEW TERM
I'M GOING TO KEEP PICKING YOU UP IN THE MORNING
SO BE READY.
ANYHOW
SEE YOU LATER.

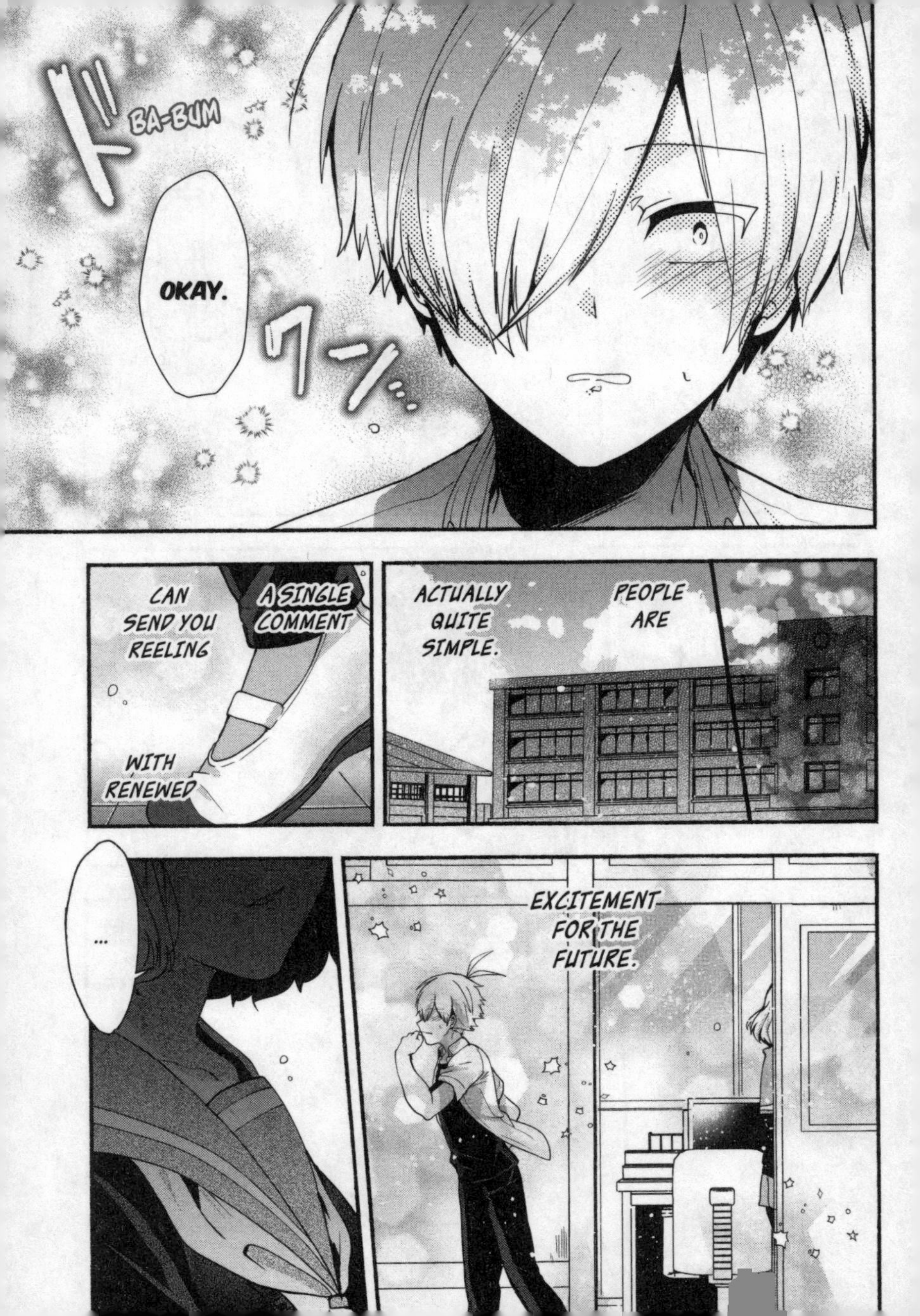
BA-BUM
OKAY.
PEOPLE ARE
ACTUALLY QUITE SIMPLE.
A SINGLE COMMENT
CAN SEND YOU REELING
WITH RENEWED
EXCITEMENT FOR THE FUTURE.
...

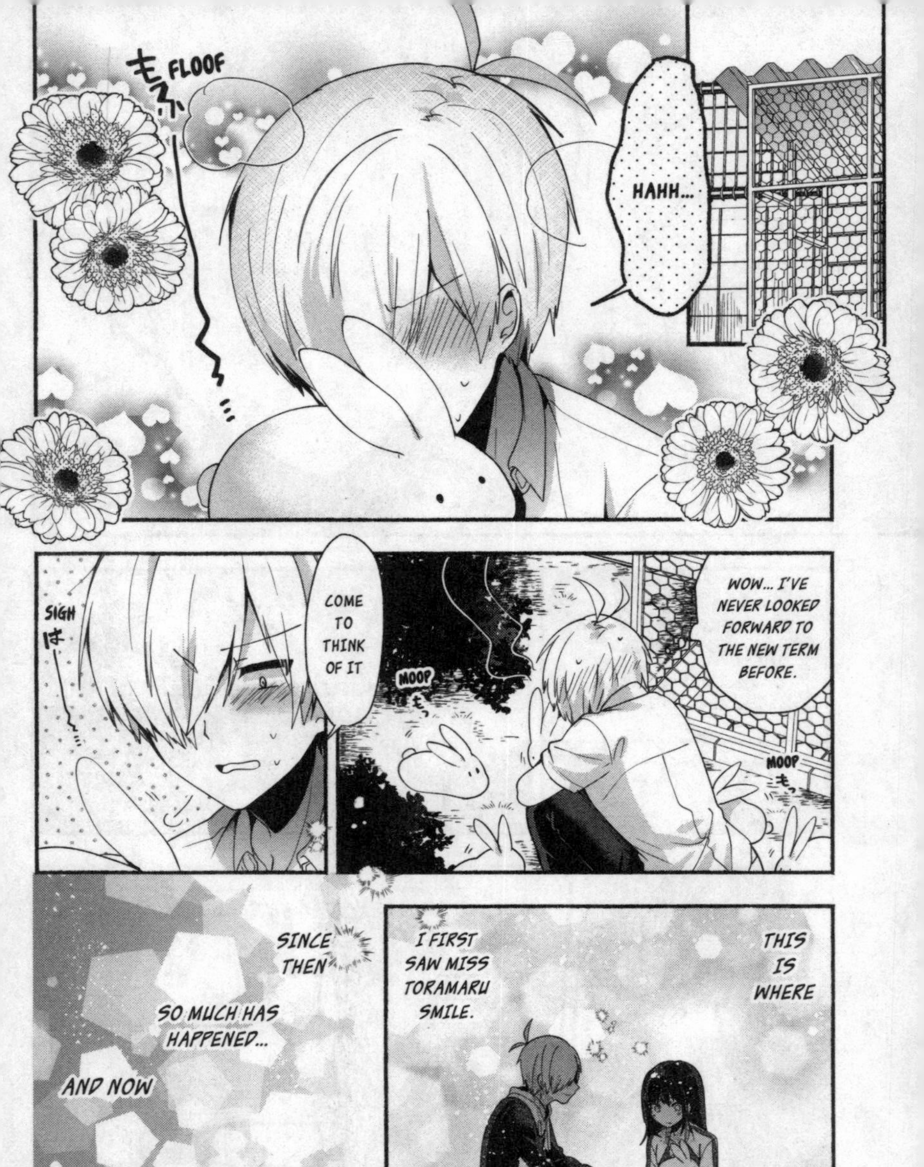
HAHH...
FLOOF
もふ
WOW... I'VE NEVER LOOKED FORWARD TO THE NEW TERM BEFORE.
MOOP
もっ
MOOP
もっ
COME TO THINK OF IT
SIGH
は
THIS IS WHERE
I FIRST SAW MISS TORAMARU SMILE.
SINCE THEN
SO MUCH HAS HAPPENED...
AND NOW

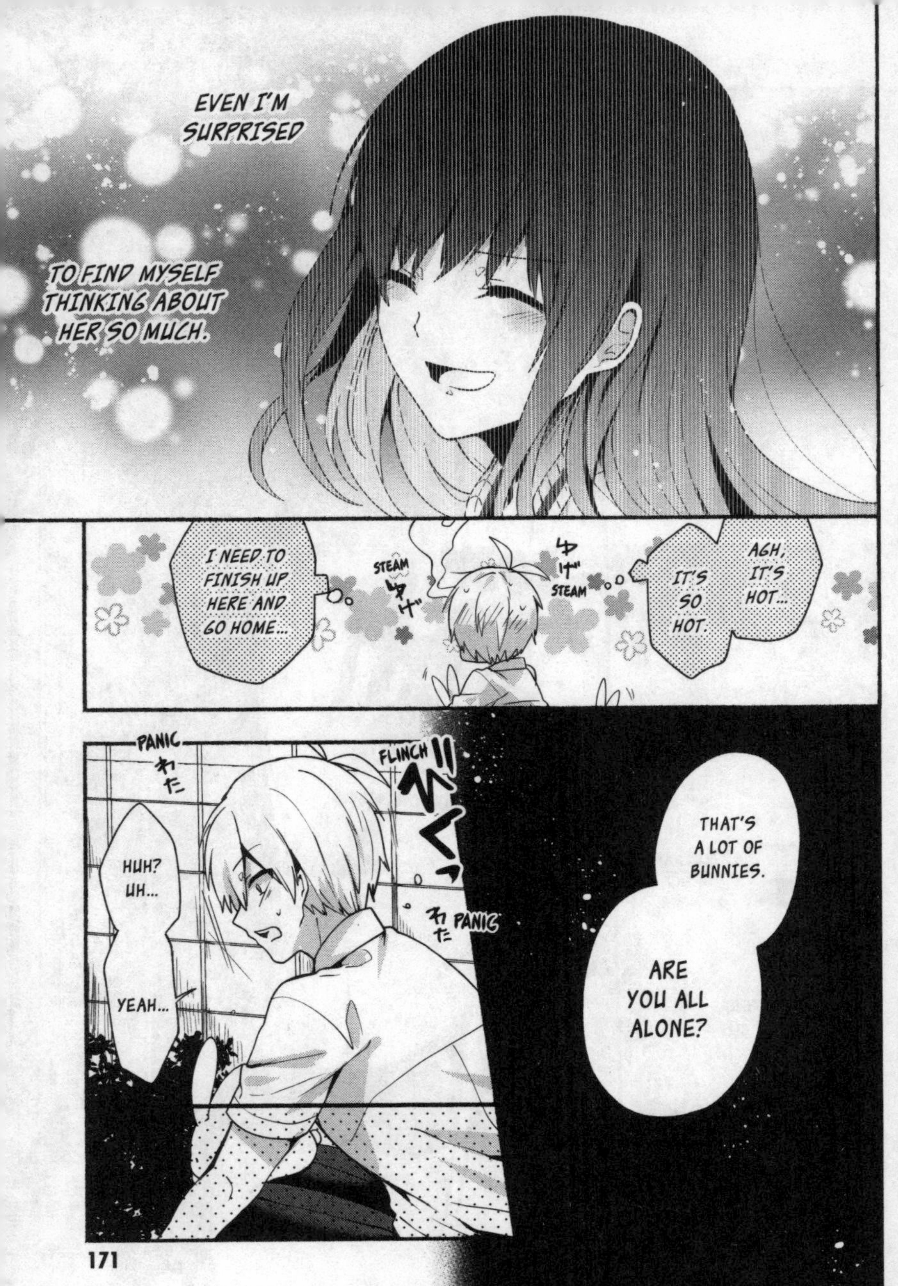
EVEN I'M SURPRISED
TO FIND MYSELF THINKING ABOUT HER SO MUCH.
AGH, IT'S HOT...
IT'S SO HOT.
STEAM
STEAM
I NEED TO FINISH UP HERE AND GO HOME...
THAT'S A LOT OF BUNNIES.
ARE YOU ALL ALONE?
FLINCH
PANIC
PANIC
HUH? UH...
YEAH...

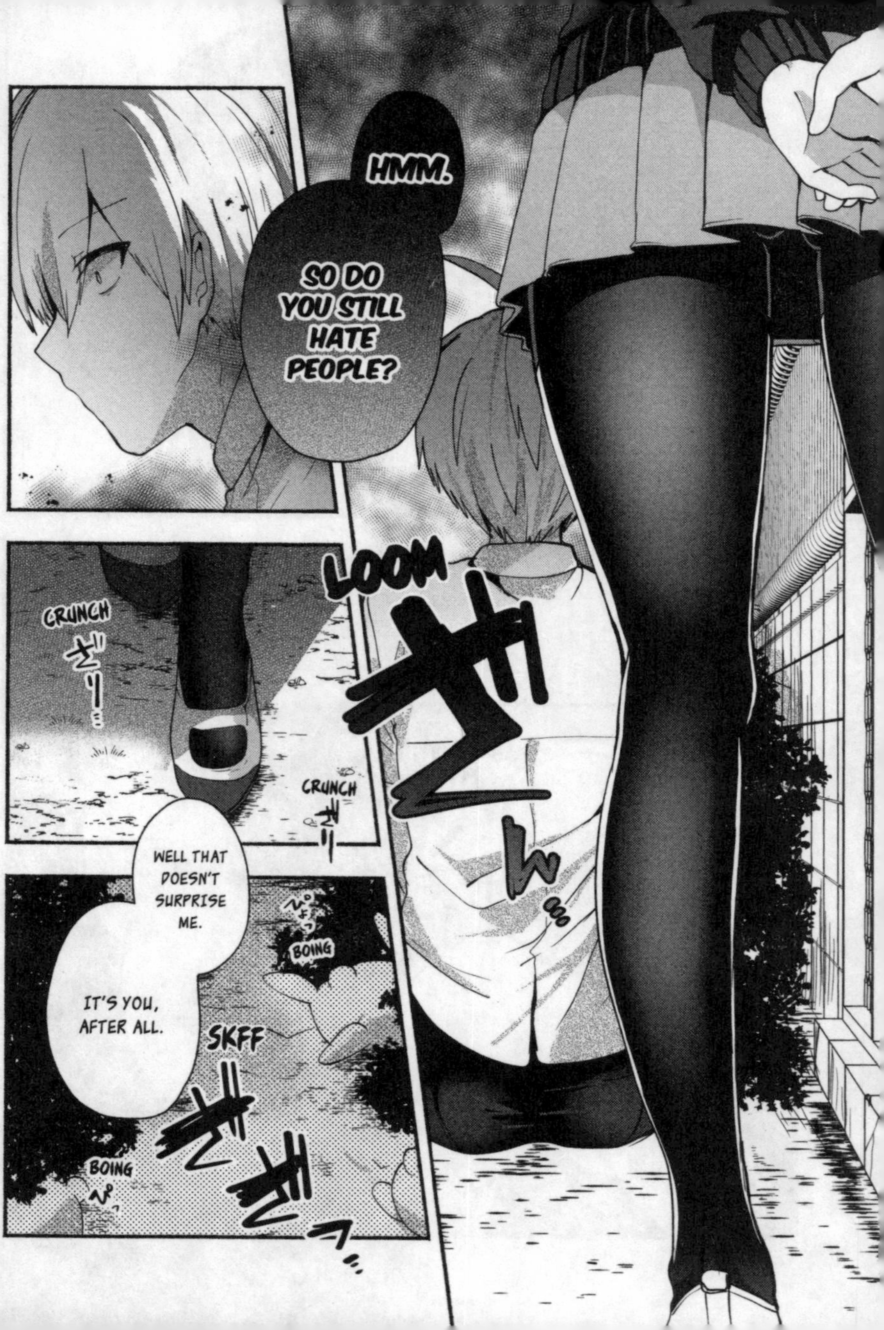
HMM.
SO DO YOU STILL HATE PEOPLE?
LOOM
CRUNCH
CRUNCH
WELL THAT DOESN'T SURPRISE ME.
BOING
IT'S YOU, AFTER ALL.
SKFF
BOING

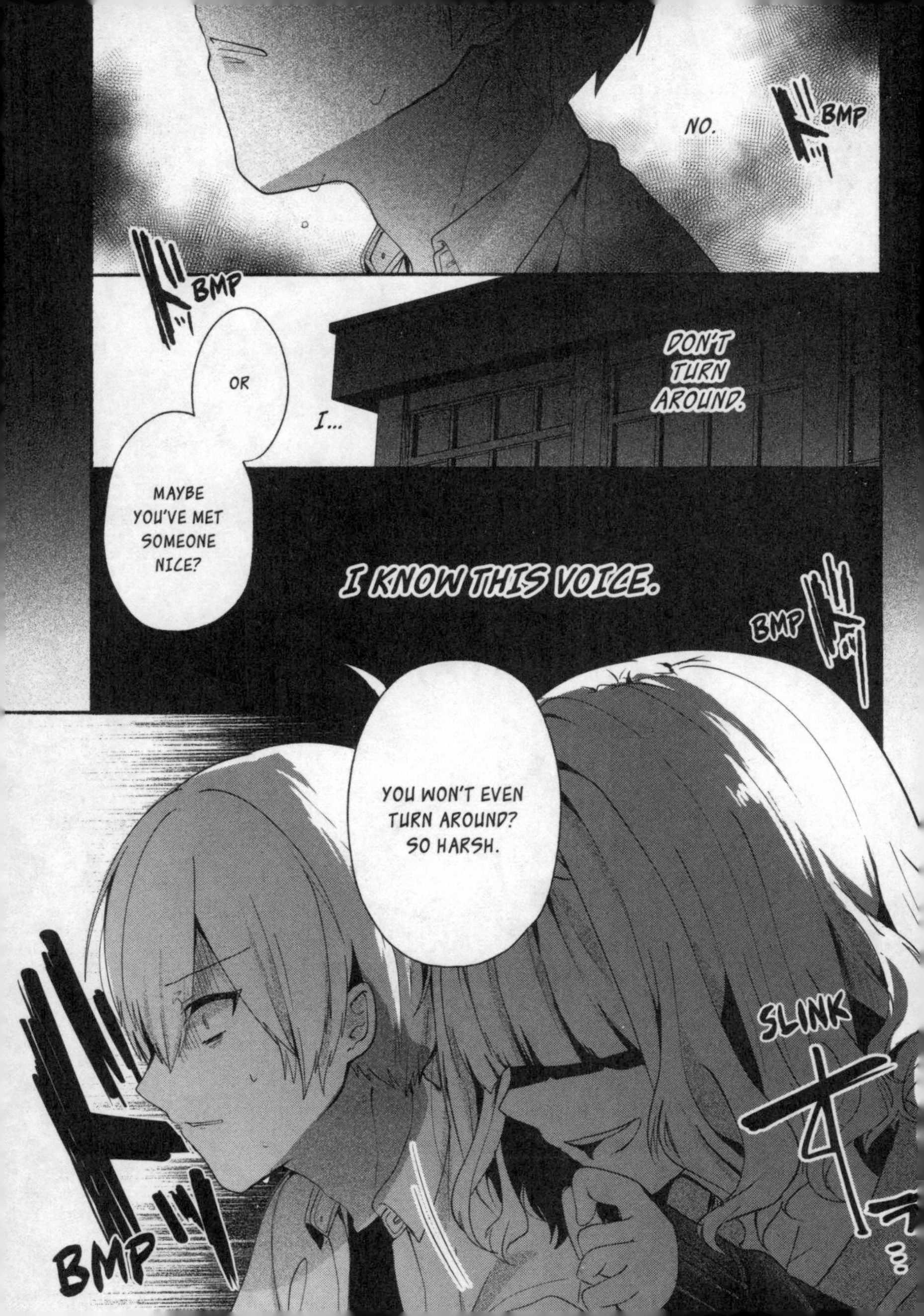
BMP
NO.
DON'T TURN AROUND.
BMP
I...
OR
MAYBE YOU'VE MET SOMEONE NICE?
BMP
I KNOW THIS VOICE.
YOU WON'T EVEN TURN AROUND? SO HARSH.
SLINK
BMP

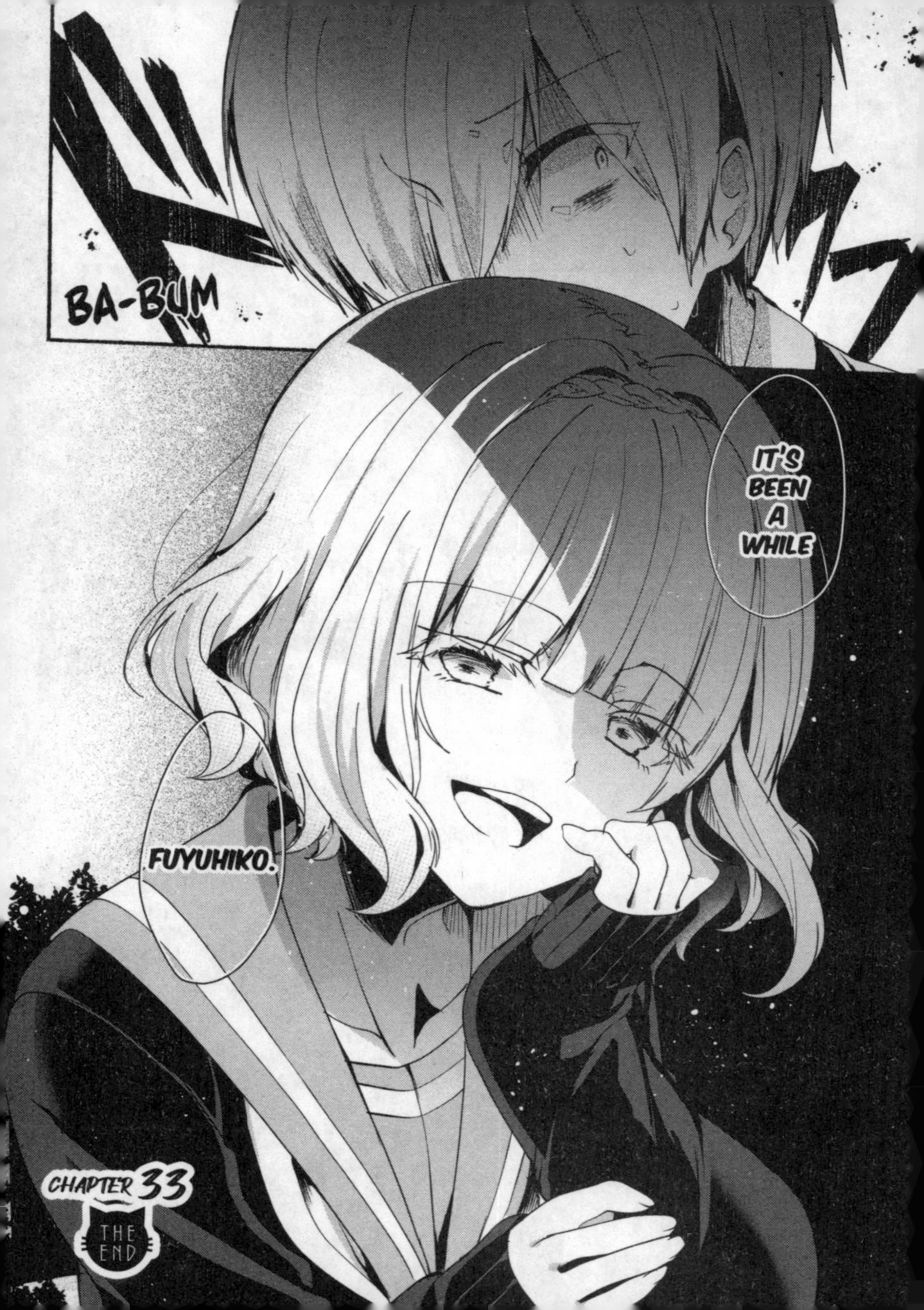
BA-BUM
IT'S BEEN A WHILE
FUYUHIKO.
CHAPTER 33
THE END

I BELONG TO THE BADDEST GIRL AT SCHOOL

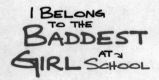

AFTERWORD

THANK YOU FOR PICKING UP VOL. 3 OF I BELONG
TO THE BADDEST GIRL AT SCHOOL.
THIS IS UI KASHIMA.

DID YOU HEAR THAT, FOLKS? THIRD VOLUME!
PERSONALLY, I THINK IT'S QUITE AN AMAZING FEAT.
AND THE SERIES ISN'T EVEN OVER YET. TRULY AMAZING.
THANK YOU.

I'M PLANNING PLENTY OF DRAMA
AND/OR LACK THEREOF,
SO I HOPE YOU'LL STICK WITH ME.

Twitter: @ui1059

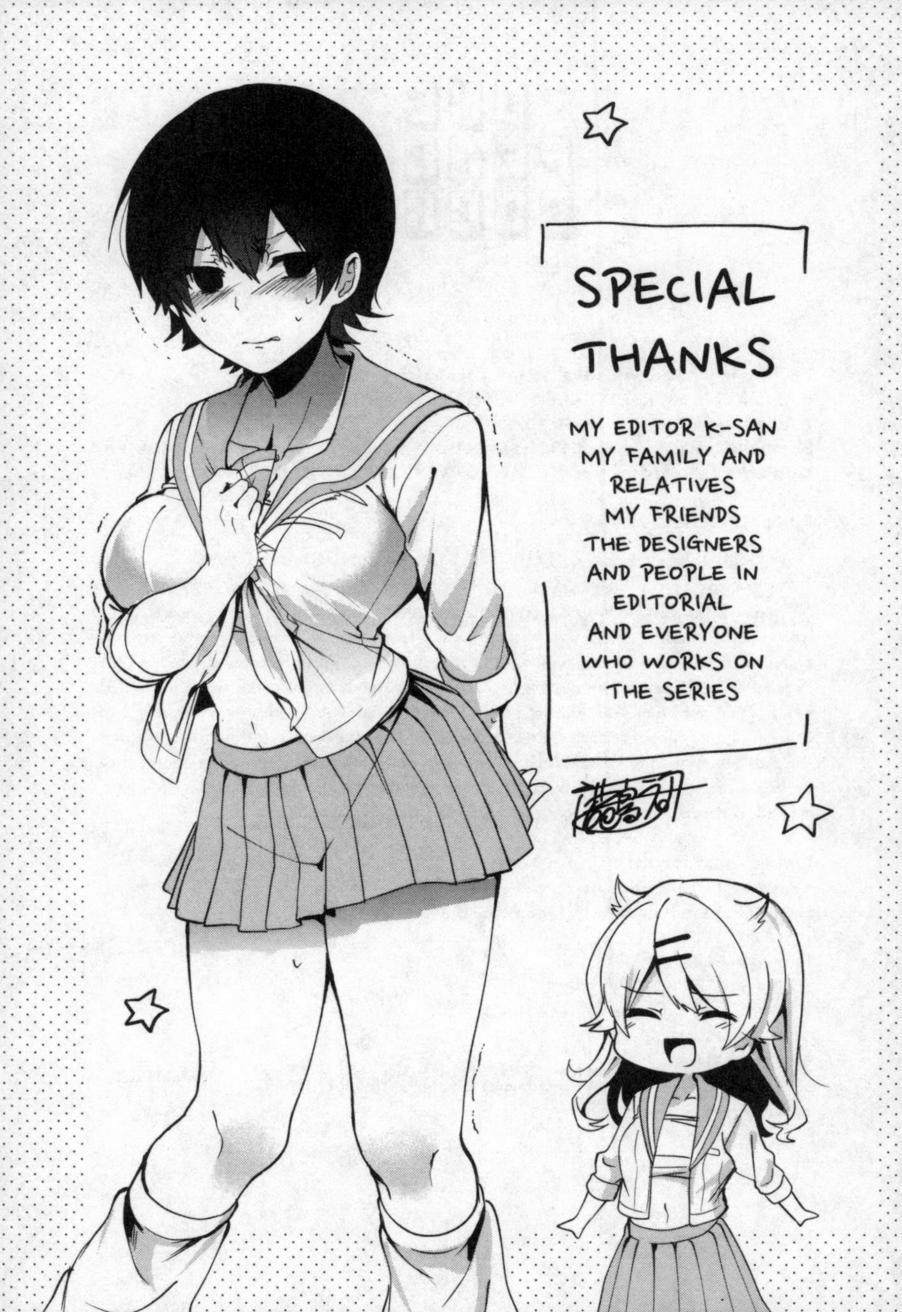
SPECIAL THANKS
MY EDITOR K-SAN
MY FAMILY AND RELATIVES
MY FRIENDS
THE DESIGNERS AND PEOPLE IN EDITORIAL
AND EVERYONE WHO WORKS ON THE SERIES

I Belong to the Baddest Girl at School Volume 03
(PASHIRI NA BOKU TO KOI SURU BANCHO-SAN Vol.3)
© Ui Kashima 2019
First published in Japan in 2019 by KADOKAWA CORPORATION, Tokyo. English
translation rights arranged with KADOKAWA CORPORATION, Tokyo.

ISBN: 978-1-64273-174-3

Written and illustrated by Ui Kashima
Translated by Emily Balistrieri
English Edition Published by One Peace Books 2021

Printed in Canada
1 2 3 4 5 6 7 8 9 10

One Peace Books
43-32 22nd Street STE 204 Long Island City New York 11101
www.onepeacebooks.com